The New Technology
of Crime, Law and Social Control

The New Technology of Crime, Law and Social Control

edited by
James M. Byrne and
Donald J. Rebovich

LYNNE
RIENNER
PUBLISHERS

BOULDER
LONDON

Published in the United States of America in 2010 by
Lynne Rienner Publishers, Inc.
1800 30th Street, Boulder, Colorado 80301
www.rienner.com

and in the United Kingdom by
Lynne Rienner Publishers, Inc.
3 Henrietta Street, Covent Garden, London WC2E 8LU

ISBN: 978-1-881798-72-9 (hc : alk. paper)
ISBN: 978-1-881798-73-6 (pb : alk. paper)
LC: 2007278942

First published in 2007 by Criminal Justice Press.
Reprinted here from the original edition.

Printed and bound in the United States of America

The paper used in this publication meets the requirements
of the American National Standard for Permanence of
Paper for Printed Library Materials Z39.48-1992.

CONTENTS

(continued)

Contents

ABOUT THE EDITORS

James M. Byrne, Ph.D. is currently a professor in the Department of Criminal Justice and Criminology at the University of Massachusetts, Lowell, where he has taught since 1984. He received his undergraduate degree in sociology from the University of Massachusetts in 1977 and his M.A. (1980) and Ph.D. degrees (1983) in criminal justice from the Rutgers University School of Criminal Justice. Dr. Byrne has over 25 years' experience in the field of evaluation research. He has served as the principal investigator for a wide range of evaluations of criminal justice initiatives, including intensive probation supervision, domestic violence control, a randomized field experiment on absconder location/apprehension strategies, and most recently, the National Institute of Corrections' Institutional Culture Change Initiative. He is a nationally recognized expert in the field of evaluation research; in addition, he is the co-editor of *The Social Ecology of Crime* (Springer Verlag, 1986), *Smart Sentencing: The Emergence of Intermediate Sanctions* (Sage, 1994) and *The Culture of Prison Violence* (Allyn and Bacon, in press). He is the author of numerous journal articles on the subjects of offender change, offender reentry, risk classification, prison/community culture, and the community context of crime and crime control. He currently serves as the Evidence-Based Review Editor of the journal *Victims and Offenders*.

Donald J. Rebovich, Ph.D. is an associate professor in the Department of Criminal Justice at Utica College and director of the college's Economic Crime Investigation Program. Before coming to Utica College, Dr. Rebovich served as research director for the National White Collar Crime Center (NW3C) and the American Prosecutors Research Institute (APRI). At NW3C, he was responsible for directing the first national analysis of Internet crime report data generated by the FBI's Internet Fraud Complaint Center and for directing the 2000 National Public Survey on White Collar Crime. He is the author of *Dangerous Ground: The World of Hazardous Waste Crime,* which presented the results of the first empirical study of environmental crime and its control in the United States. Dr. Rebovich's background also includes research in cybercrime prevention, economic crime victimization, public perceptions of fraud, fraud investigation methods, white collar crime prosecution and multi-jurisdictional task force development. Dr. Rebovich has served as advisor to the U.S. Department of Justice on tribal technology and information sharing, and on environmental crime control. He is also the Assistant Editor of the *Journal of Economic Crime Management.* Dr. Rebovich obtained his B.S. degree in Psychology from the College of New Jersey in 1973. He received his M.A. in Criminal Justice from Rutgers University in 1979 and his Ph.D. from Rutgers University in 1986.

1. INTRODUCTION – THE NEW TECHNOLOGY OF CRIME, LAW AND SOCIAL CONTROL

by

James M. Byrne

University of Massachusetts, Lowell

and

Donald J. Rebovich

Utica College

INTRODUCTION

Technology – in all its manifestations – has been at the center of every major crime control debate during the past two centuries. However, recent changes in the technology area generally – and in the area of information technology in particular – have been so dramatic and profound that they deserve special attention and critical review. Indeed, a recent FBI report argues that new technology advances have transformed both crime commission and crime control globally. According to the authors of the FBI's most recent strategic plan (2004, p. 14): "Advances in information technology, as well as other scientific and technical areas, have created the most significant global transformation since the Industrial Revolution." Technological advances and innovations have been decried by some as a *cause* of crime and embraced by others as a *solution* to our crime problem. As we demonstrate in this book, it is important to consider new technology's effects both on crime causation and on crime prevention and control, because if history is our guide (and in this case it needs to be) new technology will have effects in both areas; and there will invariably be both intended and unintended consequences for any new technological innovation (see chapter by Marx, this volume).

It is our intent to provide readers with a comprehensive review of the application of new technology in the areas of crime commission, crime prevention, and crime control (by police, courts, and corrections). In presenting this overview, we offer our assessment of the impact of each form of new technology, while also exploring key issues raised by both proponents and critics of what has come to be known as the *technology revolution*.

Our examination of the impact of new technology on crime, law, and justice will obviously raise more issues than we can possibly answer in this text. Nonetheless, three critical issues discussed at various points in the text come immediately to mind. First, perhaps the most salient issue related to the new technological innovations we examine in this text is whether – over time – we will replace *people* (police officers, court officers, judges, corrections officers, and community corrections officers) with various forms of *thing* (mechanical) technology (e.g., closed-circuit television [CCTV], cameras that detect speeders, wired courts, electronic monitoring, supermax prisons, etc.). For example, why do we need police officers patrolling the streets (and highways) when we have the technological resources (via cameras to detect speeders and red light violations, and CCTV to monitor public places) to remotely monitor activities and deploy a smaller number of police to address crime problems that are detected? The downsizing of police force manpower may be an inevitable consequence of this type of technological innovation, which is one reason that technological change may be viewed suspiciously by line personnel and the unions that represent their interests.

For those who draw parallels between domestic policing and military strategy (e.g., Kraska, 2001), it is worth noting a recent shift in the approach of the military to the question of troop strength and deployment strategy: we are now considering reducing our reliance on large, standing forces of military personnel (e.g., 150,000 troops are currently in Iraq) and instead creating a number of small, highly trained, and technology-rich quick strike Ranger-style units that can move to (and from) various "hot spot" areas as needed. This strategy may represent a possible deployment model for local, state, and federal police agencies that use various forms of hard technology (e.g., cameras, gunshot location devices, CCTV) and soft technology (e.g., crime mapping, hot spot analysis) to monitor areas (and analyze crime patterns) from a central location.

A second related issue is whether our fascination with the new technology of offender control will result in the continued development and expansion of criminal justice policies that minimize the possibility – and undermine the prospects – for individual (offender) and community change (Byrne & Taxman, 2006). One doesn't have to look any further than America's recent prison build-up to find a good example of how our reliance on offender control in institutional settings[1] has undermined our ability to provide treatment to offenders (for substance abuse, mental health, education/skill deficits) that might actually change their (criminal) behavior, both while in prison and upon reentry to the community (Gibbons & Katzenbach, 2006). To the extent that new technological innovations reinforce what David Garland (2002) has aptly labeled a "culture of control," technology may be moving our corrections system in the wrong direction. Perhaps we need to think in terms of a correctional paradigm that emphasizes the new technology of offender change, which Byrne and Pattavina (this volume) argue would represent a departure from our current emphasis on control technologies; in doing so, we would recognize a simple lesson of history: more often than not, "brute force" fails (Kleiman, 2005).

And finally, out of necessity rather than by design, we certainly need to consider the long-term consequences of privatization of key criminal justice system functions, including information management, offender/place-based monitoring, and offender control. In large part because the line staff and management in most criminal justice agencies do not currently have the necessary technology-based skill sets, we are forced to rely on the private sector today more than at any point in our history, particularly in the area of information technology. It is certainly possible to envision a "Brave New World" (Huxley, 1932) of crime prevention and control, where the private sector's helping, short-term support role (e.g., in the areas of information technology, system integration, electronic monitoring, and private prison construction/management) expands to the point where private sector crime control ultimately replaces public sector crime control in several critical areas, such as crime prevention, offender monitoring, place-based monitoring, and various forms of offender control.

HARD VERSUS SOFT TECHNOLOGY INNOVATIONS

Innovations in criminal justice technology can be divided into two broad categories: hard technology and soft technology. Hard technology innovations include new materials, devices, and equipment that can be used to either commit crime or prevent and control crime. Soft technology innovations include new software programs, classification systems, crime analysis techniques, and data sharing/system integration techniques that also provide opportunities for both crime commission and crime control. Table 1 highlights the types of hard and soft technology innovations in crime prevention, policing, the courts, institutional corrections, and com-

Table 1: The Application of Hard and Soft Technology to Crime Prevention and Control

	HARD Technology	SOFT Technology
Crime Prevention	• CCTV • street lighting • citizen protection devices (e.g., mace, tasers) • metal detectors • ignition interlock systems (drunk drivers)	• threat assessment instruments • risk assessment instruments • bullying ID protocol • sex offender registration • risk assessment prior to involuntary civil commitment • profiling
Police	• improved police protection devices (helmets, vests, cars, buildings) • improved/new weapons • less-than-lethal force (mobile/riot control) • computers in squad cars • hands-free patrol car control (Project 54) • offender and citizen IDs via biometrics/fingerprints	• crime mapping (hot spots) • crime analysis (e.g., Compstat) • criminal history data systems enhancement • information sharing within criminal justice system and with private sector
Courts	• the high-tech courtroom (computers, video, cameras, design features of buildings) • weapon detection devices • video conferencing • electronic court documents • drug testing at pretrial stage • video surveillance of courts	• case flow management systems • radio frequency identification technology • data warehousing • automation of court records • problem-oriented courts
Institutional Corrections	• contraband detection devices • duress alarm systems • language translation devices • remote monitoring • perimeter screening • less-than-lethal force in prison • prison design (supermax) • expanded use of segregation units • inmate identification and verification using biometrics	• use of simulations as training tools (mock prison riots) • new inmate classification systems (external/internal) • within prison crime analysis (hot spots; high-rate offenders) • information sharing with police, community, victims, and community-based corrections (reentry)

Table 1 *(continued)*

	HARD Technology	SOFT Technology
Community Corrections	• GPS for offender monitoring • language translators • Breathalyzers, instant drug tests • polygraph tests • laptops for line staff • GPS for staff location • reporting kiosks • remote alcohol monitoring devices • plethysmographs	• new classification devices for sex, drugs, and mentally ill offenders • new workload software • information sharing with community, police, treatment providers • computer software to monitor sex offender Internet activities

munity corrections that we will be discussing in this text. Although our list of new hard and soft technologies is not meant to be exhaustive, we suspect that it captures the range of technological innovations currently being applied in police, court, corrections, and community crime prevention programs, both in this country and abroad.

THE NEW TECHNOLOGY OF CRIME

As we consider each of these hard and soft technology applications in the field of criminal justice, it is certainly possible to think of how individuals or groups could utilize some of these same technological innovations to commit crimes and/or support ongoing terrorist activities. Indeed, this is precisely the rationale underlying the FBI's assessment of our country's cyber-crime problem:

> Cyber threats confronting the United States emerge from two distinct areas: (1) traditional criminal activity that has migrated to the Internet, such as fraud, identity theft, child pornography, and trade secret theft; and (2) Internet facilitated activity, such as terrorist attacks, foreign intelligence threats, and criminal intrusions into public and private networks for disruption or theft. The vulnerability of the United States to such activity is rapidly escalating as its economy and critical infrastructures become increasingly reliant on interdependent computer networks and the World Wide Web. (FBI, 2004)

We examine the impact of technological innovations on criminal behavior in two separate chapters. First, Kip Schlegel and Charles Cohen discuss the impact of technology on criminality. Utilizing a typology first developed by Rutgers University Professor Richard Sparks to study crimes for gain (Sparks, 1981), the authors discuss three distinct opportunity structures for committing technology-related crime: crime at work, crime as work, and crime after work.[2]

Schlegel, like us, is another former student of Richard Sparks, and his chapter written with Cohen both captures and extends Sparks's thinking on crimes for gain. As Schlegel and Cohen note in their chapter: "Simply stated, *crime as work* depicts those criminal activities which represent a way of life, that is, as a means of economic support and survival. *Crime at work* represents those criminal events (in fact, the largest category of crime) that take place in the context of one's, usually legitimate, occupation. And *crime after work* represents those events, often viewed as deviant, that are generally unrelated to one's occupation (legitimate or otherwise) and typically involve, for lack of a better word, illegal forms of leisure" (see Schlegel and Cohen, this volume). The authors provide examples of how technological innovations are utilized in each of these contexts to commit a range of technology-linked crimes, from "phishing" (an example of crime *as* work) to occupational frauds (such as the Enron case, where technology was used to commit the act and/or cover up illegal behavior; an example of crime *at* work), to sexual solicitation and illegal gambling on the Internet (crime *after* work).

The link between technology and criminal behavior is also examined in Rebovich and Martino's chapter, which particularly highlights two specific forms of technology-related crime: computer crime and identity theft. For each category of crime, the authors describe the nature and extent of the problem, the techniques used to commit the crime, and the emerging role of the private sector in the prevention and control of these forms of criminality. As Rebovich and Martino describe the new technology being developed in the private sector to prevent and control various forms of cyber-crime and identity theft (for a profit), they raise an issue that must be addressed about public-private sector partnerships: what are the consequences for crime control and for the public of the gradual encroachment of the private sector on the historical responsibilities of public criminal justice systems?

In summary, advances in both hard and soft technology have resulted in new *opportunities* for crime (through the Internet), new *forms* of criminality (e.g., Internet scams, and sex crimes on the Internet), new *techniques* for committing crimes (e.g., computer software programs, pirating, and extortion), and new *categories* of offenders and victims (e.g., on-line predators, and identity theft victims). Although this book's coverage of the new technology of crime is not meant to be exhaustive (see Taylor et al., 2006), we begin here to show that advances in both hard and soft technology have not been restricted to the criminal justice system's response to crime; they have also influenced criminal behavior in ways that are important to understand. For those readers looking for more details on the technology/ crime link, we have identified several key web-links where more information is available on a wide range of technology-related crime categories that may be of interest (see appendix for our listing of websites).

THE NEW TECHNOLOGY OF CRIMINAL JUSTICE

In addition to the two chapters we have just highlighted on the impact of new technology on crime, this text covers five separate topic areas related to the application of new technological innovations in the prevention and control of criminal behavior: (1) crime prevention, (2) police, (3) courts, (4) institutional corrections, and (5) community corrections. To the best of our knowledge, this text represents the first comprehensive review of new technological innovations across the entire criminal justice system. For each area of inquiry, we provide separate chapters on hard and soft technology innovations by some of this country's leading experts on the impact of technology on crime, law and social control. We conclude with commentary by Gary Marx, which highlights the need to distinguish rhetoric from reality in our ongoing search for "silver bullet" solutions to the crime problem. In the following section, we describe the scope of our review in each of these areas.

The New Technology of Crime Prevention

Crime prevention is a concept that has been applied in a number of different ways to the problem of crime: it has been used to refer to both *activities* (e.g., crime prevention programs and/or strategies) and *outcomes* (e.g., lower levels of crime in communities and/or lower levels of offending/re-offending by individuals). In the name of crime prevention, researchers have examined the influence/role of *formal* social control mechanisms (e.g., the deterrent effects of police, courts, and corrections) and *informal* social control mechanisms (e.g., the influence – through mechanisms such as attachment, commitment, and involvement – of family, peers, school, work, community; and the role of shame and belief systems/religion). In addition, crime prevention strategies have been targeted to different levels of prevention (primary, secondary, tertiary) and to the need for individual (i.e., private actions), parochial (group actions by neighborhood residents), and public actions (i.e., decisions to call the police) to prevent crime (Carr, 2003; Pattavina et al., 2006).

While crime prevention currently is used as a ubiquitous catch-all phrase that can be applied to both criminal justice-based and non-criminal-justice-based initiatives, our focus in this book is on strategies that utilize new technological innovations to either prevent crime (in particular places) or prevent reoffending by targeted groups of offenders (e.g., sex offenders, mentally ill offenders) and that do *not* rely exclusively on traditional actions by the police (arrest), courts (prosecution), and/or corrections (punishment, control, reform) subsystems.[3]

Our first chapter on crime prevention focuses on the new hard technology innovations being used to prevent crime in public places. According to co-authors Brandon Welsh and David Farrington: "Technological advances over the years have had a profound influence on the way we think about crime and the efforts that are taken to prevent it. Hard technologies to prevent crime cover a wide range of applications in different contexts, including metal detectors in schools, baggage screening at airports, bullet proof teller windows at banks, and security systems at homes and businesses" (this volume). There are other hard technology applications that quickly come to mind, including the use of personal protection devices (tasers, mace, lifeline/emergency call mechanisms) and ignition interlock systems with alcohol-sensor devices to prevent an individual from starting a car while intoxicated.

While there are certainly a number of possible hard technology applications to crime prevention, Welsh and Farrington's chapter focuses exclusively on the only two hard technology innovations that have had *known* effects on crime: closed-circuit television cameras (CCTV) and improved street lighting. Their chapter centers on a systematic review of the research on both forms of hard technology (Welsh & Farrington, 2002, 2004, 2006). Their findings are worth noting: "CCTV and improved lighting were more effective in reducing property crimes than in reducing violent crimes, with CCTV being significantly more effective than street lighting in reducing property crime."[4] We agree with Welsh and Farrington that, while these two strategies meet the review criteria established for identifying programs/ strategies that work, "there is still much to be learned about the optimal conditions under which CCTV and improved street lighting are most effective in reducing crime" (this volume).

The chapter by Andrew Harris and Arthur Lurigio examines a wide range of current soft technology applications in crime prevention and then provides a concise (and practical) justification for focusing on two major areas where soft technology has been applied: risk assessment and threat assessment. Harris and Lurigio provide a detailed review of the research on the design, implementation, and evaluation of the new generation of risk assessment and threat assessment instruments currently being used in this country and abroad.

Harris and Lurigio focus their review of risk assessment on two offender groups: sex offenders and mentally ill offenders. For each offender group Harris and Lurigio identify new risk assessment technology and then examine the available evidence of its effectiveness. The authors point out that: " . . . one of the major paradoxes related to the development and expansion of risk-assessment technology in the area of violence prevention is that practitioners seem obsessed by the need to assess risk in groups of individuals (e.g., sex offenders) with very low failure rates."

The application of threat assessment methods is explored in relation to school violence and terrorism. Harris and Lurigio conclude that threat assessment is only in its early stages of development and that the risk assessment field has a much sounder empirical base. Nonetheless, both represent examples of how soft technology innovations can be applied to the prevention of crime by targeted individuals (sex offenders, mentally ill) or at targeted places (schools, workplace, airports).

The New Technology of Policing

Changes in both the hard and soft technology of policing are transforming local, state, and federal policing departments in a number of fundamental ways. The two chapters we have included on technology and the police describe this transformation process, review the evidence of its impact on police practices and outcomes, and discuss the implications of technological changes in policing for the public.

Don Hummer's chapter examines several recent advances in the hard technology of policing, including: (1) non-lethal weaponry (chemical irritants, electric shock immobilizing technology, rubber, plastic, wooden bullet guns, beanbag shotguns, strobe and acoustical weaponry); (2) various non-electric immobilizing devices (water pressure, trap nets, sticky foam); (3) technology to reduce the number of vehicular pursuits (barrier strips, vehicle disabling and tracking devices); and (4) technology designed for officer safety (improved bulletproof vests, new body armor technology, improved patrol car protection technology). While there are certainly other hard technology applications in policing that can be identified (including new gunshot location devices, cameras to detect speeders and red light violations, the use of biometrics/improved fingerprint identification, and the hands-free communications systems being tested in patrol cars), Hummer has focused his review on a critical policing issue: how can we develop new technology that provides *both* officer safety and citizen safety and protection?

At the outset of his review, Hummer considers the argument that advances in new hard technology are the inevitable consequence of the militarization of domestic law enforcement (Kraska, 2001). Focusing on the issue of officer safety, Hummer concludes that: "While there are many factors in a complex dynamic associated with the significant decline in officer deaths over the past thirty years (Batton & Wilson, 2006), it seems reasonable to state that these innovations have played more than a negligible role." Apart from significant improvements in officer safety linked (generally) to advances in body armor, Hummer argues that there is little empirical evidence available to assess the impact of the other hard technology innovations on police performance. In his conclusion, he emphasizes the need for a "best practices," evidence-based review of the available research on these hard technology innovations.

Christopher Harris's chapter examines the impact of recent advances in information technology on police practices and performance. His review includes a description of new, technology-driven advances in: (1) data collection and management, including new record management systems, mobile data terminals, computer-aided dispatch (CAD) systems, and information sharing via the Internet; and (2) new data-driven police strategies, including Compstat, the use of computerized crime analysis and crime mapping software, and early warning/early intervention systems targeting police misconduct.

Harris also examines the technological and organizational challenges to the full development of information technology (IT) in local, state and federal police departments in this country. Given the current debate over the effectiveness of both problem-oriented policing and community-oriented policing strategies (Skogan & Frydl, 2004; Rosenfeld et al., 2005; Berk, 2005; Manning, 2003; Weisburd et al., 2004), Harris is cautious in his appraisal of the long-term impact of the IT revolution on police organization and administration. He concludes: "While IT has the potential to enhance police work, and perhaps fundamentally to alter traditional police practices, there is little evidence that IT has revolutionized policing when compared to the earlier eras of policing and the adoption of the telephone, two-way radio, and automobile. To the extent that newer IT mentioned throughout this chapter has contributed to policing, it appears to have largely enhanced traditional practices" (Christopher Harris, this volume).

The New Technology of Law and the Courts

Federal and state lawmakers in states across the U.S. are now scrambling to write and rewrite laws defining the elements of – and punishments for – a wide range of technology-related crimes: e.g., distribution of steroids, creation of methamphetamine labs, abuse of 911 emergency phone systems, new forms of financial and Internet fraud, sale/distribution of child pornography on the Internet, sex predation on the Internet, human trafficking on the Internet, identity theft, online credit card fraud, theft of private information and trade secrets, and disruption of computer systems, to name a few. At the same time, court administrators in these same jurisdictions are considering exactly how to integrate cutting edge technologies – some used by the new categories of techno-criminals – into traditional court processes.

The courts appear to lag behind the police in their utilization of both hard and soft technology to improve the efficiency and effectiveness of the court process while also protecting the rights of defendants, victims, witnesses, and the general public (Cornell, 2001). In addition, the courts appear to lag behind the police in their use of new technology to improve staff and courthouse safety. According to a recent review by the Joint Technology Committee of the Council of State Court Administrators and the National Association of Court Managers: "Despite the billions invested on court technology, any objective observer would have to conclude that the courts have not received the return they should have from the time, efforts, and dollars spent on court technology" (Cornell, 2001, p. 17, as quoted in Corbett, this volume). Absent an evidence-based review of the impact of technological innovations in court settings, policymakers are often forced to make critical decisions regarding new technology initiatives based only on anecdotal assessments and case studies by court managers, which may or may not be accurate.

Eric Bellone's chapter describes the application of a wide range of new technological innovations in courtroom settings across the country, including the use of CD-ROMs, desktop and laptop computers and the Internet; real-time transcription; video monitors and cameras; video conferencing; stored video/digital testimony; language translation devices; Braille systems and enhanced hearing devices; and virtual reality simulations. Bellone goes on to describe the rise of the "cyber court" (e.g., the Courtroom 21 Project at William and Mary School of Law) and to discuss the application of new technology at key decision points in the court process, including: (1) pretrial preparation, (2) the courtroom itself, (3) multi-jurisdictional and multi-court hearings, and (4) jury deliberations. In addition, he describes the use of new forms of hard technology (new weapons detection devices, shackles/restraints, video surveillance of the courthouse, and duress alarms) to improve the overall *safety* of courts. Finally, Bellone highlights the unique hard technology needs of one type of specialized court, the drug court.

Applying the evidence-based review criteria used by Sherman and colleagues (1997) to the topic of hard technology and the courts is revealing: we simply do not know "what works" in this area because the necessary independent quality evaluation research has not yet been conducted. Further clouding the picture is the cost of new technology and the likelihood that there will be differences between public defenders and private attorneys regarding access both to technology and to training on its use in the court process: these differences in access and knowledge may affect outcomes in individual cases. After considering these issues, Bellone offers the following assessment: "Given the special significance of the courts, perhaps the slow pace of hard technological integration is appropriate and leaves room for social scientists and legal scholars to properly measure the impact – and ramifications – of such changes on the judiciary as a branch of government."

The second chapter on the courts is authored by Ronald Corbett, the Executive Director of Massachusetts Supreme Judicial Court. He discusses a number of specific soft technology innovations that have been implemented in courtrooms throughout the country, including: (1) the new generation of automated court record systems, (2) court-specific web site development, (3) on-line access to case information, (4) electronic court documents, (5) new software-supported case management and court performance measurement systems (e.g., CourTools), (6) Radio Frequency Identification (RFID) technology, (7) data warehouses (e.g., Pennsylvania's Justice Network, JNET), and (8) the emergence of problem-solving courts with new soft technology requirements (e.g., drug testing, sentencing support tools). A critical issue that is now being played out in court systems (and in court cases) around the country, according to Corbett, is how do we balance the *public*'s right to know with an *individual's* right to privacy? He suggests that the answer to this question will likely determine the future course of technological innovations in the courts.

The New Technology of Institutional Corrections

Institutional corrections systems have become the testing ground for a large number of hard technology and soft technology innovations, in part through the efforts of the Office of Law Enforcement Technology Commercialization, which attempts to utilize the expertise and resources in the private sector to address problems (e.g., the detection of cell phones in prisons, safe toilet seats that cannot be turned into weapons) facing managers in public sector (Barte, 2006). According to a recent review by the National Commission on Safety and Abuse in America's Prisons, $60 billion was spent on corrections nationwide last year alone; the vast majority of these funds were used to build prisons and to house and manage prisoners (Gibbons & Katzenbach, 2006). While reliable estimates on the proportion of total corrections spending targeted for new technology development are not available, it seems safe to assert that it's a substantial sum.

Given the sheer number of prisons (1,668 in 2000) and jails (3,376 in 2000), and the amount of money we appear willing to spend to incarcerate offenders, it is not surprising that private-for-profit companies would be interested in public-private partnerships generally, and the development and testing of new technologies in particular. However, there are certainly questions that need to be answered about the impact of corrections technologies on the behavior, mental health, and physical health of offenders, both during their time in prison and upon return to the community. In the United States, inmate-line officer ratios are generally reported to be between 3:1 and 8:1 (Sourcebook, 2005), but reports of much higher ratios (100:1) are not unusual; by comparison, the ratios found in British prisons are much lower, allowing for closer interactions between staff and inmates and different strategies for staff management and offender change (Byrne et al., in press).

We rely on the technology of control in this country because we have no reasonable alternative, given our decision to use prison as the sanction of choice for certain categories of offenders (particularly drug offenders). In fact, we have made a conscious choice to imprison a large number of people (over 2 million at last count) and to supervise them using a relatively small number of line staff (270,317 custody/security staff in 2000, according to the *Sourcebook of Criminal Justice Statistics*, 2003, p. 96). While there is a continuing debate on the general deterrence-based, crime reduction effects of a prison sentence (Webster et al., 2006; Cook, 2006; Levitt, 2006), there appears to be an emerging consensus that: (1) prisons are dangerous places, (2) what happens in prison doesn't stay in prison, and, (3) *offender change* – not offender control – should be the primary mission of institutional corrections (Byrne et al., in press). It is in this broader context of sentencing policy and correctional philosophy that we now consider the new technology of prison control.

The chapter by Jacob Stowell addresses the application of new, hard technology in three general areas of institutional control: (1) facility monitoring (e.g., weapon and contraband detection, remote monitoring of inmates, officer duress systems, and perimeter security); (2) inmate/officer interactions (e.g., language translation devices, less-than lethal force); and (3) high-risk inmate control (e.g., the use of supermax prisons). According to Stowell, "With the size of the incarceration population increasing and jail and prison budgets shrinking, the ability to effectively manage prisoners has never been more difficult. One challenge that the field faces is how to strike a balance between the amount of resources dedicated to inmate *control* (technology upgrades) compared to that devoted to *treatment* (i.e., mental health services, programming) of inmates."

The chapter by Byrne and Pattavina echoes a similar theme regarding the appropriate "tipping point" between strategies designed to control offenders versus strategies designed to change their attitudes, values, and behaviors. The authors examine the implementation and impact of several new soft technology initiatives in prisons and jails, and they identify a variety of current and potential soft technology applications to problem solving in institutional settings. These applications target a wide range of inmate (classification, treatment and control) and staff (management and protection) activities, including: (1) new techniques for the initial classification and subsequent institutional placements of inmates; (2) new offender monitoring strategies (both health and behavior related); (3) crime analysis, "hot spot" identification, and problem-oriented conflict resolution strategies within prisons and jails; (4) information sharing with police, courts, corrections, public health, and public/private sector treatment providers;

(5) the application of crime mapping and neighborhood risk assessment in reentry initiatives; and, (6) staff performance measurement systems in prisons and jails.

In their conclusion, Byrne and Pattavina offer an alternative perspective on soft technology applications. They suggest that various forms of information technology – in particular, prison classification at the outset of an offender's prison experience and reclassification nearing the end of an offender's time in prison as he/she prepares for reentry – can be revised to emphasize the goal of *offender change* rather than short-term offender control. Byrne and Pattavina's chapter offers a framework for changing offenders *while in prison* by linking offender assessment to offender placement in various forms of prison treatment (for mental health problems, substance abuse problems, educational deficits, employment/skill deficits, etc.). As Gilligan and others have pointed out (Gilligan & Lee, 2004), one of the ironies of imprisonment is that some of the most compelling evidence of offender change is from evaluations of programs operated in institutional settings (e.g., prison therapeutic communities and cognitive restructuring programs located in both prisons and halfway houses). Similarly, Liebling (2004) and others have argued that prisons can and should be monitored and judged in terms of their "moral performance" (e.g., staff-inmate interactions, procedural justice, access to treatment, etc.), based on a simple axiom: the moral performance of *prisons* will affect the moral performance of *prisoners*, while in prison and upon release to the community (Byrne et al., in press).

The New Technology of Community Corrections

The growth of the nation's corrections system has not been limited to institutional corrections. Community corrections populations have actually grown at a faster pace than the populations of its institutional counterpart, but what has shrunk over the past decade and a half is the proportion of corrections spending allocated to community corrections: e.g., last year, community corrections supervised 70% of the total corrections population but received about 20% of all corrections funding. According to a recent U.S. Bureau of Justice Statistics bulletin (Glaze & Palla, 2005, p. 2): "The number of adult men and women in the United States who were being supervised on probation and parole at the end of 2004 reached a new high of 4,916,480, up from 3,757,282 on December 31, 1995. . . . Overall, the correctional population increased by nearly 2.5 million, or 57%, from 1990 to 2004. Probationers accounted for 51% of the growth (or 1,262,000), followed by prisoners (27% or 679,000), jail inmates (12% or 309,000), and parolees (9% or 234,000)." The reason these numbers matter is that as the scale of the community corrections system has increased, community corrections managers have embraced a wide range of hard and soft technologies designed to improve the community control of offenders *without adding significant numbers of new personnel.* The next two chapters highlight a variety of ways that community corrections managers can apply new technological innovations to the management of offenders under community supervision.

Patricia Harris and James Byrne's chapter identifies a number of hard technology innovations currently being used by probation and parole agencies across the country, including: (1) new electronic monitoring technology; (2) new drug testing technology (e.g., urinalysis, sweat patches, saliva samples, hair analysis, and blood tests); (3) technologies for managing alcohol-involved offenders (ignition interlock systems, and remote alcohol monitoring devices; (4) technologies for managing sex offenders (polygraph testing, the penile plethysmograph); and, (5) automated reporting systems (telephone-based reporting, kiosks, language translators). Harris and Byrne's comprehensive, evidence-based review of each of these new forms of technology provides new insights on two key issues we identified at the outset: (1) the continuing debate between advocates of treatment-versus control-based corrections strategies (Byrne & Taxman, 2005; Farabee, 2005); and, (2) the consequences of privatizing certain technology-based supervision functions (e.g., electronic monitoring) for the organization, administration, and effectiveness of community corrections.

In their chapter on community corrections and soft technology, April Pattavina and Faye Taxman review the following areas of community corrections practice that utilize new forms of soft information technology: (1) the new generation of classification instruments, (2) new approaches to offender treatment based on the Risk/Need Responsivity Model, (3) new case management information technology, and (4) new approaches to information sharing, crime mapping, and the assessment of community risk level for offenders under community supervision (and during reentry).

Pattavina and Taxman underscore the "culture of control" argument offered by Garland (2002) and others, concluding that: "Despite their good intentions, advances in soft technology in community corrections have resulted in more control over offenders. We collect more information about them, use that information to shape their future behavior and then closely monitor and control that behavior in the community."

CONCLUDING COMMENTARY

We conclude our review of the new technology of crime, law, and social control with the commentary of Gary Marx, Professor Emeritus of Sociology at the Massachusetts Institute of Technology. Dr. Marx is the author of several books and articles on the impact of technology on society generally and the role of formal agents of social control (police, courts, corrections) in particular. His chapter first presents a typology of "social engineering" strategies, which he describes as crime prevention through environmental control, and he then analyzes the consequences of these strategies for the public. Based on his review of the preceding chapters, Marx examines the unintended consequences of our ongoing search for *technological* solutions for social problems.

Marx's perspective on the use and misuse of technology in support of social control challenges much of the current thinking about the benefits of technological change. He captures a theme that runs through this entire volume: we need to find ways to apply new technology to the problems related to the monitoring and control of individuals and places; but we also need to find ways to use technology for an even more important purpose – to *reinforce moral performance at both the institutional and individual level.* As Marx wryly observes,

> A well known, if often naïve expression (given that individuals and groups do not start with equivalent resources), holds that where there is a will there is a way. This speaks to the role of human effort in obtaining goals. With the control possibilities made available by science and technology this may be reversed to where there is a way there is a will. As the myth of Frankenstein implies, we must be ever vigilant to be sure that we control the technology rather than the reverse. As Jacques Ellul (1964) argues, there is a danger of self-amplifying technical means silently coming to determine the ends or even becoming ends in themselves, divorced from a vision of, and the continual search for, the good society." (Marx, this volume)

NOTES

1. The U.S. spent $60 billion on corrections last year alone, with over three-quarters of that total allotted to prison management.
2. As former students of the late Professor Sparks, we know that he was ahead of his time in terms of his conceptualization of crimes for gain. Much of what has come to be known as the life-course perspective (Laub and Sampson, 2001) has its roots in Sparks's attempt to re-conceptualize crimes for gain (and of course Edwin Sutherland's differential association theory) during this period, by specifically considering the impact of life-course decisions (e.g., an individual choosing a life of work or a life of crime along the lines of Sutherland's *Professional Thief*, 1937) on individuals/careers (both in and out of crime). Similarly, routine activities theorists (e.g., Felson and Clarke, 1998) appear to owe a debt to Sparks as well, since he and his colleagues (e.g., Gibbs and Shelly, 1981) talked in these terms before – and more eloquently than – everyone else. Unfortunately, much of Sparks's writing on this topic is only found in technical reports to the U.S. National Institute of Justice (e.g., Sparks et al., 1982).
3. When considering the evidence of the impact of these strategies on crime, the authors of both crime prevention chapters appear to share Lawrence Sherman's view, which he presented in his influential report to Congress on *What Works* in the area of crime prevention (Sherman et al., 1997, p. 2): "Crime prevention is . . . defined not by its intentions, but by its consequences. These consequences can be defined in at least two ways. One is by the number of **criminal events**; the other is by the number of **criminal offenders** (Hirschi, 1987). Some would also define it by the amount of **harm** prevented (Reiss and Roth, 1993, pp. 59-61) or by the number of **victims** harmed or harmed repeatedly (Farrell, 1995). In asking the Attorney General to report on the effectiveness of crime prevention efforts supported by the Justice Department's Office of Justice Programs, the U.S. Congress has embraced an even broader definition of crime prevention: reduction of **risk factors** for crime (such as gang membership) and increases in **protective factors** (such as completing high school) – concepts that a National Academy of Sciences report has labeled as "primary" prevention (Reiss and Roth, 1993, p. 150). What all these definitions have in common is their focus on observed effects, and not the "hard" or "soft" content, of a program.
4. One caveat is in order when considering these findings. Both CCTV and improved street lighting strategies were found to be "far more

effective in reducing crime in the U.K. than in the U.S." (Welsh and Farrington, this volume). The obvious question is: why? The authors consider a number of possibilities for this differential effect, including length of follow-up (shorter follow-ups show better results), the actual date the study was conducted and the specific technology used (newer studies/technologies do better), whether the strategy was implemented as a stand-alone innovation or used in conjunction with another initiative (stand-alones do worse), and cultural context/public support (more public support for CCTV in U.K. than in U.S.).

REFERENCES

Austin, J. (2006, September). How much risk can we take? The misuse of risk assessment in corrections. *Federal Probation*, 58-63.

Barte, W. (2006, October). Commentary: Collaborative innovations will lead corrections into the future. *Corrections Today*, 8.

Batton, C., & Wilson, S. (2006). Police murders: An examination of historical trends in the killings of law enforcement officers in the United States, 1947 to 1988. *Homicide Studies, 10*, 79-97.

Berk, R. (2005). Knowing when to fold 'em: An essay on evaluating the impact of CEASEFIRE, COMPSTAT, AND EXILE. *Criminology & Public Policy, 4*, 451-466.

Byrne, J., & Taxman, F. (2006, June). Crime control strategies and community change. *Federal Probation*, 3-12.

Byrne, J., Taxman, F., & Hummer, D. (in press). *The culture of prison violence*. Boston: Allyn and Bacon.

Byrne, J., & Taxman, F. (2005). Crime (control) is a choice: Divergent perspectives on the role of treatment in the adult corrections system. *Criminology & Public Policy, 4*(2), 291-310.

Byrne, J., Lurigio, A., & Petersilia, J. (1992). *Smart sentencing*. Newbury Park, CA: Sage.

Carr, P. (2003). The new parochialism: The implications of the Beltway case for arguments concerning informal social control. *American Journal of Sociology, 108*, 1249-1291.

Clear, T., & Cadova, E. (2003). *Community Justice*. Belmont, CA: Wadsworth/Thomson Learning.

Cook, P. (2006). The deterrent effects of California's Proposition 8: Editorial introduction. *Criminology & Public Policy, 5*(3), 413-416.

Cornell, J. (2001). The work toward standards. *Court Manager, 16*(1), 17-24.

Ellul, J. (1964). *The technological society*. New York: Vintage Books.

Farabee, D. (2005). *Rethinking rehabilitation: Why can't we reform our criminals?* Washington, DC: AEI Press, American Enterprise Institute.

Farrington, D., & Welsh, B. (2005). Randomized experiments in criminology: What have we learned in the last two decades? *Journal of Experimental Criminology, 1*, 1-29.

Federal Bureau of Investigation (FBI), (2004). *FBI strategic plan: 2004-2009*. Washington, DC: Federal Bureau of Investigation.

Felson, M., & Clarke, R. V. (1998). *Opportunity makes the thief: Practical theory for crime prevention.* Police Research Series Paper 98. London: Home Office.

Garland, D. (2002). *The culture of control: Crime and social order in contemporary society.* New York: Oxford University Press.

Gibbons, J., & N. Katzenbach. (2006). *Confronting confinement: A report of the Commission on Safety and Abuse in America's Prisons.* New York: Vera Institute of Justice (http://www.prisoncommission.org/pdfs/Confronting_Confi nement.pdf).

Gibbs, J. J., & P. L. Shelly (1982). *Commercial theft studies project final report.* Newark, NJ: Center for the Study of the Causes of Crime for Gain, School of Criminal Justice, Rutgers University.

Gilligan, J. (1996). *Violence: Reflections on a national epidemic.* New York: Random House.

Gilligan, J., & Lee, B. (2004). Beyond the prison paradigm: From provoking violence to preventing it by creating anti-prisons. *Annals of the NY Academy of Sciences, 1036,* 300-324.

Glaze, L., & Palla, S. (2005). *Probation and parole in the United States, 2004.* Washington, DC: Bureau of Justice Statistics Bulletin, November.

Huxley, A. (1932). *Brave new world* New York: Bantam Books.

Kleiman, M. (2005). *When brute force fails: Strategic thinking for crime control.* Final report to the National Institute of Justice (NCJ # 211204).

Kraska, P. B. (2001). *Militarizing the American criminal justice system: The changing role of the armed forces and the police.* Boston, MA: Northeastern University Press.

Laub, J., & Sampson, R. (2001). Understanding desistance from crime. In M. Tonry (Ed.), *Crime and justice: A review of research,* Vol. 28. Michael Tonry. Chicago: University of Chicago Press.

Levitt, S. (2006). The case of the critics who missed the point: A reply to Webster et al. *Criminology & Public Policy, 5*(3), 449-460.

Liebling, A. (2004). *Prisons and their moral performance: A study of values, quality, and prison life.* Oxford: Oxford University Press.

Manning, P. K. (2003). *Policing contingencies.* Chicago: University of Chicago Press.

Pattavina, A. (2005). *Information technology and the criminal justice system.* Thousand Oaks, CA: Sage.

Rosenfeld, R., Fornango, R., & Baumer, E. (2005). Did CEASEFIRE, COMPSTAT, and EXILE reduce homicide? *Criminology & Public Policy, 4,* 419-466.

Sherman, L. W., Gottfredson, D. C., MacKenzie, D. L., Eck, J. E., Reuter, P., & Bushway, S. D. (1997). *Preventing crime: What works, what doesn't, what's promising.* Washington, DC: National Institute of Justice, U.S. Department of Justice.

Skogan, W., & Frydl, K. (2004). *Fairness and effectiveness in policing: The evidence.* Washington, DC: National Academies Press, National Research Council.

Sourcebook of Criminal Justice Statistics (2003). Table 1.104: Employees of Federal, State, and Local Adult Correctional Facilities. U.S. Department of Justice, Bureau of Justice Statistics, Census of State and Federal Correctional Facilities, 2000. Washington, DC: U.S. Department of Justice.

Sparks, R. F. (1981). *Center for the Study of the Causes of Crime for Gain Annual Report 1980-1981.* Newark, NJ: School of Criminal Justice, Rutgers University.

Sparks, R. F., Greer, A., & Manning, S. A. (1982). *Theoretical studies project final report.* Newark, NJ: Center for the Study of the Causes of Crime for Gain, School of Criminal Justice, Rutgers University.

Sutherland, E. H. (1937). *The professional thief.* Chicago: University of Chicago Press.

Taylor, R., Caeti, T., Loper, D., Fritsch, E., & Liederbach, J. (2006). *Digital crime and digital terrorism.* Upper Saddle River, NJ: Prentice Hall.

Taylor, R. B., & Gottfredson, S. (1986). Environmental design, crime and prevention: An examination of community dynamics. In A. J. Reiss, Jr. & M. Tonry (Eds.), *Communities and crime. Crime and justice: A review of research,* Vol. 8. Chicago: University of Chicago Press.

Webster, C., Doob, A., & Zimring, F. (2006). Proposition 8 and crime rates in California: The case of the disappearing deterrent. *Criminology & Public Policy,* 5(3), 417-448.

Weisburd, D., Mastrofski, S. D., Greenspan, R., & Willis, J. J. (2004). Reforming to preserve: Compstat and strategic problem solving in American policing. *Criminology & Public Policy,* 2, 421-455.

Weisburd, D., Mastrofski, S. D., Greenspan, R., & Willis, J. J. (2004). *The growth of Compstat in American policing.* Washington, DC: Police Foundation.

Welsh, B. C., & Farrington, D. P. (2002). *Crime prevention effects of closed circuit television: A systematic review.* Home Office Research Study, No. 252. London: Home Office.

Welsh, B. C., & Farrington, D. P. (2004). Surveillance for crime prevention in public space: Results and policy choices in Britain and America. *Criminology & Public Policy,* 3, 497-526.

Welsh, B. C., & Farrington, D. P. (Eds.). (2006). *Preventing crime: What works for children, offenders, victims, and places.* New York: Springer.

2. THE IMPACT OF TECHNOLOGY ON CRIMINALITY

Kip Schlegel

Indiana University

and

Charles Cohen

Indiana State Police

INTRODUCTION

This chapter discusses the relationship between technology and criminality. In many respects, modern technology in the 21st century is no different from the modern technology of the 20th century, modern technology of the Middle Ages, and so on: the invention and modification of tools continues to be applied to relieving victims of their money and/or property, and to moving property and money quickly. This being said, modern technology in the 21st century does depart from past history in important ways. For example, while investigators of financial crimes continue to pursue the long-established axiom to "follow the money," the impact of recent technology is that both the definition of money and avenues available to follow the illicit revenue have become increasingly obscured. Furthermore, now more than ever, technology has given certain skilled offenders an array of almost impenetrable means to engage in crime, far advanced from the skills and means available to the majority of offenders and to law enforcement. In many respects modern technology opens up possibilities for crime and, at the same time, creates a hierarchy of offending between the technological haves and have-nots. This, in turn, forces law enforcement to face technological realities that strain resources, competencies, and concepts of mission. By virtue of both its speed and scope, modern technology has also fostered a highly interactive relationship between offenders' motivations for offending and the opportunities to do so. From the standpoint of criminological theory, this relationship forces us to rethink concepts of crime and basic assumptions about the motivations for offending. In this chapter we attempt to situate the relationship between technology and crime, first with a brief discussion of technology generally, then by offering a framework to order and think about the relationship, and finally by discussing the ramifications of technology on our understanding of criminal behavior. Because issues relating to law enforcement have been discussed at length in other chapters in this book, we touch on implications for law enforcement only where relevant to the broader aims of the chapter.

Understanding the Impact of Technology on Crime

There is no way to accurately gauge the extent to which technology impacts on offending. It is of little value to turn to the statute books for help since crimes are rarely defined by their involvement with or incorporation of technology. When crimes do include technology, they are rarely distinguished by the vast array of technological tools available toward committing the offenses. We may see that someone was charged with theft and not know, on the face of the charge, whether it involved stolen credit cards and the use of a skimming device (a magnetic card reader), or simply the plucking of cash from a wallet. We may see that someone was charged with wire or mail fraud but not know, on its face, whether it was through the utilization of a traditional wire line and "snail mail" from Indianapolis to Fargo, or through the utilization of Voice Over Internet Protocols (VoIP) and electronic accounts from Miami to Chicago via the Cayman Islands, Oslo, Norway, and Zurich, Switzerland.

Similarly, there are enormous obstacles in attempting to gauge the impact of technology on rates of crime, or in trying to compare the number of crimes that include technology with crimes that don't. The U.S. Federal Bureau of Investigation (U.S. FBI, 2005), for example, estimates that in 2004 there were 401,326 robberies with an estimated total loss of $525 million or approximately $1,300 per offense. There were an estimated 7 million larceny-thefts reported in 2005 with an estimated monetary loss of $5.1 billion, or $727 per offense. The U.S. Federal Trade Commission (2006) reported that in 2005 it received approximately 431,000 complaints for fraud-related offenses such as foreign money offers, private-sweepstakes and lotteries, advance fee loans, and Internet service and computer complaints. The report estimated total fraud-related losses of over $680 million with an average median loss of $350. Of those reported frauds, 46% involved the Internet, accounting for approximately half the total losses. The commission also reported receiving an additional 255,500 identity theft complaints during 2005, including credit card frauds (26%), phone/utility frauds (18%) and bank frauds (17%). Similarly, the U.S. Bureau of Justice Statistics (2006) reported that in 2004, 3.6 million households (1 in 33) suffered some form of identity theft in the six-month period under study, and BJS estimated the total loss from identify theft to have been $3.2 billion dollars. Of course, this entire chapter could be dedicated to the problems of counting crimes and the issues that arise with making comparisons across categories and reporting mechanisms. Perhaps the safest conclusion one can draw from these numbers is that the extent of crime that involves modern technology is arguably worth writing about.

To begin to understand the scope of modern technology's effect on criminality it might be useful to turn to a case study and examine the transitional role technology has played over time with respect to one type of crime – pedophilia. Pedophiles who act on their predilections, either through the collection and dissemination of child pornography or through contact offenses involving children, have existed for centuries, not only in the United States but around the world. Through time, their crimes have morphed in response to important advances in image technology.

The first instant camera was developed in 1947 by Edwin Land: it was known as the Polaroid Land Camera. Before introduction of this technology in the marketplace, someone wanting to produce a still photographic image containing child pornography had to become skilled in the development of traditional negative-to-print film or to locate a confederate in the film developing industry. Child pornographers were able to subvert the "new" technology of instant film cameras to enhance the secrecy of their criminality. But the technology of the time still made it relatively difficult to trade in this contraband once it was manufactured. A person wishing to procure such images had to either meet the producer, or a broker, in person, or to use the mail to obtain the images. The risks and dangers associated with such a commodity trade are obvious and numerous. As a result, commercially-produced child pornography mainly constituted poor-quality magazines unlawfully imported from traditional source countries into the United States. Traditional law enforcement tools and techniques were quite successful in the interdiction of this material. Similarly, before the advent of consumer video cameras in the late 1970s to mid-1980s, those wanting to capture unlawful moving images needed to find a source for film development. As VHS and Beta format video cameras began to enter the market, law enforcement saw an influx of amateur child pornography videos produced and traded. This technology allowed contact offenders to memorialize their behaviors as never before.

The most significant technological impact on this class of criminality has resulted from the related innovations of digitalization and the Internet. Digital still and video cameras allow any interested party to become a producer of high-quality child pornography. The Internet allows for the distribution of this child pornography on a global scale in relative anonymity.[1]

Technology influences child crimes by providing a means of communication, both with other offenders and with potential victims. It takes someone with a modicum of familiarity in the World Wide Web no more than five minutes to find an active chat room where the unlawful exploitation of children is being openly discussed. Such communication with other criminals serves to enhance each offender's skills sets and provides a source of affirmation for the criminality. This is exemplified by the fact that criminals involved with child pornography collectively refer to each other as "hobbyists." Technology serves to broaden the contact offenders' predatory range. The Internet, through a myriad of methods including chat rooms, instant messaging, VoIP, Webcams, social networking sites, Internet relay chat, forums, and Web logs (blogs), provides a source through which predatory criminal can locate, cultivate, and groom potential victims.[2]

The most recent technological advances exploited by those engaged in child pornography involve the material's portability and concealment. Child pornographers are responding to law enforcement's efforts to curb the proliferation of the material by transitioning to the use of portable electronic devices, such as mobile telephones, and through the use of security software in order to cover their tracks. Mobile telephones and other mobile devices are now capable of receiving, storing, and transmitting moving and still photos, some having memory storage capacities to rival desktop computers of less than a decade ago. Many criminals now go beyond just encrypting digital files to employing techniques such as steganography, which will be examined later in this chapter.

Understanding the Role of Technology in Crime

When criminologist Edwin Sutherland was asked the best way to study and understand white-collar crime his directive was simply to ask individuals to talk about their work and the kinds of crimes that take place in their occupations. It is logical that since white-collar crimes occur in the context of the legitimate workplace, it is necessary to first understand the workplace. A similar approach might be suggested for studying the role of technology in crime. Before we discuss how it is used in crime we should first briefly consider the role of technology for socially valued and legitimate purposes. While it would be impossible to cover this topic in a book, let alone one chapter, we can outline some important points generally about technology.

First, technology is foremost a means of communication. Whether the communication conveys the announcement of a birth, the transmission of Social Security numbers, a declaration of war, a change in the price of a commodity, or support for or opposition to a cause; whether it is between individuals, groups, institutions, nation-states, or machines or devices; technology is used to convey and manage communications across time and space. The evolution of technology is grounded in part by the need and desire to manipulate the form and means of communication in ways that maximize control, efficiency, security, and effectiveness.

Second, technology serves as a production and storage tool. Technology facilitates the creation and management not only of information, but of goods and services, whether they be cars, space shuttles, toilet paper, songs and videos, pharmaceutical products, stocks or contracts on pork bellies. Technology supports the producer, intermediaries and end-user in this regard.

Third, technology is a presentation tool. In both its communication and production functions, the ability to share and convey information in the most captivating form – whether in words, numbers or images, in large quantities or to selectively targeted audiences – is vital. Importantly, technology plays a support role unto itself. A whole host of satellite technologies revolve around the core functions of communication, production, and presentation, to enhance, protect and facilitate those functions. They aid in expanding capacity, protecting by concealment, or by constructing and maintaining barriers, and they facilitate by easing and expanding access and understanding of those functions.

A recent example of the impact of technological advances on legitimate business activity can be found in the banking field. The Check Clearing Act for the 21st Century ("Check 21") was signed into law by President Bush on October 28, 2003 and became effective on October 28, 2004. Check 21 allows banks to replace original paper checks with "substitute checks" that are made from digital copies of the originals (American Bankers Association press release, June 13, 2006). This law was facilitated by advances in technology and by the functional implications of how technology is utilized in the banking industry for communication, storage, and production of records. Inter-bank electronic communications can now occur with the use of "substitute checks," allowing for the rapid transmission and approval of electronic fund transfers between financial institutions. Instead of physically moving paper checks from one bank to another, Check 21 allows banks to process more checks electronically. Banks can capture a picture of the front and back of the check along with the associated payment information and transmit this information electronically. If a receiving bank or its customer requires a paper check, the bank can use the electronic picture and payment information to create a paper "substitute check." Banks insured by the Federal Deposit Insurance Corporation are no longer required to retain original checks or similar paper negotiable instruments, but may alternatively use electronic images for archival and audit purposes. Further, the technology works to expand the industry sector of e-banking, such that a truly virtual bank can offer the same consumer services as a traditional brick-and-mortal bank.

The same factors that account for the use of technology toward socially valued and legitimate ends also account for the use of technology in crime. Along with the benefits to the banking industry and its customers, Check 21 can be exploited for criminal purposes. Investigators will no longer have the ability to retrieve the original paper instrument used by a criminal in the furtherance of his activity. Criminals must no longer worry about having left a fingerprint or trace DNA on a forged or altered check that was negotiated at a bank branch or automated teller machine. Likewise, those engaged in organized financial crime can also take advantage of the proliferation of services offered by e-banks, enabling them to more easily conceal their identity. Conversely, the traditional crime of check "kiting" (passing bad checks) is made more difficult by the speed with which the new application technology transfers money both between accounts and among banking institutions.

Technology facilitates, controls and manages communication among individuals as offenders and/or victims, or as co-conspirators or criminal networks, for purposes of engagement, management, or concealment. It may be used to bring two people together who share a rare deviant urge, as in the recent case in Germany in which one man interested in engaging in cannibalism was, through the use of the Internet, able to find a person desirous of becoming the meal.[3] It can logically be concluded that were it not for the ways in which modern technology enables communication, two people with apparently complementary fetishes would not have come in contact, facilitating the criminal act.

One example of how criminality morphs in relation to the progression of technology as a communication tool can be found in the history of network intrusion. Over time, network intrusion has evolved from "Phreaking" to "hacking" to "Phishing" and "Pharming," to "Wardriving" and most recently to "Bluesnarfing." This shows how, with every technological advance, there is a criminal element waiting to exploit the inherent weaknesses. Phreaking, now mostly defunct, is the practice of subverting pay telephones and telephone company switches to obtain free telephone service and access to telephone networks. The key to phreaking was the discovery that a tone at 2600 Hz was sent through the phone company system to signal that a user had hung up the telephone. Phreakers were able to exploit this discovery to compromise the system. The organic link between phreaking, which had its heyday in the 1950s through 1980s, and later exploits such as hacking and wardriving, is found in continued references to the 2600 Hz discovery. The most famous publication on hacking, or the exploitation of computer systems and code, is a periodical called *2600: The Hacker Quarterly*. Today, numerous Internet Relay Chat groups that include the "2600" in their names exchange information on hacking. As e-mail became the preferred method of written communication for much of the world, and the Internet entered most people's lives, generations-old fraud schemes were adapted to the new online paradigm by employing pharming and phishing (which are discussed below). As wireless networks and Wi-Fi hotspots began to proliferate, wardriving followed. Wardriving is the act of searching for wireless hotspots and then often attempting to exploit vulnerabilities to either gain access to the Internet or to compromise the information contained on the network.

"Bluesnarfing," sometimes also called Bluejacking and Podslurping, is the exploitation of Bluetooth-enabled devices. Bluetooth is a communication protocol that allows devices such as personal-digital assistants (PDAs), mobile phones, laptops, digital cameras, PCs etc., to connect to each other and exchange information. The most infamous instance of Bluesnarfing occurred in February 2005, when a Sidekick II mobile communication device owned by the celebrity Paris Hilton was compromised. Information contained on the device, including data and images, was stolen. Bluesnarfing occurs when an individual in relatively close proximity to the victim uses a Bluetooth-enabled device to remove data from a victim with another

Bluetooth-enabled device. The limiting factor for this emerging crime is the necessity for the perpetrator to be in close proximity, since the effective range of Bluetooth radio frequency is generally within 32 feet. Like many crimes exploiting emerging technologies, the risks include an uninformed pool of potential victims and the inability of public sector investigators to maintain a competitive edge. Bluesnarfing has implications that range from stalking, as arguably was seen in the Paris Hilton incident, to corporate espionage. Most large corporations expend significant resources to secure their computer networks. Nevertheless, there always must be a way for employees to gain legitimate access. Unfortunately, the law of unintended consequences is such that the more often a corporation changes the network password to mitigate the potential for improper access, and the more often it requires complex password strings to combat brute force attacks, the more likely it is that employees will record those passwords to ensure that they are not forgotten, thereby opening the door for continued problems.

Technology can be used as a communication tool toward the end of state-sponsored terrorism, or it can be used to hide identity from victims, competitors, or law enforcement. Those wanting to secretly transmit information globally can do so using technology, such as steganography, which is the technique of hiding data or an image by embedding it in the code of an innocuous image or music file. Every electronic image, whether it is located on a computer disk, hard drive, or Web site DNS server, has a virtual fingerprint called a hash value. One can tell if an image has been altered by comparing the hash value of the suspect image to that of the original image. If the values are different, the image has been altered. What many forms of steganography do is remove the least relevant portions of an electronic image and replace those portions with the hidden data or image. So, a large electronic photographic image, such as one taken with a five megapixel home digital camera may have some of the information removed, such that the alteration is not noticeable to the observer, but make room for the hidden information to be embedded such that a comparison of hash values between the altered and original image will appear the same. Additionally, the hidden data or image will be encrypted in some fashion. One advantage of steganography over encryption is that one can tell an encrypted file exists, but cannot determine its contents. It is extremely difficult, if not impossible, to determine that an image even contains steganography, much less identify the hidden information. In this manner, terrorists can secretly communicate with each other on a global scale.

The use of steganography by terrorists was reported in two *USA Today* newspaper articles by Jack Kelley on February 5, 2001, entitled "Terror Groups Hide behind Web Encryption" and "Bin Laden Notes Hidden in Sites." While much of the information contained in these and other media accounts is not verifiable, it is technologically feasible for such communication to facilitate the command and control functions of terrorist organizations. A terrorist leader, wanting to forward target information to the operational cell leader would post an innocuous image, containing the embedded information, on a prearranged Web site. Numerous free photo exchange sites could be used for this purpose. The cell leader would already know the password needed to remove the embedded information. On a prearranged date, or in response to some other cue, the cell leader would download the apparently benign image and use the password to extract the embedded information. That information could be further encrypted, potentially with a password known to another conspirator, to provide an additional level of secrecy. The various technologies both employed and exploited by this hypothetical scenario would make it almost impossible to identify the existence of the communication, much less determine the content or relevance. (Journalist Jack Kelley was later discredited for falsifying information contained in stories other than the ones cited in this chapter.) Because of the very nature of schemes such as this and the inherent secrecy of the governmental agencies tasked with investigating such crimes, it is not possible to determine the prevalence of such activity. This scenario exemplifies a quandary for investigators: how does one investigate and prove the factual elements of a crime if it is not even possible to identify its occurrence?

Another example of the illicit use of technology involves "Advance Fee Fraud." Advance fee fraud schemes disseminated through spam e-mails and originating in one African country are so ubiquitous that the scheme's common name contains that of the country of origin. Nigerian Fraud Schemes are also known as "419 fraud" schemes, making reference to the Nigerian criminal code section 419 that states, in part, "Any person who by any false pretense, and with intent to defraud, obtains from any other person anything capable of being stolen, or induces any other person to deliver to any person anything capable of being stolen" (Nigerian Law Criminal Code Act, Part 6, Division 1, Chapter 34, Section 419). This fraud scheme is possible because millions of potential victims can be contacted through e-mail, instant messaging, and other such means in a cost-effective manner. The crime is also facilitated and the identities of the criminals concealed by the exploited technology's ability to globalize the victim pool and conceal the true location of the scheme perpetrator. It has been alleged that 419 fraud schemes have been combined with another fraud scheme, known as "Pharming." Pharming occurs when a criminal launches a Web site that appears to the potential victim to be the legitimate Web site of a known business. The victim is then enticed to provide personal information through this fraudulent Web site. In an alert published through the Internet Fraud Complaint Center, the FBI reported that it had become aware of a sophisticated new technique used to obtain funds through the 419 scam. The scam contains the usual e-mail requesting assistance in transferring millions of dollars out of Nigeria. The sophistication begins when the recipient is directed to open a bank account at a Suffolk England Bank and is provided a link to the bank's Web site. After clicking the link, the victim is directed to a professional-looking bank Web site which appears to be that of Suffolk England Bank; however, it is actually a replica of the true bank site. Within hours after opening the account, a balance of millions of dollars appears to have been deposited in the victim's account. When attempting to transfer or withdraw funds from the account, the victim receives a notice requiring certain "fees" to be paid. The victim is then instructed to wire transfer the fees to Africa. If the victim makes an inquiry concerning the wire transfer, s/he is given instructions for a Bank of China branch in London and provided some reason justifying why the Suffolk England Bank cannot handle the transfer. (Review of the wiring instructions indicated the funds were actually being transferred to the Bank of China in Beijing.) This scheme uses technology to locate victims, communicate with the victims, conceal the location of the perpetrator, steal the identity of a legitimate business, and internationally transmit the criminal proceeds.

As a production tool, technology serves the same basic functions, except that the products and services are illegal. Technology can be used to facilitate money laundering through such means as international e-commerce, establishing prostitution rings, providing online betting, or promoting sex-tourism. The book and 2002 movie *Catch Me if You Can* popularized the activities of convicted criminal Frank Abagnale Jr. who, among his other criminal schemes, used a Heidelberg printing press to manufacture forged checks and other documents. In the 1960s, when Abagnale was producing forged documents, he needed to travel to Europe and use a printing press that normally required three people for its operation in order to produce genuine looking articles. Technological advances are such that relatively unskilled offenders now use free and inexpensive software to produce forged documents of a quality equal to, or better than, anything Abagnale ever did. For under $250 it is possible to purchase an inkjet printer, blank check stock, check writing software, and magnetic ink (MICR); everything necessary to produce authentic-looking forged bank checks. Alternatively, for the same cost at numerous online vendors, a would-be criminal can purchase a magnetic card reader (skimmer) used to steal consumer credit card numbers, blank magnetic cards, a magnetic card writer to encode the blank card, and the necessary software.

Technology can be used to move illegal drugs, whether the drug is methamphetamine from Mexico or cheaper Viagra from Canada. From the standpoint of crime and deviance, presentation comes into play in a vast array of activities, from counterfeiting to pornographic images. Log onto any porn site and one will find ready access to images to fit every sexual predilection, from voyeurism to bondage to images portraying, usually falsely, sex with animals, family members, transvestites, and, more noxiously, the most vulnerable – young children and the elderly. Indeed sex directories not only steer toward thousands of images, but hundreds of categories of images and videos. As a presentation tool, it also becomes a central means of fraud. Loosely defined, fraud is simply the harmful presentation and conveyance of false information, services, or products, and can involve virtually anything falling under those categories. Technology is used to falsify financial statements, home mortgages, credit information, cash register receipts, and, of course, identities.

It is in this last regard that technology is perhaps most closely linked to violent crime. Recent instances of predation on what are otherwise viewed as harmless Internet-based social networks, e.g. MyPlace and FaceBook, demonstrate the power of lure and the vast potential victim pool available to those in search of harm. Kansas State University English professor Thomas E. Murray was convicted of murdering his ex-wife, Carmin D. Ross, on March 13, 2003. During his March 2005 murder trial, prosecutors introduced evidence that before Ross was killed, Murray conducted Internet searches for terms including, "how to kill someone quickly and quietly," and "how to murder someone and not get caught" (*Lawrence Journal-World*, March 15, 2005, and March 18, 2005).[4]

Of course, violent crime is not limited to sexual assaults and "conventional" murders. The portrayal of false information and images may be used by pharmaceutical companies to hide the production of harmful drugs, or by terrorists to promote a violent end to a cause, or by manufacturing companies to conceal their dangerous pollution emissions or elimination of toxic waste.

Most importantly, of course, technology has led to the creation of a limitless space where virtually all human activities can take place. Where it has fostered our conventional sense of globalization, it also transcends the global concept in that it may expand, remove, or recreate ways in which we identify and connect ourselves to this world. Just as it can foster conventional dependencies, e.g. building economic ties between the United States and China, it allows also for boundless, dynamic, and often anonymous, relationships to emerge on the basis shared needs and interests. Those interests may lead to greater consensus around core values held in society or they might tear them apart. Moreover, as Clinard (1952) pointed out in his study of the black market, the social and cultural contexts for any social activity largely shape the degree to which that activity fosters social organization or disorganization. In other words, it is not simply the existence of technology that informs us of its use and value, but as importantly, the social and cultural conditions in which the technology exists. Surely our conceptions of the Internet have been shaped by 9/11 and the perceived rise in terrorism around the globe. Add to the fact that it is a lawless space, largely dependent on self-regulation, and one can begin to see the cracks, uncertainties, and inefficiencies that can arise with modern technology. When a space is created and open to anyone and anything, anyone and anything will participate. This, of course, is the ultimate issue for law enforcement. Technology does not cause crime, but represents a means and space for crime to occur. Law enforcement is put in the unenviable position of having to patrol this boundless space with very little, if any, legal jurisdiction and enforcement authority.

FRAMING THE ROLE OF TECHNOLOGY IN OFFENDING

It is one thing to document the uses of technology in crime and quite another to consider technology's role in offending behavior. Just as technology opens us to a boundless virtual world, it opens up to a boundless virtual world of offending. What is novel today will be old hat tomorrow, and simply to follow the changes and the ever spiraling relationship between offenders and law enforcement tells us little about the underlying contexts for the behavior. To this end it would behoove us to consider more deeply the context in which both crime and technology takes place. By framing the context of crime first, and then situating technology within that frame, we might be able to shed some additional light on the nature of offending.

Crime as Work, Crime at Work, Crime after Work

There are many ways to frame contexts for crime and no single framework tells a complete story. We borrow a framework here which we think has application in particular to issues of technology by situating crime in the context of work. Though the ideas were never fully developed, we draw reference to Richard Sparks's (1981) conceptualization of crime along the lines of "crime as work," "crime at work," and more facetiously (but relevant at least for the purposes here), "crime after work" (see Table 1). Simply stated, "crime as work" depicts those criminal activities that represent a way of life, that is, as a means of economic support and survival. "Crime at work" represents those criminal events (in fact, the largest general category of crime) that take place in the context of one's (usually legitimate) occupation. And "crime after work" represents those events, often viewed as deviant, that are generally unrelated to one occupation (legitimate or otherwise) and typically involve, for the lack of a better word, illegal forms

Table 1: Examples of Technology Crimes "As Work," "At Work" and "After Work"

CRIME AS WORK	CRIME AT WORK	CRIME AFTER WORK
Internet fraud schemes (419 letters, online auctions tourism, lottery frauds, prescription frauds)	Embezzlement Money laundering Credit card fraud by employees	Internet sex crimes (sex tourism, child pornography) Internet hate crimes
Telemarketing fraud schemes (investment scams, promotions, sales)	Theft of confidential information	Internet stalking Cyber-terrorism
Identity theft	Internet sabotage	Hacking
Credit card/Check fraud		
Extortion		
Internet pornography		
Internet piracy		

of leisure. Because we are mostly concerned with the economic benefits that accrue to offenders through crime and technology, we focus our attention here on "crime as work" and "crime at work." As we noted earlier, technology can be used for the purposes of violence and, to the extent that they do, they can occur as work, at work or after work. Obviously, this frame would not necessarily be fitting to describe violent offenses that are impulsively expressive or that lie outside of the domain of work.

Crime as Work

Crime can take place as work whether one is self-employed and acting alone, or whether one belongs to a formal organization, network or guild. According to Sutherland (1937, p. 197), "the professional thief" is one who shares particular characteristics with other professional thieves, revolving around skill sets, status, consensus, differential association and organization. For Sutherland, organization did not mean formal structure but rather a "system" in which "informal unity and reciprocity exists" (p. 209). Within this system – a system of professional thieves – "lies the knowledge which becomes the common property of the profession" (p. 210). We can think in similar terms with reference to individuals whose knowledge revolves the use of technology to commit theft. Though they are not organized in the traditional sense, they engage in crime within a system in which shared knowledge of technological skills are employed. Thus, many of the "revolutions" in technologically-oriented crimes discussed earlier, from "phishing" to "pharming" to "bluesnarfing," emerge from a progression of skills that are quickly communicated to others engaged in technologically-based crimes.

Much of "crime as work" refers to more traditional forms of organized criminal activity. Organized criminal activity may involve large organizations or small networks or teams, and in that respect it may vary in its structural and operational forms – from bureaucratically hierarchical to patron-client relationships. The criminal activity is organized in part for the purposes of continuity, but continuity can take many different forms. For the most part the activities are continuous because they are for the purposes of organizational sustenance. One is, after all, trying to make a living from them.

Here again, the technology serves as a means to perpetuate basic and quite simple criminal acts. Much of what we consider as "traditional" organized crime includes crimes such as extortion and racketeering. From the emergence of the Upright Men (the self-proclaimed chiefs of the wandering beggars in Elizabethan England), to the sectarian society known as the Assassins operating in the Near East in the mid- to late-1800s, to the Five Points and Bowery gangs controlling the docks of New York City in the 19th century, networks and organized criminal groups have made their living by the creation of protection and extortion rackets, usually under the threat of murder (Homer, 1974, pp. 31-32). Fast forward to the 20th century and we find state-of-the-art extortion conducted via the Internet. This includes the growth and use of botnets, which are networks of broadband Internet-connected computers that are disrupted by compromising software that can cause major economic loss to those involved in e-commerce through denial-of-service attacks. A related form of e-commerce extortion involves compromising the information maintained in the databases of a business. Organized crime groups attempt to compromise this information, such as the personal identifying information of customers, and then to extort the business by threatening to alert the public to the business's vulnerabilities.

Another form of "traditional" organized crime involves gambling. Gambling also comes into play in crime after work, as an illegal leisure activity engaged in by the gambler. There is little need to belabor the point that organized crime fills the void when certain desired products and services are made illegal. It is not merely a question of legality, since many states now permit some form of gambling in their jurisdictions. It is also a matter of accessibility, efficiency and cost, and certainly the rise of both electronic technology and the Internet has opened doors not only for new ways to try one's luck, but also for new avenues to take advantage of both legal and illegal markets. McMullan and Perrier (2003) note that in 2000, on average, one electronic gambling machine existed for every 329 Canadians, generating net revenue of $5.5 billion dollars. The authors detail an account of one organized crime group, for example, that targeted video gaming machines in Nova Scotia. Outfitted with a video camera and communication equipment, the "fraud team" would enter a business operating a video gaming machine and would then relay video of the gaming machine's screen to another person in a nearby van. Using several sophisticated programs, the team could determine approximately when the video machine was about to pay out and the team would then increase its bets accordingly (McMullan & Perrier, 2003, p. 6).

Wherever there is money to be made, there is money that must be moved. Illegal money typically requires a series of filters, from the illegal to the increasingly legal, in order to make its way past detection. While it has not always been the case, criminal groups have often controlled both the means to make money as well as the means to place it, layer and integrate it. Money laundering probably originated in the 1920s Prohibition era in the U.S., when it was necessary to disguise the origins of profits made from bootlegging. In the early 1930s, money laundering became increasingly sophisticated when gangster Meyer Lansky used a series of shell companies and offshore accounts to transfer gains from his slot machines in New Orleans to a Swiss back account. Laundering took a new twist in the Watergate scandal of the 1970s, as President Nixon's Committee to Re-Elect the President used connections in Mexico and Miami to move illegal campaign contributions. More recently, of course, money laundering became linked to terrorism when a major financial clearing bank based in Luxembourg, known as Clearstream, was accused of operating a system of unpublished accounts that could be used to transfer illicit funds through hundreds of banks around the world (Komisar, 2001). The complexity and size of that operation is a convincing indicator that the combination of globalization and technology have opened avenues for money to move more quickly, more inconspicuously, and more safely than at any other time in history. However, the case, and others like it, demonstrates also that globalization and technology have increased the need for specialization and more complicated interrelationships with both illegal and legal enterprises based on the particular needs when placing, layering and integrating the money. This has created its own set of problems for those involved in organized crime, to be discussed in more detail shortly.

Crime at Work

The notion of "crime as work" frames the criminal activities of groups and individuals whose living is made by their illegal activities. Crime typically requires the confluence of offender motivation, an opportunity to commit the offense, and absence of guardians to prevent the criminality. Those engaged in crime as work surely are motivated by the desire for economic gain; they seek out opportunities to engage in the crimes and work to structure and maximize those opportunities while taking advantage of, compromising, or staying ahead of those responsible for guardianship. "Crime at work," on the other hand, differs from crime as work in a number of important ways. First, to the extent that there is an organization involved, typically that organization, or workplace, is both a vehicle and a likely victim in the activity. Second, where crime as work typically involves illegal goods and services, crime at work typically occurs within the general framework and activities of the legal economy. We can think of crime at work as involving illegal activities in which the organization engages in order take advantage of perceived weaknesses in its market environment, or to protect itself from uncertainties that it is unable to control through legal operations. Crime at work may also involve illegal actions taken by an organization as the result of criminal activities of one or more of its employees, or it may involve crimes against the organization for the benefit of the individual(s) within the organization. In each of these instances technology can serve to both perpetuate and hide those crimes.

As Friedrichs (2004) and others point out, we now live in a world dominated by computers and information management and technology. It is estimated that 80% of all financial transactions occur electronically and that $100 billion in financial transactions take place each year on the Internet (p. 184). Within this larger technologically-oriented environment, there are workplaces, sometimes small start-ups, others enormous multinational corporations which vary quite dramatically in where they are situated and influenced by this environment. Within the organizations themselves, individuals vary in their knowledge, capacity and connection with technology.

Herein lies the relationship between technology and the single largest category of crime: occupational fraud. In the 2006 *Report to the Nation on Occupational Fraud and Abuse*, the Association of Certified Fraud Examiners estimated that a typical work organization loses approximately 5% of its annual revenues to fraud (p. 8), which extrapolated to the U.S. economy as a whole would suggest yearly losses exceeding $500 billion. In its study of 1,100 cases, the Association estimated that the median dollar loss was $159,000, with nearly 25% of the cases involving frauds over $1 million. Once again, it's difficult to gauge the accuracy and meaning of these figures, but it is safe to say that while we have a tendency to focus our attention on criminal events in the streets, there is a lot of mischief happening in the workplace and more attention should be given to it.

We tend not to view the Enron Corporation's recent fraud cases as crimes of technology, but those and many other corporate crimes make use of technology to either perpetuate or cover up illegal activities. In the case of Enron, both were involved. The company manipulated its financial value by creating partnerships whereby it could move its debt off its balance sheet and hide its loses. It did so primarily through a complex array of financial contracts, many of them derivative instruments. Derivative instruments are financial contracts whose value is derived on the basis of other financial contracts. Such financial contracts are common and legal means of valuation, but like property assessment and appraisal generally, the valuations are open to widely subjective interpretation and hence potential fraud. In the case of Enron, for example, some financial contracts were created on the basis of the company's stock price, even though the stock price was derived solely on the basis of the existence of those contracts. More commonly, complex algorisms are created in computer programs to provide more objectivity, or at least the appearance of objectivity to the valuation process. The more widely these programs are accepted as legitimate means of valuation, the more valuable they become as a means of covering up the criminal activity.

While a sizeable portion of occupational crime has its roots at the upper echelons, the vast majority of occupational crime occurs at lower levels within the organization and systematically impedes the daily workplace economy. The largest category of occupational fraud involves asset misappropriation, which includes the theft or misuse of an organization's assets and leads to such schemes as fraudulent invoicing, payroll fraud and the skimming of revenues. The vast majority of misappropriations involve cash, taken either before the cash is recorded by the organization (in the case of skimming) or after the cash as been recorded in the books and records (in the case of larceny). Occupational frauds also involve the manipulation or theft of disbursements, including false billing and reimbursement, check tampering, false claims for compensation, and illegal wire transfers, among others.

Two points are to be made about the relationship between technology and workplace crime. First, it is typically argued that the type of white-collar or occupational crime committed within an organization is a function of the location of the offender in the organization. This is no doubt true. Accounting frauds require, by definition, accountants, and the executives whose authority it is to sign off on what the accountants do. However, advances in the forms of technology have the potential to alter this general truth. As individuals gain access to company computers, and because they have cell phones, PDAs, wireless networks, and the like, they have the potential to widen the scope of their activity and take advantage of workplace vulnerabilities. In this respect technology may even out the playing field and render occupational position less important. A second and more obvious point is that such access also renders employee theft and occupational fraud more difficult to detect – not only by law enforcement, but more importantly by the organization itself. Similarly, while employers are often reluctant to disclose crimes committed within their organization, it may well be the case that they will be even more reluctant to do so when it involves technology. While many technologies might not easily be transferred, they are transferable, and the more difficult they are to detect, the less likely one is likely to publicize their existence.

Technology and the Interaction between Motivation and Opportunity

To what extent does technology play a role in offending behavior, whether it takes place as work or at work or after work? Routine activities theory is most relevant to crimes committed for economic gain, particularly when the criminal behavior appears grounded in utilitarian rationality. The assumption, however, that crime emerges in the confluence of a motivated offender, an opportunity and a lack of guardians is overly simplistic because it assumes almost everyone is similarly motivated: the theory therefore finds much of the causal explanation for criminal events in opportunity and the absence of effective guardianship. If this is indeed the case, the role of technology would be relevant only to the extent that it creates certain opportunities for crime that occur in the absence of a capable enforcement mechanism, either public or private, to prevent it. Without dismissing the important roles of opportunity and enforcement, it is important to reexamine the idea of offender motivation and consider how technology might affect it.

Of course, individuals are not automatons, acting in singular fashion and purpose, and influenced only by the availability of things. Individuals may or may not act rationally, if they motivated to act at all. A necessary intermediary is a process by which motive becomes activated in the first place. In other words, individuals must first come to interpret and structure both the situational and broader context of their actions. This is not to imply that people must stop, reflect on and weigh all the choices and ramifications, but it does argue for a more dynamic and complex interaction than that afforded by simply combining impulsivity, hedonism and opportunity. Given this, how might technology come to enter into this process? It might help to clarify the question by referring again to the framework of crime as work and crime at work. While both contexts for crime involve some form of instrumental gain, the process by which offenders interpret their actions must surely differ in important ways. Those who engage in crime as work obviously rationalize their actions in part by reference to a broader conception of the world of work. This may include such considerations as personal control or freedom in the workplace, the role of competition, income and leisure levels, perspectives on change and stability, longevity and retirement, safety, etc. Technology is thus more than a new opportunity to engage in old behavior but one, which can affect these different components and influence one's entry to crime as work. As technology changes and improves, so does one's dynamic interpretations of their place in that world.

Those who engage in crime at work may well be influenced by similar kinds of issues, but much of this occurs within a broader context of legality and acceptability. For example, a chief executive officer might see the need to falsify financial statements not because accounting technology and regulatory control provide convenient opportunities for crime, but because organizational and environment pressures leave the CEO to see it as either the only choice available to keep up with competition or to view lawbreaking as standard operating procedure. The age of information management and technology and the environment in which it operates may well place organizational pressures on companies in ways which set the parameters for responding. For example, the advent of global technology and the speed with which information can be communicated and shared obviously affects the ways in which investing takes place. Large volumes of stock may be traded 24 hours a day and at moments notice. This may lead to a shift in the idea of investment away from capitalization and toward speculation, where large sums can be lost and gained as a function of volume of trade and the efficiency of the market. Within this frame, modes of management may shift in response, reflecting a greater concern for protection from share instability, and of course, for keeping one's job in such an environment.

When we consider other forms of crime at work we may see similar processes taking place. One's place within the organization, the degree to which one feels loyalty or betrayal, and one's income levels all contribute to an employee's interpretation of the opportunities for crime. Technology may enter into these issues in the degree to which it creates a climate conducive to deviance, retaliation or revenge. An employee who feels dehumanized by virtue of an organization's software that treats workers like commodities may well view the theft of company assets as deserving, or perhaps metaphorically insignificant.

Though we have not addressed in detail the role of technology in crime after work, one important observation or reiteration should be made.

As mentioned earlier, technology has led to the creation of a virtual world where almost everyone can participate and everything can occur. The popularity of social networks on the Internet is, among other things, a function of the need to share ourselves with others. Shared identities emerge not merely from the degree to which common allegiances form around subjects like "American Idol," animal rights or Thai cuisine, but also around beliefs, causes and things perceived as less desired or accepted by society. Of course, what is "accepted by society" is largely an intangible idea. As beliefs, identities and urges are identified, their confirmation, either through acceptance or rejection, becomes more tangible for those who hold them. This process inevitably leads to a reformation of what is considered acceptable and what is not, and under what circumstances and conditions acceptance or disapproval occurs. The global and instant nature of virtual social networks enhances and speeds this process, and should not be underestimated as individuals come to rationalize their own actions and behaviors.

The point of much of this discussion is to move beyond the idea that technology alters crime merely by altering opportunities. While that is no doubt true, technology plays a more important role in crime than just opening doors. Technology factors in the rationalization process first by contributing to the host of aggravating and mitigating circumstances that lead one to choose whether to engage in crime or not, and second, by doing so in its very own hallmarks of speed and efficiency.

Quite obviously, technology does shape opportunity structures. Unfortunately, as scholars, and as practitioners, we know very little about how this occurs. Just as an artist doesn't create art by virtue of having a variety of paints on a palate, not everyone has the ability to take advantage of the opportunities to commit crime when they do become available. This is not simply a question of technological know-how, as important as this may be. As mentioned earlier, it is equally important that one has the chance to be situated in the social organization such that the opportunities, when they do occur, can be recognized as such and maximized. For example, let's return to the problem of money laundering. The ability to take advantage of sophisticated money laundering techniques may require an equally sophisticated knowledge of who to turn to as well as the ability to structure and negotiate relationships and manage uncertainties when they arise. These may be quite different from the structures of money laundering used in the past, in part as the result of technology itself. Thus, whereas casinos have long served as means for money laundering, the social structures of illegal gambling, at least as far as casinos went, were not particularly complex. Competitors were limited, regulators were relatively easy to control, and disputes more easily resolved. As money laundering moves to a more global domain and involves more countries), as it makes greater use of legal entities such as banks, and as it incurs greater risk of detection by law enforcement, it becomes all the more necessary for the launderers to find the right people with the right skills to navigate these concerns.

The bottom line is that we have much to learn about technology and its impact on crime. As mentioned earlier, it could be that technology evens the playing field for some kinds of crimes, such as those involving crime at work, and closes doors for others, by allowing certain criminal organizations to dominate. We also know little about the impact that technology has on the relationship between offenders and victims. It has been a general axiom that offenders and victims tend to look alike; that is, the poor tend to victimize the poor, whites tend to victimize whites, and so on. It is logical to assume that access to technology can change those relationships because one is no longer bound to geography, and the anonymity provided by the Internet allows offenders to victimize a much larger pool of victims.

The final observation is that if there is anything to be learned by examining the relationship between technology and crime it is that it our perceptions of crime, as scholars and as law enforcers, is remarkably monocular. We draw stereotypes of theft, of violent crime, of sexual assault and predation that are sculpted by conceptions of geography, income, gender and race, and we create our theories of crime from data that seldom go beyond what occurs on the street. We concentrate law enforcement resources and define the enforcement mission on the basis of often valid, but narrow, perceptions of public's needs and concerns and we punish accordingly. The apparent increase in the number of Internet-related frauds, the voluminous monetary loss from corporate scandals, the vast globalization of crime and the ability to offend and virtually disappear with the press of a button are likely to push us to redirect our attention and redefine, or at least broaden, our concerns. We should hope this broadening comes sooner rather than later.

◆ ◆ ◆ ◆

NOTES

1. This information is from one of the author's personal interviews with collectors of child pornography. Many self-report that they would not

have engaged in criminal acts associated with child pornography were it not for the availability of the material on the Internet. It is important to note that these reports may be partially attributed to an attempt on their part to rationalize the activity. It can be concluded, though that technology serves to make the contraband more readily available. One must wonder if a person with pedophilic tendencies, living in rural America, would undertake the effort and risk necessary to obtain such images if it were not as close as his broadband connection. On a related note, a contact offender making still or moving images for self-gratification may be less likely to disseminate the unlawful material were it not for these technologies.

2. One nationally publicized example of the intersection of technology and child pornography involves Justin Berry, who for five years starred in his own Webcam child pornography business. Berry became a victim of child pornography at 13 years of age, after he acquired a Web camera as part of a deal with an Internet service provider. A lonely kid of a divorced family without many friends, Berry hoped to use the device to make friends his own age. Instead, a pedophile sent him an instant message within minutes of Berry's image landing on a Web site called Spotlife.com. Webcam encounters with child pornographers escalated into personal meetings with contact offenders. One offender helped him open his own pornographic Web site for money. Another rented him an apartment to conceal the criminal behavior from Berry's mother (CBS News, April 4, 2006). During congressional testimony, Berry told the House Energy and Commerce Committee: "At 13, I believed these people were my friends. They were kind. They complimented me. They wanted to know about my day." Berry also told the panel: "I believed that the government would protect the children being abused. I believed they would act quickly. I was wrong" (*Congressional Record*, Volume 152 [2006]).

3. This was the case when Armin Meiwes, a computer technician placed an advertisement on the Internet for "a well-built male prepared to be slaughtered and then consumed" (BBC, May 9, 2006). Future victim Bernd-Jurgen Brandes, a computer engineer, began to converse with Meiwes in an Internet chat room after responding to the advertisement. According to German court testimony, Meiwes told investigators Brandes met him at his home in Rotenburg in March 2001. Brandes agreed to have his penis cut off, which Meiwes then flambéed and they both ate. Meiwes subsequently fatally stabbed the victim and continued to

cannibalize the corpse. Meiwes used available technology to memorialize the event in a two-hour video, recovered by investigators. This video, along with chat logs and a will, corroborated the assertion that Brandes was a willing victim. Meiwes came to the attention of law enforcement after an Austrian student reported an online advertisement in which Meiwes attempted to find additional victims (Reuters, January 1, 2006).

4. Lt. Col. Dave Grossman, U.S. Army (Retired) conducts research in the areas of human aggression and violence. He asserts that violent video games, particularly those that are extremely realistic, both desensitize juveniles to violence and make those who carry out violence more effective (www.killology.com). In December 1997, 14-year-old Michael Carneal fired a handgun at students engaged in an informal prayer group on the steps of a West Paducah, Kentucky high school. The result the shooting left two dead and six injured (CNN, December 1, 1997. In an October 1999 statement before the New York legislature, Grossman pointed to this incident as an example in which realistic video games acted as a training simulator for juvenile killers. Carneal, who had never fired a handgun until the night before the killing, fired eight shots. Of those, all eight hit a target, including four head shots and three upper-torso shots. From witness statements, Carneal placed one shot per victim, rather than shooting individual victims multiple times. Grossman argues, and it is this author's experience, that an untrained shooter will shoot multiple times at a target, after engaging it, before acquiring another target. It is only with extensive training and practice that a shooter develops the discipline to quickly acquire and transition among targets. This type of shooting is taught in military and law enforcement settings, but is also required to become proficient in the "first person shooter" genre of video games. Additionally, it is unlikely that an untrained and unpracticed shooter would display the accuracy of shot placement seen in Carneal.

REFERENCES

Association of Certified Fraud Examiners. (2006). *2006 report to the nation on occupational fraud and abuse.* Retrieved from: http://www.acfe.com/documents/2006-rttn.pdf

Clinard, M. B. (1952). *The black market: A study of white-collar crime.* Montclair, NJ: Patterson Smith.

Felson, M. (2002). *Crime and everyday life* (3rd ed.). Thousand Oaks, CA: Pine Forge.

Fredrichs, D. (2004). *Trusted criminals: White-collar crime in contemporary society*. New York: Wadsworth.

Homer, F. D. (1974). *Guns and garlic: Myths and realities of organized crime*. West Lafayette, IN: Purdue University Press.

Kosimar, L. (2001, October 4). *Tracking terrorist money – too hot for us to handle?* Pacific News Service. Retrieved from: http://www.webcom.com/hrin/magazine/money.html.

McMullan, J. L., & Perrier, D. C. (2003). Technologies of crime: The attacks on electronic gaming machines. *Canadian Journal of Criminology and Criminal Justice, 45*(2), 154-186.

Roman, M. E. (2006, March 4). Smith and Wessons get replaced by computers: High-tech robbers grab more loot, take less risk than crooks of yesteryear. *Worcester Telegram and Gazette*.

Sparks, R. F. (1981). *Crime as work: An illustrative example*. Draft report to the National Institute of Justice. Newark, NJ: Rutgers University, Center for Studies of Crime for Gain.

Sutherland, E. H. (1937). *The professional thief*. Chicago: University of Chicago Press.

U.S. Bureau of Justice Statistics, United States Department of Justice. (2006). *First Estimates from the National Crime Victimization Survey Identity Theft, 2004*. Retrieved from: http:/www./ojp.usdoj.gov/bjs/pub/ascii/it04.txt

U.S. Federal Bureau of Investigation (FBI). (2005). Press release dated October 17, 2005, and retrieved, from: http://www.fbi.gov/pressrel/pressrel05/factsheet101705.htm

United States Federal Trade Commission (2006). *Consumer Fraud and Identity Theft Complaint Data, January-December 2005*. Retrieved from: http://www.consumer.gov/sentinel/pubs/Top10Fraud2005.pdf

3. TECHNOLOGY, CRIME CONTROL AND THE PRIVATE SECTOR IN THE 21ST CENTURY

by

Donald J. Rebovich
Utica College

and

Anthony Martino
Utica, New York Police Department

INTRODUCTION

On March 2, 2006, at George Washington University in Washington DC, the Global Security Consortium held a widely publicized summit on technologies required for effective security on a national level. The consortium, dedicated to enhancing security on all levels through the formation and management of public/private partnerships, devoted its summit conference to the access and use of open source intelligence to enhance security towards the goal of preventing terrorist acts. Many of the summit's panels were dedicated to methods of perfecting rapid, structured correlations of large volumes of unstructured data on people, places and events to effect timely assessments of threats and their significance. While fundamentally targeting the threats of terrorism, the list of corporate sponsors and panelists read like a virtual "Who's Who" of private sector entities that have been increasingly shifting their attention to the more general needs of public sector crime control and prevention. Some were familiar names like IBM, Lockheed Martin, General Dynamics, Google, and LexisNexis. Others not quite as well known were SAIC, Basis Technology, Factiva, Cyveillance and Veritas Analysis, among others (Atkins, 2006).

Summits like the one held by the Global Security Consortium are becoming more of a fixture in the crime control landscape as our society marches through the technology age and as our public law enforcement agencies struggle to improve process efficiency and keep in step with the evolution of criminal offenders' technological advances. Less common a decade ago, the ongoing and direct engagement of the private sector in improving crime control and prevention technologies in the U.S. has been received with open arms in some sectors while raising eyebrows in others along the way. For, while there is little doubt that the technological expertise that the private sector can provide to the criminal justice system is invaluable, it has been accompanied by a sense of at least mild anxiety about what some consider the gradual encroachment of the private sector on the historical responsibilities of public criminal justice systems and the possible erosion of privacy of personal records.

As a provider of technology designed to complement the tasks of law enforcement, private sector-generated technology has enabled law enforcement agencies to enhance its information-based capabilities in a variety of areas. On occasion, private firms join forces to tackle particularly perplexing needs for law enforcement. One example is Choicepoint's partnership with Voyager Systems, Inc. to create Voyager Query, which addresses the needs of law enforcement agencies as they relate to mobile technology. The introduction of Voyager Query raised capabilities for mobile law enforcement technology by providing a fully integrated wireless data application for furnishing instantaneous record checking to securely run on virtually any handheld device or wireless network. In effect, this technology allows law enforcement to reasonably explore alternatives to mobile computer terminals. Taking it another step further from being tied to stationary computers, private sector technology like this permits law enforcement to shorten the time it takes for the review of criminal records, the verification of subjects' identities, the tracking of outstanding warrants (via local, state and federal databases) and the verification of positive identification through the instantaneous viewing of mug shots. With continuous network operations center support, Voyager Query is designed to provide immediate information access, without requiring dispatcher involvement, in an average of 4 to 10 seconds' response time (ChoicePoint, 2006).

As a company, ChoicePoint's other efforts that promise to reduce active time in background searches extends to its development of products like AutoTrackXP, providing Internet access to more than 17 billion records on individuals and businesses. AutoTrack XP was created to simplify what are normally cumbersome tasks of cross-referencing public and proprietary records. Such records reflect real property transactions, deed transfers and information on the subject's businesses and associates (ChoicePoint, 2006).

Another publicized technological advance was LexisNexis's Accurint LE Plus, created for the law enforcement market to efficiently search, locate and map sexual offender addresses. LexisNexis originally developed its product in response to troubling findings from two research studies. The first were U.S. Bureau of Justice Statistics' (BJS) findings that released sex offenders are four times as likely to be rearrested for similar crimes than are other types of offenders (Bureau of Justice Statistics, 2003). The other study, conducted by the group Parents for Megan's Law, reported that 24% of the 550,000 registered sex offenders in the U.S. were ignoring residency requirements under the states' "Megan's Laws" (Curtis, February 7, 2003). The Advanced Sexual Offender Search capabilities of Accurint LE Plus are designed to improve efficiency in the investigation of child abduction cases by determining the location of sex offenders who have not followed proper protocol in reporting their addresses to authorities. The desktop application, besides serving as a gateway to countless public records, integrates methods for identifying logical associations between individuals, events and geographic locations. in one package. As described by LexisNexis' CEO for Risk Management, James Peck, LexisNexis's goal for introducing Accurint LE Plus was to supply law enforcement with a tool that could effectively increase the chances of safely reuniting as many abducted children as possible with their parents (Atkins, 2006).

New, privately developed technology like Voyager Query, AutoTrackXP and Accurint LE Plus are only a few of many tools aimed at the law enforcement market, designed to make difficult jobs easier for law enforcement personnel. But, it is in two specific crime control areas that the private sector has been particularly active (and highly competitive) in creating so much relevant technology that the "supplemental" role of the private sector has blurred into a more encompassing "surrogate" role for traditional criminal justice responsibilities. In the areas of computer crime and identity fraud, the private sector has taken a path that can best be described as (1) analytic, (2) responsive, and (3) metamorphic. Enterprising firms have been "analytic" in recognizing the ripe market for products and services that are not otherwise available to the public law enforcement sector. The private sector has also demonstrated an entrepreneurial understanding of the new market for "alternative corrective services" sought by victimized businesses to not only help control these crimes, but prevent them as well. And, finally, the private sector has been "metamorphic" in embracing a philosophy of perpetual evolution of products and strategies to match the prowess of their most wily competitor, the criminal offender.

COMPUTER CRIME AND THE PRIVATE SECTOR

Hardening the Target of Computer Crime

Statistics on the frequency of computer/Internet crimes demonstrate how computer crime has moved toward the front of crime concern priorities for the nation. The Computer Security Institute/Federal Bureau of Investigation's (CSI/FBI) 2005 Computer Crime and Security Survey of over 700 computer security practitioners in corporations and government agencies across the U.S. reported that 56% had experienced unauthorized use of computer systems. Virus attacks had caused the greatest financial losses, representing 32% of overall losses. Unauthorized access rose dramatically from the previous year's survey results, and demonstrated a significant rise in average losses incurred, from $51,545 to $130,234. Average loses per respondent due to theft of proprietary information also rose sharply, from $168,594 to $355,552. Over all, more than $30 million was lost due to theft of proprietary information. Web site defacements were also reported to be on the rise (Computer Security Institute, 2005).

Many years ago, before anyone heard or could conceive of computers, much less the Internet, banks and safe manufacturers were facing a perplexing problem. It seemed that those who wanted access to the treasures contained in safes were willing to go to great lengths to achieve that access. They were first able to perfect skills at picking the combination locks on the safes. Safe manufacturers responded by making combination locks that were tamper-proof. The thieves resorted to devising instruments that could literally remove the combination locks. Safe manufacturers took to constructing safes in which the combination locks could not be removed. Safecrackers then poured nitroglycerin in the seams between the doors and the body of the safes and blew the doors off. Safes were made with seams so narrow that it was impossible to inject nitro into them. Enter the acetylene torch. And on it went. Skill development and competition continued between the world of crime and the world of business. One side dedicated to "hardening the target" and the other side determined to "penetrate the target." What complicated the problem for the safe manufacturers was that, although safecrackers are far from being even loosely organized, they did share information on penetration techniques.

Today, target hardening has become the primary aim in the battle to contain computer crime, and, as they did for banks of the past to thwart the efforts of safecrackers, private sector vendors have been enlisted to aid law enforcement to fight this battle. Situational factors present special opportunities for the commission of crimes. According to Felson's routine activities theory relating to crime commission, any predatory crime requires three minimal elements: (1) a likely offender, (2) a suitable target, and (3) the absence of a capable guardian. The offender measures the "suitability" through his assessment of dimensions such as the target's "value," inertia (e.g., rejection of theft of some items due to physical hurdles making theft impractical), his anticipated visibility to detection and the chance to exit easily (Felson, 1998).

Computer crime can be viewed as a result of situations in which offenders capitalize on perceived opportunities to invade computer systems to achieve criminal ends or use computers as instruments of crime, figuring that the "guardians" do not possess the means or knowledge to prevent or detect criminal acts. These, then, become old battles fought with new weapons to access "unguarded" targets and permit quick and unencumbered entry and exit. Cohen and Felson (1979) stress the importance of "target hardening" to counteract the criminal acts and help deter decisions leading to future criminal acts. Enhancing the technological capabilities of the "guardians," the criminal investigators, is one of a number of ways to harden criminal targets.

While computer technology has opened doors to upgraded conveniences for many, this same technology has paradoxically offered new opportunities for criminals. Businesses that used to rely upon computerization to collect and assemble sensitive information on their critical resources now must increasingly confront the daunting, and costly, task of protecting this information from those who wish to achieve illegal access to it. Criminals are now able to easily encrypt information containing evidence of their criminal acts, store the information and even transmit it, with little fear of detection by law enforcement. Due to the extraordinary impact of the Internet, a computer crime scene can now extend worldwide from the geographical point of the victimization (e.g., the victim's personal computer) to any other point on the planet, further complicating criminal investigative efforts (Gordon et al., 2002).

Businesses Responding to the Problem

To keep up with the rapidly evolving use of computers not only to commit crime but also to hide evidence of crimes, the private sector has intensified its efforts to establish high-end businesses specializing in the field of computer forensics. Companies have sprouted throughout the U.S. dedicated to diving into the DNA of computers to extract seemingly deleted data that, when detected and analyzed, can form the basis for both civil and criminal actions against both outside intruders as well as offenders in the workplace. These computer forensics companies represent a growth industry serving business managers in gathering computerized evidence related to on-the-job offenses ranging from embezzlement, to theft of proprietary information, to acts of sexual harassment.

Much of this evidence exists in the form of simple e-mails, yet extraction of this "deleted" evidence often requires the skilled hands and minds of those working for computer forensics firms. Personnel in these computer forensics firms hold advanced degrees and have backgrounds not only in computer science, but also in the areas of fraud investigation and computer security. They are the "tech age" crime scene investigators, and they are thriving in the private sector.

Computer forensics firms have been addressing the recent trend of hackers developing anti-forensics software specifically for counteracting attempts to analyze computers for evidence of criminal activity. Software packages like The Defiler's Toolkit have been released anonymously on the Internet to undermine forensic analyses of systems subsequent to remote break-ins. It does so by creatively tracking all changed data and using random bits to automatically overwrite the data. Vogon is one data recovery company that has developed countermeasures to new forensic tools, like the Defiler's Toolkit, by exploiting the physical characteristics of a hard disc to dig deeper into its past. Vogon uses machines called spin stand testers to uncover pieces of residual information of data once stored on the hard disc even after cybercriminals have used anti-forensic tools to erase data. If enough pieces can be gathered, incriminating data, thought by the offender to be wiped out, can be successfully reconstructed. The ability of computer forensics firms to recover such information becomes more difficult with the continual increase of hard disc memory, yet firms like Vogon remain hard at work in an effort to maintain a competitive edge over cybercriminals (Knight, 2004).

The use of computer forensics has already begun to be commonplace in many large investigations. For example, the trial of Scott Peterson in

2004 for the murder of his wife lasted for months and garnered daily coverage in the nation's major media outlets, becoming one of the most followed cases in recent history. During the trial, the key evidence presented by the prosecution detailed Internet search items and e-mails sent and received by the defendant. A forensic investigator from the Stanislaus County Sheriff's Department testified that he had used the Forensic Toolkit software produced by Access Data to analyze computers used by the defendant. According to the testimony, Peterson had used his computer to search for information on the locations of boat launches and currents in San Francisco Bay, which were key points in corroborating the prosecution's theory of the murder and disposal of the victim's body (Associated Press, 2005). The defense in the trial countered with its own computer forensic experts, leading to a showdown of legal arguments based on the ones and zeros of digital evidence.

In the near future, computer forensics tool development can be expected to grow rapidly in response to our increasingly digital, interconnected world. Already, law enforcement and private industry investigators are scrambling to keep up with the frenzied pace at which new electronic devices become potential containers of critical evidence. Cellular telephones and personal digital assistants (PDAs) have become almost ubiquitous in modern society. Many contemporary models of these devices go far beyond carrying voice communications and storing appointments, to the point that they are now fully qualified miniature computers. With capabilities such as e-mail, playing digital videos and text messaging, these are devices that are essential to include in any investigation. Companies such as Paraben Forensics are at the forefront of this new digital evidence revolution, producing Cell Seizure Toolkit and PDA Seizure Toolkit packages that enable a forensic investigator to gain access to these non-traditional digital storehouses. With electronic devices continuing to become more powerful, smaller, and more integrated in everyday life, it is not a stretch to expect that investigative needs will soon require the tool to conduct forensic examination of a whole new array of devices such as wrist watches, automobile computers and video game systems.

As time goes on, cybercriminals have been adopting some of the entrepreneurial activities of legitimate technology vendors to ply their trade. Nowhere has this been more evident than in recent proliferation of malicious programming code that, when embedded and activated, seizes control of the victim's computer and converts the computer into a "bot," a remote-controlled robot used for a range of activities from sending spam to stealing data. The SANS Institute estimates that an average of 250,000 Internet Protocol addresses are infected each day by such bots, with half attacking home personal computers (PCs) and half going after large and mid-sized firms. Cybertrust has reported that the number of new bot codes increased by over 500% through the year of 2005. Convicted offenders like Jeanson James Ancheta of Downey, California have reaped great profits by not only developing the bots, but also selling them and providing consulting help with their use. A 21-year-old who has a high school equivalency diploma, Ancheta sold and rented bots to send spam, launch denial-of-service attacks and defraud online advertising companies by instructing bots to install ads on overtaken computers. At one point Ancheta's pricelist on his "botz4sale" online channel advertised up to 10,000 compromised PCs at a time for as little as 4 cents apiece. The design, use and marketing of bots have emerged as especially vexing problems for cyber-enforcers because they are so difficult to eradicate. Efforts by average computer owners to clean their PCs of bots and patch them often are hindered by the introduction of new bots designed to exploit different vulnerabilities (Gage, 2006a).

Continuing advances in computer technology have presented new problems for cybercrime enforcers. One of the most popular of these advances is "Wi-Fi," the industry's marketing term for technology that runs most wireless data networks. Hackers have taken quick advantage of the growth of the number of laptops equipped with Wi-Fi network-connecting hardware and the widening scope of Wi-Fi hotspots created by service providers to "wardrive" searching for vulnerable networks. Security experts have agreed that, regrettably, most businesses with wireless networks have taken few responsible actions to secure those networks. Many companies rely on the encryption protocol Wired Equivalent Privacy (WEP), introduced in 2000, to thwart wireless intruders, but offenders now find it fairly easy to hack. The introduction of a newer, more secure technology, Wi-Fi Protected Access (WPA), has improved matters, but the private sector has, once again, been busy developing new counteractive technology to fill gaps in that protocol. Companies like WiMetrics, Network Chemistry, AirMagnet and AirDefense have created new security technologies designed to detect unauthorized users in targeted areas through intensified monitoring of the radio spectrum in those areas. The best of these technologies identify locations of vulnerable "rogue" access points within businesses and detect situations in which hackers disguise their computers as legitimate wireless access points in an effort to steal passwords (e.g., "evil twin" schemes). In addition to developing enhanced protective technologies, wireless network technology vendors have formed the Wi-Fi alliance, a consortium dedicated to improving awareness of "best" security standards and practices (Spangler, 2005).

The intersection of new technology and security vulnerabilities is often first found and exploited by those with harmful intentions, and wireless networks are no exception. Wi-Fi networks are often the weakest link in the armor protecting a corporate or government network, and they pose a soft target for hackers, crackers, and other unauthorized cyber-trespassers. One of the first reported wireless weaknesses occurred in January 2002 at Denver International Airport. American Airlines, responding to new federal regulations on passenger-luggage matching after the September 11th terrorist attacks, installed wireless networks to support its curbside check-in operations. A consultant hired by a technology magazine to cover the story of the innovative use of this new technology discovered that security was lacking in American's Wi-Fi network, and in fact watched as others in the terminal were able to gain access to the airline's computer system (Brewin et al., 2002). This technology misstep was soon followed by others, including the September 2003 hacking of a Lowe's hardware store wireless network in Southfield, Michigan by a group of young credit card thieves. In this case, an FBI investigation led to the capture of the suspects and a 9-year prison sentence for the ringleader (Associated Press, 2005). While our thirst for new technology in business and personal venues is almost insatiable, the consequences of operating behind the curve of information security and investigative personnel can sometimes lead to unintended results.

The concern over the serious negative impact that insecure wireless networks can have on a private business has led one New York State county to pass a law mandating that all business Wi-Fi network owners operate their systems utilizing at least a minimum standard of security practices. Westchester County, which occupies the geographic region just north of New York City, is home to corporate residents such as IBM, Morgan Stanley and Reader's Digest. The county enacted a law in April of 2006 that mandates that all business wireless networks be operated in a manner consistent with common Wi-Fi security practices, including data encryption and network components that do not constantly broadcast their presence (Westchester County, 2006). Proponents of the new law believe that private wireless network owners have done too little to protect themselves from harmful cyber-predators, and that the risk to both private and public infrastructure is significant enough that legislation to protect the societal interest in these assets is warranted. Critics argue that the law is difficult to enforce and targets the victim instead of the criminal who preys on the data sent over these networks. In either case, this act provides an interesting solution to a problem affecting private entities failing to adequately protect their wireless networks and law enforcement's difficulty in successfully coping with the crimes that result.

Not only have the methods of cybercriminals been changing, but also the types of offenders themselves. Because the conventional criminal justice system is poorly positioned to achieve a reasonable proactive balance, businesses are turning to computer security companies to ward off the looming threat of digital espionage committed by private sector competitors. In 2005, high-profile digital espionage cases brought this problem into sharp relief. In one 2005 case, Robert McKinney, the former chief technology officer at Business Software Corp. of San Francisco pled guilty to downloading trade secrets from rival firm Niku Corp. In another California case, Brent Alan Woodward, San Jose-based Lightwave Microsystem's former information technology director, pled guilty to trying to sell backup tapes containing trade secrets for network equipment to Lightwave's competitor, JDS Uniphase. New laws have prompted firms to clamor for assistance from the private sector to properly meet standards for protection of proprietary information. The federal Health Insurance Portability and Accountability Act (HIPPA) holds executives legally accountable for securing the privacy and transmission of health care data, and under the federal Sarbanes-Oxley Act private firms must ensure the viability of internal controls. Companies like Pro-Tec Data are responding to the private sector's demand for guidance on compliance with these laws by providing expert consultation on the identification and classification of company assets. And new vendors like Vontu and Liquid Machines are offering innovative products that effectively track and control internal and external access to companies' electronic information. Some of these companies, like Ra Security Systems, also aid companies in vulnerability assessments for digital snooping in the workplace, heightening employee awareness of secrecy protection and fine-tuning methods for limiting access to proprietary information (Gage, 2005b).

Daunted by the hacker's ability to usurp almost any commonly implemented network defenses, and the slow or insufficient response by law enforcement to electronic crimes, some businesses have elected to utilize countermeasures that go beyond traditional post-incident responses. A new category of tools known as "strike-back" systems allows for instantaneous responses to perceived threats. Depending on the severity of response desired by the operator, countermeasures can range from relatively mild steps such as e-mails sent to an intruder or their Internet service provider and up to the automatic launching of a denial-of-service attack that shuts down a perceived attacker's servers. In December 1999, while large-scale protests choked the streets of Seattle, Washington during meetings of the World Trade Organization, a group of cyber-activists took aim at the WTO's web site. A denial-of-service attack focused at Conxion, the host of the WTO site, was quickly determined to originate in a server operated by a group in the U.K. Conxion rerouted all incoming packets from this location back to the group, shutting down both the attack and the attacker (Radcliff, 2000).

Although Conxion's actions in the WTO case sparked criticism from many, interest in electronic countermeasures as a network defense has only grown, sparking product development from private vendors and open source developers. Tools such as Zombie Zapper produced by Bindview (now owned by Symantec) show that network security professionals are looking beyond simple passive defenses and demanding systems that offer a range of incident-response options. While hack-back reactions such as Conxion's arise from the frustration felt by cyber-security experts and cyber-crime investigators, their use is mired in ethical and legal controversy. Although it can be argued that cyber-vigilantism is simply a new-age solution to a new-age problem, the jury is still out on this topic.

"Behind the Curve": The Changing Needs of Law Enforcement in Counteracting Offenders' Expertise

Enterprising and opportunistic criminals have consciously turned to the computer to commit their illegal acts in situations in which the computer serves as the instrument of the crime or the means by which the crime is committed. Of course, the victim's computer, or computer system can often become the target, or objective, of the act as well. And in some situations the computer is used to house and protect information that represents evidence tying the offender to criminal acts. A commonality among these types of crimes is that the offender, to a great degree, depends upon the lack of technological skills of law enforcement to successfully commit the offenses and escape undetected. Based upon the empirical evidence of the self-assessed skills of investigators in this area, computer criminals would have good reason to feel some confidence in their chances to evade detection of their crimes (Gordon et al., 2002).

Unfortunately, it has become apparent that the expertise required of law enforcers to competently battle the emerging menace of computer crime may not be matching the expectations of a public becoming increasingly aware of the gravity of the effects of computer crime. A U.S. National Institute of Justice (NIJ) survey of some of the most experienced law enforcement officials in computer crime, representing over 100 law enforcement agencies at local and state government levels, found that three-quarters of the investigators believed "they do not possess the necessary equipment or tools to effectively detect and identify computer or electronic intrusion crimes." Over 80% believed they required additional training in computer crime investigation to do their jobs properly and rated their abilities to deal with encrypted data as "low" or "doesn't exist." It is not surprising that investigator participants in NIJ's study cited the availability and understanding of up-to-date forensic cyber-tools as one of the most critical needs for computer crime investigators today (Stambaugh et al., 2001).

Investigators, like those surveyed in NIJ's computer crime needs assessment, have increasingly assumed the responsibilities of enforcing relatively new laws on computer crime. Specially trained computer crime investigators now work in state attorney generals' offices as well as in county prosecutors' offices and police departments throughout the U.S. Of course, simply having sufficient numbers of investigators dedicated to the computer crime area does not, in itself, guarantee effective enforcement of computer crime-related laws. The "rub" is that the "new breed" of offender who takes advantage of the public's increasing use of computers requires a new breed of investigator who is adequately equipped with the knowledge and tools to level the new playing field of crime.

One of the most pronounced differences between traditional crimes and computer crimes is that the perpetrator of a traditional crime is likely to dispose of a crime tool once successfully used. Many cybercrime tools, however, are most effective when left behind by the perpetrator, similar to a covert listening device. This is done to assist the perpetrator in future criminal actions against the victim's computer. The location of such covert devices aids the investigator with a starting point for tracing back to the offender, as well as for delivering valuable evidence in the development of a criminal case.

Today's cybercriminals avail themselves of arsenals of scanning tools to map out individual networks as well as entire Local Area Networks (LANS) to identify security weaknesses and, consequently, isolate those forensic tools most effective in exploiting the weaknesses for illegal system penetration. Such virtual "doorknob rattling" becomes, in essence, the criminal reconnaissance for further cybercriminality, laying the groundwork for widespread system invasion. Widely available and robust software tools enable cybercriminals to "crack" passwords, "wardial" modem tones to assess details of computer systems to which the modems are attached, crash systems through Denial of Service (DOS) attacks (including e-mail flooding programs), and "spoof" their own IP addresses to achieve virtual anonymity in their attacks. Further, widely available tools permit savvy offenders to employ computer "packet sniffers" to analyze the victim's network traffic, log the victim's keystrokes, and implant Trojan horse programs (i.e., malicious computer programs disguised as legitimate software). Offenders readily avail themselves of "rootkits" easily accessible through countless hacker web sites. These tools are potent mechanisms designed to hide criminal activity on compromised systems by replacing system commands that would ordinarily be employed to reveal criminal intrusions (Gordon et al., 2002).

A potent technological threat to cybercrime enforcers is the presence and use of steganography tools by cybercriminals. With these tools, offered through commercial and freeware programs, offenders take advantage of unused data areas on computer files to conceal secret information, often in computerized images or audio clips. More than 100 such tools now available can be used in the commission of crimes of child pornography exchange, information warfare and industrial espionage. Because steganography allows information to be hidden in another file, potential evidence is virtually unobtainable. Consequently, steganography stands as one of the most difficult problems for the cybercrime enforcers (Gordon et al., 2002).

Private Sector Tools Used by Law Enforcement

In surveys of Cybercrime enforcers, they have complained that, while the gap has been closing, there is still a significant disparity between the tools cybercriminals use and those available to the criminal justice community. Some of the most popular forensic tools have been identified by cybercrime enforcers as EnCase, SafeBack, DriveSpy, and Ilook. Private sector-developed tools like these have been commended for their attributes of reliability, ease of use, graphical interfaces (GUI) and technical support services. However, cybercrime law enforcers have repeatedly voiced concern about the paucity of tools for operation and analysis on alternate operating systems like Linux and Unix as well as the lack of adequate tools to view obscure file formats like those typically used by child pornography offenders to store pornographic images. Enforcers also lament the lack of tools that assist in the efficient analysis of data generated from systems dedicated to detecting evidence of external attempts to invade computer systems. Enforcers find that many of the tools that are commercially available, because of their proprietary nature, cannot be easily modified to suit the enforcers' exact needs (Gordon et al., 2002).

Yet, the private sector has stepped forward and consistently strived to develop and offer new, improved tools to help keep enforcers in pace with advancing uses of technology by cybercriminals. As an example, The Coroners Toolkit (TCT) represents an automated investigation tool in the Unix environment that accelerates as well as standardizes digital forensic examination processes. This tool also permits the cyber-investigator not only to collect static evidence from computers but also to collect volatile evidence like memory and contents of a computer screen that can disappear in an instant (Gordon et al., 2002).

The work of companies like Wetstone, Technologies Inc. has demonstrated that some companies have been vigilant in developing tools that address cybercrime enforcer needs on both a specific "micro" level and a more holistic "macro" level. On a "micro" level, much of Wetstone's recent work has centered on developing what the company calls "blind steganography detection." This application uses mathematical modeling to determine "normal" ranges of color, intensity, saturation and hue of images, and then automatically compares them to given images to detect any deviations from the norm. These deviations provide distinct clues to the level of purity of image data and can, thus, confirm the presence of steganographic hidden messages in computerized images. On a "macro" level, Wetstone has created SI FI (Synthesized Information from Forensic Investigations), which is a secure distributed evidence repository designed to pool information from intrusion detection programs from multiple locations and also from past forensic investigations. The tool addresses the critical need for organization in optimizing analysis capabilities, especially between criminal justice agencies working on multijurisdictional cases and wishing to share information in a secure web based environment. It allows investigators the options to correlate and graph information on any number of attacks and employ data mining capabilities to tease out common patterns between them. SI FI is widely viewed as a tool that can help identify how such attacks are performed and can also serve as a test bed for the creation of future forensic tools to control these attacks (Gordon et al., 2002).

The Nexus between Cybercrime Enforcers and the Private Sector

Undeniably, the private sector has emerged as an indispensable element in the ever-changing equation to effectively impede the illegal achievements of today's cybercriminals. Without the private sector, the law enforcement community would be incapable of even remotely offering minimal resistance to this formidable enemy. The technological benefits inherent in private sector involvement in the fight against cybercrime are evident. But, are there drawbacks as well? In a quest to control and prevent cybercrime, might there not be a danger of an overreliance on the creativity and resources of the business world? Some in the law enforcement community think so. They have expressed some inner conflict over the dynamics of criminal justice system/private sector interactions. Law enforcers have become torn between appreciation for the availability for existing technology, regret over the absence of needed technology not yet developed, and, somewhat ironically, a sense of resentment over their critical dependence on resources originating outside of the criminal justice system. Some of this uneasiness stems from the dread of relinquishing command to an outside entity, not unlike the experience of having to yield a criminal investigation to another law enforcement agency as a result of jurisdictional disputes. Some dissatisfaction is rooted in the belief that the private sector's dominant role has contributed to a transformation of the public perception that law enforcement is relatively weak in cybercrime enforcement and has also encouraged businesses to treat law enforcement as an afterthought.

Given the technological implications of the private sector's role in fighting cybercrime, it is easy to lose sight of the fact that the criminal justice system/private sector relationship is symbiotic; the private sector depends on the criminal justice system almost a much as the criminal justice system depends on it. The computer security/forensics technology industry is, to a degree, beholden to the criminal justice system, virtually guaranteeing a sustained, viable market for the purchase and use of private sector products and services. That is why the most astute managers of these businesses realize that it is in their companies' best interests to forge meaningful partnerships with law enforcement agencies to steer those agencies toward greater self-reliance.

An example of such a partnership on a local law enforcement level is the one developed by the Wayne County, Michigan Sheriff's Office. The office turned to the private sector for help when the cost of developing a cybercrime unit and training cybercrime investigators was determined to be unmanageable. To help it meet the objectives, the Wayne County Sheriff's Office actively enlisted the assistance of 20 private corporations, including General Dynamics, Xerox, Novell, Ameritech, and Electronic Data Systems (EDS). Each of the firms donated valuable resources and training to the unit and some, like EDS, also donated expert consultation for the office's investigations of computer network intrusions. While such relationships show promise, there are some inherent pitfalls, including potential law enforcement conflicts of interest, particularly if the businesses donating products/services run into legal trouble themselves down the road (McKay, 2001).

The private sector can learn much from the cultivation of working relationships with law enforcement, some of it beyond the scope of the normal undertakings of the business world. Much of this information centers on a precise understanding of the inner workings and strategies of criminal groups in the commission of cybercrimes, insights that would suitably equip the private sector to more accurately tailor products/services to changing needs. Recent events have demonstrated how the intersection of key dimensions of computer crime have signaled greater complexity of attack from the criminal world. One such intersection is the growing use of bots in cases of digital espionage. In Israel, for example, Ruth and Michael Haepharti were recently convicted of building spying bots that they sold to executives at Israeli competitive intelligence firms, who, in turn, illegally collected proprietary information by transferring the software to their clients' vulnerable computers. Similar activity is being seen in the U.S., and private-public teams are organizing to tackle this problem. "Bot Fighters" like Assistant U.S. Attorney James Aquilina and Special Agents Cameron Malin and Kenneth Mcguire of the FBI are a few of the pioneers in these teams that are responsible for cracking bot-related crimes (Gage & Nash, 2006).

An even more troublesome intersection is the one of organized crime and the criminal use of bots on the Internet. The U.S. Secret Service brought down Shadowcrew in October of 2004 after extensive investigation into this "web mob" responsible for wide scale auctioneering of stolen and counterfeit credit and identification cards on the Internet. The group was organized into "administrators" directing "moderators" who ran discussion forums, "reviewers" responsible for evaluating the worth of the to-be auctioned products and "vendors" responsible for selling the products. Over 4,000 general "members" visited Shadowcrew's Internet marketplace to get information on committing fraud. The group used a number of effective techniques to escape enforcement like encrypted text and "proxy" servers to impede tracing. The group added another layer of protection through the use of virtual private network (VPN) "anonymizers" that hide the Internet Protocol addresses of the users. While the U.S. Secret Service turned to available technology to override the VPN defense, it was their ability to use an informant who was secretly placed within the group that cracked the case. An informant running one of the group's servers assisted the Secret Service in operating its undercover operation, and the Secret Service was able to use software to "trap and trace" filtered Internet traffic and pinpoint offenders' IP addresses (Gage, 2005a; Naraine, 2006). While this Web mob was vanquished, other, more recently developed ones have arisen armed with sophisticated bots, further complicating the job of cyber-enforcers.

Private sector teams like the Rapid Response Team at iDefense, and enforcement agencies like the Secret Service and the FBI are uncovering evidence that the new breed of Web mobsters has strong connections to conventional organized crime, specifically the Russian mob and loosely affiliated mob groups. These groups have set up Russian web sites that offer to infect computers for use in botnets at $25 per 10,000 hijacked personal computers. There is now fierce competition among criminal groups to control the resources of infected computers with documented attempts to hijack botnets. The Web mobs' use of Trojans like MetaFisher that are connected to Web-based command and control interfaces has already spread to countless PCs. These mobs use career web sites to recruit "money mules" to help launder and transfer funds, "under the radar" from hijacked online bank accounts. They are using more malicious programs to destroy software developed by rival crime groups and are directing threats against these criminal competitors, as well as against anti-virus vendors. They have even gone as far as using violence against known hackers to force them to join their operations. In short, the new Web mobs have resorted to the long-established criminal traditions of syndicate crime (Naraine, 2006).

Enforcement agencies and private firms are recognizing the importance of working together to help ensure a potent effort to contain these new Web mobs. Speaking at the RSA Security Conference in San Jose, California in February of 2006, FBI Director Robert Mueller called the private sector the "first line of defense" against cybercrime and pointed out that the FBI had been most successful with cybercrime cases when they had involved major technology industry players. The director of iDefense's Rapid Response Team, Ken Dunham, has added that government-corporate collaborations lay the critical groundwork for improved responses to cyberthreats. However, the Vice President of Threat Research at WebRoot sees need for improvement on the public sector side, most notably in enhancing development of international cooperation and breaking away from an overdependence on reactive methods devoid of any reasonable analysis of possible future trends in criminality (Lyman, 2006).

THE PROBLEM OF IDENTITY FRAUD

Scope of the Identity Fraud Problem

Identity fraud has arisen as a major problem for both the criminal justice system and the private sector, especially in its overlap with other crime areas like terrorism, money laundering, drug trafficking, alien smuggling, and weapons smuggling. Identity fraud is the criminal process of using false identifiers, fraudulent documents, or stolen identities (identity theft) in the commission of a crime. It has been employed by criminals and criminal organizations in an effort to facilitate criminal activities and to avoid detection of those acts. While identity theft specifically refers to the theft of an actual person's identity, identity fraud encompasses the wider scope of the fraudulent use of any real or fictitious, identity. The rocketing rise of Internet use, allowing illegal access to personal identifiers through hacking and to websites that demonstrate how to create and/or obtain fraudulent documents, has exacerbated this problem. Complicating the law enforcement difficulties is the fact that there is no discrete data source responsible for the compiling and reporting of all incidences of identity fraud. Consequently, there is no foolproof way to effectively measure the size and scope of identity fraud. Much of the information on identity fraud that does exist is must be culled indirectly from information on other crimes that are facilitated by identity fraud. At present, no federal criminal justice repository, such as the UCR (Uniform Crime Reports) or NIBRS (National Incident-Based Reporting System), is responsible for collecting identity fraud data (Gordon et al., 2004).

Understanding the size and scope of identity fraud is difficult, to say the least. Many entities try to collect information on these dimensions, but, in large part, they represent piecemeal efforts. Collected statistics are affected by shifts in law enforcement approaches and by the fact that identity fraud has not entirely been recognized as a discrete "crime area." The collection of data on identity fraud is carried out by an amalgam of federal, state and local agencies (e.g., General Accountability Office, Federal Trade Commission, Social Security Administration, state Attorney Generals' offices) with little cross-communication. The resulting lack of coordination between interested enforcement entities is blamed by some for the extended periods of time within which offenders can sustain their criminal activities.

Exacting a true measure of the extent of identity theft in the U.S. today is, thus, one of the most formidable tasks facing the law enforcement community. This is a crime area in which the bulk of the richest data resides within the domain of the private sector, with some aggregate information collected by public entities like the Federal Trade Commission (FTC). In its annual report entitled *National and State Trends in Fraud and Identity Theft – December 2004*, the FTC reported that identity theft had topped the list of fraud-related complaints for five consecutive years (Federal Trade Commission, 2004). One dependable private sector source of data has been the credit card industry, which started collecting data on identity theft and account takeovers in the mid-1990s. Despite the limitations of data on offenses, both the criminal justice system and the private sector have been compelled to devise quick solutions due to the potentially devastating effects identity fraud victimization can have on victims' credit ratings and financial stability. Besides officially establishing identity theft as an illegal act, the federal Identity Theft and Assumption Deterrence Act of 1998 established the Federal Trade Commission (FTC) as a central repository for the reporting the crime of identity theft and now stands as the recognized source of aggregate identity theft data (Federal Trade Commission, 2000).

Identity fraud not only represents the criminal activities inherent within the act itself, but it also serves as a facilitator of other, more traditional crimes. Offenders who use identity fraud as a crime facilitator acquire or fashion "breeder" documents (e.g., birth certificates) and use them to procure other identification documents (e.g., passports), gaining more credibility as they move along. Some may cross borders using this fraudulent documentation, eventually obtaining drivers' licenses and Social Security cards, allowing them to open bank accounts and establish a "purer" identity. This identity purifying process has been recognized as a key component of increasing the chances of successful criminal activities in the areas of drug smuggling, human trafficking, money laundering as well as activities enabling acts of terrorism (Gordon et al., 2004).

Smugglers of illegal immigrants have used fraudulent documents to obtain immigration benefits (e.g., permanent residency and work authorization) for aliens smuggled into the United States, and have taken advantage of the Visa Waiver Pilot Program (VWPP) which allows nationals from some countries to enter the U.S. with no documents other than a valid passport. Incidents in which smugglers using both counterfeit and genuine passports from VWPP countries to smuggle non-VWPP nationals have been on the rise. An even thornier problem is posed by cases in which alien smugglers create fictitious companies for which the aliens ostensibly work. Such fraud has occurred in over 90% of the Immigration and Naturalization Service's analysis of 5,000 L-1 visa petitions, representing a "new wave in alien smuggling" (General Accounting Office, May 2000).

Replacing a Criminal Justice Control Model with a Private Sector Prevention Model

The criminal justice system has attempted to address the growth of identity fraud through the same processes that it has addressed evolving crime areas in the past: by creating new and tougher laws prohibiting undesirable behavior. The Identity and Assumption Deterrence Act, the Internet False Identification Prevention Act and the "Safe ID" Act have all tried to tackle the problem of identity fraud control and prevention. While the Identity and Assumption Deterrence Act spelled out definitions of the criminal act and delineated penalties, the Internet False Identification Prevention Act and the "Safe ID" Act went further to criminalize the electronic transmission of counterfeit identification through websites and the trafficking in false authentication features (e.g., holograms, watermarks). Legislation like the Customer Identification program of Section 326 of the federal U.S.A. Patriot Act reaches still further by creating minimum standards for financial institutions to ensure the identification of customers. But most related criminal justice system generated responses to identity fraud cling to the familiar crime control/punishment model.

Once again, the private sector has become actively engaged in 21st century crime problems by offering a fresher model invested more in preventing identity fraud through a pronounced emphasis on authentication. This model is based on methods employed by credit card companies to cut their losses through fraud, particularly as they relate to e-commerce fraud. Business surveys like that of GartnerG2, which revealed over $700 million lost in online sales (McCabe, 2002), and the Pew Internet Project public surveys, showing that over 85% of the public fears online credit card theft, have impelled the private sector to develop more sophisticated methods to thwart e-commerce identity fraud by enhancing credit card authentication systems (Fallows, 2005).

New consumer-friendly authentication systems have been introduced by both Visa (i.e., Verified by Visa) and MasterCard (i.e., Universal Cardholder Authentication Field Secure Payment Application [SPA]). Each has entailed some inconvenience by requiring the consumer to momentarily leave the merchant checkout page of the merchant's web site, but they have strengthened security through password-based authentication systems and by attaching authentication information to authorization messages. The actions taken by Visa and MasterCard form the basis of technology-based actions to prevent credit card fraud in general. They include the employment of credit card processing firms that use powerful technology that tracks "identifiers" of unusual use patterns. Firms like First Data have engineered artificial intelligence methods for understanding potentially fraudulent transactions. First Data's development and use of neural networks flags spending deviations from past transactional amounts and transactions taking place at the same time (i.e., simultaneous use by the legitimate user and a fraudster), and then produces metamorphic models that predict fraudulent credit card transactions, the formulas for which are kept top secret.

A growing number of private firms are dedicating the lion's share of their business to tracking credit card use patterns to detect identity fraud. ID Analytics, for instance, developed ID Score to track purchasing behavior as a way to detect identity fraud. An enhanced component of ID Score, Graph Theoretic Anomaly Detection, spots unusual patterns with two separate models. Its retroactive model analyzes the past and determines where and when fraud has occurred. Its predictive model replicates past behavior patterns to detect future identity fraud. The firm Fair Isaac has developed its own model, Strategy Science, which factors in criteria such as the retail environment, the transaction amount, and the time of transaction. This model also weighs the likelihood of false positives, reducing the chances of needlessly alarming legitimate cardholders (MacDonald, 2006).

In responding to the identity fraud crime problem, many other companies are now developing technology exclusively for front-end applications.

Atlanta-based InterCept Payment Solutions has touted its "fraud scrubber," which analyzes a consumer's payment behavior to determine the potential for fraud, weighing those patterns against fraud patterns. New Jersey-based Retail Decisions is emblematic of the new direction taken by firms. The company uses a proprietary database of 75 million records of credit card accounts, shipping, e-mail and Internet Protocol addresses suspected of being connected to acts of fraud. Retail Decisions uses the database for its fraud detection tool called ebitGuard, tracking static data used by fraudsters like the same phone numbers or mailing addresses. Since fraudsters will often test the validity of stolen account numbers by initiating, but not completing, long distance calls, ebitGuard is designed to search account numbers that had charges for such unbilled long distance calls. In his assessment of how the private sector has analyzed the identity fraud problem and quickly responded, Peter Lucas of Credit and Collections World has proclaimed that great inroads have finally been made. As Lucas puts it, "With so many new weapons now available to combat fraud and create greater operating efficiencies, creditors and collections agencies appear well armed to battle criminals and recover dollars more efficiently without dramatically increasing operating costs" (Lucas, 2006).

Fraud protection technology vendors are incrementally devoting more of their resources to criminal methods research (i.e., methods used by identity fraudsters) to effectively stay "ahead of the curve." In 2005, ID Analytics conducted such a study of over 300 million account applications with some fascinating results. The form of identity fraud gaining most in popularity for identity fraudsters is something called "synthetic" identity fraud. Some identity fraudsters are abandoning the standard ways of committing identity fraud through using a victim's name and other personal data to access the victim's financial or credit card accounts, and instead assembling bits and pieces of real identities to create a "synthetic" new identity. In the synthetic approach, criminals may modify a valid Social Security number to create multiple variations of similar names across the numerous identities. The goal is to fashion a fictitious identity and construct a credit history, thereby allowing them to apply for credit cards or borrow money. ID Analytics found that these "synthetic" identity fraudsters like to open up wireless accounts to help substantiate their false identities and operate quickly to victimize individuals and businesses, abandon the identities and move on to create new synthetic identities. While ID Analytics found that only 15% of synthetic identity fraud attempts were successful, compared to 28% of standard identity frauds, they also found that synthetic fraud now accounts for over 83% of identity fraud incidents and over 73% of funds lost through identity fraud. As a result of their research findings, ID Analytics is hard at work devising technology to specifically detect observable patterns in synthetic identity fraud, such as the use of variations of names and the use of celebrity names, making them easier to remember. Their work is cut out for them given the growing proliferation of synthetic identity fraud "how to" kits available on the Internet (Wolfe, 2005; *Electronic Payments Week*, 2005).

Adapting Private Sector Models to the Justice System: Information Sharing on a National Level

In the national post-9/11 atmosphere, the private sector has been looked to for the development of a technology and information-based model to prevent identity fraud that could culminate in terrorist acts. These new models assess the "threat" to an "asset" and the appropriate level of protection needed for that asset. Pioneered by the financial service industry (e.g., credit reviews prior to the granting of credit cards, approval of loans), these models are dependent on the effective structuring of incremental levels of risk assessment, for identity authentication, based on factors like cost, speed of decision making, availability of information, and sophistication of those making the threats. The models avoid reliance on simple identity document matching, and are composed of three parts: validation, verification and authentication.

LexisNexis is one company that has mastered such an authentication model called Radiant Trust, and has offered it as a blueprint for a national identity fraud prevention system. At its initial, and most basic validation phase, Radiant Trust determines if identification information is fictitious by consulting tables of records to confirm that the identifier information conforms to an established format and satisfies an existing logic that the person is "real." The next, more sophisticated, level of verification uses parallel searching of multiple databases to determine if certain "identifiers" logically "belong" together. Balanced against cost and the need for precision, discrepancies at this level can lead to deeper analysis. The final and most sophisticated level, authentication, builds on the first two levels to create a modeling/scoring engine, mirroring private sector credit risk models that determine authenticity based on variables of existing records (e.g., addresses, Social Security numbers). In this engine, each variable is assigned a weight based on the assessed strength of prediction of real identification.

The engine is continually updated as new data is entered into the system and scores are created in near-real time. "Exception" scores are isolated for deeper analysis through the searching of specialized databases (Gordon et al., 2004).

Authentication models like Radiant Trust appear to be the wave of the future in the private sector to prevent identity fraud. They can be complex for they not only include the building of the models and the development of scoring processes, but they require the procuring of appropriate data and the access to data to develop effective and secure national repositories. This presents the greatest challenge to success, for the effectiveness of the model is based on the extent to which the public and private sectors will share the data to populate data repositories and specialized databases needed for these decision systems to work. Private firms like LexisNexis are promoting a new direction in which criminal justice agencies, as well as other components of the public sector, acknowledge their inability to administer such a system and partner with the private sector to ensure its success. Such a partnership is intended to relieve the public sector of the burden of mammoth costs, but would mean the liberal sharing of types of national information heretofore viewed as too sensitive to entrust to the private sector. Acknowledging the effectiveness of the private sector's authentication models, the burning question of whether such information is secure in the hands of private sector remains (Gordon et al., 2004).

Partnerships for Identity Fraud Control

Traditional crime fighting has relied on a "time of flight" factor since the beginning. This formula held that a perpetrator of a crime could only travel a certain distance within the time that has elapsed since the occurrence of the offense. The speed with which a police agency could mobilize forces would then determine the size of the area that most likely contained the suspect. This concept has been significantly affected by advances such as motorized vehicles and air travel, but it has been all but nullified by the advent of electronic communications.

The challenges to law enforcement posed by identity fraud crimes demand the use of creative solutions such as applying older statutes to new-age criminal acts, and utilizing partnerships that blur the line between government and industry. For example, in the Chicago metropolitan area, a coalition of government, enforcement agencies and private corporations have joined forces to address identity fraud. The Chicago Metropolitan

Identity Fraud Task Force (CMIFTF) uses the combined resources, skills and knowledge of its member agencies to "arrest and prosecute criminals that engage in organized identity fraud crimes, seize assets, educate Law Enforcement and private sector Investigators, and serve as a deterrent to suspects." With members such as the FBI, American Express and Circuit City (CMIFTF, 2003), the CMIFTF provides a modern model for fighting what is surely an uphill battle against identity thieves.

A bright light in creative partnerships addressing identity fraud is the information sharing partnership between the Identity Theft Assistance Center (ITAC) and the Federal Trade Commission. ITAC is a center operated by the Washington DC-based private non-profit Identity Theft Assistance Corporation. The center is supported by 48 large financial service companies, members of the industry group The Financial Services Roundtable and its information technology sister organization, BITS, a consortium dedicated to addressing emerging issues involving financial services, technology and commerce. Among the supporting companies are Ford Motor Credit Co., U.S. Bancorp, and Wells Fargo & Co. ITAC shares identity theft information, like the types of scams reported by victims, with the FTC, which then shares the information with appropriate law enforcement agencies. Information is only shared with the permission of victims. The information sharing is an effort to overcome problems like the lack of necessary cross-jurisdictional information for law enforcement agencies operating in cities or counties located near the borders of other states or municipalities. Identity fraud cases that have no obvious links to cases in bordering jurisdictions would otherwise garner little law enforcement attention. Financial service firms would, in the past, share identity fraud information with local law enforcement agencies, but a national data-sharing effort was unheard off. That situation has changed with the private-public partnership developed through ITAC (Gross, 2005).

SUMMARY

From producing non-lethal weaponry to subdue resistant suspects, to designing substance testing and protective equipment for the investigators of environmental crimes, to the perfection of DNA matching techniques, the private sector has a long history of aiding the criminal justice system as it reinvents itself in the age of technology. One would be hard pressed, though, to find arenas within which the private sector has become as dominant in this role as it is in the control and prevention of computer crime and identity fraud. In recent years, the private sector has carefully analyzed the complexities of meeting the challenges presented by these two crime areas and has admirably responded by turning out products and services that not only assist the criminal justice system to reach its objectives, but has also filled in crime control/prevention "gaps" that the criminal justice system has been unable to satisfactorily address. In addition, the private sector has assumed a prescient "metamorphic" role in that it has strived to perpetually adapt its innovations to pattern changes of offender methods and predict possible courses offenders might take in the future.

The private sector response to the accelerated rate of computer crime has, in effect, led to the birth of a growth industry: computer crime forensics. Law enforcement agencies increasingly reach out to the private sector to avail themselves of the necessary forensic tools to detect and track acts of computer crime. Companies like PG Lewis and Associates and Protiviti have sprouted throughout the U.S. offering highly valued forensic services to businesses hoping to uncover computerized criminal evidence. With the majority of written communication now being digitally created, computer forensics has now become essential to the successful disposition of corporate investigations and litigation support in civil and criminal matters. These computer forensic firms are able to unearth criminal evidence in the form of e-mail communications, web sites visited, file destruction and account alteration thought by the perpetrators to have been deleted or destroyed. Such firms also serve a vital function to the business community by: (1) predicting potential for fraud through fraud vulnerability assessments; (2) protecting businesses from costly lawsuits by analyzing suspect employees and preserving all data in advance of potential litigation; and (3) preventing potential problems by ascertaining if proprietary information had been copied, e-mailed or printed without authorization.

There is no end in site for the need of the private sector to move rapidly forward to manufacture fresh new tools and services in the race to impede the criminal actions of those who use the computer as a weapon, target and repository of criminal evidence. There are clear signs that neither the private sector nor the criminal justice system believes that "targeting hardening" in the physical sense alone will markedly stunt the progress of the offenders. Collaborative efforts between the private sector and the criminal justice system are becoming more common in the computer crime area. The new wrinkle, though, is that past one-sided dependence of the criminal justice system on the private sector is beginning to slowly, but surely, change. The private sector is demonstrating a clearer willingness to recognize the wealth of information the criminal justice system possesses with regard to changes in crime commission methods, particularly information relating to acts of conspiracy and group/organized crime. Needless to say, such "soft technology" collaborations are required for optimization of computer crime control/prevention efforts.

As for identity fraud, it is more insidious than computer crime in that it has become the enabling agent for such diverse crimes as terrorism, money laundering, drug trafficking, alien smuggling and weapons smuggling. Effective responses to this problem are hampered by the lack of any reliable, organized reporting system that accurately reflects all reported identity fraud, across agencies and jurisdictions as well as international borders. While the criminal justice system has clung to the "deterrence-through punishment" model, private sector identity fraud control/prevention models that are rooted in neural network pattern tracing and proactive authentication methods have gained popularity, especially within the business community. The private sector is busy creating new tools to effectively enhance the capabilities of these authentication models. This approach, however, will not work on a national scale unless there can be some agreement on the sharing of public and private information such models. Model systems, such as Radiant Trust, provide examples of potential solutions for sharing appropriate information in order to facilitate identity authentication.

Without private/public systems in place to authenticate individuals on a national scale, identity fraud is destined to spread. As it is now, decision makers are unable to administer accurate and expeditious authentication assessments without access to specialized databases and trusted technology, and the education and training necessary to operate them. There are many challenges to successfully developing the means to slow down this growing problem. These challenges include the sharing of public and private information, issues surrounding protection of privacy and the availability of and easy access to false identification sources. The private sector must continue to perfect authentication methods and proven risk management strategies that provide the basis for faster and more effective determinations of identity. For these refined models, effective information analysis, including scoring and modeling, is essential. Information sharing and data integration across the private and public sectors is the core element for the provision of sophisticated information analysis, which can then be shared across the affected parties within a trusted environment (Gordon et al., 2004).

Government/private sector partnerships are the key for reigning in both computer crime and identity fraud. While law enforcement agencies struggle in an attempt to stay current with emerging trends in electronic crimes and identity fraud, many are overlooking a resource that already is prepared with the knowledge they need. The limited financial, academic and human resources available in most government entities are constraints that are often not shared in private industry. Although possibly limited to the specific industry in which they do business, private companies will likely have knowledge, resources and skills that cover modern technology in a breadth and depth not possible in a government funded agency. Since they are the major consumers of high technology, private businesses will continue to have personnel on staff who are well versed in how these systems function, as well as in security measures and methods that can be used to collect evidence of use and misuse.

Cooperation between private industry and law enforcement agencies is historically limited, and in some cases non-existent. This lack of trust is a two-way street that stems from a fundamental failure to understand the missions and needs of each other. This lack of knowledge is echoed in the findings of the FBI/CSI studies, which anonymously poll private companies on the subject of computer crime victimization. The results of these studies have repeatedly shown that even though the instances of hacking, intrusions and electronic espionage are on the rise, only approximately one-third of these instances are reported to law enforcement. The reasons for this large-scale underreporting are varied, but most agree that they include business decisions made by private companies to limit negative publicity and the belief of many in private industry that law enforcement agencies can't be trusted with sensitive company information and are incapable of investigating high technology crimes anyway.

The failures that have plagued law enforcement task forces in the past, coupled with the challenges of fighting modern day crimes, all point to the need for a new model for forming these collaborative ventures. Criteria for this model are the inclusion of a highly diverse membership that is both multi-jurisdictional and multi-disciplinary, and partnership with academic and private industry entities that can bring cutting edge knowledge, skills and resources to the group. With little fanfare, one of the best examples of this model at work has been running for over a decade in New York

City. In 1995, the U.S. Secret Service founded the New York Electronic Crimes Task Force. This task force was created with a mission to combat high technology and financial fraud crimes in and around the greater metropolitan area. When creating a membership structure for the task force, the Secret Service used a "form follows function" approach, realizing that embracing non-traditional partners from the private sector would be critical to fighting crime in a city that is the business capital of the world. Boasting partners such as the State University of New York's John Jay College of Criminal Justice, and some of the most well known Wall Street financial firms, the New York task force has successfully created an atmosphere of government/private sector trust, sharing and partnership that has thrived where many others have failed. It is incumbent upon both the criminal justice system and the private sector to underscore productive endeavors like these and may, hopefully, effect change so that it becomes the norm for the future.

◆ ◆ ◆ ◆

REFERENCES

Associated Press (2004). Lowe's hardware hacker gets nine years. *USA Today*. Retrieved May 08, 2006 from: http://www.usatoday.com/tech/news/computer security/hacking/2004-12-15-lowes-hack_x.htm

Associated Press (2005). Officer: Computer shows Peterson researched currents in Bay. *USA Today*. Retrieved May 02, 2006 from: http://www.usatoday.com/news/nation/2004-08-03-peterson_x.htm

Atkins, K. (2006, March 2). Global security consortium holds summit on technologies requires for effective collection and exploitation of Open Source Intelligence. *LexisNexis*. Retrieved April 4, 2006 from: http://www.lexisnexis.com/about/releases/GlobalSecurity.asp

Brewin, B., Verton, D., & DiSabatino, J. (2002, January 14). Computerworld: Wireless LANs: Trouble in the Air. Retrieved May 07, 2006 from: http://www.computer world.com/industrytopics/travel/story/0%2C10801%2C67344%2C00.html

Bureau of Justice Assistance (November, 2003). *Recidivism of sex offenders released from prison in 1994*. (NCJ 198281.) Washington, DC.

Carr, D. (2005, December 15). Quick strike. *Baseline*, 42-43.

Cohen, L., & Felson, M. (1979). Social changes and crime rate trends: A routine activity approach. *American Sociological Review, 44*, 588-608.

Chicago Metropolitan Identity Fraud Task Force (CMIFTF). (2003). *Mission*. Retrieved from: http://www.CMIFTF.org

Curtis, K. (2003, February 7). Where are they? States losing track of sex offenders, survey shows. *USA Today.*

ChoicePoint (2006). Voyager query. Retrieved March 1, 2006 from: www.choice point.com/industry/government/public_le_3.htm l

Computer Security Institute (2005). *2005 CSI/FBI Computer Crime and Security Survey.* San Francisco: Computer Security Institute.

Electronic Payments Week (2005, February 15). A window into identity theft. Retrieved May 4, 2005 from: www.idanalytics.com/pdf/electronics_Payment_Article.pdf.

Fallows, D. (2005, December 28). *How women and men use the Internet.* Pew Internet and American Life Project. Retrieved April 2, 2006 from: www.pewinternet.org/pdf/PIP-women_and_men_online.pdf

Federal Trade Commission (2004). *National and state trends in fraud and identity theft – 2004.* Retrieved April 24, from: www.consumer.gov/sentinel/pubs/Top10 fruad2003.pdf

Federal Trade Commission (2000, August 30). *Identity theft complaints triple in last six months: FTC victim assistance workshops to be convened October 23-24.* Retrieved April 13, 2006, from: www.ftc.gov/opa/2000/08/caidttest.htm

Felson, M. (1998). *Crime and everyday life.* Thousand Oaks, CA: Pine Forge Press.

Gage, D. (2005a, December 15). Getting mobbed. *Baseline,* 22-24.

Gage, D. (2005b, December 15). When competitors attack. *Baseline,* 20-21.

Gage, D., & Nash, K. (2006, April 6). Security alert: when bots attack. *Baseline.* Retrieved April 11, 2006 from: www.baselinemag.com/article2/0,1540,1946399, 00.asp

Gordon, G., Willox, N., Rebovich, D., Regan, T., & Gordon, J. (2004). Identity fraud: A critical national and global threat. *Journal of Economic Crime Management,* 2(1), 3-47.

Gordon, G., Hosmer, C., Siesdma, C., & Rebovich, D. (2002). *Assessing technology, methods and information for committing and combating cyber crime.* National Institute of Justice Report. Washington, DC: U.S. Department of Justice.

Gross, G. (2005, July 11). Financial firms to share identity theft data with FTC. *Computerworld Security.* Retrieved April 19, 2005 from: www.computerworld.com/security/topics/security/story/010801,103112,00.html

H.R. 3162 - USA Patriot Act of 2001 section 105 (2001). Retrieved 05/08/06 from: http://www.house.gov/judiciary_democrats/usapatriotsecbysec102301.pdf# search='patriot%20act%20new%20york%20electronic%20crime%20task% 20force

Kerner, S. (2005, February 1). FTC: Identity theft, fraud on the rise. Ecommerce. Retrieved November 13, 2005 from: www.internetnews.com/ec-news/article. php/3467171

Knight, W. (2004, May 8). Chasing the elusive shadows of e-crime. *NewScientist,* 26-29.

Lucas, P. (2006). Tech tools unplugged. *Credit and Collections World.* Retrieved April 1, 2006 from: www.collectionsworld.com/cgi-in/readstory2.pl?story=2003 0801CCRA501.xml

Lyman, J. (2006, February 17). FBI chief calls for cybercrime-fighting collaboration. *TechNews World.* Retrieved April 23, 2006 from: www.technewsworld.com/story/ 48945.html

MacDonald, A. (2006). The anti-fraud battle rages on. *Credit and Collections World*. Retrieved March 1, 2006 from: www.collectionsworld.com/cgi-bin/read story2.pl?story=20031201CCRU387.xml

McCabe, M. (2002, March 4). Gartner G2 says 2002 online fraud losses were 19 times as high as offline fraud losses. Retrieved from: www.gartner.com/5

McCabe, S. (2005, September 25). LexisNexis upgrades Accurint LE Plus to help law enforcement locate and map addresses for sex offenders. *LexisNexis*. Retrieved March 1, 2006 from: www.lexisnexis.com/about/releases/0831.asp

McKay, J. (2001, September 31). Partnerships in crime. *Government Technology*. Retrieved April 7, 2006 from: www.govtech.net/magazine/story.php?id=5771& issue=9:2001

Naraine, R (2006, April 13). Return of the webmob. EWeek.com. Retrieved April 11, 2006 from: www.eweek.com/article2/0,1895,1947884,00.asp

P.G. Lewis Associates LLC (2005). Overview. Retrieved November 11, 2005 from: www.pglewis.com/services.asp

Radcliff, D. (2000). Can you hack back? *Network World*. Retrieved May 02, 2006 from: http://cnnstudentnews.cnn.com/2000/TECH/computing/06/01/ hack.back.idg/

Ross, M. (2006, March 2). Global security consortium holds summit on technologies required for effective collection and exploitation of open source intelligence. *LexisNexis*. Retrieved March 1, 2006 from www.lexisnexis.com/about/releases/ Global%20Security.asp

Spangler, T. (2005, December 15). Swiped into thin air. *Baseline*, 38-40.

Stambaugh, H., Beaupre, D., Icove, D., Baker, R., Cassardy, W., & Williams, W. (2001). *Electronic crime needs assessment for state and local enforcement, National Institute of Justice report*. Washington, DC: U.S. Department of Justice.

U.S. General Accounting Office (2002). *Identity theft: Greater awareness and use of existing data are needed*. Washington, DC: U.S. Government Printing Office.

U.S. General Accounting Office (2000). *Alien smuggling: Management and operational improvements needed to address growing problem*. Washington, DC: U.S. Government Printing Office.

U.S. General Accounting Office (1998). *Information on prevalence, cost and impact is limited*. Washington, DC: U.S. Government Printing Office.

Weaver, B. (2002). *Statement of Mr. Bob Weaver before the House Committee on Science U.S. House of Representatives*. Retrieved April 23, 2006 from: http://www.house.gov/ science/hearings/full02/jun24/weaver.htm

Westchester County (2006). *Wireless Security Law*. Press release. Retrieved May 2, 2006 from: http://www.co.westchester.ny.us/currentnews/2006pr/Wifi new.htm

Wolfe, D. (2005, May 27). In brief: Synthetic fraud said rising. *American Banker Online*. Retrieved May 4, 2006 from: www.idanalytics.com/pdf/am_Banker_ synthetic_fraud_Said_ rising_053105.pdf

4. CRIME PREVENTION AND HARD TECHNOLOGY: THE CASE OF CCTV AND IMPROVED STREET LIGHTING

by

Brandon C. Welsh

University of Massachusetts, Lowell

and

David P. Farrington

Cambridge University

Technological advances over the years have had a profound influence on the way we think about crime and the efforts that are taken to prevent it. Hard technologies designed to prevent crime cover a wide range of applications in different contexts, including metal detectors in schools, baggage screening at airports, bulletproof teller windows at banks, and security systems at homes and businesses.

Closed-circuit television (CCTV) cameras and improved street lighting are two other hard technologies that have been put to much use over the years in an effort to prevent crime in a wide range of public and private contexts. Known more widely in the criminological literature as techniques of situational crime prevention (Clarke, 1995), each performs a surveillance function. Clarke and Homel (1997) differentiate among three types of surveillance, each aimed at increasing offenders' perceived risks of committing a crime: formal surveillance, natural surveillance, and surveillance by employees (i.e., by virtue of their position they perform a surveillance function, e.g., parking lot attendants, bus drivers).

Formal surveillance aims to produce a "deterrent threat to potential offenders" through the deployment of personnel whose primary responsibility is security (e.g., police, security guards) or through the introduction of some form of technology, such as CCTV, to enhance or take the place of security personnel (Clarke, 1997, p. 20). Natural surveillance shares the same aim as formal surveillance, but involves efforts that seek to "capitalize upon the 'natural' surveillance provided by people going about their every-day business." Examples of natural surveillance include the installation or improvement of street lighting, the removal of objects from windows of convenience stores that obscure lines of sight into the store, and the removal or pruning of bushes in front of homes so residents may have a clear view of outside (Clarke, 1997, p. 21).

This chapter focuses specifically on the effects of CCTV and improved street lighting on crime. It does so because to our knowledge only these two hard technologies have been the subject of an empirical assessment of effectiveness using the highest quality methodology of systematic review incorporating meta-analytic techniques. In short, evidence-based crime prevention is a main interest of this chapter.

HOW MIGHT CCTV AND STREET LIGHTING REDUCE CRIME?

Explanations of the way that CCTV surveillance cameras and improvements in street lighting could prevent crime can be found in situational approaches that focus on reducing opportunity and increasing perceived risk through modification of the physical environment (Clarke, 1995), and in perspectives that stress the importance of strengthening informal social control and community cohesion through more effective street use (Jacobs, 1961) and investment in neighborhood conditions (Taub et al., 1984; Taylor & Gottfredson, 1986).

The situational approach to crime prevention suggests that crime can be prevented by environmental measures that directly affect offenders' perceptions of increased risks and decreased rewards. This approach is also supported by theories that emphasize natural, informal surveillance as a key to crime prevention. For example, Jacobs (1961) drew attention to the role of good visibility combined with natural surveillance as a deterrent to crime. She emphasized the association between levels of crime and public street use, suggesting that less crime would be committed in areas with an abundance of potential witnesses.

Other theoretical perspectives have emphasized the importance of investment to improve neighborhood conditions as a means of strengthening community confidence, cohesion, and social control (Wilson & Kelling, 1982; Skogan, 1990). Sampson et al. (1997) argued that a low degree of "collective efficacy" in a neighborhood (a low degree of informal social control) caused high crime rates. As highly visible signs of investment,

CCTV and improved street lighting might reduce crime if they physically improved the environment and signaled to residents that efforts were being made to invest in and improve their neighborhood. In turn, this might lead residents to have a more positive image of the area and increased community pride, optimism, and cohesion. In turn, this might lead residents to exert greater informal social control over potential offenders in an area. It should be noted that this theoretical perspective predicts a reduction in both daytime and nighttime crime. Consequently, attempts to measure the effects of improved street lighting on crime should not concentrate purely on nighttime crime. The same is true for evaluations of CCTV because infrared and other night vision technology allows CCTV to operate just as effectively during nighttime as during daytime.

The relationship among visibility, social surveillance, and criminal opportunities is a consistently strong theme to emerge from the literature. A core assumption of both opportunity and informal social control models of prevention is that criminal opportunities and risks are influenced by environmental conditions in interaction with resident and offender characteristics. Street lighting and CCTV are tangible alterations to the built environment, but they do not constitute a physical barrier to crime. However, they can act as a catalyst to stimulate crime reduction through a change in perceptions, attitudes, and behavior of residents and potential offenders.

Based on these theoretical perspectives, the ways that CCTV and street lighting can prevent crime are similar. Of course, there are a number of differences between these two situational crime prevention measures. One of these differences rests on the widely held perception that CCTV is far more threatening to law-abiding citizens' civil liberties (Clarke, 2000, p. 104).

It is important to acknowledge that CCTV and improved street lighting could also cause crime to *increase.* In the case of CCTV, it could give potential victims a false sense of security and make them more vulnerable because they relax their vigilance or stop taking precautions, such as walking in groups at night and not wearing expensive jewelry. It may encourage increased reporting of crimes to the police and increased recording of crimes by the police. If an offender is detected through CCTV, the offense may be recorded and detected at the same time, leading to an increase in police clearance rates. Hence, in order to disentangle criminal behavior from reporting and recording, both surveys and recorded crime measures are needed in any evaluation. CCTV may also cause crime to be displaced to other locations, times, or victims.

In the case of street lighting improvements, they could, in certain circumstances, increase opportunities for crime. They may bring a greater number of potential victims and potential offenders into the same physical space. Increased visibility of potential victims may allow potential offenders to make better judgments of their vulnerability and attractiveness (e.g., in terms of valuables). Increased social activity outside the home may increase the number of unoccupied homes available for burglary. Increased illumination may make it easier for offenders to commit crimes and to escape. Like CCTV, improved street lighting may also cause crime to be displaced to other areas, times, or victims.

METHODS

This chapter brings together the findings of two separate systematic reviews that were carried out to assess the effects of CCTV and improved street lighting on crime (Farrington & Welsh, 2002a, b; Welsh & Farrington, 2002, 2003, 2004a, b). It is important to comment briefly on the methodology of systematic reviews in general and the methods employed specifically in the two systematic reviews.

Systematic Reviews

Systematic reviews use rigorous methods for locating, appraising, and synthesizing evidence from prior evaluation studies, and they are reported with the same level of detail that characterizes high quality reports of original research. According to Johnson et al. (2000, p. 35), systematic reviews "essentially take an epidemiological look at the methodology and results sections of a specific population of studies to reach a research-based consensus on a given study topic." They have explicit objectives, explicit criteria for including or excluding studies, extensive searches for eligible evaluation studies from all over the world, careful extraction and coding of key features of studies, and a structured and detailed report of the methods and conclusions of the review. All of this contributes greatly to the ease of their interpretation and replication by other researchers. It is beyond the scope of this chapter to discuss all of the features of systematic reviews, but interested readers should consult key reports on the topic (see e.g., Farrington & Petrosino, 2001; Welsh & Farrington, 2006).

Criteria for Inclusion of Evaluation Studies

In selecting evaluations for inclusion in the reviews, the following criteria were used:

1. CCTV or improved street lighting was the focus of the intervention. For evaluations involving one or more other interventions, only those evaluations in which CCTV or improved street lighting was the main intervention were included.

2. The main aim of the schemes was the reduction of crime, and that there was an outcome measure of crime. The most relevant crime outcomes were violent and property crimes.

3. The evaluation design was of high methodological quality, with the minimum design involving before-and-after measures of crime in experimental and comparable control areas. Control areas are needed in order to counter threats to internal validity. According to Cook and Campbell (1979) and Shadish et al. (2002), this is the minimum design that is interpretable. It corresponds to level 3 on the Scientific Methods Scale (Farrington et al., 2002; Sherman et al., 1997).

4. The total number of crimes in each area before the intervention was at least 20. The main measure of effect size was based on changes in crime rates between the before and after time periods. It was considered that a measure of change based on an "N" (sample) below 20 was potentially misleading. Also, any study with less than 20 crimes before would have insufficient statistical power to detect changes in crime. The criterion of 20 is probably too low, but we were reluctant to exclude studies unless their numbers were clearly inadequate.

Search Strategies

The following four search strategies were carried out to identify CCTV or improved street lighting evaluations meeting the criteria for inclusion in the two systematic reviews:

1. Searches of on-line databases. The following databases were searched: SPECTR, *Criminal Justice Abstracts,* National Criminal Justice Reference Service (NCJRS) Abstracts, *Sociological Abstracts, Social Science Abstracts* (SocialSciAbs), Educational Resources Information Clearinghouse

(ERIC), Government Publications Office Monthly Catalog (GPO Monthly), *Psychology Information* (PsychInfo), and Public Affairs Information Service (PAIS) International. These databases were selected because they had the most comprehensive coverage of criminological, criminal justice, and social science literatures. They are also among the top data bases recommended by the Campbell Crime and Justice Coordinating Group, and other systematic reviews of interventions in the field of crime and justice have used them (e.g., Braga, 2006).

For the CCTV systematic review, the following terms were used to search these databases: closed-circuit television, CCTV, cameras, social control, surveillance, and formal surveillance. When applicable, "crime" was then added to each of these terms (e.g., CCTV and crime) to narrow the search parameters. For the street lighting systematic review, the following terms were used to search the databases: street lighting, lighting, illumination, and natural surveillance. When applicable, "crime" was then added to each of these terms, again to narrow the search parameters.

2. Searches of literature reviews on the effectiveness of the interventions in preventing crime (Eck, 2002; Fleming & Burrows, 1986; Nieto, 1997; Painter, 1996; Pease, 1999; Phillips, 1999; Poyner, 1993; Ramsay & Newton, 1991; Tien et al., 1979).[1]

3. Searches of bibliographies of CCTV and street lighting reports.

4. Contacts with leading researchers.

Both published and unpublished reports were included in the searches. Furthermore, the searches were international in scope and were not limited to the English language (one non-English language evaluation report is included in the CCTV review).

The search strategies resulted in the identification of 83 evaluations (49 for CCTV and 34 for street lighting). Of these, 76 were obtained and analyzed; the other 7, which may or may not have met the criteria for inclusion, could not be obtained. Of these 76 evaluations, 32 met the criteria for inclusion (19 for CCTV and 13 for street lighting) and 41 did not (25 for CCTV and 16 for street lighting) and thus were excluded from the systematic reviews. The three remaining studies (all CCTV) met the criteria for inclusion, but did not provide the needed data to be included in the meta-analysis (see below).[2]

RESULTS

The main aim of this chapter is to assess the effects of CCTV and improved street lighting on crime, using the highest quality available research evidence. (Table 1 presents summary information on each of the 32 included studies.) To address this and other questions of interest, results obtained in the included evaluations are analyzed using the statistical technique of meta-analysis.

A meta-analysis is essentially a statistical summary of comparable effect sizes reported in each evaluation. In order to carry out a meta-analysis, a comparable measure of effect size and an estimate of its variance are needed in each program evaluation (Lipsey & Wilson, 2001; Wilson, 2001). In the case of CCTV and street lighting evaluations, the measure of effect size had to be based on the number of crimes in the experimental and control areas before and after the intervention, because this was the only information that was regularly provided in these evaluations.

The odds ratio (OR) is used to measure the effect size. The OR is calculated from the following table:

	Before	After
Experimental	a	b
Control	c	d

Where a, b, c, d are numbers of crimes

$$OR = ad/bc$$

The OR is meaningful because it specifies the relative change in crime in a control area compared with an experimental area. For example, if the weighted average OR was 1.25, this would show that crime increased by 25% more in control areas than in experimental areas, or conversely that crime decreased 20% more in experimental areas than in control areas (using the inverse of the OR = 1/1.25).

The variance of OR is calculated from the variance of LOR (the natural logarithm of OR). The usual calculation of this is as follows:

$$V (LOR) = 1/a + 1/b + 1/c + 1/d$$

In order to produce a summary effect size in a meta-analysis, each effect size is weighted according to the inverse of the variance. This was another reason for choosing the OR, which has a known variance (Fleiss, 1981, pp. 61-67).[3]

Table 1: Summary of CCTV and Improved Street Lighting Evaluations

Author and Publication Date	Place	Period (months) Pre	Period (months) Post	Other Interventions	Outcome Measure
CCTV in City Centers					
Brown (1995)	Newcastle UK	26	15	No	Survey
Brown (1995)	Birmingham UK	12	12	No	Records
Short & Ditton (1996)	Airdrie UK	24	24	No	Records
Skinns (1998)	Doncaster UK	24	24	Yes	Records
Armitage et al. (1999)	Burnley UK	12	12	No	Records
Farrington et al. (2007)	Cambridge UK	11	11	No	Survey/ Records
Mazerolle et al. (2002)	Cincinnati N[a]	23	6	No	Records
Mazerolle et al. (2002)	Cincinnati H[a]	23	4	No	Records
Mazerolle et al. (2002)	Cincinnati F[a]	24.5	3.5	No	Records
Street Lighting in City Centers					
Poyner & Webb (1997)	Birmingham UK	12	12	No	Records
Atlanta RC[b] (1974)	Atlanta	12	12	No	Records
DIFL[c] (1974)	Milwaukee	12	12	No	Records
Wright et al. (1974)	Kansas City MO	12	12	No	Records
Sternhell (1977)	New Orleans	51	29	No	Records
CCTV in Residential/Public Housing					
Musheno et al. (1978)	New York	3	3	No	Survey
Street Lighting in Residential/Public Housing					
Shaftoe (1994)	Bristol UK	12	12	No	Records
Painter & Farrington (1997)	Dudley UK	12	12	No	Survey/ SR[d]
Painter & Farrington (1999)	Stoke UK	12	12	No	Survey
Inskeep & Goff (1974)	Portland OR	6 or 11	6 or 11	No	Records
Harrisburg PD[c] (1976)	Harrisburg	12	12	No	Records
Lewis & Sullivan (1979)	Fort Worth	12	12	No	Records
Quinet & Nunn (1998)	Indianapolis	6-9	6-9	Yes	Records

Table 1 *(continued)*

Author and Publication Date	Place	Period (months)		Other Interventions	Outcome Measure
		Pre	Post		
CCTV in Car Parks (parking lots)					
Poyner (1991)	Guildford UK	24	9	Yes	Records
Tilley (1993)	Hartlepool UK	15	30	Yes	Records
Tilley (1993)	Bradford UK	12	12	Yes	Records
Tilley (1993)	Coventry UK	8/16[f]	8/16[f]	Yes	Records
Sarno (1996)	Sutton UK	12	12	Yes	Records
Street Lighting in Car Parks (parking lots)					
Poyner (1991)	Dover UK	24	24	Yes	Records
CCTV in Public Transportation					
Burrows (1979)	Underground S[g]	12	12	Yes	Records
Webb & Laycock (1992)	Underground B[g]	46	26	Yes	Records
Webb & Laycock (1992)	Underground C[g]	28	32	Yes	Records
Grandmaison & Tremblay (1997)	Montreal	18	18	No	Records

Notes: a. Cincinnati: N = Northside, H = Hopkins Park, F = Findlay Market.
b. RC = Regional Commission.
c. DIFL = Department of Intergovernmental Fiscal Liaison.
d. SR = self-reports.
e. PD = police department.
f. 8/16 = 8 for experimental, 16 for control (in both pre and post).
g. Underground: S = Southern sector, N = Northern line, C = Central.

We also investigated the important issues of displacement of crime and diffusion of crime prevention benefits. Displacement is often defined as the unintended increase in targeted crimes in other locations following from the introduction of a crime reduction scheme.[1] Reppetto (1976) identified five different forms of displacement: temporal (change in time), tactical (change in method), target (change in victim), territorial (change in place), and functional (change in type of crime). Diffusion of benefits is defined as the unintended decrease in crimes following from a crime reduction scheme, or the "complete reverse" of displacement (Clarke & Weisburd, 1994).

Pooled Results

Separate meta-analyses of the 19 CCTV evaluations and the 13 improved street lighting evaluations provided evidence that both interventions were effective in reducing (total) crime. In the case of CCTV, the weighted mean OR was 1.09 (95% confidence interval 0.97 – 1.22, ns).[5] This means that crimes increased by 9% after CCTV in control areas compared to experimental areas, or conversely that crimes decreased by 8% in experimental areas compared to control areas. In the case of improved street lighting, the weighted mean OR was 1.23 (95% confidence interval 1.10 – 1.39), which was a highly significant effect (p = .0002). This means again that crimes increased by 23% after improved street lighting in control areas compared with experimental areas, or conversely crimes decreased by 19% in experimental areas compared with control areas. Improved street lighting was significantly more effective in reducing crime than CCTV (p = .040).[6]

Setting

All of the 19 CCTV evaluations and the 13 improved street lighting evaluations were carried out in one of four settings: city center, residential or public housing, car parks, or public transportation (see Table 2). With the exception of CCTV in residential/public housing (only one study), all of the settings in which either CCTV or improved street lighting schemes could be evaluated showed desirable effects on crime, as measured by the weighted mean OR. CCTV in car parks had the largest effect on crime, with an overall OR of 1.70 (95% confidence interval 1.40 – 2.07, p < .0001).

Table 2: Meta-Analysis of CCTV and Improved Street Lighting Evaluations, by Context of Intervention

Context of Intervention	CCTV (N = 19)	Street Lighting (N = 13)
City Center	OR = 1.08 (0.92 – 1.27) (n = 9; Newcastle, Birmingham, Airdrie, Doncaster, Burnley, Cambridge, Cincinnati N, Cincinnati H, Cincinnati F)	OR = 1.18 (0.91 – 1.52) (n = 5; Birmingham, Atlanta, Milwaukee, Kansas City, New Orleans)
Residential/ Public Housing	OR = 0.89 (0.30 – 2.62) (n = 1; New York)	OR = 1.26* (1.10 – 1.45) (n = 7; Bristol, Dudley, Stoke, Portland, Harrisburg, Fort Worth, Indianapolis)
Car Parks	OR = 1.70* (1.40 – 2.07) (n = 5; Guildford, Hartlepool, Bradford, Coventry, Sutton)	OR = 1.14 (0.49 – 2.67) (n = 1; Dover)
Public Transportation	OR = 1.06 (0.77 – 1.47) (n = 4; Underground S, Underground N, Underground C, Montreal)	n.a.

* p < .05.
Notes: OR = weighted mean odds ratio (and 95% confidence interval); Cincinnati: N = Northside, H = Hopkins Park, F = Findlay Market; Underground: S = Southern sector, N = Northern line, C = Central; n.a. = not available.

Crime Type

Table 3 shows that CCTV and street lighting were more effective in reducing property crimes (OR for CCTV = 1.50, $p < .0001$; OR for lighting = 1.19, $p = .05$) than violent crimes (OR for CCTV = 1.03, ns; OR for lighting = 1.12, ns). However, CCTV was significantly more effective in reducing property crime ($p = .010$). Property crimes included burglary, vehicle crimes, and theft, while violent crimes included robbery and assault.

Country Comparison

Of the 19 CCTV evaluations, 14 were from the U.K. and the other five were from North America (four from the U.S. and one from Canada). Of

Table 3: Meta-Analysis of CCTV and Improved Street Lighting Evaluations, by Crime Type

Crime Type	CCTV	Street Lighting
Violent	OR = 1.03 (0.83 – 1.28) (n = 6; Airdrie, Burnley, Cambridge, Underground N, Underground C, Montreal)	OR = 1.12 (0.90 – 1.39) (n = 9; Bristol, Dudley, Stoke, Atlanta, Milwaukee, Portland, Kansas City, Harrisburg, New Orleans)
Property	OR = 1.50* (1.26 – 1.79) (n = 11; Newcastle, Airdrie, Burnley, Underground S, Underground C, Montreal, Guildford, Hartlepool, Bradford, Coventry, Sutton)	OR = 1.19* (1.00 – 1.42) (n = 11; Dover, Bristol, Birmingham, Dudley, Stoke, Atlanta, Milwaukee, Portland, Kansas City, Harrisburg, New Orleans)

*p < .05. Notes: OR = weighted mean odds ratio (and 95% confidence interval); Underground: S = Southern sector, N = Northern line, C = Central.

the 13 improved street lighting evaluations, eight were from the U.S. and the other five were from the U.K. As illustrated in Table 4, when the pooled meta-analysis results for each intervention were disaggregated by country, CCTV and improved lighting were more effective in reducing crime in the U.K. (OR for CCTV = 1.16, ns; OR for lighting = 1.40, p < .0001) than in North America (OR for CCTV = 0.99, ns; OR for lighting = 1.08, ns). Street lighting was significantly more effective than CCTV in the U.K. (p = .024)

Table 4: Meta-Analysis of CCTV and Improved Street Lighting Evaluations, by Country

Country	CCTV	Street Lighting
United Kingdom	OR = 1.16 (0.98 – 1.36) (n = 14)	OR = 1.40* (1.19 – 1.65) (n = 5)
U.S. and Canada	OR = 0.99 (0.94 – 1.04) (n = 5)	OR = 1.08 (0.96 – 1.21) (n = 8)
Total	OR = 1.09 (0.97 – 1.22) (N = 19)	OR = 1.23* (1.10 – 1.39) (N = 13)

*p < .05.
Note: OR = weighted mean odds ratio (and 95% confidence interval).

and street lighting was significantly more effective in the U.K. than in North America (p = .0002).

CCTV and Improved Street Lighting

Five of the 19 CCTV evaluations (Bradford, Coventry, Guildford, Sutton, and Underground N; see Table 1) used improved lighting as a secondary intervention. (None of the 13 improved street lighting evaluations used CCTV as a secondary intervention.) A meta-analysis of these five evaluations provided evidence that the combination of CCTV and improved lighting can be highly effective in reducing crime, with a weighted mean odds ratio of 1.62 (95% confidence interval 1.29 – 2.02, p < .0001). A meta-analysis of the other 14 evaluations (4 of which used other interventions, such as security officers and notices of CCTV) produced a much smaller weighted mean odds ratio of 1.08 (95% confidence interval 0.95 – 1.23, ns). From these results, it can be seen that the combination of CCTV and improved lighting (as primary and secondary measures, respectively) was the more effective form of surveillance in reducing crime, and the difference was significant (p < .0001). It is important to note, however, that four of these five evaluations took place in car parks (parking lots) and only measured the schemes' impact on vehicle crimes. Therefore, the powerful result evidenced from combining CCTV surveillance cameras and improved street lighting may be limited to targeting vehicle crimes in car parks.

Displacement of Crime and Diffusion
of Crime Prevention Benefits

Eleven of the 19 CCTV studies and 12 of the 13 street lighting studies measured displacement of crime, diffusion of crime prevention benefits, or both. Across the CCTV studies, mixed results were found for territorial displacement and diffusion of benefits. For example, in the case of the seven city center CCTV studies that measured displacement, diffusion, or both, four studies reported at least some evidence of territorial displacement and three studies reported at least some evidence of diffusion of benefits. Different results were found for the street lighting studies. Only three of these studies reported some or possible evidence of territorial displacement, and the other nine reported no evidence of displacement, with two of these studies (Birmingham & Stoke; see Table 1) also reporting at least some evidence of diffusion.

In order to investigate displacement of crime and diffusion of crime prevention benefits, the minimum design should involve one experimental area, one adjacent area, and one non-adjacent comparable control area. If crime decreased in the experimental area, increased in the adjacent area, and stayed constant in the control area, this might be evidence of displacement. If crime decreased in the experimental and adjacent areas and stayed constant or increased in the control area, this might be evidence of diffusion of benefits. Unfortunately, few CCTV or street lighting studies used this minimum design. Instead, most had an adjacent control area and the remainder of the city as another (non-comparable) control area. Because of this, any conclusions about displacement or diffusion effects of CCTV and street lighting seem premature at this time.

DISCUSSION AND CONCLUSIONS

On the basis of the highest quality available research evidence, both CCTV surveillance cameras and improved street lighting are effective situational measures for reducing crime, with street lighting being the more effective of the two. For city managers, business owners, or others this may be useful information if a decision needs to be made about implementing one or the other measure. Hopefully, as Moore (2002) argued in another context, a cost-effectiveness analysis or comparative cost-benefit analysis would also be carried out to inform this decision.

What may be more helpful to practitioners and more useful for policy discussions is information about the specific conditions under which improved street lighting and CCTV are most effective in reducing crime. The present research showed that CCTV and improved street lighting were effective in reducing total crime (with one exception) in each of the four settings where they were evaluated, with the largest effect on crime being for CCTV in car parks. This finding provides further direction for the allocation of scarce public resources.

Also of importance was evidence showing that CCTV and improved lighting were more effective in reducing property crimes than in reducing violent crimes, with CCTV being significantly more effective than street lighting in reducing property crime. Regular crime analysis by the police, such as used in Compstat (Weisburd et al., 2003), could be used to identify those places that are at greatest risk for property crimes, particularly vehicle crimes, which, in turn, could be used to guide the deployment of CCTV surveillance cameras or improved lighting. The advent of mobile and removable CCTV units may make this a more feasible and perhaps less costly option (but see Waples & Gill, 2006). There was also some empirical support, albeit limited, for combining the two measures. Arguably, there is no conflict in implementing these two measures alongside each other.[7]

Another interesting finding to emerge from the present research is that both forms of surveillance were found to be far more effective in reducing crime in the U.K. than in the U.S.[8] What might account for this? Or, more importantly, what lessons can be drawn from the U.K. studies to help improve the effectiveness of CCTV and improved street lighting in the U.S.? There were some differences in key characteristics between the U.K. and U.S. CCTV schemes and between the U.K. and U.S. improved street lighting schemes, which may help to address these questions.

First, the average follow-up period of the five U.S. CCTV schemes was substantially shorter than for the 14 U.K. CCTV schemes: 6.9 months versus 17.7 months. Four of the U.S. evaluations had the shortest follow-up periods of all 19 CCTV evaluations, ranging from a low of three months to a high of six months. Because of the short follow-up periods in the U.S. studies, it is possible that the CCTV schemes were not given enough time to produce a clear effect on crime, either desirable or undesirable (all five of the U.S. studies showed evidence of either a null or uncertain effect on crime). Longer follow-up periods, as in the majority of the U.K. studies, seem to be warranted for future U.S. CCTV evaluations. No difference was found in the average follow-up period for the U.K. and U.S. improved street lighting evaluations (14.4 months vs. 13.6 months, respectively).

Second, and perhaps most importantly, not one of the five U.S. CCTV evaluations used other interventions alongside CCTV, while nine of the 14 U.K. schemes used one or more other type of intervention, such as improved lighting or police patrols. It is possible that the absence of lighting, policing, or other situational crime prevention measures in the U.S. CCTV schemes may be a contributing factor to their overall poor effect in reducing crime. CCTV on its own may not represent a sufficient deterrent threat to influence an offender's decision-making process to commit a crime or not. No difference was found between the U.K. and U.S. improved street lighting schemes on their use of other interventions.

Another important issue that may be a contributing factor to the difference in effectiveness between the U.K. and the U.S. schemes, both for CCTV and improved street lighting, is cultural context. In the U.K., there is a high level of public support for the use of CCTV cameras in public settings to prevent crime (Norris & Armstrong, 1999, pp. 60-62;

Phillips, 1999, pp. 139-140), while in the U.S. the public is less accepting of and more apprehensive of Big Brother implications arising from this surveillance technology (Murphy, 2002). In the U.S., resistance to the use of CCTV in public space also takes the form of legal action and constitutional challenges under the U.S. Constitution's Fourth Amendment prohibition against unreasonable searches and seizures (Nieto, 1997, p. 1).

It could very well be that the poor showing of the U.S. CCTV schemes was due in part to a lack of public support (and maybe even political support) for the schemes, which, in turn, may have resulted in cuts in program funding, the police assigning lower priority to the schemes, or attempts to discourage desirable media coverage, for example. Each of these factors could potentially undermine the effectiveness of CCTV schemes. In contrast, the Home Office, which funded many of the U.K. evaluations, would have liked to find that CCTV was effective (in order to justify the massive government investment in CCTV).

While cultural context could play a role in the differential effectiveness of street lighting in the two countries (to our knowledge there have been no recent surveys of the public in either country), it is our opinion that this is not likely. This is mainly because this form of surveillance is generally viewed as having few harmful social consequences, unlike CCTV.

For improved street lighting there may be something of an age effect that has contributed to the difference in effectiveness between the U.K. and U.S. schemes. With the exception of one of the eight U.S. street lighting evaluations, all of them were carried out at least 10 to 15 years earlier than the first U.K. street lighting evaluation. Could it be that the U.K. street lighting evaluations drew upon the knowledge gleaned from the individual U.S. evaluations and the detailed review by Tien et al. (1979), and that this played some role in the effectiveness of the U.K. lighting schemes? This is quite possible, because there was a great awareness of this U.S. research, as evidenced in U.K.-based reviews of the literature (Ramsay & Newton, 1991; Painter, 1996) and in some of the U.K. lighting studies included here. Another factor that may have contributed to the difference in effectiveness between the U.S. and U.K. street lighting schemes is the possibility that offenders during the 1990s (in the case of the U.K. studies) may have been influenced by different factors compared to those over a decade earlier.

There is still much to be learned about the optimal conditions under which CCTV and improved street lighting are most effective in reducing crime. But at this time these two measures demonstrate the effectiveness of two key applications of hard technology to the prevention of crime.

◆ ◆ ◆ ◆

NOTES

1. The review by Tien et al. (1979) identified 103 street lighting projects carried out in the United States in the 1970s, but only considered that 15 (listed on their pp. 51-54) met their minimum methodological standards. We attempted to obtain 11 of these 15 evaluation reports. For the other four studies (conducted in Baltimore; Chicago; Richmond, Virginia; and Washington, DC), Tien et al. (1979) could not determine from the reports that there was any kind of experimental-control comparison. Hence, we did not attempt to obtain and screen every possible study on street lighting and crime conducted prior to Tien et al. (1979), only studies that conceivably might meet our criteria for inclusion. We did attempt to obtain and screen every possible study conducted after Tien et al.'s (1979) review.

2. Information on the unobtainable and excluded evaluations is available from the first author.

3. The estimate of the variance is based on the assumption that total numbers of crimes (a, b, c, d) have a Poisson distribution. Thirty years of mathematical models of criminal careers have been dominated by the assumption that crimes can be accurately modeled by a Poisson process (Piquero et al., 2003). However, the large number of changing extraneous factors that influence the number of crimes may cause overdispersion; that is, where the variance of the number of crimes VAR exceeds the number of crimes N.

$$D = VAR/N$$

specifies the overdispersion factor. Where there is overdispersion, V(LOR) should be multiplied by D. Farrington et al. (2005) estimated VAR from monthly numbers of crimes and found the following equation:

$$D = .0008 \times N + 1.2$$

D increased linearly with N and was correlated .77 with N. The median number of crimes in a CCTV study was 760, suggesting that the median value of D was about 2. However, this is an overestimate because the monthly variance is inflated by seasonal variations, which do not apply to N and VAR. Nevertheless, in order to obtain a conservative estimate,

V(LOR) calculated from the usual formula above was doubled in all cases. This adjustment corrects for overdispersion within studies but not for heterogeneity between studies.

4. For a discussion of "benign" or desirable effects of displacement, see Barr & Pease (1990).

5. These effect size estimates are based on a fixed effects model when heterogeneity was not significant. When heterogeneity was significant, the usual additive random effects model gave misleading results, because all studies (small or large) were given similar weightings. It is desirable to give more weight to results obtained in larger studies. Therefore, we used a random effects model with a multiplicative variance adjustment (Jones, 2005). This model adjusts for both overdispersion and heterogeneity and exactly fits the data. In it, the weighted mean odds ratio is the same as in the fixed effects model but the confidence interval is greater.

6. The significance of the difference between two ORs was calculated from each LOR (logarithm of the OR), VLOR (variance of LOR), and N (number of studies on which each OR was based).

$$z = (LOR_1 - LOR_2) / \sqrt{\text{pooled variance}}$$

Pooled variance =
$$[(N_1 - 1) \times VLOR_1 + (N_2 - 1) \times VLOR_2] / (N_1 + N_2 - 2)$$

7. Some may view the combination of CCTV surveillance cameras and street lighting as trivial, based on the notion that CCTV requires natural or artificial lighting to work. This is not the case. Technological innovations in CCTV cameras, such as infra-red, allow cameras to work without other lighting. Thus, improved street lighting and CCTV should be viewed as distinct interventions. There may be a conflict between the two measures if improved lighting increases community cohesion and CCTV cameras give the impression that a place is unsafe, thus detracting from social cohesion because residents are afraid to go there.

8. Reference is hereafter made to the U.S. because, with the exception of the Grandmaison & Tremblay (1997) CCTV evaluation, all of the CCTV and improved street lighting evaluations were conducted in either the U.K. or the U.S.

REFERENCES

Armitage, R., Smyth, G., & Pease, K. (1999). Burnley CCTV evaluation. In K. Painter & N. Tilley (Eds.), *Surveillance of public space: CCTV, street lighting and crime prevention.* Crime Prevention Studies, vol. 10. Monsey, NY: Criminal Justice Press.

Atlanta Regional Commission (1974). *Street Light Project: Final Evaluation Report.* Atlanta: Author.

Barr, R., & Pease, K. (1990). Crime placement, displacement, and deflection. In M. Tonry & N. Morris (Eds.), *Crime and justice: A review of research* (Vol. 12). Chicago: University of Chicago Press.

Braga, A. A. (2006). Policing crime hot spots. In B. C. Welsh & D. P. Farrington (Eds.), *Preventing crime: What works for children, offenders, victims, and places.* New York: Springer.

Brown, B. (1995). *CCTV in town centres: Three case studies.* Crime Detection and Prevention Series Paper, No. 68. London: Home Office.

Burrows, J. N. (1979). The impact of closed circuit television on crime in the London Underground. In P. Mayhew, R. V. G. Clarke, J. N. Burrows, J. M. Hough, & S. W. C. Winchester, *Crime in public view.* Home Office Research Study, No. 49. London: Her Majesty's Stationery Office.

Clarke, R. V. (1995). Situational crime prevention. In M. Tonry & D. P. Farrington (Eds.), *Building a safer society: Strategic approaches to crime prevention. Crime and justice: A review of research* (Vol. 19). Chicago: University of Chicago Press.

Clarke, R. V. (1997). Introduction. In R. V. Clarke (Ed.), *Situational crime prevention: Successful case studies* (2nd ed.). Monsey, NY: Criminal Justice Press.

Clarke, R. V. (2000). Situational crime prevention, criminology, and social values. In A. von Hirsch, D. Garland, & A. Wakefield (Eds.), *Ethical and social perspectives on situational crime prevention.* Oxford, England: Hart Publishing.

Clarke, R. V., & Homel, R. (1997). A revised classification of situational crime prevention techniques. In S. P. Lab (Ed.), *Crime prevention at a crossroads.* Cincinnati: Anderson.

Clarke, R. V., & Weisburd, D. (1994). Diffusion of crime control benefits: Observations on the reverse of displacement. In R. V. Clarke (Ed.), *Crime prevention studies* (Vol. 2). Monsey, NY: Criminal Justice Press.

Cook, T. D., & Campbell, D. T. (1979). *Quasi-experimentation: Design and analysis issues for field settings.* Chicago: Rand McNally.

Department of Intergovernmental Fiscal Liaison (1974). *Final Report - Milwaukee High Intensity Street Lighting Project.* Milwaukee: Author.

Eck, J. E. (2002). Preventing crime at places. In L. W. Sherman, D. P. Farrington, B. C. Welsh, & D. L. MacKenzie (Eds.), *Evidence-based crime prevention.* New York: Routledge.

Farrington, D. P., Bennett, T. H., & Welsh, B. C. (2007). The Cambridge evaluation of the effects of CCTV on crime. In G. Farrell, K. Bowers, S. Johnson, & M. Townsley (Eds.), *Imagination for crime prevention: Essays in honor of Ken Pease.* Crime Prevention Studies. Monsey, NY: Criminal Justice Press (in press).

Farrington, D. P., Gill, M., Waples, S. J., & Argomaniz, J. (2005). *Studying the effects of CCTV on crime: Meta-analysis of a national evaluation.* Unpublished paper.

Farrington, D. P., Gottfredson, D. C., Sherman, L. W., & Welsh, B. C. (2002). The Maryland scientific methods scale. In L. W. Sherman, D. P. Farrington, B. C.

Welsh, & D. L. MacKenzie (Eds.), *Evidence-based crime prevention*. New York: Routledge.

Farrington, D. P., & Petrosino, A. (2001). The Campbell Collaboration Crime and Justice Group. *Annals of the American Academy of Political and Social Science, 578,* 35-49.

Farrington, D. P., & Welsh, B. C. (2002a). Improved street lighting and crime prevention. *Justice Quarterly, 19,* 313-342.

Farrington, D. P., & Welsh, B. C. (2002b). *Effects of improved street lighting on crime: A systematic review.* Home Office Research Study, No. 251. London: Home Office.

Fleiss, J. L. (1981). *Statistical methods for rates and proportions* (2nd ed.). New York: Wiley.

Fleming, R., & Burrows, J. N. (1986). The case for lighting as a means of preventing crime. *Home Office Research Bulletin, 22,* 14-17.

Grandmaison, R., & Tremblay, P. (1997). Évaluation des effets de la télé -surveillance sur la criminalité commise dans 13 stations du Métro de Montréal. *Criminologie, 30,* 93-110.

Harrisburg Police Department (1976). *Final Evaluation Report of the "High Intensity Street Lighting Program."* Harrisburg, PA: Planning and Research Section, Staff and Technical Services Division, Harrisburg Police Department.

Inskeep, N. R., & Goff, C. (1974). *A preliminary evaluation of the Portland Lighting Project.* Salem, OR: Oregon Law Enforcement Council.

Jacobs, J. (1961). *The death and life of great American cities.* New York: Random House.

Johnson, B. R., De Li, S., Larson, D. B., & McCullough, M. (2000). A systematic review of the religiosity and delinquency literature: A research note. *Journal of Contemporary Criminal Justice, 16,* 32-52.

Jones, H. E. (2005). *Measuring effect size in area-based crime prevention research.* Unpublished M.Phil. thesis. Cambridge, England: Statistical Laboratory, Cambridge University.

Lewis, E. B., & Sullivan, T. T. (1979). Combating crime and citizen attitudes: A case study of the corresponding reality. *Journal of Criminal Justice, 7,* 71-79.

Lipsey, M. W., & Wilson, D. B. (2001). *Practical meta-analysis.* Thousand Oaks, CA: Sage.

Mazerolle, L., Hurley, D., & Chamlin, M. (2002). Social behavior in public space: An analysis of behavioral adaptations to CCTV. *Security Journal, 15,* 59-75.

Moore, M. H. (2002). The limits of social science in guiding policy. *Criminology & Public Policy, 2,* 33-42.

Murphy, D. E. (2002, September 1). As security cameras sprout, someone's always watching. *New York Times,* 22.

Musheno, M. C., Levine, J. P., & Palumbo, D. J. (1978). Television surveillance and crime prevention: Evaluating an attempt to create defensible space in public housing. *Social Science Quarterly, 58,* 647-656.

Nieto, M. (1997). *Public video surveillance: Is it an effective crime prevention tool?* Sacramento: California Research Bureau, California State Library.

Norris, C., & Armstrong, G. (1999). *The maximum surveillance society: The rise of CCTV.* Oxford, England: Berg.

Painter, K. (1996). Street lighting, crime and fear of crime: A summary of research. In T. H. Bennett (Ed.), *Preventing crime and disorder: Targeting strategies and responsibilities.* Cambridge Cropwood Series. Cambridge, England: Institute of Criminology, Cambridge University.

Painter, K., & Farrington, D. P. (1997). The crime reducing effect of improved street lighting: The Dudley project. In R. V. Clarke (Ed.), *Situational crime prevention: Successful case studies* (2nd ed.). Monsey, NY: Criminal Justice Press.

Painter, K., & Farrington, D. P. (1999). Street lighting and crime: Diffusion of benefits in the Stoke-on-Trent project. In K. Painter & N. Tilley (Eds.), *Surveillance of public space: CCTV, street lighting and crime prevention*. Crime Prevention Studies, vol. 10. Monsey, NY: Criminal Justice Press.

Pease, K. (1999). A review of street lighting evaluations: Crime reduction effects. In K. Painter & N. Tilley (Eds.), *Surveillance of public space: CCTV, street lighting and crime prevention*. Crime Prevention Studies, vol. 10. Monsey, NY: Criminal Justice Press.

Phillips, C. (1999). A review of CCTV evaluations: Crime reduction effects and attitudes towards its use. In K. Painter & N. Tilley (Eds.), *Surveillance of public space: CCTV, street lighting and crime prevention*. Crime Prevention Studies, vol. 10. Monsey, NY: Criminal Justice Press.

Piquero, A. R., Farrington, D. P., & Blumstein, A. (2003). The criminal career paradigm. In M. Tonry (Ed.), *Crime and justice: A review of research* (Vol. 30). Chicago: University of Chicago Press.

Poyner, B. (1991). Situational crime prevention in two parking facilities. *Security Journal, 2*, 96-101.

Poyner, B. (1993). What works in crime prevention: An overview of evaluations. In R. V. Clarke (Ed.), *Crime prevention studies* (Vol. 1). Monsey, NY: Criminal Justice Press.

Poyner, B., & Webb, B. (1997). Reducing theft from shopping bags in city center markets. In R. V. Clarke (Ed.), *Situational crime prevention: Successful case studies* (2nd ed.). Monsey, NY: Criminal Justice Press.

Quinet, K. D., & Nunn, S. (1998). Illuminating crime: The impact of street lighting on calls for police service. *Evaluation Review, 22*, 751-779.

Ramsay, M., & Newton, R. (1991). *The effect of better street lighting on crime and fear: A review*. Crime Prevention Unit Paper, No. 29. London: Home Office.

Reppetto, T. A. (1976). Crime prevention and the displacement phenomenon. *Crime & Delinquency, 22*, 166-177.

Sampson, R. J., Raudenbush, S. W., & Earls, F. (1997). Neighborhoods and violent crime: A multilevel study of collective efficacy. *Science, 277*, 918-924.

Sarno, C. (1996). The impact of closed circuit television on crime in Sutton town centre. In M. Bulos & D. Grant (Eds.), *Towards a safer Sutton? CCTV one year on*. London: London Borough of Sutton.

Shadish, W. R., Cook, T. D., & Campbell, D. T. (2002). *Experimental and quasi-experimental designs for generalized causal inference*. Boston: Houghton Mifflin.

Shaftoe, H. (1994). Easton/Ashley, Bristol: Lighting improvements. In S. Osborn (Ed.), *Housing safe communities: An evaluation of recent initiatives*. London: Safe Neighbourhoods Unit.

Sherman, L. W., Gottfredson, D. C., MacKenzie, D. L., Eck, J. E., Reuter, P., & Bushway, S. D. (1997). *Preventing crime: What works, what doesn't, what's promising*. Washington, DC: National Institute of Justice, U.S. Department of Justice.

Short, E., & Ditton, J. (1996). *Does closed circuit television prevent crime? An evaluation of the use of CCTV surveillance cameras in Airdrie Town Centre*. Edinburgh: Central Research Unit, Scottish Office.

Skogan, W. G. (1990). *Disorder and decline: Crime and the spiral of decay in American neighborhoods.* New York: Free Press.

Skinns, D. (1998). *Doncaster CCTV Surveillance System: Second Annual Report of the Independent Evaluation.* Doncaster, England: Faculty of Business and Professional Studies, Doncaster College.

Sternhell, R. (1977). *The limits of lighting: The New Orleans experiment in crime reduction: Final impact evaluation report.* New Orleans, LA: Mayor's Criminal Justice Coordinating Council.

Taub, R. P., Taylor, D. G., & Dunham, J. D. (1984). *Paths of neighborhood change: Race and crime in urban America.* Chicago: University of Chicago Press.

Taylor, R. B., & Gottfredson, S. (1986). Environmental design, crime and prevention: An examination of community dynamics. In A. J. Reiss, Jr., & M. Tonry (Eds.), *Communities and crime. Crime and justice: A review of research* (Vol. 8). Chicago: University of Chicago Press.

Tien, J. M., O'Donnell, V. F., Barnett, A., & Mirchandani, P. B. (1979). *Street lighting projects: National evaluation program.* Phase 1 Report. Washington, DC: National Institute of Law Enforcement and Criminal Justice, U.S. Department of Justice.

Tilley, N. (1993). *Understanding car parks, crime and CCTV: Evaluation lessons from safer cities.* Crime Prevention Unit Series Paper, No. 42. London: Home Office.

Waples, S. J., & Gill, M. (2006). The effectiveness of redeployable CCTV. *Crime Prevention and Community Safety, 8,* 1-16.

Webb, B., & Laycock, G. (1992). *Reducing crime on the London underground: An evaluation of three pilot projects.* Crime Prevention Unit Paper, No. 30. London: Home Office.

Weisburd, D., Mastrofski, D. D., McNally, A. M., Greenspan, R., & Willis, J. J. (2003). Reforming to preserve: Compstat and strategic problem solving in American policing. *Criminology & Public Policy, 3,* 421-456.

Welsh, B. C., & Farrington, D. P. (2002). *Crime prevention effects of closed circuit television: A systematic review.* Home Office Research Study, No. 252. London: Home Office.

Welsh, B. C., & Farrington, D. P. (2003). Effects of closed-circuit television on crime. *Annals of the American Academy of Political and Social Science, 587,* 110-135.

Welsh, B. C., & Farrington, D. P. (2004a). Evidence-based crime prevention: The effectiveness of CCTV. *Crime Prevention and Community Safety, 6,* 21-33.

Welsh, B. C., & Farrington, D. P. (2004b). Surveillance for crime prevention in public space: Results and policy choices in Britain and America. *Criminology & Public Policy, 3,* 497-526.

Welsh, B. C., & Farrington, D. P. (Eds.), (2006). *Preventing crime: What works for children, offenders, victims, and places.* New York: Springer.

Wilson, D. B. (2001). Meta-analytic methods for criminology. *Annals of the American Academy of Political and Social Science, 578,* 71-89.

Wilson, J. Q., & Kelling, G. L. (1982, March). Broken windows: The police and neighborhood safety. *Atlantic Monthly,* 29-38.

Wright, R., Heilweil, M., Pelletier, P., & Dickinson, K. (1974). *The impact of street lighting on crime.* Ann Arbor, MI: University of Michigan.

5. CRIME PREVENTION AND SOFT TECHNOLOGY: RISK ASSESSMENT, THREAT ASSESSMENT, AND THE PREVENTION OF VIOLENCE

by

Andrew J. Harris

University of Massachusetts, Lowell

and

Arthur J. Lurigio

Loyola University Chicago

INTRODUCTION

The prevention of violent offenses encompasses a broad spectrum of activities and milieus, ranging from primary prevention approaches that address the underlying causes of violent behavior in urban areas, to secondary and tertiary prevention approaches that address specific at-risk populations or individuals in jails, schools, or other settings. A wide range of strategies and models can be included under the rubric of "soft" crime prevention technologies. These include community policing, information-sharing protocols among law enforcement agencies, advances in computer protection technology, new anti-theft/target devaluation technologies, and social policy measures designed to ameliorate the environmental, economic, and psychosocial factors that encourage violent crime (Sherman et al., 1996).

This chapter is relatively modest in scope. We acknowledge the expansive nature of the crime prevention literature and focus on a subset of soft technologies that can assist practitioners in the prevention of certain violent crimes.

We explore two related, but distinct, approaches to the systematic collection, analysis, and communication of information: risk and threat assessment. The first soft technology application is risk assessment, which attempts to evaluate the potential for certain types of violence (e.g., sex offenses, murder, domestic violence) among targeted populations of high-risk individuals, such as known offenders, particularly those who have a history of mental illness or substance abuse problems, or both). One of the major paradoxes related to the development and expansion of risk-assessment technology in the area of violence prevention is that practitioners seem obsessed by the need to assess risk in groups of individuals (e.g., sex offenders) with very low failure rates. For example, recidivism studies of sex offenders place the risk of reoffending during a standard, one-year follow-up period at no more than 5-10% (Sample & Bray, 2006). Hence, high-stakes (sex offenders, murderers) but low-recidivism-risk offenders are now being targeted for risk-assessment strategies based on the notion that unique subgroups of these offenders can be identified even in populations with very low, overall base rates for reoffending.

The second soft technology application is threat assessment, which involves instruments or protocols to prevent violent incidents that rarely occur (e.g., an individual's risk of being a murder victim in a school shooting is less than one in a million), but that nonetheless create great fear and anxiety in the general population, such as terrorism and violence in the school and workplace. The purpose of threat assessment strategies is to prevent events of *targeted violence* (e.g., at schools and in the workplace) in which assessing a particular individual's inherent risk of violence is secondary the trajectory of behaviors leading up to the planned attack.

RISK ASSESSMENT

From "Dangerousness" to Risk Assessment

The practice of assessing an individual's risk of violence has evolved considerably during the past two decades. Once dominated by dichotomous predictions and loosely defined notions of "dangerousness," the field now encompasses a more multifaceted conception of violence risk that is becoming increasingly aligned with the practical demands of violence prevention (Douglas & Kropp, 2002). Much of the contemporary field of risk assessment has been shaped by a conceptual distinction between clinical and actuarial approaches to evaluating the risk of violence.

The clinical-actuarial debate has been framed traditionally in terms of the distinction between unstructured, purely subjective (clinical) judgments versus objective (actuarial) standardized measures that predict risk levels based on statistical formulations (Dawes et al., 1989; Meehl, 1954). However, contemporary risk-assessment practices have demanded a more nuanced view of this traditional distinction. Clinical methods are becoming increasingly grounded in empirical research (Webster et al., 1997), and actuarial approaches are more closely mirroring the process of clinical decision making (Monahan et al., 2005).

For much of the twentieth century, the assessment of violence risk in a legal context was the responsibility of "clinical experts" – typically psychiatrists – who were deemed to be sufficiently qualified to render predictions solely on the basis of their clinical expertise. This model flourished during the era of psychiatric institutionalization in the decades leading up to the early 1960s. At the peak of institutionalization in 1955, more than half a million individuals were held in state-run psychiatric institutions. Many were placed in these facilities as a form of preventive detention pursuant to psychiatric determinations of dangerousness (Grob, 1995).[1]

In the 1960s, a convergence of factors – notably state budget pressures, the burgeoning civil rights movement, and new developments in the practice of psychiatry – led to a widespread movement to reduce the use of institutionalization as a means of social control (Grob, 1995). Operating in this general context, the 1966 U.S. Supreme Court ruling in *Baxstrom v. Herold* questioned the methods employed in assessing dangerousness for the purpose of involuntary civil psychiatric commitment. As a consequence, over 900 individuals who had been civilly committed in New York State were released following the completion of their prison sentences (Baxstrom v. Herold, 1966).

The *Baxstrom* case awakened simmering doubts about clinicians' ability to effectively predict violence. In their follow-up study of individuals released pursuant to the Baxstrom ruling, Steadman and Cocozza (1974) found strong support for the contention that clinicians making dangerousness determinations tended to over-predict future violence. Of the 966 individuals the study followed – all of whom had been committed pursuant to a psychiatric determination of dangerousness – only 20% had been criminally convicted during a four-year follow-up period, the majority for non-violent offenses (Steadman & Cocozza, 1974).

Throughout the 1970s, legal scholars and researchers expressed dwindling faith in the legality and accuracy of clinical predictions of violent behavior. Summarizing their review of the evidence concerning psychiatry's role in the prediction of dangerousness, Ennis and Litwack (1975, p. 752) concluded:

The professional literature confirms (that) . . . psychiatrists have bitten off more than they can chew. The fault, however, is not theirs alone, for legislatures and courts, in an attempt to shift responsibility for making the determinations of who shall be allowed to remain free and who shall be confined, have turned to psychiatry for easy answers when there are none.

Concurrent with these developments, structured studies of actuarial methods, as an alternative to subjective determinations of dangerousness, attracted the attention of researchers and practitioners (Grove & Meehl, 1996). Often traced to Meehl's seminal monograph *Clinical Versus Statistical Prediction* (Meehl, 1954), the actuarial approach to predicting violence maintained that statistically-based mechanical models were superior to impressionistic judgments. Beginning in the late 1970s and over the next two decades, an emphasis on empirically-validated actuarial models would profoundly shape the nature of contemporary risk assessment (Monahan, 1988; Monahan & Steadman, 1994).

The intense focus on actuarial methods marked a significant transition between older notions of "dangerousness" and contemporary risk-assessment practices. In 1981, Monahan (1981) clarified the boundaries between clinical and actuarial approaches, citing the apparent superior predictive capacity of actuarial methods in assessing *a priori* risk through largely static variables and the potential role of clinical judgment in addressing dynamic factors that might inform short-term efforts at mitigating risk. (Static variables are factors such as gender that do not change over time, while dynamic variables are factors like employment status that are subject to change over time.)

Over the years, the field of violence risk assessment has flourished, producing a steadily expanding evidence base and a refinement of conceptual and theoretical models (Hanson, 2005; Monahan, 1988; Monahan & Steadman, 1994).

Along with these developments, in the past decade, there have been numerous efforts to bridge the divide between research and practice, and specialized risk-assessment technologies have proliferated for a range of groups, including sexual offenders, individuals with mental illness, perpetrators of domestic violence, and juvenile offenders. In addition, a wealth of recent research continues to show that actuarial approaches are far superior to clinical approaches in predicting violent behavior (Hilton et al., 2006).

Contemporary Risk-Assessment Practices

The changing nature of violence risk assessment during the past two decades has been guided by three notable themes. First, traditional monolithic notions of "dangerousness" have been deconstructed, and changes have been made in how risk is defined and communicated. For example, in 1989 the National Research Council suggested that the term "dangerousness" should distinguish among risk factors (i.e., variables associated with the probability that violence will occur), outcomes (the nature and severity of the consequences of the violent behavior), and risk levels (the probability that violence will occur; National Research Council, 1989). These elements have been implemented in the risk-assessment field through a range of methodological improvements including:

- extending the range of factors that are used as independent variables (that is, variables that may influence violent behavior) in the risk assessment process;

- broadening the definition of "violent behavior" to encompass actions that were not captured by prior research (notably, moving away from sole reliance on violent behaviors that resulted in arrest and conviction); and,

- shifting from models that rely on dichotomous determinations of dangerousness (i.e., "dangerous" or "not dangerous") to models that specify risk in a more continuous manner (Steadman et al., 2000).

Second, the fundamental orientation of risk assessment has evolved from a predominant focus on one-time predictions of risk to emphasizing the ongoing prevention of violence (Douglas & Kropp, 2002; Hart, 1998). In the assessment and management of violence risk, this change occurred with the growing awareness of the complementary roles of static variables (factors that are immutable and potentially correlated with long-term risk of violence) and dynamic variables (factors that are contextual and/or otherwise amenable to change, and potentially correlated with immediate or short-term risk of violence).

In distinguishing between predictive- and management-oriented risk-assessment approaches, Heilbrun (1997) suggested that the identification of *a priori* risk – the baseline risk that someone is deemed to present based on prior research on individuals with similar characteristics – might have limited practical utility when the goal is to prevent violence through the evaluation of the actual risk that the person represents. Taking this one step further, the prediction-management distinction bridges the actuarial-clinical divide, with actuarial methods (typically dependent on static variables) most applicable in contexts that call for longer-term prediction, and clinical methods (focused on dynamic factors) most applicable in contexts that call for the evaluation and management of short-term risk (Dvoskin & Heilbrun, 2001).

Third, attempts to better appreciate the nature of clinical decision making have influenced the direction of risk-assessment practices. The role of professional judgment,[2] once derided as arbitrary and unstructured, has been altered dramatically with the development of empirically guided instruments to support the risk-assessment process. Structured professional guidelines allow the evaluator to consider a range of empirically validated risk factors, which are then applied to a general estimate of risk (Webster et al., 1997). In contrast to pure actuarial instruments, which leave no room for subjective interpretation, structured professional guidelines provide a general decision framework that allows the evaluator to exercise some measure of independent judgment. Examples of structured professional guidelines include the HCR-20 (Webster et al., 1997) and the SVR-20 (Boer, Hart, Kropp & Webster, 1997), each of which is described in the next section of this chapter.

The confluence of these developments – the deconstruction of "dangerousness" with the move from fixed predictive models to more dynamic systems of risk management, the emergence of empirically grounded professional judgments, and an enhanced focus on bridging research and practice – has reshaped the range and emphasis of decision-support technologies for violence prevention in high-risk populations. In the process, these developments have also facilitated a movement toward a middle ground between the traditional boundaries of clinical and actuarial approaches, with professional determinations that are now framed by empirical evidence and actuarial tools that are now more closely aligned with the clinical decision making process.

SPECIALIZED APPLICATIONS OF VIOLENCE RISK ASSESSMENT

The risk-assessment field's growing evidence base has encouraged the development and validation of general tools to assess the risk of violence risk and specialized methods to assess the risk of specific categories of violence, including sexual offenses (Epperson et al., 1999; Hanson & Thornton, 1999; Hart et al., 2004), domestic violence (Kropp et al., 1999), and violence committed by juveniles (Borum et al., 2002) and individuals with mental disorders (Monahan et al., 2005; Quinsey et al., 2006). This section examines the application of violence risk-assessment models with two populations that have, for different reasons, attracted considerable attention in the risk-assessment field – sexual offenders and individuals with mental disorders.

Sex Offenders

Throughout the twentieth century, potential sex offenders have figured prominently in the evolution of psychiatric evaluations of dangerousness and risk-assessment practices. The assessment of sex offenders' dangerousness can be traced as far back as Richard von Krafft Ebbing's 1886 publication, *Psychopathia Sexualis*, and it reached its zenith during the peak passage of "sexual psychopath" laws between the 1930s and 1950s. During that period, hundreds of thousands of sexual offenders were preventively detained in psychiatric facilities on the basis of dangerousness determinations (Jenkins, 1998).

Developments in the field of specialized risk assessment for sexual offenders have accelerated dramatically since the early 1990s. Dozens of studies have contributed to a growing evidence base on sexual offender recidivism risk factors and the effectiveness of treatment and other interventions (Hanson & Bussiere, 1998; Hanson & Morton-Bourgon, 2004). On the basis of these findings, a broad array of specialized actuarial and guided clinical assessment instruments have been introduced and continue to be tested and refined (Doren, 2004).

Accelerations in research activity and instrument development were spurred in part by a number of significant policy shifts. Prompted by federal legislation, registration and community notification laws have been adopted nationwide and they have called for effective systems for classifying risk levels (Adams, 2002). The underlying assumption of these initiatives is that the public needs information on the identity and location of sex offenders in order to protect their families and themselves from victimization. When viewed in this context, *knowledge* – of a sex offender's identity and location – empowers the public to initiate one of a variety of crime prevention techniques (e.g., target hardening, offender removal, victim removal), including, for example, the use of personal protection devices (mace, tasers), new/improved locks on doors, better street lighting, closer child supervision patterns, direct monitoring of children's movements to and from school and play, involvement in community groups, neighborhood watch groups, and other collective actions targeting sex offender monitoring and/ or removal from a particular location.

When these crime prevention actions do not work, an individual can always move to a new location. Unfortunately, one unintended consequence of sex offender registration is the use of violence by community residents (assault, murder) and the threat of violence to remove sex offenders from a particular neighborhood. Some have argued that it is fear of this type of victimization that has motivated a significant number of sex offenders (estimates are about 1 in 4) to fail to register as sex offenders and/or to inform the registry of changes in location. It is one of the paradoxes of sex offender registration and community notification that in order to *prevent* one form of victimization (by sex offenders who recidivate) we *create* the opportunity for another form of victimization (against sex offenders).

In addition to sex offender registration, a number of states have passed laws allowing for the removal of sex offenders from the community altogether, utilizing sexually dangerous offender legislation. Since 1990, 17 states in the U.S, have adopted civil commitment laws for sexual predators – policies that were predicated on predictions of future violence and required states to address the complex issues associated with an individual's suitability for community release (Harris, 2005). Individuals committed under these statutes will likely spend over a decade in a locked institutional setting. This is an excellent example of a crime prevention strategy based on the exclusion of a known offender group classified as sexually dangerous from the community. In these cases, the courts have decided that it is simply too risky to leave crime prevention in the hands of the general public and the police.

Despite the existence of involuntary civil commitment legislation, only a fraction of all known sex offenders will be considered for involuntary civil commitment; and of those considered, less than 5% will actually be committed. For the vast majority of sex offenders, placement under community supervision – in lieu of prison or as a condition of release from prison – is the most likely scenario. Specialized models for the supervision of sexual offenders in the community have demanded effective means for the application of risk-assessment strategies (English et al., 1997). In addition, the introduction of risk-based sentencing systems has produced demands for evidence-based decision tools that can both inform the sentencing process and ensure due process (Kern & Farrar-Owens, 2004). As of 2006, legislative activity shows few signs of slowing down as the issue of sex offenders remains at the top of state legislative crime control agendas (National Conference of State Legislatures, 2006). However, research has demonstrated that sex offenders are a heterogeneous group with respect to the likelihood of rearrest, which suggests that the blanket application of sex offender registration and community notification laws does little to promote public safety (Sample & Bray, 2006).

Applied Risk-Assessment Technologies

The above policy initiatives – ostensibly designed to prevent future sexual crimes – created a substantial market for sex-offender risk-assessment technologies. Doren (2004) cited at least 20 instruments in the contexts of sentencing, pre-release determinations, post-release supervision, community notification laws, and civil commitment proceedings. Of these, the majority have been adapted or developed exclusively for sex offenders. Below, we consider several examples of the more widely used methods: three traditional actuarial instruments (RRASOR, Static-99, and the MnSOST-R), one more recent actuarial instrument that attempts to capture dynamic variables (SONAR), and one structured clinical decision guide (SVR-20).

RRASOR. The Rapid Risk Assessment for Sexual Offense Recidivism (RRASOR) is brief and simple to use; it consists of only four variables, all of which can be easily retrieved from official records (Hanson, 1997). These four factors – previous sexual offenses, extra-familial victims, offender age under 25, and male child victims – were based on research that demonstrated a strong correlation between these factors and the risk of reoffending. Although it is moderately accurate in the prediction of risk, the RRASOR omits several variables that are highly correlated with the risk of reoffending, such as deviant sexual preferences, antisocial orientation, and treatment compliance.

Static-99. A second, commonly used tool, the Static-99, addresses some of the *RRASOR's* shortcomings by combining it with a second scale, the Structured Anchored Clinical Judgment-Minimum (Hanson & Thornton, 1999). Beyond the variables contained in the RRASOR, the Static-99 considers a range of additional factors, including sexual deviance, types of available victims, persistence, and pattern of antisocial behaviors (Hanson & Thornton, 1999, 2000). In a comparative review, the Static-99 added to the predictive accuracy of the RRASOR in the measurement of long-term risk potential (Hanson & Thornton, 2000).

SORAG. Compared with the Static-99, the Sex Offender Risk Appraisal Guide (SORAG) measures a different, although closely related, group of factors (Quinsey et al., 1998). This scale, adapted from a general violence prediction tool known as the VRAG (described in the next section), integrates psychiatric and psychological variables, such as psychopathy and other mental disorders. Its relative predictive value is comparable to the Static-99 in the prediction of sexual recidivism, and the tool more effectively predicts nonsexual violent recidivism than does the Static-99 (Hanson & Thornton, 2000).

MnSOST. In contrast with the above instruments, which are designed for general use, some states have developed customized instruments, which generally fall under the auspices of a state agency and have been designed for specific use with sex offenders. The Minnesota Sex Offender Screening Tool (MnSOST) was originally developed in the early 1990s by the Minnesota Department of Corrections as a means of codifying the factors that place an individual at high risk of reoffending (Huot, 1999). Revised in 1996, the MnSOST-R (Epperson et al., 1999) was explicitly designed for use by nonclinical staff. Research on the MnSOST has demonstrated a moderate predictive capacity comparable to other commonly used actuarial instruments (Barbaree et al., 2001; Hanson & Morton-Bourgon, 2004).

SONAR. As with most actuarial instruments, the above tools depend almost exclusively on the prediction of long-term (i.e. *a priori*) risk through the application of static or highly stable variables. More recently, researchers have begun to test sex offender-specific actuarial approaches that integrate dynamic risk factors into their prediction scales. The SONAR (Sex Offender Needs Assessment Rating) was designed in 2001 as an actuarial tool based on dynamic variables (Hanson & Harris, 2000). Viewed as an adjunct to actuarial instruments based on static factors, the SONAR captures information on both stable and acute dimensions. Stable factors include intimacy deficits, negative social influences, attitudes toward sex offending, and self-regulation. Acute factors include substance abuse, negative moods, anger, and victim access.

The SONAR was subsequently adapted into two scales, the STABLE 2000 and the ACUTE 2000. These scales, combined with the Static-99, form the basis for a blended approach toward community supervision that captures the long-term, intermediate, and short-term factors associated with sexual recidivism (Harris & Hanson, 2003).

SVR-20. In contrast with the other tools presented above, the Sexual Violence Rating Scale (SVR-20) was developed not as an actuarial instrument but as a structured clinical decision tool. Applying an approach similar to the HCR-20 – a tool used to structure clinical decisions regarding the risk of general violence (Webster et al., 1997) – the SVR-20 encompasses 20 variables categorized into three broad domains. These domains include psychosocial adjustment (e.g., sexual deviance, history of childhood sexual abuse, psychopathy, relationship problems, employment instability, and offending history); the nature of sexual offending (e.g., levels of violence employed, escalation in severity of offense, and attitudes toward offending behaviors), and future plans (e.g., responsiveness to interventions). One essential characteristic of the SVR-20 is its potential to capture and integrate an individual's responses to treatments and interventions. The SVR-20 has recently been modified into a new instrument known as the Risk for Sexual Violence Protocol (RSVP; Hart et al., 2004).

INDIVIDUALS WITH A MENTAL DISORDER

The quest for understanding the link between violence and mental disorder has been a dominant factor in the evolution of contemporary risk-assessment practices. From Steadman and Cocozza's (1974) groundbreaking study in the wake of the Supreme Court's 1966 Baxstrom decision, to Monahan's (1981) reframing of the clinical-actuarial debate, to the recent work of the MacArthur Violence Risk-Assessment Project, the interaction between psychopathology and potential violence has been at the forefront of research and practice.

The criminality of the mentally ill has been a topic of scholarly debate for more than 70 years. Fueled by sensational media reports, negative stereotypes concerning the dangerousness of persons with mental illness are long standing and widespread, and they seem to have become more entrenched (Link & Stueve, 1994; Monahan, 1992; Phelan et al., 1997; Shah, 1975; Shain & Phillips, 1991). Misconceptions and unfounded fears often determine the responses of both the general public and criminal justice professionals to the mentally ill and can greatly affect social policies and legal practices relating to their sentencing, treatment, and care (Barlow & Durand, 1999; Steadman et al., 1998).

The risk of serious mental illness for violence is probably less than or equal to the added risk that is associated with age, educational level, and gender (Link et al., 1992; Swanson et al., 1990). Serious mental illness and violent behaviors both have low base rates in the general population and are unlikely to occur together. Hence, the contribution of mental illness to overall levels of violence in the United States is probably trivial (Swanson, 1994). For example, Torrey (1997) estimated that persons with mental illness commit 4% of all homicides in the United States. Yet data have suggested that the mentally ill are being arrested and incarcerated at levels that exceed their representation in the general population and their tendencies to commit serious crimes (Teplin, 1991).

In the broader framework of risk assessment in the criminal justice arena, the link between violence and mental disorders figures prominently for several reasons. First, from a methodological perspective, the development and validation of risk-assessment tools and methods within psychiatric populations has produced a range of approaches that might be applied to broader offender populations. One prominent example is the Iterative Classification Tree model developed through the work of the MacArthur Research Network on Mental Health and the Law, which is described later in this chapter.

Second, although the dynamics between mental illness and violence carry certain particular characteristics, many of the strongest predictors of violence among individuals with mental illness are also strong indicators of violence in the general criminal population. For example, psychopathy and antisocial personality, while not synonymous, are closely related to each other and play a role in the general propensity for violence in both psychiatric and nonpsychiatric populations (Quinsey et al., 2006).

Third, although the boundaries between the mental health and criminal justice systems have always been somewhat blurred, policymakers, researchers, and practitioners widely recognize that the growing numbers of individuals with serious mental illness and criminal involvement present substantial challenges to virtually every aspect of the criminal justice system (Council of State Governments, 2002).

Violence Risk Appraisal Guide (VRAG)

Resulting from a major longitudinal study of 800 serious offenders released from a maximum-security psychiatric facility in Canada, the Violence Risk Appraisal Guide (VRAG) translated empirically derived risk factors into an actuarial scale (Quinsey et al., 1998). The VRAG consists of 12 items that address a range of demographic, criminal history, and psychometric characteristics, and it produces a score that indicates the percentage likelihood that an individual will commit a violent act within a circumscribed time period.

Hare Psychopathy Checklist – Revised (PCL-R)

One of the VRAG's major predictive factors is the level of psychopathy, as measured by the Hare Psychopathy Checklist-Revised (PCL-R) (Hare, 1991). This measure, which is contained in several other actuarial scales, has been cited repeatedly in contemporary literature as a strong predictor of future violence. PCL-R scores are based on a 20-item scale, with each item assigned between 0-2 points, producing a maximum, possible score of 40 points. On each item, zero points indicate the absence of psychopathy, one point indicates a partial or non-definitive presence of psychopathy, and two points indicate a definitive presence of psychopathy. Although psychopathy is typically operationalized as a score of 30 or greater, some studies have used lower cut-off scores.

HCR-20

The Historical/Clinical/Risk Management-20 (HCR-20) was originally developed in 1995 and revised in 1997. The instrument has emerged as a prototype for structured clinical decision making, representing an alternative approach to the relative rigidity of pure actuarial models. The HCR-20 captures many factors that are similar to those contained in the PCL-R and is balanced in terms of static, stable, and dynamic variables. Its 20 items (also rated on a 0-2 scale like the PCL-R) are divided into three sections that integrate key information from the past ("Historical"), present ("Clinical") and future ("Risk Management"; Webster et al., 1997).

Iterative Classification Tree (ICT) and Classification of Violence Risk (COVR)

ICT. Stemming from what is arguably the most extensive and ambitious violence risk-assessment study ever undertaken, the MacArthur Violence Risk-Assessment Study employed a new paradigm for evaluating the risk of violence. The research involved a multiyear longitudinal design that tracked approximately 1,000 civil psychiatric patients after their release to the community, and information was gathered on more than 100 variables. The study's findings were fairly consistent with other studies showing that psychopathy and substance dependence interact with mental illness to produce violence. However, the significance of the MacArthur study lies largely in its ambitious approach to overcoming many of the methodological shortcomings that have characterized previous risk-assessment research (Banks et al., 2004; Monahan et al., 2000; Monahan et al., 2005).

During the formative stages of the MacArthur Study, two of its principal investigators identified four major methodological challenges facing risk-assessment research: a limited range of predictor variables (those factors that are validated as reliable predictors of violent); weak criterion variables (i.e., the manner in which violence is measured); constricted validation samples (particularly, overreliance on research drawn from institutionalized populations); and unsynchronized research efforts (referring to a lack of consensus among researchers on matters such as definitions, methods and terminology; Steadman & Monahan, 1994). These challenges laid the groundwork for the study's comprehensive design. For example, whereas previous studies depended primarily on a one-dimensional view of violence (generally drawn from arrest or conviction data), the MacArthur study drew from a variety of sources, including official records and collateral contacts with people who had regular interactions with the individual in the community. This expanded reach enabled the study to capture a wide range of interpersonal violence, ranging from serious acts of felonious assault to more mild forms of violence, such as shoving or other minor alter-cations.

As an extension of the study, the authors established a new vision for violence risk-assessment practices – one predicated on a more nuanced and interactive view of violence and its causes. This vision was implemented through the Iterative Classification Tree (ICT) model, which was predicated on the recognition that members of the clinical community had largely resisted the use of actuarial tools, which are of considerable interest to researchers. This resistance was attributed partly to the tendency of actuarial tools to treat all cases uniformly and to classify risk across a single dimension. This approach contrasts sharply with the manner in which clinicians view and evaluate risk. Clinical assessments utilize a more multi-faceted ap-proach, beginning with broader case characteristics and subsequently "dril-ling down" to more specific risk factors. This approach uses "decision tree" logic in which the answers at one stage of the evaluation process will inform the questions that must be asked during subsequent stages. The ICT approach was conceived to more closely mirror the clinical decision-making process by using these decision trees and establishing dual thresh-olds for isolating high-risk and low-risk cases[3] (Steadman et al., 2000).

COVR. Based on the ICT model, MacArthur researchers developed a computer-assisted program of decision making dubbed the Classification of Violence Risk (COVR); in 2005 they released a prospective validation study testing this new approach (Monahan et al., 2005). The study demonstrated that the COVR approach is an effective means of predicting differential outcomes between low- and high-risk populations, but it was unable to draw firm conclusions about the instrument's discriminatory value for moderate-risk cases.

Further studies of the COVR tool should be conducted, and it has yet to be validated beyond psychiatric populations. However, the tool's conceptual, methodological, and operational foundations appear to hold significant promise. Through its multidimensional view of risk and technology-supported administration, the COVR tool has significant implications for decision making in high-risk populations in the fields of community corrections and law enforcement.

THREAT ASSESSMENT

The Exceptional Case Study Project

In the mid-1990s, the United States Secret Service commissioned a study of 83 individuals known to have attacked or approached with the intent of attacking, a prominent public official or public figure. Known as the Exceptional Case Study Project (ECSP), the study found considerable variability among subjects in terms of their psychological and demographic characteristics. Researchers concluded that attempts to develop a useful profile of potential assassins were essentially futile. Nonetheless, they identified a key characteristic shared by all of its subjects, namely, patterns of behaviors in the period leading up to the assassination or assassination attempt (Fein & Vossekuil, 1999).

Based on the ECSP's findings, the Secret Service developed and disseminated a threat-assessment approach that eschewed the inductive and prediction-oriented methods of traditional violence risk assessment in favor of a deductive, behaviorally-focused system of incident prevention (Borum et al., 1999; Fein & Vossekuil, 2000). From its inception, experts recognized that the threat-assessment approach could be extended beyond the limited purview of assassinations; its framers viewed the system as a viable means of preventing acts of "targeted violence," including stalking-related attacks and school and workplace shootings (Fein et al., 1995).

Core Principles

Threat assessment is based on several core principles. First, the approach explicitly rejects the notion that there is a "typical profile" – psychological, demographic, or otherwise – that can be applied to perpetrators of targeted violence. The ECSP found certain characteristics present in a substantial portion of the study's sample, but the attackers studied were remarkably diverse, varying in demographic factors, such as marital status, educational levels, age, and employment, and in mental health variables, such as history of mental instability, substance use, and the presence of delusions. In short, the study found that any attempts to develop a profile of targeted-violence perpetrators would be neither specific enough to have any real discriminatory value nor sensitive enough to effectively identify potential attackers who might fall outside of the "typical profile" (Fein & Vossekuil, 1999).

Second, threat assessment draws a critical distinction between making a threat and posing a threat. The working premise is that the majority of individuals who make specific threats of violence never carry them out, and that many cases of specific violence involve no explicit threats before any action is taken. Noting that some individuals who make direct threats might, in fact, carry out their actions (77% of the ECSP sample had communicated their threat to someone before the incident), threat assessment views articulated threats as neither necessary nor sufficient for the presence of an actual threat.

Third, acts of targeted violence are not spontaneous events but are planned activities that typically permeate the thoughts of potential perpetrators in the period leading up to the violence. As a corollary, threat assessment views virtually all acts of targeted violence as preceded by a chain of behaviors, and, hence, a series of behavioral warning signs that are amenable to identification and interdiction.

Fourth, threat assessment takes a dynamic view of the etiology of targeted violence, holding that the trajectory from idea to execution is highly influenced by interactions between would-be attackers, their views of and perceived relations with the target, and a range of situational variables. As such, effective prevention and interdiction involves evaluating interactions among potential perpetrators, situational and opportunistic contexts, and potential targets.

Threat Assessment and Protective Intelligence

The threat-assessment model depends on a system of protective intelligence to prevent acts of targeted violence. The protective intelligence program contained in the threat-assessment model consists of three main elements: identification, assessment, and case management (Fein & Vossekuil, 2000).

Identification. The identification phase attempts to isolate potential cases of targeted violence and formulates initial responses to those cases. In certain cases, individuals will self-identify with a particular target either through the articulation of an explicit threat or the expression of inappropriate interest in it. In these situations, the information conveyed by the potential attacker becomes a data point for the subsequent assessment of the potential threat.

In most instances, identification requires the input of secondary sources, including law enforcement agencies, school personnel, mental health providers, family members, neighbors, and others. This range of potential sources requires effective criteria for threat identification, systems of outreach that facilitate the dissemination of those criteria, and clear means of communication through which potential threats can be conveyed.

Assessment. After a potential threat has been identified, the protective intelligence process progresses to the assessment phase. This phase includes both an initial determination of whether further investigation is warranted and, if so, a more in-depth threat-assessment investigation that might inform effective case management. The first question to be answered involves the extent to which further investigation is warranted.

Fein and Vossekuil (2000) noted that this preliminary assessment should be based partially on the information that led to the identification of the initial case. For cases in which the referral was based on inappropriate or unusual interest in a target (as opposed to directly-articulated threats), they suggested that it is reasonable to presume that the person will not be found to pose a threat and the investigator should attempt to identify information that rebuts this presumption. The fundamental investigatory focus at this stage is whether the person has taken action on the inappropriate interest, such as attempting to contact the potential target or seeking weapons.

In cases involving threats – whether made through explicit self-identification or anonymously – Fein and Vossekuil (2000) suggested that investigators proceed with the presumption that the threat is serious. Failure to investigate self-identified threats could be perceived by the potential perpetrator as encouragement to attack or could increase the desperation (and violence potential) of individuals who have made the threat in an effort to draw in authorities. Along similar lines, individuals who make anonymous threats might be ambivalent about their planned attack, and communicate their threats in the hope that they might be stopped.

Following this initial determination, the assessment phase moves to a detailed investigation. Working with both subjects and collateral sources, the evaluation focuses on several variables related to the subject's background, motives, interests, and behaviors. Some of the key questions that guide the assessment are presented in Table 1.

Case management. The third and final prong of a protective intelligence system involves the ongoing management of cases deemed to present a threat of targeted violence. The precise strategies associated with case management are highly dependent on the established facts of the case. Approaches could include periodic law enforcement contact with the subject and individuals in the subject's family or social environment, ongoing monitoring and surveillance as well as tactics to redirect the potential attacker through social support systems and service interventions. Case management continues until the investigator gathers information affirming that the individual's thoughts and behaviors and the contextual variables associated with the assumed threat have been sufficiently modified.

CONTRASTING THREAT ASSESSMENT AND RISK ASSESSMENT

The fundamental distinction between risk assessment and threat assessment is that the former is inductive and predicated on empirically based predictions, whereas the latter is deductive and predicated on presumed outcomes of ascertainable patterns of thoughts and behaviors. The risk-assessment approach to preventing violence depends on the application of empirically observed phenomena (i.e., the propensity of individuals with certain characteristics to commit acts of violence) in order to identify cases of likely violence. Conversely, a threat-assessment approach examines the circumstances of a particular situation, deduces the trajectory of those circumstances, and uses that information to develop interventions to alter that trajectory.

Considering this distinction, researchers have concluded that, for cases involving targeted violence – such as terrorism, stalking-related attacks, school and workplace shootings, and assassinations, for example – traditional risk-assessment tools are simply inapplicable (Borum et al., 1999;

Table 1: Questions to Ask in a Threat Assessment (adapted from Borum et al., 1999)

What motivated the subject to make the statement or take the action that caused him or her to come to attention?

What has the subject communicated to someone else (target, law enforcement, family, friends, colleagues, associates) or written concerning his or her intentions?

Has the subject shown an interest in assassination, weapons, militant of radical ideas/ groups, murderers and/or mass murderers, and workplace violence and stalking incidents?

Is there evidence that the subject has engaged in menacing, harassing, and/or stalking-type behaviors? Has the subject engaged in attack-related behaviors such as:

- Developing an attack idea or plan.
- Approaching, visiting, and/or following the target.
- Approaching, visiting, and/or following the target with a weapon.
- Attempting to circumvent security.
- Assaulting or attempting to assault a target.

Does the subject have a history of mental illness involving command hallucinations, delusional ideas, feelings of persecution, etc., with indications that the subject has acted on those beliefs?

How organized is the subject? Does the subject have the ability to plan and execute a violent action against a target?

Is there evidence that the subject is experiencing desperation and/or despair? Has the subject experienced a recent personal loss and/or loss of status? Is the subject now, or has the subject ever been, suicidal?

Is the subject's "story" consistent with his or her actions?

Are those who know the subject concerned that he or she might take action based on inappropriate ideas?

What factors in the subject's life and/or environment might increase or decrease the likelihood that the subject will attempt to attack a target (or targets)?

Reddy et al., 2001). In contrast to generalized forms of violence, in which potential perpetrators select targets randomly or based on circumstantial opportunity, targeted violence involves fixating on a particular target and planning an attack.[4] Targeted violence involves an intense direct relationship – real or perceived – between the potential perpetrator and the potential target; therefore, the individual's proclivity towards violence might not be evident. Furthermore, despite the significant public attention paid to events such as school and workplace shootings, stalking-related murders, and acts of terrorism, these remain extremely low base-rate events. From an empirical standpoint, they simply do not lend themselves to the inductive techniques inherent in most risk-assessment practices.

SELECTED APPLICATIONS OF THREAT ASSESSMENT

School Violence

School-based shootings are relatively rare occurrences but they tend to evoke considerable soul-searching and anxiety among educators, officials, and the general public. In the wake of such incidents during the 1980s and 1990s, a common response was to focus on the characteristics of the individuals involved in order to establish a useful profile of the school shooter (McGee & DeBernardo, 1999, 2002; Verlinden et al., 2000a).[5] Implicit in these and other individual-centric approaches, is the notion that effective prevention stems from the ability to identify and intervene with potential school shooters. This approach has several shortcomings.

For reasons we previously described, profiles might have limited or no utility in the prevention of school-based incidents. Beyond the fact that the base rate of such incidents remains far too low to build a solid empirical foundation, such profiles are bound to be either so limiting that they exclude potential threats or so overly inclusive that they have little discriminatory value (Reddy et al., 2001; Sewell & Mendelsohn, 2000). In addition, the practice of prospective profiling has particular problems. Specifically, its tendency toward false positives can lead to unnecessary (and potentially damaging) stigmatization of youth who fit the profile but present no actual threat (Reddy et al., 2001; Sewell & Mendelsohn, 2000).

Recognizing both the limitations and the promise of the threat-assessment approach, the FBI's National Center for the Analysis of Violent Crime (NCAVC), in the spring of 1998, embarked on a behavioral and situational analysis of 18 school-based shooting incidents. In July of 1999, approximately three months after the shootings at Columbine High School in Colorado, the NCAVC convened a symposium to work toward setting parameters that would apply the threat-assessment model to the prevention of school shootings. Among the symposium's 160 participants from education and law enforcement were representatives from each of the 18 schools involved in the study (O'Toole, 2000).

O'Toole describes a four-pronged approach to the application of threat assessment in order to effectively prevent school-based shootings.[6] This approach examines the personality of the student; family dynamics; school dynamics, including the student's relationship and interaction with the school; and social dynamics. In each of these dimensions, the NCAVC's School-based Threat-Assessment Model considers numerous variables to help evaluators assess the nature of the student's motives, intentions, and relationships with others.

Beyond the assessment process, the NCVAC model formulates an intervention strategy involving communication with students and parents, centralized coordination of the threat-assessment process, and multidisciplinary threat management that involves law enforcement officers. The approach also presents guidelines for setting thresholds for law enforcement involvement, based on threat levels that are identified through the assessment process.

School Violence and Threat Assessment in Perspective

In a 2001 review, Reddy and colleagues (including the initial framers of the threat-assessment model) critically evaluated the evidence regarding risk assessment, threat assessment, and other approaches to the prevention of school-based violence (Reddy et al., 2001). They concluded that, for many of the reasons we enumerated earlier, the traditional risk-assessment tools were unlikely to be effective in the prevention of planned school attacks. At the same time, they recognized that the application of the threat-assessment approach is constrained by the absence of any substantive empirical study. Their report concludes:

> We recognize that although the threat assessment approach is based upon empirical research on targeted violence, it too lacks the benefit of comprehensive empirical knowledge on targeted violence in schools. The most effective approach for understanding and preventing planned school-based attacks will be the one that is informed by empirically derived knowledge about the antecedents, motives, idea development, communications, and planning behaviors of all known perpetrators of targeted school violence. We see these as the most critical unanswered questions that school and law enforcement professionals currently face in attempting to prevent targeted violence in schools. (Reddy et al., 2001, pp. 169-170)

The essential message here is that the threat-assessment approach, while appearing conceptually sound, remains largely undeveloped as an applied technology.

Terrorism

A second potential application of the operational, behavioral-based approach embodied in threat assessment lies in the model's potential contributions to the prevention of terrorist violence. The initial framers of the threat-assessment approach have addressed the application of threat assessment's basic principles to the problem of terrorism, emphasizing the adoption of behavior-based operational research as an alternative to the profiling approach that has dominated much of the discussion of terrorism prevention (Borum et al., 2004). Their approach is based on three key principles:

- operationally-informed research built on the primary questions and threshold decisions that must be made during the course of counter-terrorism assessment, intelligence gathering and interdiction;

- a fundamental orientation that emphasizes analysis of behavior patterns, rather than characteristics of specific individuals; and,

- a fundamentally deductive method of interpreting results and extracting lessons, concentrating on which behaviors precede the outcome rather than the causes of the behaviors.

Terrorism and Threat Assessment: Areas of Convergence and Divergence

In many respects, terrorist acts converge with threat assessment's general conceptions of targeted violence. At the same time, applying the threat assessment model to counter-terrorism efforts presents a range of unique challenges. The first point of convergence relates to threat assessment's rejection of composite profiling as a means of identification and evaluation. In his extensive analysis of the psychology of terrorism, Borum (2004) refutes the notion that there is a "terrorist personality" or any valid psychological, demographic, or behavioral profile of a terrorist (see also Horgan, 2003). Although some practitioners have attempted to develop such profiles (Russell & Miller, 1983), the problem with this approach is its lack of both specificity (the ability to exclude "false positives") and sensitivity (the ability to avoid "false negatives"). On one level, the common traits shared among terrorists provide few cues to distinguish those who are likely to commit acts of violence from those who are not (Borum et al., 2003). On the other hand, there is little evidence that any composites of a typical terrorist would identify all individuals who might pose a threat (Borum et al., 2003; Silke, 2003a).

The second key point of convergence relates to threat assessment's fundamental premise that targeted violence almost always involves a powerful and compelling inner rationale for one's planned actions, along with the expectation that committing the planned act will result in the fulfillment of goals (Fein & Vossekuil, 2000). Acts of terrorism are implicitly goal-directed behaviors, accompanied by strong convictions that the violent behavior is a viable means to a desired end.

A third key link between terrorism and general targeted violence, as conceived by the threat-assessment model, is that terrorism is never a spontaneous act, but rather involves considerable forethought and planning. Moreover, the acts of terrorism include several precursor activities that ultimately form the basis for interdiction.

Despite these similarities, there are also key points of divergence. First, in terms of the identification process specified by the threat-assessment model, the identification of potential terrorists requires strategies that are generally far more complex than those required to thwart other potential perpetrators of targeted violence. Those planning school or workplace attacks generally live and operate in social environments that are aligned with the goal of preventing violent acts – a context in which family members, peers, co-workers, teachers, and others might serve as secondary sources for the identification process. In contrast, potential terrorists typically operate in more closed communities, avoiding social situations that might bring their plans to the attention of authorities. Accordingly, the identification and assessment of terrorism risk becomes far more dependent on sophisticated systems of intelligence than assessment of most other forms of targeted violence.

Second, unlike individuals who act alone or in concert a small number of friends or associates, terrorists generally carry out their activities supported by significant organizational resources and planning capacity. This enhanced sophistication presents additional challenges to investigators and those charged with threat management.

Third, terrorists can be distinguished from many other perpetrators of targeted violence in terms of their relative mental state and emotional factors underlying the violent act. The framers of the threat-assessment model point out that mental disorder is not a sufficient basis for identifying potential perpetrators of targeted violence, but they also acknowledge that targeted violence is often tied up in the perpetrator's emotional needs (Borum et al., 1999; Fein & Vossekuil, 2000). For individuals such as stalkers or perpetrators of school and workplace violence, inner emotional turmoil plays a major role in their rationale for violence and, in turn, their likelihood of executing an attack.

Terrorists are characterized by a noticeable absence of psychopathology (McCauley, 2002; Silke, 1998). Studies of suicide bombers, for example, have found a remarkable absence of the typical markers of suicidal risk associated with major mental disorder (Silke, 2003b). Moreover, despite the callous nature of terrorist acts, individuals committing terrorist violence on behalf of a cause generally do not meet standards for antisocial personality or psychopathy, which include a selfish focus on fulfilling one's individual needs and desires. In contrast, terrorists typically maintain rather strong ties to a social group and shared ideologies (Pynchon & Borum, 1999).

In summary, although the threat-assessment approach is somewhat synergistic with counter-terrorism efforts, the model's specific application to the prevention of terrorist violence requires that a unique set of questions and issues must be addressed. As with the case of school violence, the model's ultimate utility rests largely with the expansion of its operational research base.

CONCLUSION: RISK ASSESSMENT AND THREAT ASSESSMENT IN CONTEXT

The past quarter-century has witnessed significant strides in the practice of violence risk assessment. Researchers have overcome earlier methodological hurdles in variable specification and decision modeling. The field's expanding evidence base and a growing demand for specialized applications has moved it from a "one-size-fits-all" approach to the development of population-targeted instruments. Perhaps most important, the focus of risk assessments has shifted from a predominant research orientation to the applied context of violence prevention.

Threat assessment remains nascent. As risk assessment emerged from a research-oriented foundation and evolved into operational practice, threat assessment was conceived in a predominantly operational context and is now faced with the challenge of expanding its empirical base. Although the approach remains conceptually promising for the prevention of targeted violence in many contexts, its ultimate effectiveness hinges on valid research to inform its future development.

Certainly, there are key points of overlap between the two approaches. Notably, threat assessment can be viewed as an extension of the risk-assessment field's de-emphasis of prediction-oriented approaches and the associated shift toward applied, management-oriented models. In this sense, the threat-assessment approach can be viewed as part of a broader trend in the risk-assessment field to adopt a more deductive, operationally-driven approach to the ongoing management of risk.

◆ ◆ ◆ ◆

NOTES

1. In addition to "sexual psychopaths," the inpatient psychiatric population contained significant numbers of individuals deemed psychopathic personalities and at substantial risk of committing acts of violence.
2. Some have suggested abandoning the term "clinical" judgment in favor of the more inclusive "professional judgment," acknowledging the potential role of non-clinical personnel such as law enforcement or correctional staff (Hart, 1998).
3. Other actuarial instruments utilize a singular "cut-off" score to distinguish between "high-risk" and "low-risk" cases. For example, if the rating scale was from 0 through 100 and the cut-off is set at a score of 50, individuals scoring 49 would be deemed "low risk" (as would individuals scoring at the far low end of the scale), while those scoring a 51 would be deemed "high risk" (along with those who score at the extremely high end of the range). The ICT's "dual threshold" approach addresses this limitation by establishing separate cut-off scores for cases to be regarded as "high" or "low" risk, therefore accommodating cases that are on "middle ground."
4. This is not to infer that certain types of cases described under the risk assessment approach above do not involve some measure of target selection and fixation. Certain child molesters, for example, will carefully select and "groom" their victims, planning their activities well in advance. These cases, however, typically involve the opportunistic targeting of specific victims to fulfill a general need, and not the type of exclusive fixation on a particular target that characterizes most perpetrators of targeted violence.
5. In at least one of these instances, the authors eventually retracted their study, noting significant problems with their data (Verlinden et al., 2000b; Verlinden et al., 2001).

6. The proposed approach set forth in the NCAVC report focuses predominantly on the "Assessment Phase" as noted in the threat assessment overview. This presumes that a particular individual has been identified through either self-identification or through a secondary source. For more information on the identification process, see Fein and Vossekuil (2000).

REFERENCES

Adams, D. (2002). *Summary of state sex offender registries, 2001.* Washington, DC: Bureau of Justice Statistics.

Banks, S., Robbins, P. C., Silver, E., Vesselinov, R., Steadman, H. J., Monahan, J., Mulvey, E. P., Appelbaum, P. S., Grisso, T., & Roth, L. H. (2004). A multiple-models approach to violence risk assessment among people with mental disorder *Criminal Justice and Behavior, 31,* 324-340.

Barbaree, H. E., Seto, M. C., Langton, C. M., & Peacock, E. J. (2001). Evaluating the predictive accuracy of six risk assessment instruments for adult sex offenders. *Criminal Justice and Behavior, 28,* 490-521.

Barlow, D. H., & Durand, M. V. (1999). *Abnormal psychology* (2nd ed.). New York: Brooks/Cole.

Baxstrom v. Herold (1966). 383 U.S. 107.

Boer, D., Hart, S., Kropp, P., & Webster, C. (1997). *Manual for the sexual violence risk-20: Professional guidelines for assessing risk of sexual violence.* Burnaby, British Columbia: Mental Health Law and Policy Institute, Simon Fraser University.

Borum, R. (2004). *Psychology of terrorism.* Tampa: University of South Florida.

Borum, R., Bartel, P., & Forth, A. (2002). *Manual for the Structured Assessment for Violence Risk in Youth (SAVRY).* Tampa: Florida Mental Health Institute, University of South Florida.

Borum, R., Fein, R., Vossekuil, B., & Berglund, J. (1999). Threat assessment: Defining an approach for evaluating risk of targeted violence. *Behavioral Sciences and the Law, 17,* 323-337.

Borum, R., Fein, R., Vossekuil, B., & Gelles, M. (2003). Profiling hazards: Profiling in counterterrorism and homeland security. *Counterterrorism and Homeland Security Reports, 10,* 12-13.

Borum, R., Fein, R., Vossekuil, B., Gelles, M., & Shumate, S. (2004). The role of operational research in counterterrorism. *International Journal of Intelligence and Counterintelligence, 17,* 420-434.

Council of State Governments. (2002). *Criminal Justice-Mental Health Consensus Project Report.* New York.

Dawes, R. M., Faust, D., & Meehl, P. E. (1989). Clinical vs actuarial judgment. *Science, 243,* 1668-1674.

Doren, D. M. (2004). *Bibliography of published works relative to risk assessment for sexual offenders.* Retrieved October 15, 2005 from: http://www.atsa.com/pdfs/riskAssessmentBiblio.pdf

Douglas, K., & Kropp, P. (2002). A prevention-based paradigm for violence risk assessment. *Criminal Justice and Behavior, 29,* 617-658.

Dvoskin, J., & Heilbrun, K. (2001). Risk assessment and release decision making: Toward resolving the great debate. *Journal of the American Academy Psychiatry Law, 29,* 6-10.

English, K., Pullen, S., & Jones, L. (1997). *Managing adult sex offenders in the community: A containment approach* (163387). Washington, DC: U.S. National Institute of Justice.

Ennis, B., & Litwack, T. (1975). Psychiatry and the presumption of expertise: Flipping coins in the courtroom. *California Law Review, 62,* 693-723.

Epperson, D., Kaul, J., Huot, S., Hesselton, D., Alexander, W., & Goldman, R. (1999). *Minnesota Sex Offender Screening Tool – Revised.* St. Paul: Minnesota Department of Corrections.

Fein, R., & Vossekuil, B. (1999). Assassination in the United States: An operational study of recent assassins, attackers, and near-lethal approaches. *Journal of Forensic Sciences, 44,* 321-333.

Fein, R. A., & Vossekuil, B. (2000). *Protective intelligence and threat assessment investigations: A guide for state and local law enforcement officials.* Washington, DC: U.S. National Institute of Justice.

Fein, R. A., Vossekuil, B., & Holden, G. A. (1995). *Threat assessment: An approach to prevent targeted violence.* U.S. Department of Justice, Office of Justice Programs, National Institute of Justice.

Grob, G. (1995). *The mad among us: A history of the care of America's mentally ill.* Cambridge: Harvard University Press.

Grove, W. M., & Meehl, P. E. (1996). Comparative efficiency of informal (subjective, impressionistic) and formal (mechanical, algorithmic) prediction procedures: The clinical-statistical controversy. *Psychology, Public Policy, and Law, 2,* 293-323.

Hanson, R. K. (1997). *The development of a brief actuarial scale for sex offender recidivism.* (User Report No. 1997-04). Ottawa, Canada: Department of the Solicitor General of Canada.

Hanson, R. K. (2005). Twenty years of progress in violence risk assessment. *Journal of Interpersonal Violence, 20,* 212-217.

Hanson, R. K., & Bussiere, M. T. (1998). Predicting relapse: A meta-analysis of sexual offender recidivism studies. *Journal of Consulting and Clinical Psychology, 66,* 348-362.

Hanson, R. K., & Harris, A. J. R. (2000). *The Sex Offender Needs Assessment Rating (SONAR): A method for measuring change in risk levels.* Ottawa: Department of the Solicitor General of Canada.

Hanson, R. K., & Morton-Bourgon, K. (2004). *Predictors of sexual recidivism: An updated meta-analysis.* Ottawa: Public Safety and Emergency Preparedness Canada.

Hanson, R. K., & Thornton, D. (1999). *Static-99: Improving actuarial risk assessments for sex offenders.* (User Report No. 99-02). Ottawa: Department of the Solicitor General of Canada.

Hanson, R. K., & Thornton, D. (2000). Improving risk assessments for sex offenders: A comparison of three actuarial scales. *Law and Human Behavior, 24,* 119-136.

Hare, R. (1991). *The Hare Psychopathy Checklist-Revised: Manual.* North Tonawanda, NY: Multi-Health Systems.

Harris, A. (2005). *Civil commitment of sexual predators: A study in policy implementation.* New York: LFB Scholarly Publishing.

Harris, A. J. R., & Hanson, R. K. (2003). The Dynamic Supervision Project: Improving the community supervision of sex offenders. *Corrections Today, 64,* 63-65.

Hart, S. D. (1998). The role of psychopathy in assessing risk for violence: Conceptual and methodological issues. *Legal and Criminological Psychology, 3,* 123-140.

Hart, S. D., Kropp, P. R., & Laws, R. L. (2004). *The Risk for Sexual Violence Protocol (RSVP).* Burnaby, BC: Mental Health, Law, and Policy Institute, Simon Fraser University.

Heilbrun, K. (1997). Prediction versus management models relevant to risk assessment: The importance of legal decision making context. *Law and Human Behavior, 21,* 347-359.

Hilton, N. Z., Harris, G. T., & Rice, M. E. (2006). Sixty-six years of research on the clinical versus actuarial prediction of violence. *The Counseling Psychologist, 34,* 400-409.

Horgan, J. (2003). The search for the terrorist personality. In A. Silke (Ed.), *Terrorist, victims, and society: Psychological perspectives on terrorism and its consequence.* London: John Wiley.

Huot, S. (1999). The referral process. In A. Schlank & F. Cohen (Eds.), *The sexual predator: Law, policy, evaluation and treatment.* Kingston, NJ: Civic Research Institute.

Jenkins, P. (1998). *Moral panic: Changing concepts of the child molester in modern America.* New Haven: Yale University Press.

Kern, R. P., & Farrar-Owens, M. (2004). Sentencing guidelines with integrated offender risk assessment. *Federal Sentencing Reporter, 16,* 165-169.

Kropp, P. R., Hart, S. D., Webster, C. D., & Eaves, D. (1999). *Manual for the Spousal Assault Risk Assessment Guide.* Toronto: Multi-Health Systems.

Link, B., Andrews, H., & Cullen, F. (1992). The violent and illegal behavior of mental patients reconsidered. *American Sociological Review, 57,* 275-292.

Link, B., & Stueve, A. (1994). Psychotic symptoms and the violent/illegal behavior of mental patients compared to community controls. In J. Monahan & H. Steadman (Eds.), *Violence and mental disorder: Developments in risk assessment.* Chicago: University of Chicago Press.

McCauley, C. (2002). Psychological issues in understanding terrorism and the response to terrorism. In C. Stout (Ed.), *The psychology of terrorism: Theoretical understandings and perspectives.* Westport, CT: Praeger.

McGee, J. P., & DeBernardo, C. R. (1999). The classroom avenger: A behavioral profile of school based shootings. *Forensic Examiner, 8,* 16-18.

McGee, J. P., & DeBernardo, C. R. (Eds.), (2002). *The classroom avenger.* San Francisco, CA: Jossey-Bass.

Meehl, P. (1954). *Clinical versus statistical prediction: A theoretical analysis and review of the literature.* Minneapolis: University of Minnesota Press.

Monahan, J. (1981). *Predicting violent behavior: An assessment of clinical techniques.* Beverly Hills: Sage Publications.

Monahan, J. (1988). Risk assessment of violence among the mentally disordered: Generating useful knowledge. *International Journal of Law and Psychiatry, 11,* 249-257.

Monahan, J. (1992). Mental disorder and violent behavior: Perceptions and evidence. *American Psychologist, 47*, 511-521.

Monahan, J., & Steadman, H. J. (1994). *Violence and mental disorder: developments in risk assessment.* Chicago: University of Chicago Press.

Monahan, J., Steadman, H. J., Robbins, P. C., Silver, E., Appelbaum, P., Grisso, T., Mulvey, E. P., & Roth, L. H. (2000). Developing a clinically useful actuarial tool for assessing violence risk. *British Journal of Psychiatry, 176*, 312-319.

Monahan, J., Steadman, H. J., Robbins, P. C., Appelbaum, P., Banks, S., Grisso, T., Heilbrun, K., Mulvey, E. P., Roth, L., & Silver, E. (2005). An actuarial model of violence risk assessment for persons with mental disorders. *Psychiatric Services, 56*, 810-815.

National Conference of State Legislatures (2006). *State crime legislation in 2005.* Denver: National Conference of State Legislatures.

National Research Council (1989). *Improving risk communication.* Washington, DC: National Academy Press.

O'Toole, M. (2000). *The school shooter: A threat assessment perspective.* Quantico, VA: Federal Bureau of Investigation.

Phelan, J., Link, B., Stueve, A., & Pescosolido, B. (1997). *Public conceptions of mental illness in 1950 and today: Findings from the 1996 General Social Survey Module on Mental Health.* Paper presented at the annual meeting of the American Sociological Association, Toronto, Ontario.

Pynchon, M., & Borum, R. (1999). Assessing threats of targeted group violence: Contributions of social psychology. *Behavioral Sciences and the Law, 17*, 339-355.

Quinsey, V. L., Harris, G. T., Rice, M. E., & Cormier, C. (1998). *Violent offenders: Appraising and managing risk.* Washington, DC: American Psychological Association.

Quinsey, V. L., Harris, G. T., Rice, M. E., & Cormier, C. A. (2006). *Violent offenders: Appraising and managing risk* (2nd ed.). Washington, DC: American Psychological Association.

Reddy, M., Borum, R., Berglund, J., Vossekuil, B., Fein, R., & Modzeleski, W. (2001). Evaluating risk for targeted violence in schools: comparing risk assessment, threat assessment, and other approaches. *Psychology in the Schools, 38*, 157-172.

Russell, C. A., & Miller, B. H. (1983). Profile of a terrorist. In L. Freedman & Y. Alexander (Eds.), *Perspectives on terrorism.* Wilmington, DE: Scholarly Resources.

Sample, L. L., & Bray, T. M. (2006). Are sex offenders different? An examination of rearrest patterns. *Criminal Justice Policy Review, 17*, 83-102.

Sewell, K. W., & Mendelsohn, M. (2000). Profiling potentially violent youth: Statistical and conceptual problems. *Children's Services: Social Policy, Research, and Practice, 3*, 147-169.

Shah, S. A. (1975). Dangerous and civil commitment of the mentally ill: Some public policy considerations. *American Journal of Psychiatry, 132*, 501-505.

Shain, R., & Phillips, J. (1991). The stigma of mental illness: Labeling and stereotyping in the news. In L. Wilkins and P. Patterson (Eds.), *Risky business: Communicating issues of science, risk, and public policy.* Westport, CT: Greenwood Press.

Sherman, L., Gottfredson, D., MacKenzie, D., Eck, J., Reuter, S., & Bushway, S. (1996). *Preventing crime: What works, what doesn't, what's promising.* Washington, DC: U.S. National Institute of Justice.

Silke, A. (1998). Cheshire-cat logic: The recurring theme of terrorist abnormality in psychological research. *Psychology, Crime and Law, 4,* 51-69.

Silke, A. (2003a). Profiling terror. *Jane's Police Review 8/7/03.*

Silke, A. (2003b). The psychology of suicidal terrorism. In A. Silke (Ed.), *Terrorist, victims, and society: Psychological perspectives on terrorism and its consequence.* London: John Wiley.

Steadman, H. J., & Cocozza, J. (1974). *Careers of the criminally insane: Excessive social control of deviance.* Lexington, MA: Lexington Books.

Steadman, H., & Monahan, J. (1994). Toward a rejuvenation of risk assessment research. In J. Monahan & H. Steadman (Eds.), *Violence and mental disorder.* Chicago: University of Chicago Press.

Steadman, H. J., Silver, E., Monahan, J., Appelbaum, P. S., Clark Robbins, P., Mulvey, E. P., Grisso, T., Roth, L. H., & Banks, S. (2000). A classification tree approach to the development of actuarial violence risk assessment tools. *Law and Human Behavior, 24,* 83-100.

Steadman, H. J., Mulvey, E. P., Monahan, J., Robbins, P. C., Appelbaum, P. S., Grisso, T., Roth, L. H., & Silver, E. (1998). Violence by people discharged from acute psychiatric inpatient facilities and by others in the same neighborhoods. *Archives of General Psychiatry, 55,* 393-401.

Swanson, J. W. (1994). Mental disorder, substance abuse, and community violence: An epidemiological approach. In J. Monahan & H. J. Steadman (Eds.), *Violence and mental disorder: Developments in risk assessment.* Chicago: University of Chicago Press.

Swanson, J., Holzer, C., Ganju, V., & Jono, R. (1990). Violence and psychiatric disorder in the community: Evidence from the Epidemiologic Catchment Area surveys. *Hospital and Community Psychiatry, 41,* 761-770.

Teplin, L. A. (1991). The criminalization hypothesis: Myth, misnomer or management strategy. In S. Shah & B. Sales (Eds.), *Law and mental health: Major developments and research needs.* Washington, DC: U.S. Department of Health and Human Services.

Torrey, E. F. (1997). *Out of the shadows: Confronting America's mental illness crisis.* New York: John Wiley.

Verlinden, S., Hersen, M., & Thomas, J. (2000a). Risk factors in school shootings. *Clinical Psychology Review, 20,* 3-56.

Verlinden, S., Hersen, M., & Thomas, J. (2000b). Risk factors in school shootings: Erratum. *Clinical Psychology Review, 20,* 679.

Verlinden, S., Hersen, M., & Thomas, J. (2001). Risk factors in school shootings: Retraction. *Clinical Psychology Review, 21,* 158.

Webster, C., Douglas, K., Eaves, D., & Hart, S. (1997). *Manual for the HCR-20: Assessing risk for violence.* Burnaby, British Columbia: Mental Health Law and Policy Institute, Simon Fraser University.

6. POLICING AND "HARD" TECHNOLOGY

by

Don Hummer

Penn State University, Harrisburg

The purpose of this chapter is to illustrate the advances in weapons technology currently in use by police agencies as well as to report on the "next generation" of non-lethal weaponry designed to increase officer and citizen safety and minimize damaging effects on offenders taken into custody. While some of these devices were created exclusively for law enforcement use (Silberman, 2005), many of these technological advances originated from the U.S. military, the National Aeronautics and Space Administration, DARPA (the Defense Advanced Research Projects Agency), other national research laboratories, and private sector corporations (Alexander, 2001; Hubbs and Klinger, 2004; Nunn, 2001). This "next generation" of weapons technology spans the gamut from electromagnetic pulses and lasers to super sticky polymers (Silberman, 2005). The challenge for police is to incorporate technology designed for the battlefield and tailor its use to a crime prevention/suppression mandate in a way that is not only functional, but also practical. One of the unintended by-products of the current "War on Terror" could very well be that technology designed for urban warfare against insurgent groups abroad allows domestic law enforcement agencies to incorporate cutting-edge technology directly from Department of Defense laboratories to American cities (Conser et al., 2005).

A community-focused model of policing necessarily lends itself to minimizing injuries to civilians when the use of force is necessary. In spite of problem-specific training, increased educational requirements for new officers, innovative recruiting techniques, and specific departmental policies drafted in the wake of *Tennessee v. Garner* (1985),[1] incidents of deadly force by police officers remain in the headlines. Rappert (2001) asserts that in comparison to other potential weapons that can be used for nonviolent purposes, guns are inherently more dangerous and designed specifically to cause physical trauma. Advocates of non-lethal weapons[2] have argued for decades that police reliance on firearms has resulted in scores of preventable deaths (Homant and Kennedy, 2000; Tennenbaum and Moore, 1993).

Civil cases filed by the survivors of the victim in a deadly use-of-force incident can result in major monetary awards paid by municipalities on top of legal fees incurred during a defense of such cases. An analysis of wrongful death settlements in Texas demonstrates that cases settled by the parties involved averaged $55,411 per award, while those that went to trial averaged nearly $100,000 per case (Vaughn et al., 2001). Of course not every wrongful death lawsuit involving the police is the result of shots fired by an officer, but a recent analysis of civil cases over a 10-year period (1995-2005) indicates that the second most frequent manner of death in deadly force lawsuits is by shooting, accounting for roughly 30% of all deaths in such incidents (Fishel et al., 2006).

While the debate continues regarding whether these incidents are declining or on the rise (see Bailey, 1996), many police departments have incorporated non-lethal weapons technology into their arsenals in an effort to lessen the possibility of fatal injury at the hands of the police (see Terrill, 2003). The universal justification given for the diverse array of non-lethal weapons is that they allow for an intermediate step between possible deadly force (use of a sidearm) and no force at all (Rappert, 2001).[3] Policing agencies around the globe have long utilized irritants such as tear gas to disperse unruly crowds, and the concept is merely being refined as chemical irritants are presently in widespread employ in the United States and abroad for the same purpose (Noakes et al., 2005). Police responding to large-scale unrest today do so with traditional firearms held back as weapons of absolute last resort, although anecdotal evidence is used by skeptics of non-lethal weapons to question whether such weapons are indeed "non-lethal."[4] Chemical irritants are also well suited for incapacitating an individual subject, and their use has been widely accepted and endorsed by policing agencies in the United States due to their potential for reducing excessive force complaints, lessening injuries to subjects and officers, and fairly speedy recovery periods for those who have the spray used against them (Nowicki, 2001).

"HARD" TECHNOLOGY IN POLICING: PRESENT USE, INNOVATIONS, AND QUESTIONS[5]

Despite the rapid progress in non-lethal weapons technology, and the application of this technology to law enforcement use, one simple fact remains: police officers continue to view their sidearms as the most valuable tool in their arsenal. Conventional wisdom states that non-lethal weapons are most effective against an unarmed opponent (Robin, 1996), and that an offender armed with a gun requires a commensurate level of force exhibited by the officer. While this assertion will not be argued here, it can be stated that non-lethal weapons are a potentially useful alternative to firearms when confronting an unarmed but violent perpetrator (Meyer, 1992) or an offender armed with a crude, but potentially lethal weapon such as a knife or bat (Robin, 1996). The majority of people taken into custody by the police are not in possession of a firearm: thus, the possibilities for using non-lethal alternatives are frequent. The following is a discussion of non-lethal weapons currently in widespread use by law enforcement agencies in the United States and abroad.

Chemical Irritants

No other non-lethal weapon is used by more police departments than oleoresin capsicum (OC), commonly known as "pepper spray." In fact, a survey of more than 600 law enforcement and correctional personnel found that most practitioners believe that, when properly deployed, OC pepper spray is a highly effective means of incident management (McEwen and Leahy, 1994). A single dose of this highly irritating substance is normally sufficient to disable most offenders long enough for them to be safely placed into custody. By the early 1990s, police departments had begun experimenting with OC, but its use had already become prevalent among park rangers, postal carriers and others who required protection from belligerent animals such as dogs and bears (Adams, 2001). Refinements in the concentration of the chemical in pepper spray allow officers to administer a very heavy dose or just enough to gain compliance. Law enforcement personnel can scatter the chemical using darts, guns, spray cans, and grenades depending upon the circumstances at hand (Tennenbaum and Moore, 1993). OC typically results in intense burning in the eyes and mucus membranes of the nose and throat, which renders an individual unable to forcibly resist officer orders or attempts to take that individual into custody. Once restrained, the effects of pepper spray can be counteracted with extensive flushing of the exposed areas with water, so that a normal, healthy adult will have recovered fully from the effects of the spray within an hour of exposure.

Despite over a decade's use and positive reviews from officers and departments who have successfully utilized OC in potentially volatile situations (e.g., Edwards et al., 1997), vocal criticism has come from groups such as the American Civil Liberties Union regarding the decision to use pepper spray in a given scenario. One of the most common complaints is that officers are too quick to use non-lethal weapons such as pepper spray because the potential for serious injury or death resultant from its use is statistically very low. Since there are few repercussions, the argument goes, why not use OC whenever the need arises? Widespread application of pepper spray has led some police departments to draft guidelines for pepper spray use which include stipulations that a) verbal commands must be attempted first and have failed, and b) the target for OC use must not be a minor, an elderly person, an individual known to be mentally ill, or a person known to have serious/chronic health issues. England's Parliament has gone as far as to discuss legislation delineating the parameters for pepper spray use (Rappert, 2001).

Another criticism addresses the use of pepper spray in a crowded setting. A large number of civil lawsuits pertaining to police use of pepper spray have come from bystanders who consider themselves "collateral damage" in a widespread application (or misapplication) of OC by law enforcement. A large-scale dispersal of OC is subject to the vagaries of weather conditions, the concentration of bystanders relative to the incident, and the accuracy of those dispensing the chemical. Lastly, but by no means less important, are those rare instances where "non-lethal" pepper spray use indeed becomes deadly. A debate continues regarding the primary contributing factor in deaths attributed to an adverse reaction to OC exposure: empirical research examining in-custody deaths attributed to the chemical has failed to implicate oleoresin capsicum exposure as the primary cause of death in any of the cases reviewed (Granfield et al., 1994; Steffee et al., 1995). Further, OC advocates assert there is no means available to quantify how many deaths have been *prevented* by officers utilizing a chemical irritant against a violent target instead of opting for their sidearms, which arguably would pose a much higher risk of fatal injury. There are well-documented cases of fatalities attributable to OC use, but these cases are not deaths due to exposure to pepper spray; rather they are fatalities associated with the *dispersal* of the chemical and can often be categorized as "blunt force trauma" (see end note 5). This risk of fatality when using pepper spray can be reduced if officers receive training and certification in the proper use of OC diffusion devices.

Electric-Shock Immobilizing Technology

A close second to chemical irritants, in terms of breadth of use by law enforcement, is the broad classification of electric-shock immobilizers. Commonly referred to as a "stun gun" or "TASER,"[6] this class of non-lethal weapon administers a low-level electric shock to the intended target and disables the subject for a period of time until s/he may be safely taken into custody. In the example of the TASER, two darts are fired from a gun-like device toward the intended target. The darts trail wires that remain connected to the gun. Once the darts have penetrated the subject's skin, the officer in control of the weapon can administer an electric current that causes involuntary muscle contraction and intense pain, stunning and subsequently incapacitating the perpetrator (Conser et al., 2005). Discontinuation of the electric charge ceases the effect of the weapon and the subject typically recovers from the shock in a few minutes. Other similar devices are designed to work in close proximity to the offender, with the electric charge applied directly from the weapon onto the target's skin or garments.[7]

Other electric-shock immobilizers are incorporating technology that does not require close contact with the subject or hard wires to connect the perpetrator with the stunning device. These include weapons that fire electrically conductive fibers toward an assailant, lasers that produce long filaments of electrically charged plasma, and others that project ionized gas designed to disable vehicle electronics (Conser et al., 2005). Advances in this area of weaponry are currently in development and/or have limited availability (i.e., military or law enforcement use only). As is the case with most technological innovation, the new class of electric-shock immobilizers are cost prohibitive for adoption by smaller police agencies.

As with chemical irritants, the criticisms surrounding stunning technology center around premature use or misapplication of the weapon and potentially lethal effects of electric shock on certain offenders. Further, the level of electric shock necessary to disable a target varies by physiological factors such as body weight (McDonald et al., 2005) and is frequently insufficient for subjects under the influence of drugs or alcohol, thereby necessitating an increased level of force used by officers (Robin, 1996). TASER International, the leading manufacturer of electrical stun devices, was put into a damage control posture in early 2005 after a scathing report by Amnesty International detailing abuses by law enforcement officers employing the device on "questionable" subjects, such as the mentally impaired, minors, and individuals who police felt were merely "in noncompliance" (Amnesty International, 2004), and an investigation into TASER-related deaths by the Arizona Attorney General's Office. The manufacturer countered with empirical evidence absolving the device in the majority of cases where death was attributed to TASER shock (e.g., Kornblum and Reddy, 1991; McBride and Tedder, 2005). The debate continues regarding the positive net effects of electrical-shock immobilizer use, with the fundamental questions centering upon police decisions to utilize the device in various scenarios and the fatalities or more serious injuries that have been prevented by police use of a "non-lethal" technology.[8]

Rubber, Plastic, and/or Wooden Bullet Guns and Beanbag Shotguns

The variations of "non-ballistic" guns that utilized by law enforcement serve a purpose similar to that of traditional firearms in so far as they are meant to either incapacitate a subject, gain compliance, or disperse unruly crowds. The key difference is that these weapons do so with far less risk of fatal injury for the actors involved. The projectiles fired from these weapons disperse their kinetic energy over a greater area, and thus are designed not to penetrate the skin of the target, if used properly. This class of weaponry was used with a modicum of effectiveness, but also with a high degree of ignominy in the Northern Ireland conflict. Opponents of the British Army's presence in the disputed territory chronicled the injuries and misapplication of rubber bullets in and around Belfast (White and White, 1995).[9] Conser et al. (2005) assert that the use of such devices by police personnel has a highly effective psychological component as well because from a distance it appears that officers are firing conventional weapons (with the accompanying noise, flash, and smoke), and thus compliance with commands is more likely when subjects are confronted with what they mis-perceive as potential deadly force.

Use of projectile weaponry comes with a stringent set of manufacturers' guidelines regarding parts of the body at which to fire (extremities preferable, never at the neck or shoulders), distance from target (e.g., optimal firing range of between 75 and 100 feet), and firing technique (e.g., rubber bullet rounds skip-fired at the ground in front of a target so that the perpetrator is hit at knee level and incapacitated; White and White, 1995). There is an assumption that users of such devices will have proper training and certification, but the extent of injuries and fatalities attributable to non-ballistic projectiles has been well documented. A recent study of eye injuries caused by rubber bullets indicated that orbital bone fractures are common when the area around the eye is struck by a rubber projectile, and that even rounds that do not enter the eye itself can result in blindness or permanent reduction in visual acuity (Lavy and Abu Asleh, 2003). Furthermore, a direct impact with the eye itself can easily be fatal, and if the injured survives, the eye itself is rarely salvageable (Lavy and Abu Asleh, 2003).

Perhaps due to the troublesome political history of rubber bullet use (in the Northern Ireland and Israeli-Palestinian conflicts), U.S. law enforcement agencies have made increasingly frequent use of the traditional 12-gauge shotgun loaded with a "beanbag" round (Mertz, 2002; Ijames, 2001). This device has garnered favor in law enforcement circles because it can be fired using the same pump-action shotgun most officers carry in their patrol units and it can be employed against a perpetrator at relatively close range (optimal firing distance is typically 15 to 45 feet). Regardless of popularity, the weapon is not without its critics and controversies. Recent fatal incidents in both the United States and Canada resulting from beanbag round usage illustrate its potential dangers. Hubbs and Klinger (2004) found that 8 individuals in 373 "impact munitions" incidents died at the hands of law enforcement. Six of the 8 deaths occurred when the projectile was fired from a range of *less than* 30 feet. These impacts resulted in broken ribs that then punctured the lungs, heart, or both (Hubbs and Klinger, 2004).[10]

While firing range is the primary determinant in fatalities associated with beanbag rounds, other serious injuries have resulted from the round missing the intended target on the subject's body. Rounds striking the head or neck are particularly troublesome, and they exemplify the inaccuracy of firing a non-rigid projectile. Studies of the aerodynamics of non-lethal projectiles demonstrate that when a round is less able to retain its shape after being fired, the projectile is more likely to veer off target (Mertz, 2002). "Soft" ammunition like beanbag pouches is not as reliable or stable in the air as a harder projectile, such as a rubber bullet, would be (Mertz, 2002). The fatalities and serious injuries associated with beanbag round use have led to a reevaluation of beanbag shotgun use in California, and some manufacturers have amended their recommendations for optimal firing ranges and weapon usage.[11]

Strobe and Acoustical Weapons Technology

One military tactic that has been borrowed and customized by U.S. law enforcement is the use of "sensory weapons." These were made famous (or infamous) when American troops blasted heavy metal music day and night in an effort to draw former Panama dictator Manuel Noriega out of the Papal Nuncio's residence and into U.S. custody. Such weaponry follows a rather simplistic framework whose long-term effects are virtually null (save for a possible permanent distaste for contemporary rock music). Similar technology has been experimented with for use in hostage or barricaded-perpetrator situations, and even for crowd control. However, due to its specialized application, this weaponry is reserved almost exclusively for Special Weapons and Tactics (SWAT) units, and frequently is not the first choice among several alternatives available for the aforementioned scenarios.

Sensory weapons cause low-level pain and physiological/psychological discomfort, and serve to temporarily disorient subjects in order for officers to make a safe entry into a structure. But the effectiveness of such weapons is questionable. In testing, percussive weaponry could not be limited to the intended target, while strobe technology either did not incapacitate the perpetrator for a sufficient period of time or the officers involved became as disoriented as the target (Conser et al., 2005). Furthermore, there are logistical considerations with this class of weaponry as well (applicable also to high-pressure water, trap nets and sticky foam, as explained below). Police officers can only transport so much gear to have ready at a moment's notice. The typical scenario where strobe and/or acoustical weapons technology is currently applied allows for sufficient time for equipment to be brought to the incident scene and set up. But as mentioned earlier, such scenarios are relatively rare events in comparison to the total number of uncooperative subjects police are required to subdue and take into custody annually.[12]

Non-Electric Immobilizing Devices

A number of devices have been experimented with to immobilize targets without the use of chemicals, projectiles, or electricity in an attempt to minimize any harm to the individual. The devices outlined below have not been overwhelmingly endorsed for use by law enforcement, and the weaknesses associated with these various technologies are thought to far outweigh their potential usefulness.

Water Pressure

Visual documentation from the urban riots that affected many cities in the United States in the 1960s typically contain images of demonstrators and protestors being doused with high-pressure streams of water, and the refrain "Get the hoses!" has become synonymous with crowd control. In reality, the use of water pressure as a means of dispersing unruly mobs was all but abandoned with the emergence of rubber bullets and pepper spray, which proved to be much more effective. Experimentation with water pressure to subdue combative individuals has continued sporadically, but logistical issues of running high-pressure lines in dynamic situations and the inability of water pressure to sufficiently incapacitate subjects have prevented the technique from being widely adopted (Tennenbaum and Moore, 1993).

Trap Nets

Police officers working in the 1980s lived in constant fear of exposure to HIV when confronting an uncooperative subject whose blood, hypodermic needles, or other bodily fluids could potentially transmit the disease that causes AIDS. This era saw an increase in experimentation with devices that reduced direct contact with targets. While HIV remains a potential threat to any personnel working with an infected population, the use of "people netting" never truly caught on, and the technology is not considered a primary component of the police arsenal. Modeled after the trap netting used to capture wild animals, the purpose of trap nets is to ensnare an individual in a fishnet style device and entrap them so that officers can more easily take the offender into custody (Conser et al., 2005). Although there are a myriad of designs, the basic configuration consists of a large net strung between two rigid handles that can be wrapped around the target, forcing the subject to the ground. Officers then overpower the disabled target. As the above scenario indicates, use of trap netting requires the participation of multiple officers (at least two to operate the net, and then a number to place the individual into custody). It also requires a contained apprehension area, so that officers carrying the net can effectively surround the subject. Lastly, direct contact with a perpetrator cannot be completely avoided since officers must subdue the combative subject by hand after they are netted and eventually disentangle them.

Sticky Foam

Sticky foam, also referred to as "super sticky" gel, is an example of technology that has found its way from military application to law enforcement experimentation. A Department of Energy (DOE) report states:

> In late 1992, the National Institute of Justice (NIJ), the research arm of the Department of Justice, began a project with SNL [Sandia National Laboratory] to determine the applicability of sticky foam for law enforcement usage. The objectives of the project were to . . . develop a dispenser capable of firing sticky foam, to test the developed gun and sticky foam effectiveness on SNL volunteers acting out prison and law enforcement scenarios, and to have the gun and sticky foam further evaluated by correctional representatives. (Scott, 1996, p. 1)

This report details the effectiveness of the technology, and why the substance is better suited to a correctional setting than for law enforcement use. First, the immobilizing capability of sticky foam is negligible unless the target is adhered to an immobile object such as a floor or wall (Scott, 1996). Second, accuracy with the dispenser is fairly easy to master, however maximum range was only about 25 feet (Scott, 1996). Lastly, clean up of the substance can be cumbersome and labor intensive, requiring healthy applications of mineral oil and an average of 30 seconds of cleaning time per square inch of exposed skin (Scott, 1996).

It is no wonder that police departments would shy away from this material, given that an alternative like pepper spray can provide similar (if not more effective) results without the mess. A subject cannot be taken into custody until the foam is effectively cleansed off the body, and the amounts necessary to adequately incapacitate can be voluminous. Further, while the foam itself is considered harmless (assuming no long-term exposure), the substance *must* be applied only from the waist down to prevent the risk of suffocation if the substance were to enter breathing passages (Scott, 1996). In the decade since the initial tests of sticky foam for law enforcement application, little progress or adoption of the technology by law enforcement agencies has occurred.[13]

Technology to Reduce the Number of Vehicular Pursuits

Barrier Strips

Police pursuits of offenders fleeing in vehicles have almost become a part of American folk heritage. We can watch pursuits live on television, filmed out the windows of media helicopters, while national news channels depict the "car chase of the day" on evening programs, and citizens come out of their homes to cheer on drivers who lead police on chases through neighborhoods. The deadly sidebar to these pursuits is that they are the primary basis for wrongful death lawsuits filed against police departments (Fishel et al., 2006). Vehicular pursuits endanger suspects, officers, and innocent bystanders. Most police departments across the United States now have stringent guidelines detailing when a high-speed pursuit is justified and when officers should fall back and try to apprehend the fleeing suspect at a later juncture. Recently law enforcement has added an extra tool to its arsenal in an effort to end in-progress pursuits quickly, before innocent bystanders are put into harm's way. Barrier or "Spike" strips are devices that, when applied, can quickly disable a speeding vehicle with a minimal potential for death or serious injury. Barrier strips also serve as an alternative to the traditional "bump" technique widely used to end pursuits. One recognized expert in the area of police field operations summarizes this technique as follows:

> By pulling up alongside the suspect vehicle on either the right or left side, it is possible to turn into the vehicle and strike the rear quarter panel at about the rear wheel. If the maneuver is performed correctly, the police vehicle should continue forward and out of danger, while the suspect vehicle should spin around in a 180-degree turn and end up facing the opposite direction. (Adams, 2001, p. 205)

Such a maneuver on the part of pursuing officers can be extremely dangerous, with unpredictable results (Adams, 2001). The most pressing concern is that an out-of-control suspect vehicle could be at risk of striking an oncoming vehicle, innocent bystanders or private property (Adams, 2001).

Very simply, barrier strips are deployed across a roadway (usually manually, but also via remote control), and they contain a series of sharp spikes that deflate a vehicle's tires, either disabling the vehicle altogether or reducing the speed at which the vehicle can be driven. Some models of barrier strips have spikes that detach and are hollow, thus slowly deflating the tires of fleeing vehicles instead of resulting in "blowouts" that could send a vehicle careening out of control (National Security Research, Inc., 2004).[14]

Technology under development and testing is designed to terminate pursuits by debilitating a fleeing vehicle from a distance. Most barrier strips are manually deployed by an officer as the suspect vehicle passes by and are then retrieved via a cord or chain so as not to damage other vehicles using the roadway. Two experimental technologies would allow law enforcement to disable a vehicle from a safe distance. The first delivers ionized plasma that short-circuits the vehicle's electrical system (see "Electric-Shock Immobilizing Technology" above). The second device is akin to a GPS tracking device similar to that currently being used to monitor the movements of certain offenders who are under correctional supervision in the community. The device would be fired at the vehicle and the "tag" would allow officers to monitor the vehicle's movement from a safe distance, without endangering the public (Conser et al., 2005). A similar device is a remote-controlled transmitter that can be used to shut the vehicle's engine down (Conser et al., 2005). This technology is very similar to that currently used by On Star in General Motors' vehicles. Owners who lock their keys in their vehicle can have the vehicle's doors opened remotely once a user name and password are provided. The technology is somewhat costly at the present time, and it is not yet known how easily the technology may be disabled.[15]

Technology Designed for Officer Safety

In 1998, the federal Bureau of Justice Assistance announced the Bulletproof Vest Partnership (BVP), a program that would fund up to half the purchase price of a new bulletproof vest for all criminal justice personnel (employed in policing, courts, or corrections). As of 2004, the program has provided $118 million to purchase nearly half a million bulletproof vests (Bureau of Justice Assistance, 2005). The efficacy of "ballistic-resistant" technology is unquestioned. Batton and Wilson (2006) assert that one correlate in the decline in homicides of police officers since the mid-1970s was the federal Law Enforcement Assistance Administration's (LEAA) funding of bullet-proof vests, begun shortly after that agency was founded in 1968. Similarly, a recent empirical assessment of serious assaults on police officers in the city of Boston (Kaminski et al., 2003) mentioned the wearing of bulletproof vests as a possible confounding variable in the research, because a vest could very well offer officers enough protection that it might change the subjective meaning of the term "serious" assault. Evidence of this concept comes from a report on deaths and injuries sustained by members of the South African Police Service (SAPS). Of 92 officers who had received gunshot wounds and were admitted to a level-one trauma center in Johannesburg, South Africa between 1993 and 2002, only 15 had been wearing bulletproof vests, and none of those injured officers who had been wearing body armor suffered lethal gunshot wounds (Plani et al., 2003).

The National Law Enforcement and Corrections Technology Center (NLECTC) has been a component of the federal National Institute of Justice (NIJ) since 1984 and its headquarter is in Rockville, Maryland. This is perhaps the most comprehensive and exhaustive testing center in the world for ballistic body armor (NLECTC, 2001). The current generation of body armor technology is capable of arresting the majority of ballistic rounds available in the United States, reducing the possibility of officer fatality or serious injury, and the next generation of vests under development is designed to withstand even higher-caliber ammunition. However, the effectiveness of the technology is dependent upon officers wearing their vests at all times while on duty. Officers give a plethora of reasons why they do not always wear body armor on duty, ranging from forgetfulness to restriction of movement to oppressive heat (NLECTC, 2001). Indeed, even the most advanced protective vests are to a certain degree bulky, confining, and extremely hot to wear in summer weather, especially if an officer is on foot or bike patrol (NLECTC, 2001). Based on feedback from officers, body armor manufacturers are experimenting with lighter weight materials with the same level of ballistic-resistance, as well as with alternate materials such as gels that harden when a projectile makes impact with the vest.

Protection of Police Property

In response to injuries sustained by officers when a combative suspect kicks out a patrol car window or security screen, airbag-style padding is available that prevents a perpetrator from damaging the inside of a patrol car and possibly injuring the arresting officer or the subject themselves (Conser et al., 2005). When traditional restraints cannot be used, these "back seat airbags" facilitate the protection of law enforcement personnel and property, while simultaneously frustrating the combative subject's efforts to damage or injure.

And in an interesting coda to the above discussion of bulletproof vests, outdated body armor is finding new life within police departments by becoming part of ballistics-resistant barriers in the doors of patrol cars, office furniture, and at firing ranges (NLECTC, 2001). The logic is part of a greater mission in law enforcement to prevent fatalities associated with intentional or accidental discharge of a firearm in an environment where such weapons are pervasive.[16]

CONCLUSIONS AND FUTURE DIRECTIONS

Technological innovation in the realm of police weaponry and equipment has undoubtedly saved lives and lessened the severity of injuries suffered by both perpetrators and officers. While there are many factors in a complex dynamic associated with the significant decline in officer deaths over the past 30 years (Batton and Wilson, 2006), it seems reasonable to state that these innovations have played more than a negligible role. The use of non-lethal weapons is a rare exemplar in law enforcement policy today; a tactical decision that has received widespread support both from the public and within police ranks as well. Officers have seen firsthand how the use of non-lethals can neutralize offender resistance to police intervention and decrease the likelihood of an officer using deadly force. At the same time, in the "public relations" era of policing, citizens are reassured knowing officers have options at their disposal other than brute force or a sidearm.

This shift in the use-of-force continuum is not without its examples of misapplication or tragedy, but it is indicative of a policing model more attuned to the preservation of individual well being. From a political stand-point, what is required is empirical evidence to support and justify the continued use and development of non-lethal weapons. Law enforcement needs an evidence-based assessment of the extent to which non-lethal weaponry has reduced serious injuries or deaths to both perpetrators and police officers. To this point we have little scientific evidence demonstrating the direct *impact* that non-lethal weaponry has had in this area; therefore, advocates of non-lethal weapons use have been forced to rely upon anec-dotal evidence to support their agendas. While there are no guarantees that non-lethals have led to *significant* decreases in serious injury or death, any positive results will keep the momentum of non-lethal weapons initia-tives moving forward and assist in maintaining the level of political support necessary to fund further research and development in non-lethal weapons technology. It has been said that the possibilities for the future are infinite, and the only limitations on this technology are available funds and a lack of creativity (Tennenbaum and Moore, 1993). In visualizing the ideal non-lethal weapon, scientists must look toward technological innovation in the disciplines of engineering, medicine, and business (as well as in the military), and examine how advances in those fields may be applied to law enforcement weapons technology. Policing has only just begun to experiment with lasers and advanced chemical compounds as potential non-lethal weapons technology, and law enforcement needs to become a principal collaborator in research efforts aimed at bringing new technology to the market.

◆ ◆ ◆ ◆

NOTES

1. The United States Supreme Court ruled in *Tennessee v. Garner* that police officers who use deadly force to apprehend a fleeing offender who poses no risk to the officers or the citizenry, violate the reasonableness requirement pertaining to seizure contained within Fourth Amendment. Such actions are, thus, unconstitutional. This case more clearly delineates the circumstances where deadly force is acceptable and, conversely, circumstances where law enforcement agencies are viewed as culpable.

2. The nomenclature "less lethal" or "less than lethal" weapon is also used to reference the same class of weapons discussed in this chapter, but acknowledges that virtually any weapon used against an individual can result in lethal injury (see Borello, 2000; Jussila and Normia, 2004; Rappert, 2005). For the sake of simplicity, the term "non-lethal weapon" will be used throughout this chapter as an umbrella term for all weapons meant to reduce the possibility of civilian death.

3. A similar argument, albeit in reference to a very different dynamic, is that the use of non-lethal weapons decreases the likelihood that a perpetrator will sustain serious injury, or even death, at the hands of a *group* of officers apprehending a dangerous individual without drawing their firearms but using flashlights, nightsticks, or bare hands. Employing an alternative such as pepper spray implies less physical force over all as well as a reduction in the *number* of officers necessary

to take a belligerent individual into custody. For a police management perspective on this issue, see Cooper, 1997.

4. An incident that occurred in Boston after the hometown Red Sox defeated the New York Yankees on the way to their first World Series Championship in 86 years gave face to fears expressed about the dangers associated with firing any projectile into a crowd, made over a decade ago (see Tennenbaum and Moore, 1993). In the aforementioned incident, a 21-year old college student named Victoria Snelgrove was celebrating with fans outside Fenway Park in Boston after the Red Sox clinched the American League Championship when a city police officer inadvertently shot her through the eye with a pepper-spray pellet. Ms. Snelgrove died shortly thereafter. An independent commission investigating the fatal shooting concluded that officers at the scene were complicit in Ms. Snelgrove's death because some of the officers firing the pepper-spray guns were not certified to use them. The Snelgrove family settled with the case with the city of Boston for a reported $5.1 million.

5. While police utilization of "Hard Technology" has existed since the time of the first watch system, this chapter is devoted to *recent* technological innovations and those that are currently under development. Therefore, instruments such as batons, nightsticks, sap gloves, and others are not considered, as the purposes and implications associated with using these devices are well chronicled. Further, while firearms technology has progressed as well, this chapter also has also adopted the theme of non-lethal technology as a priority of law enforcement. This focus is by no means meant to imply that sidearms are not an integral and vital component of an officer's arsenal

6. TASER is an acronym for Thomas A. Swift Electric Rifle (Wrobleski and Hess, 2003).

7. Although such weapons have many slight variations in design and strength of electrical current, "stun guns" such as these are not a novel technology, as California police agencies utilized early versions of electrical stun technology for nearly three decades.

8. Another philosophical question emerges from electric stun technology, but becomes a question for all "non-lethal" weaponry, and that is "Who should have access to these weapons?" Aside from the deaths attributed to TASERS in Arizona, the Attorney General's Office was as concerned with the availability of electrical stun devices for the general public. While TASER international's target market has always

been law enforcement agencies, these weapons are widely advertised as personal protective devices in print and on the Internet. A concern regarding all "non-lethal" weapons is that if perpetrators are armed commensurate with the police, will law enforcement be "forced" to utilize their sidearms to resolve such a scenario, thus negating the intended purpose of "non-lethal" technology?

9. White and White (1995) contend that the widespread use of rubber bullets by the British Army in Northern Ireland was an indicator of the greater issue of state repression based on religious bias and depressed economic conditions.

10. Hubbs and Klinger's (2004) study also alludes to a potentially troublesome issue associated with the expansion of law enforcement arsenals: Two deaths included in this report were the result of officers mistakenly firing *lethal* rounds from what they thought were non-lethal weapons. Because different munitions (lethal and non-lethal) can be fired from the same weapon, officers must be able to load an appropriate round for the situation at hand. Under conditions of uncertainty or stress, it is apparent that mistakes are possible.

11. It is important to note that beanbag rounds are used primarily as a substitute for 00 buckshot pellets typically loaded into the pump-action shotguns officers carry in their cruisers. Discussion of fatalities and serious injuries should be framed in reference to the probability of death or serious injury when "live" ammunition is fired from the shotgun, as, ostensibly, beanbag rounds are replacing buckshot in specific incidents or scenarios. While reducing fatalities and serious injuries is of course a primary consideration, the police incidents where shotguns are utilized typically revolve around close-quarters situations with the threat of officers coming under fire. Manufacturers of impact munitions stress that, even with the fatal incidents reported with their weapon's use, the "real" number of fatalities has been dramatically reduced by police agencies converting to non-lethal technology.

12. In examining police preference for non-lethal alternatives, the primary considerations for new weapons technologies include effectiveness, ease of use, portability, and the threat of serious injury to officers, subjects or bystanders (see McEwen and Leahy, 1994).

13. Sticky foam has been evaluated and applied to correctional settings. The initial DOE study did find potential for use of the substance in correctional settings, specifically in subduing a single inmate in a

contained area. More recent applications of sticky foam are as a close-in defense and access delay surrounding sensitive targets (Scott, 1996). After the 9/11 terrorist attacks, there was a renewal in testing of sticky foam application, but not specifically in the law enforcement arena.

14. Early versions of barrier strip technology utilized spikes that punctured vehicle tires almost instantly, frequently leading to high-speed crashes. Also, car tire technology has advanced as well so that fewer punctures of any sort result in an instant loss of tire pressure. Instead, air is released at a slower rate, increasing driver control of the vehicle. The improved technologies of both barrier strips and tires have significantly decreased the risk associated with deploying spike strips.

15. Devices such as car alarms and even ignition locks are effective only so long as the knowledge regarding how to defeat the devices is absent. Skilled car thieves have demonstrated an ability to defeat any technology thus far introduced, and there is no reason to believe the technology currently being developed would not meet the same fate. One can therefore envision a constant cycle of upgrading technology and having it defeated, only to be replaced by the next generation of theft-proofing.

16. With the federal government facilitating easier access to bulletproof vests for even the smallest police departments on limited budgets, it has become increasing difficult to find willing takers for body armor used by larger departments. Because the materials in bulletproof vests do not readily break down, they cannot be discarded with regular municipal waste, so the only recycling options available are the small number of manufacturers that possess the technology to break down the materials in older vests for inclusion in new body armor (NLECTC, 2001). This difficulty in disposal has led to novel thinking about how older, yet still serviceable, armor can be utilized within a law enforcement organization.

REFERENCES

Adams, T. F. (2001). *Police field operations* (5th ed.). Upper Saddle River, NJ: Prentice Hall.

Alexander, J. B. (2001). An overview of the future of non-lethal weapons. *Medicine, Conflict and Survival, 17,* 180-193.

Amnesty International (2004). *Excessive and lethal force? Amnesty international's concerns about deaths and ill-treatment involving police use of TASERS.* New York: Amnesty International.

Bailey, W. C. (1996). Less-than-lethal weapons and police-citizen killings in U.S. urban areas. *Crime & Delinquency, 42,* 535-552.

Batton, C., & Wilson, S. (2006). Police murders: An examination of historical trends in the killing of law enforcement officers in the United States, 1947 to 1998. *Homicide Studies, 10,* 79-97.

Borello, A. (2000). The terminology trap: Non-lethal, less-than-lethal, less-than or lethal? *The Law Enforcement Trainer, 15,* 60-65.

Bureau of Justice Assistance (2005). *Solutions for safer communities: FY2004 Annual Report to Congress.* Washington, DC: Department of Justice, Office of Justice Programs, Bureau of Justice Assistance.

Conser, J. A., Russell, G. D., Paynich, R., & Gingerich, T. E. (2005). *Law enforcement in the United States* (2nd ed.). Sudbury, MA: Jones and Bartlett.

Cooper, M. (1997, March 27). Hoping for less lethal force. *New York Times,* B3.

Edwards, S. M., Granfield, J., & Onnan, J. (1997). *Evaluation of pepper spray.* Washington, DC: Department of Justice, Office of Justice Programs, National Institute of Justice.

Fishel, J., Gabbidon, S. L., & Hummer, D. (2006). *An analysis of wrongful death lawsuits involving police officers in the United States.* Paper presented at the Academy of Criminal Justice Sciences annual meeting, March 3, 2006, Baltimore, MD.

Granfield, J., Onnen, J., & Petty, C. S. (1994). *Pepper spray and in-custody deaths.* Alexandria VA: International Association of Chiefs of Police.

Homant, R. J., & Kennedy, D. B. (2000). Effectiveness of less than lethal force in suicide-by-cop incidents. *Police Quarterly, 3,* 153-171.

Hubbs, K., & Klinger, D. (2004). *Impact munitions use: Types, targets, effects.* Washington, DC: Department of Justice, Office of Justice Programs, National Institute of Justice.

Ijames, S. (2001, July). Impact in the field. *Police,* 16-20.

Jussila, J., & Normia, P. (2004). International law and law enforcement firearms. *Medicine, Conflict and Survival, 20,* 55-69.

Kaminski, R. J., Jefferis, E., & Gu, J. (2003). Community correlates of serious assaults on police. *Police Quarterly, 6,* 119-149.

Kornblum, R. N., & Reddy, S. K. (1991). Effects of the TASER in fatalities involving police confrontation. *Journal of Forensic Sciences, 36,* 434-448.

Lavy, T., & Abu Asleh, S. (2003). Ocular rubber bullet injuries. *Eye, 17,* 821-824.

Lyman, M. D. (2005). *The police: An introduction* (3rd ed.). Upper Saddle River, NJ: Pearson Prentice Hall.

McBride, D. K., & Tedder, N. B. (2005). *Efficacy and safety of electrical stun devices.* Arlington, VA: Potomac Institute for Policy Studies.

McDonald, W. C., Stratbucker, R. A., Nerheim, M., & Brewer, J. E. (2005). Cardiac safety of neuromuscular incapacitating defensive devices. *Pacing and Clinical Electrophysiology, 28,* 284-287.

McEwen, T., & Leahy, F. J. (1994). *Less than lethal force technologies in law enforcement and correctional agencies.* Washington, DC: Department of Justice, Office of Justice Programs, National Institute of Justice.

Mertz, L. (2002). Weapons of choice. *New Science Magazine, 15,* 1-4.

Meyer, G. (1992). Nonlethal weapons: Where do they fit? Part II. *Journal of California Law Enforcement, 26,* 53-58.

National Law Enforcement and Corrections Technology Center (NLECTC), (2001, Summer). Body armor on board. *TechBeat*, 1-5.

National Security Research Inc. (2004). *Department of Defense nonlethal weapons and equipment review: A research guide for civil law enforcement and corrections.* Washington, DC: Department of Justice, Office of Justice Programs, National Institute of Justice.

Noakes, J. A., Klocke, B. V., & Gillham, P. F. (2005). Whose streets? Police and protester struggles over space in Washington, DC, 29-30 September 2001. *Policing & Society, 15*, 235-254.

Nowicki, E. (2001). OC spray update. *Law and Order, 49*, 28-29.

Nunn, S. (2001). Police technology in cities: Changes and challenges. *Technology in Society, 23*, 11-27.

Plani, F., Bowley, D. M., & Goosen, J. (2003). Death and injury on duty – A study of South African police officers. *South African Medical Journal, 93*, 851-853.

Rappert, B. (2001). The distribution and resolution of the ambiguities of technology, or why Bobby can't spray. *Social Studies of Science, 31*, 557-591.

Rappert, B. (2005). Prohibitions, weapons and controversy: Managing the problems of ordering. *Social Studies of Science, 35*, 211-240.

Robin, G. D. (1996). The elusive and illuminating search for less-than-lethal alternatives to deadly force. *Police Forum, 6*, 1-8.

Scott, S. H. (1996). *Sticky foam as a less-than-lethal technology.* Albuquerque, NM: Department of Energy, Sandia National Laboratory.

Silberman, J. (2005). Non-lethal weaponry and non-proliferation. *Notre Dame Journal of Law, Ethics and Public Policy, 19*, 347-354.

Steffee, C. H., Lantz, P. E., Flannagan, L. M., Thompson, R. L., & Jason, D. R. (1995). Oleoresin capsicum (pepper) spray and "in-custody deaths." *American Journal of Forensic Medicine and Pathology, 16*, 185-192.

Tennenbaum, A. N., & Moore, A. M. (1993). Non-lethal weapons: Alternatives to deadly force. *The Futurist, 27*, 20-23.

Terrill, W. (2003). Police use of force and suspect resistance: The micro-process of the police-suspect encounter. *Police Quarterly, 6*, 51-83.

Vaughn, M. S., Cooper, T. W., & del Carmen, R. V. (2001). Assessing legal liabilities in law enforcement: Police chiefs' views. *Crime & Delinquency, 47*, 3-27.

White, R. W., & White, T. F. (1995). Repression and the liberal state: The case of Northern Ireland, 1969-1972. *Journal of Conflict Resolution, 39*, 330-352.

Wrobleski, H. M., & Hess, K. M. (2003). *Introduction to law enforcement and criminal justice* (7th ed.). Belmont, CA: Thomson Wadsworth.

7. THE POLICE AND SOFT TECHNOLOGY: HOW INFORMATION TECHNOLOGY CONTRIBUTES TO POLICE DECISION MAKING

by

Christopher J. Harris

University of Massachusetts, Lowell

The police have always been infatuated with technological innovations, even as far back as the 1800s when they first adopted uniforms, patrol wagons, and call boxes (Maguire and King, 2004). While some innovations are merely tools that officers use to perform their usual tasks, other technologies have fundamentally altered the way the police function. The first technological revolution in policing that produced a notable change in their function came about with the advent of the telephone, the two-way radio, and the automobile (Walker, 1984). Prior to this time, officers patrolled their beat with nightstick in hand, cut off from communication with agency headquarters, with little prospect of assistance in case of some urgent need. Citizens who required police assistance had to wander into the street looking for an officer, or walk miles to a police station for help.

With the proliferation of telephones in the early 20th century, policing changed. Citizens called – and in fact were encouraged to call – the police to deal with a multitude of problems, and the police responded to those calls from dispatch via a two-way radio, and sped quickly to locations via patrol cars. These technological advances, along with changes in police administrative practices, helped to create the police as we know them today. Now, anyone is the United States can pick up a phone and summon the police to deal with any crises that arise, criminal or otherwise. While the effects of these technologies are too broad to enumerate here, suffice it to say that the technology of the telephone, the two-way radio, and the automobile fundamentally changed how the police interacted with citizens, how they fulfilled their various roles, and how the police were supervised.

Some scholars claim that we may be in an era marked by a new policing revolution, one brought about both by changes in police philosophy and advances in information technology (IT[1]; Dunworth, 2000; Stroshine, 2005). Traditional police strategies have stressed routine preventive patrol, rapid response to crime calls, and general follow-up investigations as the core police functions. Such an overall operation made patrol officers and detectives primary users of information regarding crime and suspects, and this information was generally developed by police through their intimate area knowledge. Supervisors used data collected on arrests made, number of citations issued and etc. to evaluate subordinates, and occasionally used crime analysis to direct the activity of their units (Dunworth, 2000). Top police executives used crime information for decisions regarding patrol deployment and resource allocations, and they disseminated crime reports to inform the public and other criminal justice institutions of overall trends and conditions.

Newer strategies based on Problem-Oriented Policing (POP) and Community-Oriented Policing (COP) now encourage police to make greater use of the data they routinely collect, and to be more analytic with regards to the data they utilize for tactical and strategic decision making (Goldstein, 1979; Greene and Mastrofski, 1998; Manning, 1988). Both strategies encourage police to go beyond individual calls for service, and instead take on the problems underlying them. To do so, police are encouraged to collect data from a wide variety of sources, some of which may be traditional information sources, while others may be newer, untapped sources of information, such as community members or organizations. Moreover, police are also encouraged to disseminate this new information to external (non-police) constituents, who will become increasingly responsible for assisting police in identifying problems and developing solutions for dealing with them. Since these strategies move beyond the limited information police routinely collect (e.g., from witnesses, victims, and suspects), adjustments to information systems within departments will become necessary as police shift their focus from individual calls for service to community problems and concerns.

This chapter discusses the new developments in police IT, and focuses upon the ways in which police are using IT to enhance their operational and administrative decision making. While there is too little research to determine whether these IT tools are prolific enough that they constitute a fundamental trend in the policing industry, they nevertheless merit consideration due at least to their potential for changing police practices and effectiveness. Specifically, this chapter focuses on advances in the ways in which police capture, store, manipulate, analyze, retrieve, and share data, and how that data is (or is not) deployed for a variety of tactical, strategic, and administrative purposes.

POLICE AND INFORMATION

The police have always kept records of their activities. In fact, this was one of the fundamental mechanisms of police administration expressed by Robert Peel, who founded the world's first police department in London in 1829 (Cordner et al., 2005). The police also have a long history of gathering information on crime. The Uniform Crime Reports (UCR), one of the first systematic collections of criminal activity nationally, was designed during the 1920s and has served as a means to analyze crime for numerous police departments. While most of these records have historically been captured on paper, computerization in law enforcement has become increasingly widespread, allowing police to capture more information than ever before. Additionally, demand for police information has been vastly increased, with many institutions such as insurance companies, public health and welfare agencies, schools, and private companies relying on the police to assist them in risk management (Ericson and Haggerty, 1997). Because of these factors, police are inundated with information, some of it captured without any inherent purpose or reason, but is recorded "just in case." Yet police are in the position to use IT in ways that are unique when compared to other criminal justice agencies. As Dunworth (2000, p. 379) writes: "In many respects, police departments have the greatest need among criminal justice agencies for a clear understanding of their environment and the ways they can adapt to it. This makes them . . . the neediest consumers of the new information systems and technology. . . . "

Indeed, by all accounts, police are rapidly acquiring IT, but the vital question remains: how are police using this IT? If police are acquiring systems to simply switch from a paper to an electronic system, they are missing out on the ways in which IT can have a profound impact on the core policing technology – decision making (Manning, 1992). Developing the capacity to capture and retrieve data electronically may increase efficiency and minimally alter some police behaviors, but being able to gather more data more quickly says nothing about what the police are doing with it. If police are acquiring IT and employ it to continue "business as usual," meaning a focus on short-term, case-driven decision making, then they will be utilizing a mere fraction of their IT capacity.

What follows is a brief overview of IT that assists police in data management. Specifically, I focus upon Record Management Systems (RMS) and Computer Aided Dispatch (CAD) systems, along with the use of Mobile Data Terminals (MDTs) in patrol cars and the use of the Internet by police. Then I go on to discuss IT that makes use of data captured by police and which aid in police decision making at operational and administrative levels.

DATA COLLECTION AND MANAGEMENT

Record Management Systems (RMS)

As mentioned above, police have always kept records of their activities. A RMS is a way to manage this information, from criminal reports and arrest records to personnel records and fingerprints, and will be utilized by almost all staff in any given department. Thus, a fully functioning RMS is vital to the performance of any police agency. Without records of its past and current activities, a police agency loses its "institutional memory" and is essentially "flying blind" (Bratton, 1998).

At first, police department records were manually recorded by officers with pen and paper, and were later entered using a typewriter. With the increasing use of mainframe computers in the 1970s and 1980s, many police department records, especially crime and arrest reports, were captured electronically by entering in handwritten or typed reports for storage and later retrieval (Dunworth, 2000). Even today, most police RMS systems lack sophistication, being merely recordkeeping tools serving as little more than electronic file cabinets. While most police departments (60%) use computers for records management, significantly fewer serve to do fairly simple tasks such as automated booking, resource allocation, or compiling UCR statistics (Hickman and Reaves, 2003). In fact, many agencies have only partial computerization of recordkeeping: their lack of experience and limited understanding of computers have led to a haphazard adoption of this technology (Manning, 2003). Key RMS functions are not automated, leaving personnel to do data entry by hand, and stored information may not be easily retrieved. For example, most RMS records are stored by case, and are accessed by the name of the person for whom the file was created. It may not be possible to search records by the date or type of an event

(Craig-Moreland, 2004). Thus, a fragmented RMS can be far less than even an average system that adequately serves agency purposes, and these dysfunctional systems currently appear to be more the rule than the exception.

Ideally, a state-of-the-art RMS would be fully automated, and it would allow users to search various relational databases as part of an integrated system. Moreover, the RMS would be more than an independent system. It would be connected with other databases within the department (such as dispatch records, property and evidence records, etc.), and with other databases compiled at the city, county, state, and federal levels. The system would also include a user-friendly interface, and would have built-in editing and error checking so that incorrect information would be identified before it is stored (Dunworth, 2000). While such capabilities offer significant potential for increasing the efficiency and effectiveness of police organizations, the development and implementation for such an advanced RMS is not an easy task. A large amount of time and resources are required for the adoption of such a system, which may be difficult for a police department to justify under shrinking municipal budgets. Nevertheless, a modern RMS will make it easier to deploy other important IT advancements. As Dunworth (2000, p. 382) writes: "In a real sense, all other IT applications depend on RMS. If it is absent or deficient, then a domino effect seems inevitable. The other applications either will not realize their full potential, or they will fail outright."

Computer-Aided Dispatch (CAD) Systems

Rapid response to calls for service has been a vital police function ever since the adoption of the telephone, automobile, and two-way radio by police. Historically, calls for police service were treated equally, with each call being dispatched to an officer as quickly as possible. Records kept by the agency about these calls were handwritten, until computers were adopted to create electronic records of these calls and police responses to them. Such computer systems collected and stored information about the caller, the call, the operator, the incident, and its routing, assignment, and disposal (Manning, 1992).

With the advent of the 911 system in 1968 as a means of reporting emergency situations, police experienced a steady increase in public demand for police service as this system was gradually adopted nationwide. The system was heavily advertised, and the mandates of police professionalism began to view quick service-call response as a measure of organizational effectiveness. Citizen perceptions changed too, and they increasingly expected their calls for service to be responded to quickly by a uniformed officer.

However, as awareness of usage of 911 by the public increased, resources were not kept commensurate with demand. People began calling 911 for all sorts of concerns, most of which were non-emergency in nature. In fact, some research estimates that most calls to 911 (50-90%) are non-emergency in nature (Harris, 2003). Some of these systems became overloaded at times, resulting in some callers being put on hold or receiving an automated message when the system was overloaded. This resulted in tremendous inefficiency, with significant backlogs that placed citizens with actual emergencies in peril. Currently, more than 97 million calls for service to 911 are made annually, and the number has been increasing, especially with the proliferation of cellular phones (Dunworth, 2000).

One solution adopted by some cities was to develop a non-emergency number, such as 311. Another response is to attempt to sustain rapid police response to true emergencies (e.g., crimes in progress), while either eliminating police response to calls that do not ultimately demand their attention or "stacking" calls that require police attention but where a delayed response is adequate. New features to existing CAD systems have been developed as a technology to serve this role.

CAD systems now not only automate the recordkeeping of calls for service and their responses, but can also provide a means for classifying and prioritizing these calls (Stroshine, 2005). Such systems were adopted by the larger U.S. police departments such as New York, Boston, and Detroit in the early 1970s, and now just over half (56%) of police departments serving populations of 50,000 or more use such CAD systems (Hickman and Reaves, 2001). Newer CAD systems not only allow police to identify the location and number of an incoming call, but can now communicate directly with computers in patrol cars, national databases, and a department's RMS, and some can provide mapping capabilities (Dunworth, 2000).

Mobile Data Terminals (MDTs)

Along with enhanced CAD systems has been another important development in police response capacity: MDTs. While these in-field computers are far from commonplace in U.S. police departments (only 40% of police agencies used MDTs as of 2000), they represent a technology with the capacity to increase the efficiency with which departments capture, report, disseminate, and share information (Hickman and Reaves, 2003).

Early forms of MDTs were simple machines used to transmit information wirelessly to and from officers and the station (Dunworth, 2000). Here, officers could record information electronically, such as the time of arrival at a call scene. As miniaturization of computers has progressed, MDTs have now become essentially in-car laptop computers, capable of performing the same tasks as a desktop computer. Such MDTs can be used to obtain information about a call for service (e.g., previous calls from that address), and about persons (e.g., criminal histories) with whom they have contact. This helps eliminate airtime use with requests for information from dispatchers, and also increased police ability to proactively run license plate checks on automobiles without having to stop them.

MDTs can also be used to obtain information from officers. They can be used to fill out routine paperwork in the field, submit warrant requests and approvals, etc. Also, since these forms are filed electronically, they can increase uniformity in reporting and ensure reporting accuracy. This could increase the efficiency of agencies, as supervisors are presumably relieved of spending a sizable amount of time checking their subordinates' paperwork. If MDTs are tied into an agency's RMS, much of the paperwork done by an agency can be electronic, which facilitates information sharing within the agency, and perhaps with other agencies. This also allows forms to be directly imported into RMS, instead of requiring personnel to enter paperwork into RMS manually.

Information Sharing and the Internet

Accompanying better IT systems such as RMS and CAD, there has been an increase in the number of police departments that use internal networks – called *intra*nets – to connect computers within agencies, as well as the number of agencies using *inter*nets (which connect networks across agencies), and in the number of departments that have home pages on the World Wide Web (Dunworth, 2000).

The Internet has evolved rather rapidly, presenting with it a host of new problems and challenges for police agencies, such as cybercrime. However, this technology of networking computers has also allowed police agencies – which have been typically fragmented from each other for historical reasons – to share large amounts of information about crimes and criminals, and it has also facilitated the streamlining of the administration of this information. Agencies are now not only linked horizontally across various local police departments, but vertically as well with local, state, and federal agencies sharing information. Some states have established repositories for criminal histories, and the FBI maintains criminal histories for federal offenders and national criminal record systems, such as the National Crime Information Center (NCIC), the Interstate Identification Index, and an automated National Fingerprint File (Dunworth, 2000).

While information sharing among law enforcement agencies certainly has the potential to increase the productivity of officers and to increase officer safety, little research has been done on the effects of increased information sharing. A recent study based in San Diego County compared two sheriffs' departments, one with access to a countywide information sharing system (called ARJIS) and another without such access. The researchers found that while officers with ARJIS access felt that the system improved their job performance, the personnel of the two agencies did not differ in their perceptions of how information sharing can lead to arrest productivity (Zaworski, 2006). Objective indicators such as clearance rates showed no difference between the two sheriffs' departments with regard to violent crimes, even though officers with access to ARJIS felt it aided them in their ability to investigate and solve crimes. Also, the department *without* ARJIS actually had twice the property crime clearance rate of the department with ARJIS, and some of this might have been attributable to the fact that officers who used ARJIS suffered from information overload. There was little training offered to officers on how to use ARJIS, and so officers with access to this system found it difficult to locate the information for which they were searching. Thus, even though ARJIS offered access to more information, it is likely that the search time required of officers to locate information had increased, perhaps in some cases greatly (depending on an officer's computer savvy). This may have led to an actual decrease in officer efficiency, as they spent *more* time trying to find vital information. These findings are consistent with other research noting that IT can actually increase paperwork, paper files, and the amount of time officers spend in an office than on the street, thereby decreasing efficiency instead of increasing it (Manning, 1992).

The ultimate goal of employing information sharing technology is to create an integrated justice system. Not only would computer networks link law enforcement agencies at various levels together, but such IT would also involve linkages to court and corrections systems. This would allow criminal justice agencies to track individuals through the system, thereby improving the quality and accuracy of data, the speed with which it is available, and the elimination of redundant or superfluous data entry (Dunworth, 2000). This potential is tremendous, and could possibly aid in the elimination of a criminal justice system which is often criticized for being fragmented and uncoordinated. However, significant obstacles will have to be overcome, such as the incompatibility of information systems and the way in which they record information, competition among criminal justice agencies for limited resources, lack of understanding about IT and its uses, and the myriad difficulties in attempting to coordinate the direction of multiple agencies. While some argue that the potential outweighs the drawbacks, and therefore that integrated justice information systems should be pursued (Dunworth, 2000), one should remain skeptical regarding criminal justice agencies' ability to surmount these hurdles, even if the technology is attainable.

Another common law enforcement application of Internet technology, and one that has been increasing steadily in recent years, is the building of police web sites. These sites largely serve as a means of enhancing communication between the police and the public, which is done through a variety of means. First, police web sites can aid the public with contact information, providing a personnel directory with the names, phone numbers, and e-mail addresses, facilitating the ability of the public to contact appropriate police personnel. Second, the web site can serve to disseminate important information, such as crime prevention brochures, crime reports and advisories, a "most wanted" criminals list, clarification on laws or a frequently-asked-questions page, or provide prospective employees with job information (Dunworth, 2000; Manning, 2003; Stroshine, 2005). Some police web sites can even produce crime statistics and crime maps with a few mouse clicks. Third, police web sites can receive information from the public. Some police web sites allow citizens to file complaints or commendations, submit crime reports about minor incidents, and provide tips or information about a crime. Given the ease with which the public can access an Internet home page, it is suspected that police web sites will enhance communication with citizens, since it is quicker and easier than driving to a local police station. This of course applies only to citizens with Internet access, and therefore is likely to exclude many lower-class citizens from availing themselves of this information.

Given that the equipment requirements and expertise necessary to create an Internet home page are relatively low, the proliferation of police web sites is very likely to continue. In fact, some Internet Service Providers are donating time and expertise to help police agencies create a home page (Sulewski, 1997). Many departments have found web pages to be very cost-effective. Once an Internet site is established, maintenance costs are low (especially when compared to other IT), and it can even reduce the costs of publicizing records or hiring personnel (Dunworth, 2000).

NEW DATA-DRIVEN POLICE STRATEGIES

We have seen that IT has enhanced the potential of police agencies to store, process, and disseminate information. Advances in computerization allow RMS and CAD systems to store large amounts of information that would have been inconceivable a few decades ago. Moreover, these advances have allowed police to reduce the error made in capturing information by formatting computer records, to reduce the time it takes to make information available by automating some recordkeeping processes, and enhance information sharing through the networking of computer systems. Also, the miniaturization of computers has made such technology available to the officer in the field, allowing MDTs to record, transmit, and retrieve valuable information from a police vehicle or hand-held device.

But the vital question remains: what are police *doing* with all this information? If police are simply using IT to streamline "business as usual," then the potential for IT to change how police operate will ultimately be lost. More specifically, if police use technologies such as CAD, RMS, and MDTs to do traditionally reactive, or what Goldstein (1979) calls "fire brigade" policing, they will miss the most significant contribution IT can make to a department: to enhance decision making, both tactical and strategic, based on a systematic review of sound information at the operational and administrative level. To fulfill such potential, IT must be integrated into the organization in such a way that it contributes to, and even may fundamentally change, the way police operate.

Fortunately, some police departments are integrating IT into their organization as a way to enhance decision making, and are using IT to do more than just enhance recordkeeping. The next section reviews some examples of this technology and how police are utilizing data-driven strategies for decision making, including crime analysis and mapping, the Compstat program, and early intervention systems.

Computerized Crime Analysis and Crime Mapping

Crime analysis is a process by which data drawn from crime incidents is systematically analyzed with a view towards identifying patterns, instead of simply focusing on single incidents. To some extent, the police have always been engaged in crime analysis in some form or another. In fact, since even the earliest police departments deployed officers according to a predefined beat during a specific shift, officers likely engaged in informal crime analysis when comparing their investigations with their past experiences and with those of other officers. But given the limitations of this form of crime analysis – namely that officers are limited by the number of hours they work and the number of experiences that are shared between officers – a more systematic process of crime analysis is desired. If crime analysis remains this simple, it risks being haphazard and anecdotal, and is likely to overlook important crime patterns that emerge. Modern crime analysts no longer rely on their own memory or observations of crime incidents; they now utilize computer systems for the application of various techniques, ranging from simple patterns analysis to complex statistical analysis (Boba, 2005).

The IT innovations mentioned above have greatly contributed to law enforcement's capacity for crime analysis. The computerization of records has been a boon for the power and speed with which police departments can conduct analyses. For example, CAD systems routinely collect information necessary for crime analysis – such as the date, time, and location of a call for service – which can be made available to analysts for detection of crime patterns. Given the advances in IT, police departments are making increasing use of computerized crime analysis. According to a 2000 survey of police departments, about a third of them are using computers for crime analysis (Hickman and Reaves, 2003).

What specifically are police doing with their enhanced crime analysis capabilities? In concrete terms, Reuland (1997) identifies four specific functions of crime analysis:

1. *To support resource deployment* – Crime analysis for this purpose involves detecting patterns in crime or the potential for crime to enhance effectiveness of daily patrol operations, surveillance, stakeouts, and other police tactics. These analyses influence personnel deployment and resource allocation.

2. *To assist in investigating and apprehending offenders* – By comparing files that contain modus operandi characteristics with files of new suspect attributes, departments hope to make more and better arrests.

3. *To prevent crime* – Crime analysts focus on identifying locations, times of day, or situations where crimes appear to cluster so that departments can take steps to harden these potential targets to make them less likely targets of crime.

4. *To meet administrative needs* – Law enforcement administrators need to provide other individuals and agencies with crime-related information, including city agencies, courts, government officers, community groups, and the media. Administrators may need to use crime analysis in this context for legislative, political, and financial purposes.

Probably the most prominent crime analysis technique advanced by IT improvements in recent years has been computerized crime mapping. While police have mapped crime with large maps and colored pushpins since the early 1900s, the relatively recent development of inexpensive, PC-based mapping software capable of sophisticated analysis has increased the frequency with which police departments map crime. As Pattavina (2005, p. 147) writes: "Advances in computer hardware and software during the past 20 years or so have made it cheaper, faster, and easier to map significant amounts of information and have resulted in the development and application of more sophisticated spatial analytic techniques that can be used by researchers and practitioners to study criminal activities."

These advances are linked to those of geographic information systems (GIS), which are computer-based tools that allow users to modify, visualize, query, and analyze geographic and tabular data (Boba, 2005). These systems not only allow for the production of maps, but also allow users to view and manipulate the data behind the maps, to combine various geographic data, and to perform statistical functions. Crime mapping, in turn, is used to refer to the process of using GIS to conduct spatial analysis of crime problems and other police-related issues (Boba, 2005).

Crime mapping is sometimes thought to be a separate field from crime analysis, largely due to the nature of the software that is used as well as its distinct connection to environmental criminology (an approach that emphasizes the geographic context of crime; Pattavina, 2005). However, crime mapping is actually a subfield of crime analysis, and, according to Boba (2005) mapping serves three main functions in relation to crime analysis:

1. It facilitates visual and statistical analyses of the spatial nature of crime and other types of events.

2. It allows analysts to link unlike data sources together based on common geographic variables (linking census information, school information, and crime data for a common area).

3. It provides maps that help to communicate analysis results.

Thus, crime mapping serves a complimentary role in crime analysis. Analysts can create a number of maps to depict geographic information, such as an electronic *pinmap* of all the homicides in a police beat in a given year, which places a colored dot or symbol at each crime location. An example of a pinmap is displayed in Figure 1. Such a map would be relatively simple, and it would draw upon a database (e.g., CAD) that stores information on the location of crimes. This map could be used in deployment decisions or crime prevention planning. A more complicated map might display the homicides throughout a city for a given year. Because such a map could be a blur of symbols (depending on the frequency of the crime of interest), mapping the concentrations of crime rates using a symbol range, which is called a *thematic map*, would be more intelligible. An example of a thematic map is displayed in Figure 2. This map could also be used for deployment or crime prevention decisions. Specifically, these maps help to engage police in *visual thinking* – to notice relationships among environmental factors that may have gone unnoticed and generate ideas to explain them (Harries, 1999). However, these types of maps are descriptive only, and rely on visual inspection of patterns that are ultimately subjective in their interpretation.

Maps can also be created based on statistical methods to identify patterns, thus removing the subjectivity of descriptive maps. The most common method for identifying such patterns involves hot spot analysis. Simply put, hot spots are places where greater than expected numbers of crimes occur (Sherman et al., 1989). There are currently several available types of hot spot analysis, with no consensus as to which method is best (Eck et al., 2005). By identifying hot spots of criminal activity, police departments can engage in tactical planning regarding manpower distribution, or strategic planning to design an intervention strategy based on resolving the underlying problem(s) at the location(s). Such activities have already been accomplished under the Strategic Approaches to Community Safety Initiative (SACSI), and are currently underway through Project Safe Neighborhoods (PSN). Both programs seek to gather data from criminal justice and social

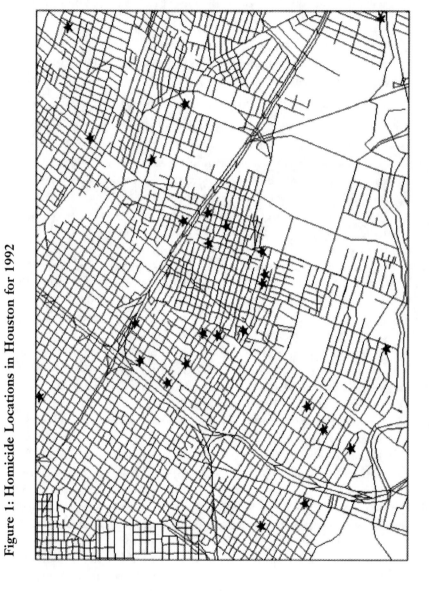

Figure 1: Homicide Locations in Houston for 1992

Source: Data obtained from Paulsen & Robinson, 2004

Figure 2: Homicide Rates per 1,000 in Houston for 1992

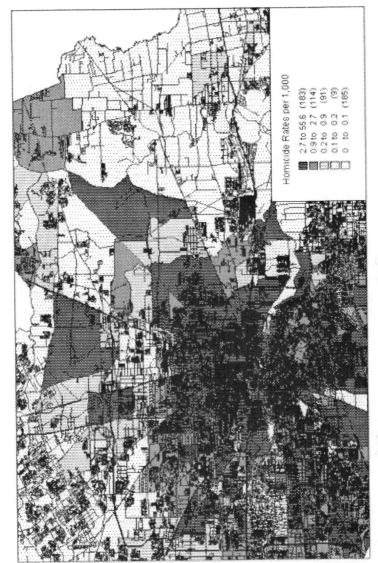

Source: Data obtained from Paulsen & Robinson, 2004

service agencies and to merge them to help sites analyze crime problems, develop comprehensive intervention strategies to combat them, and make adjustments to such strategies based on rigorous feedback (Rich, 1999).

In addition, new analytic techniques are being developed to forecast where crime is likely to occur, a process known as projective analysis, by identifying factors related to crime production (Pelfry, 2005). Such analysis can, for example, examine the temporal and spatial relationships between signs of physical disorder (e.g., abandoned cars, graffiti, etc.) and serious crime hot spots (Rich, 1999). Other methods of crime mapping are also in development, such as geographic profiling. This technique is based on routine activities theory, and it suggests that serial criminals are likely to commit crimes in a specific pattern. Based on what criminologists know about an offender's journey to crime, geographic profiling is designed to locate areas with the greatest likelihood of an offender's residence. While the analysis is not designed to produce a specific address, it does attempt to identify the neighborhoods from which offenders most likely have traveled to commit their crimes (Pelfry, 2005). While both projective analysis and geographic profiling are relatively new and still in development, and thus their utility has not been firmly established, there have been some success stories (see, for example, *NIJ Journal* #253, 2006).

Despite the widespread innovation, many police departments have not embraced computerized crime analysis and mapping. Those that do employ crime analysis and mapping tend to use the technology for focusing on criminal apprehension or identifying high-crime areas. This suggests that police departments use crime analysis for tactical, short-term planning, which supports traditional, crime-oriented police functions instead of enhancing them. More long-term strategic planning is rare, as is problem analysis directed towards identifying and responding to persistent community problems (O'Shea and Nicholls, 2003). This limited use of crime analysis and mapping by police agencies demonstrates that many law enforcement agencies have yet to fully capitalize on the capabilities of this technology, thus limiting their potential impact.

One of the primary obstacles to this limited utility may be the fact that police agencies lack the ability to readily interpret crime statistics and maps. As Manning (2003, p. 97) insightfully notes, "Crime maps (and other analytic models), while often colorful, fascinating, and provocative, have no intrinsic actionable meaning. A picture may need a thousand words to explain it." Moreover, even if the maps can be interpreted for police personnel by crime analysts, their implications for action may be unclear. As one police lieutenant confided to the author, showing his agency's command staff crime maps was like "showing a monkey fire . . . they were very impressed with it, but had no idea what to do with it." Thus, if agencies invest in crime analysis without much planning or forethought as to how the information generated will be utilized, the statistics, maps, and other crime analysis products will be regarded as a mere novelty that may only be utilized by a limited number of police personnel.

Other obstacles serve to exacerbate this initial concern. Many police officers on the street see crime analysis as only marginally related to their day-to-day work, which typically involves little activity one would categorize as crime-fighting. This problem is compounded by the fact that the vast majority of crime analysis is done by civilians, who are viewed as outsiders in a police agency. Many officers resent the idea that a civilian can tell them anything about their job which they do not already know, and so crime analysts lack standing in a department to point out the implications of their work for decision making, which is ultimately left to police managers. Another element in this equation is time. Careful crime analyses, especially those used for strategic decision making, take time, which often runs counter to the traditional notion of reactive police work.

Other obstacles are more routine in nature, involving problems such as inadequate funding to purchase and maintain IT equipment, inadequate training of personnel on crime analysis, difficulty with compatibility of hardware and software, and challenges in obtaining necessary data from other agencies. These obstacles may be a bit more easily overcome as IT acquisition costs decline, user expertise improves, and systems become increasingly integrated.

This is not to say that computerized crime analysis and crime mapping cannot be an integral part of the decision making in a police agency. What follows is an example of how this process might operate: it shows how crime analysis can serve to guide departmental decision making, and moreover, hold administrators accountable for those decisions. The example is New York City's Computer Comparison Statistics (Compstat) program.

Compstat

Introduced in 1994 by then-commissioner William Bratton of the New York City Police Department (NYPD), Compstat has been a widely acclaimed innovation in American policing. The program has received awards from Harvard University and then-Vice President Al Gore, and has been largely credited by its creators and proponents with the large reduction of crime in New York City in the late 1990s (Bratton, 1998; Silverman, 1999). In a recent survey of police departments with over 100 sworn officers, Weisburd et al. (2004) found that one-third of the agencies surveyed had implemented a "Compstat-like program" and another quarter were planning one.

So what exactly is Compstat? It has been referred to as a "strategic control system" by some, incorporating both technological and management systems as a way for the NYPD to gather and disseminate information on its crime problems and track efforts to deal with them (Weisburd et al., 2003). Thus, Compstat combines state-of-the-art IT and crime analysis with modern management principles to focus an organization squarely on crime reduction.

Essentially, Compstat is based on four principles designed to make police organizations rational and responsive to management direction: (1) accurate and timely information made available at all levels of the organization; (2) the selection of the most effective tactics for specific problems; (3) rapid, focused deployment of people and resources to implement those tactics; and (4) relentless follow-up and assessment to learn what happened and make subsequent tactical assessments if necessary (Willis et al., 2006). These principles are most visible in the NYPD's twice-weekly Compstat "Crime-Control Strategy" meetings, where precinct commanders are brought before the department's top brass to report on the crime problems in their district and what they are doing about them (Weisburd et al., 2004).

These Compstat meetings are also illustrative of the important role IT plays in Compstat. In these meetings, recent precinct crime statistics (e.g., arrests, shooting incidents, etc.), crime maps (typically electronic pin maps), and other relevant data (e.g., workload data, demographic data, etc.) are prominently displayed on overhead screens. These data provide a framework in which commanders display their knowledge of local crime problems and discuss future strategies for dealing with them. These plans are documented, and when the commander is brought again before the top brass he or she must demonstrate follow-up on these strategies. Sometimes members of the press or other agencies, as well as peers and subordinates, are invited to Compstat meetings, thus providing a "great theater" and generating an increased public awareness of how the department is managed (Weisburd et al., 2004). Supervisors then grill commanders on their knowledge of crime problems and their strategies for solving these issues. Failure to provide a satisfactory answer may lead to criticism, or even removal from command for consistently poor performance. Such a process greatly increases information sharing within the agency and with the city at large, thereby preventing commanders from unjustly hoarding information and expertise (Geller, 1997).

Weisburd et al. (2003), in an attempt to discern the common features that are central to the development of Compstat-like programs, identify six key elements:

1. *Mission clarification* – A police agency must have a clear mission that specifies management's commitment to specific goals for which the organization can be held accountable, such as reducing crime by 10% in a year.

2. *Internal accountability* – Police managers must be held accountable and should expect consequences for not being knowledgeable about, or not having responded to, problems that fit within the department's mission.

3. *Geographic organization of operational command* – Operational command is focused on the policing of territories, so central decision-making authority on police operations is delegated to commanders with territorial responsibility (e.g., precincts). Specialist units (e.g., narcotics, vice, etc.) are placed under command of the precinct commander so as to be responsive to his/her needs.

4. *Organizational flexibility* – Compstat requires that the organization develop the capacity of changing established routines to mobilize resources when and where they are needed for strategic application.

5. *Data-driven problem identification and assessment* – Compstat requires that data be made available to identify and analyze problems to track and assess the department's response. Data must be made available to all relevant personnel on a timely basis and in a readily usable format.

6. *Innovative problem-solving tactics* – Managers are expected to select responses to crime problems that offer the best prospects of success, and not to cleave to traditional strategies. Thus, experimentation and innovation are encouraged from knowledge gained from personal experience, the experience of other departments, and research about crime prevention.

As one can observe from the above six elements, IT has an integral part in Compstat. Data on crime is needed in a timely fashion, it needs to be distributed throughout the agency, and it needs to be in a format that is accessible to those who will use it. Moreover, this crime analysis serves as the basis to identify problems and develop responses to them. Then, data is collected to evaluate responses and adjust strategies as necessary. Without crime analysis and crime mapping, the Compstat program cannot occur. But instead of simply having a crime analysis unit generate maps and statistics, Compstat specifies exactly how that information is to be utilized by the agency for tactical and strategic decision making, and goes further by gathering data to evaluate those decisions, thereby holding police managers accountable.

But does it work? Is there any demonstrable evidence that Compstat is an effective crime-fighting strategy? Based on the rapid rate of adoption of this program by American police agencies, one would certainly think so, but the available evidence is far from definitive. While New York City experienced large, double-digit drops in rates of non-negligent manslaughter, robbery, burglary, and motor vehicle theft after the implementation of Compstat, thus far there has not been any scientifically rigorous study of the impact of Compstat on crime (Willis et al., 2006). In fact, if anything, there is reasonable evidence to be suspicious about the claims of Compstat supporters that it is solely responsible for reducing crime rates in New York City and elsewhere.

First, Compstat was implemented in New York City alongside several other changes in the NYPD, including a dramatic increase in the number of officers, a zero-tolerance policing policy, and a greater focus on gun enforcement (Eck and Maguire, 2000). As a result, it is difficult to attribute the crime drop in New York City to any one of these specific police changes.

Second, while the implementation of Compstat in New York City coincided with a decline in crime rates, it may be more a case of coincidence than causation. Examining New York City's homicide rate between 1986 and 1998, Eck and Maguire (2000) demonstrated that homicides declined before the implementation of Compstat. In fact, homicides peaked and *began to fall three years before* Compstat began. Moreover, other large U.S. cities experienced similar drops in homicide during the same time period, and these places had no Compstat program. This led Eck and Maguire (2000, p. 233) to conclude, " . . . these data do not support a strong argument for Compstat causing, contributing to, or accelerating the decline in homicides in New York City. . . . "

Another Police Foundation study by Willis et al. (2003) also reported similar findings. These researchers examined the crime trends before and after the implementation of Compstat by the police departments in Lowell,

Massachusetts, Minneapolis, Minnesota, and the Newark, New Jersey. According to UCR data, crime rates were already declining before the implementation of Compstat in all three cities. After the program was implemented, the declines in crime rates were as steep or less steep in all three cities (Willis et al., 2003). In fact, Lowell experienced a rise in crime rates two years after implementation of Compstat. While the authors readily admitted that a simple pre-post test at three sites is far from sufficient to draw any definitive conclusions of Compstat's impact on crime, their findings were consistent with Eck and Maguire's (2000) earlier study. Over all, based on these assessments of Compstat, one should remain skeptical regarding advocates' claims that Compstat is responsible for the crime drop in New York City or elsewhere.

Why then, in face of evidence that should lead one to remain skeptical of Compstat, are police departments so quick to adopt it? Two explanations present themselves. First, Compstat empowers police administrators and allows them to innovate without changing the strategies, tactics, or traditional organization of policing (Willis et al., 2006). Other policing programs such as Community Oriented Policing (COP) readily encourage innovation, but require drastic changes in the way the police do business. COP stresses more discretion at the line officer level, thereby decreasing the power of police management, it advocates community involvement in the co-production of public safety by identifying problems (often noncriminal in nature) and contributing to their resolution, and it encourages a flattening of the traditional top-heavy police hierarchy. Compstat, by comparison, demands none of these things, and instead places emphasis on harnessing the power of the traditional command hierarchy to achieve crime reduction.

Second, police departments are under constant pressure to appear "cutting-edge," using state-of-the-are technologies to enhance their operations (Willis et al., 2006). Since Compstat has been touted by well known police leaders and political representatives, as well as professional police organizations, police departments who adopt this program are likely to achieve increased legitimacy within their own environment (Willis et al., 2006). As the rhetoric surrounding Compstat continues to promulgate its success, departments that use this program also benefit from this rhetoric. Departments that fail to adopt this program, or adopt some other police strategy like COP, may not receive the benefit of appearing to be cutting-edge, and may not receive as much organizational legitimacy.

Whether truly effective or not, it is likely that Compstat-like programs are going to be utilized by police departments quite expansively in the near future. In fact, Compstat has such widespread appeal that elements of the program are appearing in other government organizations. For example, Baltimore has created CitiStat, a program that utilizes Compstat-style features such as measuring outcomes and holding managers accountable. But CitiStat applies to all city agencies and is not focused squarely on police (Clines, 2001). The problem with increased use of Compstat-like programs, of course, is that they are largely adopted with an inherent belief in their effectiveness, which may result in unintended or unanticipated outcomes. Already some research is demonstrating that Compstat can conflict with existing organizational values, and its potential is appreciably limited by traditional organizational constraints such as work shifts, shift assignments, and the agency's budget (Willis et al., 2003). Whether or not these challenges can be overcome remains in question.

Early Intervention Systems

Police agencies are also utilizing IT not only to enhance their crime-fighting capacity, but to also enhance internal accountability by combating police misconduct. We have already noted how Compstat increased police accountability by holding managers (e.g., precinct captains) responsible for developing solutions to crime problems, but Compstat does not monitor, nor is it intended to monitor, police misconduct. But in the wake of high-profile incidents – such as the infamous beating of Rodney King by Los Angeles police officers in the early 1990s, increasing civil litigation against police officers and their supervisors for mistreatment of citizens, and the proliferation of consent decrees to settle such lawsuits – police departments have great incentive to be concerned with misconduct. Many departments are now utilizing new strategies and tools to enhance agency accountability, such as critical incident reporting, accessible citizen complaint procedures and external monitoring by citizens, and early intervention systems (Walker, 2005). These strategies constitute a new paradigm in police accountability, and all involve some form of new or routine data collection and systematic analysis. Such analysis helps to produce a "fact-based picture" of what officers are doing, with the notion of identifying any behavioral problems in the department that merit some form of corrective action (Walker, 2005). Below, I cover in detail one of these tools as an example of this data-driven strategy for police accountability, early intervention systems.

Early warning (EW) systems, or early intervention (EI) systems as they are currently labeled, are behavior-monitoring systems used by police ad-

ministrators to identify officers who display symptoms of frequent misconduct and then to direct those officers to some form of intervention (e.g.,
counseling, retraining, etc.). This type of proactive intervention in officer
careers has the potential to prevent a substantial amount of police misconduct, especially as research has found that a small number of officers are
responsible for a disproportionate amount of misconduct (Harris, 2006).
A national evaluation of EI systems conducted by the Police Executive
Research Forum (Walker et al., 2000) concluded that, "[EI] systems are a
significant and growing aspect of American law enforcement. . . . " About
one-quarter of local police agencies serving populations of 50,000 or more
had some version of an EI system at the time of the survey in 1999, and
another 12% were planning such systems (Walker et al., 2000).

Specifically, EI systems gather data on various aspects of police performance, such as personnel complaints filed, use-of-force incidents, involvement in civil litigation, police vehicle accidents, and the like. These
indicators serve as selection criteria to identify potentially problematic
officers whose patterns of performance warrant intervention. Some systems
rely on only one indicator, such as personnel complaints, while others
utilize multiple criteria for selection. The EI system in Oakland, California
for example, utilizes 20 indicators, while the Minneapolis, Minnesota Police
Department relies only on citizen complaints (Walker, 2005). Many EI
systems function as simple "time-and-numbers" systems that provide specific
numerical thresholds over specific time periods for selection, such as three
personnel complaints in a 12-month period. Currently there is no consensus
among experts as to the optimal number of performance indicators to be
included in an EI system, nor is there consensus regarding the optimal
thresholds to be utilized for those selection criteria. Some departments,
however, do treat identification and selection of officers as two separate
stages, such that supervisors conduct a full review of officers who have
exceeded identification thresholds, and then discern whether those officers
indeed present problems that require intervention, or whether their activities have other legitimate explanations (Walker, 2005).

If an officer exceeds pre-defined thresholds that are used to indicate
problem behavior, he or she is flagged for an intervention. The intervention
can include a review by the officer's immediate supervisor, a training class
regarding particular tactics, or a recommendation that an officer seek
professional counseling. Generally, the intervention is based on a combination of deterrence and education (Walker et al., 2000). Some departments
have conducted interventions with classes of officers who were selected by

the EI system, but such interventions have met with difficulty. First, scheduling is a concern, and classes do not allow individual attention to individual problems. Second, bringing such officers together can give them a sense of solidarity as the "bad boy" group (Walker, 2005). Other departments provide for individualized interventions, and provide a specific list of programs to supervisors from which to choose. These can include stress management programs or other psychological services.

Once an officer receives a specified intervention, his or her performance is closely monitored following the intervention. This post-intervention period can be informal, with supervisors monitoring behavior for an unspecified period of time, or it can be formal, with specified conditions of monitoring, evaluation, and reporting for a specified time period (Walker et al., 2000).

It is interesting to note the similarity of EI systems to Compstat-like programs (Walker, 2005). Both attempt to increase accountability within an agency through systematic collection and analysis of data. Procedurally, both require managers to scan data to identify problems, develop responses to those problems, and follow-up on those responses. Both employ some form of IT, which is vital to the program's success. The only difference is that Compstat focuses on crime problems in the external environment, while EI systems focus on misconduct problems in the internal environment.

While certainly IT plays a vital role in EI systems, with data on officer performance entered into a preexisting database or combined with information from various other departmental systems (RMS, for example), the development of EI systems is in the early stages. A National Institute of Justice-sponsored evaluation by Walker and others (2000) in three police departments employing an EI system found reductions in the use of force and citizen complaints among officers following an EI intervention. This indicates some measure of effectiveness, but it is unclear yet whether such systems led officers to engage in less police activity in the post-intervention period as a means of avoiding citizen complaints, having to use force, or engaging in other actions that may flag them again for additional intervention (Worden et al., 2005).

Other issues with EI systems also remain in question. While police departments have been increasingly concerned about actively curtailing unwanted problematic behavior on the part of their officers, the validity of the selection criteria upon which these systems are based has not been established by research (Worden et al., 2003). Thus, one should remain skeptical that an officer with, say, three complaints in twelve months would continue to display problematic behavior in the absence of some EI system intervention. Moreover, the indicators of police misconduct that form the basis of EI systems are often ambiguous. The use of force, and even citizen complaints, could be expected to occur even when police perform their jobs properly. Also, many EI systems do not take into account other important factors – such as the nature of an officer's assignment – that may affect the likelihood that s/he will use force or be the subject of citizen complaints. Thus, many existing EI systems leave room for improvement.

There have also been documented problems with the planning and implementation of EI systems, as such systems require considerable investment of resources and administrative attention (Walker, 2005). If a department wishes to use multiple indicators for the selection criteria, it must determine where within the agency those indictors are to be found and devise a method for collecting those indicators for EI system purposes. For example, citizen complaint data may be stored in the internal affairs unit, while information on civil litigation may be stored in the legal department, and data on officers' sick leave may be stored in the accounting office. These divergent sources of data may be maintained on different IT systems, may reference that data based upon different officer identification criteria (e.g., officer name, or officer shield number, or officer Social Security number), and may be of vastly differing quality.

Once an EI system has been planned and implemented, it must be clear to managers how the program is to be used, and resources must be deployed for ongoing support to ensure it is viable. If the system does not hold a prominent place in the organization, it will lack effectiveness and may degrade into a symbolic gesture with little to no content (Walker et al., 2000). Presumably, EI systems will work best when they are part of an increasing trend to enhance accountability within an agency, and not simply regarded as a panacea for police misconduct.

CHALLENGES TO INFORMATION TECHNOLOGY IN POLICING

While IT improvements and data-driven police strategies certainly possess the potential to improve police performance and enhance police accountability, a number of obstacles must be overcome before such innovations realize their full potential. Some of these obstacles are technological, while others have more to do with the police themselves; but all of them limit or at least temper the impact that IT can have over all. I shall try to enumerate these obstacles here, but this list is by no means comprehensive or exhaustive.

Technological Issues

As was stated earlier, police are awash in data, and it is up to each particular agency to turn that data into useful information. A number of challenges impede this process, however, the first of which has to do with the accuracy of collected data (Dunworth, 2000). For any information to be useful, it must be accurate. If data is inaccurately recorded on a form by an officer, or if a data entry system allows for inaccurate recording of information, at the very least such errors can impede progress on other fronts, or at worst they can lead to poor tactical or strategic decision making. For example, if officers routinely enter in the wrong addresses for various crime incidents, it will prove difficult, if not impossible, to map those incidents for crime analysis purposes, to use the data for deployment of agency resources and personnel, or to ground other tactical decision making on this information.

Even if data is properly recorded, there are technological issues with how that data is shared within the agency or across other agencies. Many police departments have outdated computer systems and have neither the money nor expertise to update their computers or their software. Moreover, many departments make *ad hoc* changes to their existing systems as they try to backfit various technologies to their existing systems (Manning, 2003; Stroshine, 2005). This process results in a series of unrelated and incompatible technologies within the agency, such as: RMS, CAD, and MDT systems having no way to "talk" to each other; crime analysts having to extract data from RMS to enter by hand into their own databases for analytic purposes; and crimes reported and recorded not being linked to arrest records. Also, as police departments and other criminal justice agencies increasingly recognize the value of sharing information, compatibility of computer and software systems across agencies is a significant obstacle. Many departments have idiosyncratic systems specifically tailored to their agency, adopted without the forethought that such data would need to be shared with other systems. Thus, sharing information is often done by extracting data from one system, and then entering it, often by hand, into another. This process is tedious and time consuming, and it draws from agency resources that could be better deployed elsewhere.

Along with sharing information comes the concern of how that information is going to be utilized, and how that information, if confidential, can be protected. Traditionally, paper records were stored in a file cabinet in a police station. Such filing created a physical barrier and restricted access to those files. Police rarely shared the information they had, even with other law enforcement agencies. Now, police records are kept on computers, which may be networked to other systems and to the Internet. This technological change, combined with the increasing demand for police to share information with external bodies (for risk management purposes and increased cooperation with other law enforcement agencies), has changed the way information is distributed (Ericson and Haggerty, 1997). Data can quickly be made available for any who require it, provided there is some legitimate reason for its distribution. However, once police relinquish information – whether it is to another police agency, an insurance company, or a landlord inquiring about a potential tenant – control of that information is lost (Dunworth, 2000). This may or may not be a desirable standard, but neither the police nor the public has given much thought concerning policy on this matter.

Another related issue is protection of information. Any computer connected to the Internet can be subject to outside attack, either from computer viruses that can corrupt files or computer hackers who breach security looking for confidential information. National databases thought to have been safe from external attack have already been breached, and the police should also be concerned with the security of their files.

Organizational Issues

The potential for IT and other technologies is also limited by the police organization itself. There are few empirical studies of the effect of IT on policing, but those that exist note that the organization shapes IT as much as, and in many cases even more than, IT shapes the organization (Manning, 1992). Thus, any evaluation of the potential for IT must be concerned with more than just technical capacity – one must consider the social, psychological, political, and cultural factors that exist within an organization and how it may impact any new technology. As Chan (2001, p. 147) writes: "The impact of technology on policing is dependent on how technology interacts with existing cultural values, management styles, work practices, and technical capabilities." To consider only technology and its capabilities will result in an overly optimistic view of the ways in which these various technologies, including IT, can transform or "revolutionize" police agencies in the future.

Not only is IT limited by the police organization, it is shaped by police work itself. No matter how much a police agency attempts to adhere to new police philosophies such as COP or POP, it will never escape the fact that much of police work is reactive, and driven by emergent crises. As Bittner (1972) concisely expressed, police work comprises "that-which-not-ought-to-be-happening-about-which-someone-ought-to-be-doing-something-NOW." Thus, police work will always be reactive to some degree, and technologies that can be employed pragmatically and immediately by officers in accordance with traditional practices are those that will be (or at least perceived to be) most useful. It is also likely that this technology will be the least disruptive (e.g., new weapons, breathalyzers, etc.).

Other technologies that shape decisions or choices of officers (e.g., CAD systems, electronic report filing) are probably less useful to officers, since they limit discretion in what officers report and how they report it. Such technologies are most likely to be viewed with suspicion by officers, and may even be perceived as threatening (Manning, 2003). Thus, officers may limit the information they record, especially if such information leaves the officer vulnerable to lawsuits or departmental discipline. The bottom line: police officers will tend to manipulate, adapt, or somehow bend technologies to fit their traditional operations, not because of any desire to be overly subversive, but because the pressure to respond quickly and effectively to calls for service demands as much.

Finally, other technologies that have little day-to-day impact, such as those that enhance strategic decision making (e.g., crime analysis and mapping), are likely to be viewed by officers as distant, irrelevant, and trivial (Manning, 2003). As Manning (2003, p. 137) writes, "In many respects, the 'technologies' of problem solving, crime analysis, and prevention, crime mapping and other more analytic tools, are honored in the abstract but seldom if at all used by officers." As stated before, police departments have tremendous pressure to appear state-of-the-art, but adoption of cutting-edge technologies by a department may have little impact on the day-to-day operations of the patrol officer, who are still the primary sources of information for any police agency.

CONCLUSION

While IT has the potential to enhance police work, and perhaps fundamentally alter traditional police practices, there is little evidence that IT has revolutionized policing when compared to the earlier eras of policing and the adoption of the telephone, two-way radio, and automobile. To the extent that the newer forms of IT mentioned throughout this chapter have contributed to policing, they appear to have largely enhanced traditional practices. Still, some research has shown changes in police time use and skill levels among younger officers, as well as positive attitudes toward IT innovation (Chan, 2001). Other studies conducted outside the U.S. have demonstrated improvement in detective work through IT (Harper, 1991), and the research by Ericson and Haggerty (1997), who argue police information gathering is being increasingly influenced by external institutions, is certainly provocative.

Whether IT systems can be adapted to readily serve police information needs for COP, POP, and other new police roles or functions (e.g., intelligence gathering) remains to be seen. Perhaps as IT becomes more widespread, less expensive, and more user-friendly, we will see less resistance to such technology by police officers. Nevertheless, we must bear in mind that police work is unlikely to radically change in the future, and thus IT will most likely continue to serve police needs in short-term, tactical decision making, despite its potential to accomplish a great deal more.

NOTES

1. Technology is defined here as the means by which raw materials are transformed into outputs (Manning, 1992). Information technology is defined here as the development, installation, and implementation of computer systems and their applications for the distribution of information.

REFERENCES

Bittner, E. (1972). *The functions of police in modern society.* Rockville, MD: National Institute of Mental Health.

Boba, R. (2005). *Crime analysis and crime mapping.* Thousand Oaks, CA: Sage.

Bratton, W. (with P. Knobler) (1998). *Turnaround: How America's top cop reversed the crime epidemic.* New York: Random House.

Chan, J. B. (2001). The technological game: How information technology is transforming police practice. *Journal of Criminal Justice, 1,* 139-159.

Clines, F. X. (2001, June 10). Baltimore uses databank to wake up city workers. *The New York Times,* Section 1, p. 24.

Cordner, G. W., Scarborough, K. E., & Sheehan, R. (2004). *Police administration* (5th ed.). Cincinnati: Anderson, LexisNexis Group.

Craig-Moreland, D. E. (2004). Technological challenges and innovation in police patrolling. In Q. C. Thurman & J. Zhao (Eds.), *Contemporary policing: Controversies, challenges, and solutions*. Los Angeles, CA: Roxbury.

Dunworth, T. (2000). Criminal justice and the IT revolution. In J. Horney, R. Peterson, D. MacKenzie, J. Martin, & D. Rosenbaum (Eds.), *Policies, processes, and decisions of the criminal justice system*, volume 3 of *Criminal Justice 2000*. Washington, DC: U.S. National Institute of Justice.

Eck, J. E., Chainey, S., Cameron, J. G., Leitner, M., & Wilson, R. E. (2005). *Mapping crime: Understanding hot spots*. Washington, DC: U.S. National Institute of Justice.

Eck, J. E., & Maguire, E. R. (2000). Have changes in policing reduced violent crime? An assessment of the evidence. In A. Blumstein, J. Wallman, & D. Farrington (Eds.), *The crime drop in America*. Cambridge, UK: Cambridge University Press.

Ericson, R. V., & Haggerty K. D. (1997). *Policing the risk society*. Toronto, CAN: University of Toronto Press.

Geller, W. A. (1997). Suppose we were really serious about police departments becoming learning organizations? *NIJ Journal # 243*, 2-8.

Goldstein, H. (1979). Improving policing: A problem-oriented approach. *Crime & Delinquency, 25*, 236-258.

Greene, J. R., & Mastrofski, S. D. (1988). *Community policing: Rhetoric or reality?* New York: Praeger.

Harper, R. R. (1991). The computer game: Detectives, suspects, and technology. *British Journal of Criminology, 31*, 292-307.

Harries, K. (1999). *Mapping crime: Principle and practice*. Washington, DC: U.S. National Institute of Justice.

Harris, E. (2003). *311 for non-emergencies: Helping communities one call at a time*. Washington, DC: U.S. Department of Justice, Community Oriented Policing Services.

Harris, C. J. (2006). *Police misconduct careers: Lessons from a developmental perspective*. Unpublished doctoral dissertation, University at Albany, New York.

Hickman, M. J., & Reaves, B. A. (2001). *Local police departments, 1999*. Washington, DC: U.S. Department of Justice, Office of Justice Programs, Bureau of Justice Statistics.

Hickman, M. J., & Reaves, B. A. (2003). *Local police departments, 2000*. Washington, DC: U.S. Department of Justice, Office of Justice Programs, Bureau of Justice Statistics.

Maguire, E. R., & King, W. R. (2004). Trends in the policing industry. *Annals of the American Academy of Political and Social Science, 593*, 15-41.

Manning, P. K. (1984). Community policing. *American Journal of Police, 3*, 205-227.

Manning, P. K. (1988). *Symbolic communication: Signifying calls and the police response*. Cambridge, MA: MIT Press.

Manning, P. K. (1992). Information technologies and the police. In M. Tonry & N. Morris (Eds.), *Modern policing*, volume 15 of *Crime and justice: A review of research*. Chicago: University of Chicago Press.

Manning, P. K. (2003). *Policing contingencies*. Chicago: University of Chicago Press.

NIJ Journal #253 (2006). Washington, DC: U.S. National Institute of Justice.

O'Shea, T. C., & Nicholls, K. (2003). *Crime analysis in America: Findings and recommendations*. Washington, DC: U.S. Department of Justice, Office of Community Oriented Policing Services.

Pattavina, A. (2005). Geographic information systems and mapping in criminal justice agencies. In A. Pattavina (Ed.), *Information technology and the criminal justice system*. Thousand Oaks, CA: Sage.

Paulsen, D. J., & Robinson, M. B. (2004). *Spatial aspects of crime: Theory and practice*. New Jersey: Allyn & Bacon.

Pelfry, W. V. (2005). Geographic information systems applications for police. In R. G. Dunham & G. P. Alpert (Eds.), *Critical issues in policing* (5th ed.). Longrove, IL: Waveland Press.

Reuland, M. M. (1997). *Information management and crime analysis: Practitioners' recipes for success*. Washington, DC: Police Executive Research Forum.

Rich, T. (1999). Mapping the path to problem solving. *NIJ Journal, 241*, 2-9.

Sherman, L. W., Gartin, P. R., & Buerger, M. E. (1989). Hot spots and predatory crime: Routine activities and the criminology of place. *Criminology, 27*, 27-55.

Silverman, E. B. (1999). *NYPD battles crime: Innovative strategies in policing*. Boston: Northeastern University Press.

Stroshine, M. S. (2005). Information technology innovations in policing. In R. G. Dunham & G. P. Alpert (Eds.), *Critical issues in policing* (5th ed.). Longrove, IL: Waveland Press.

Sulewski, K. D. (1997). Faxback response: Previous question: How has the Internet helped your agency? *FBI Law Enforcement Bulletin, 66*, 23-25.

Walker, S. (1984). "Broken windows" and fractured history-the use and misuse of history in recent police patrol analysis. *Justice Quarterly, 1*, 75-90.

Walker, S. (2005). *The new world of police accountability*. Thousand Oaks, CA: Sage.

Walker, S., Alpert, G. P., & Kenney, D. J. (2000). *Responding to the problem police officer: A national study of early warning systems*. Washington, DC: U.S. National Institute of Justice.

Weisburd, D., Mastrofski, S. D., Greenspan, R., & Willis, J. J. (2003). Reforming to preserve: Compstat and strategic problem solving in American policing. *Criminology & Public Policy, 2*, 421-455.

Weisburd, D., Mastrofski, S. D., Greenspan, R., & Willis, J. J. (2004). *The growth of Compstat in American policing*. Washington, DC: Police Foundation.

Willis, J. J., Mastrofski, S. D., & Weisburd, D. (2003). *Compstat in practice: An in-depth analysis of three cities*. Washington, DC: Police Foundation.

Willis, J. J., Mastrofski, S. D., & Weisburd, D. (2006). The myth that Compstat reduces crime and transforms police organizations. In R. Bohm & J. Walker (Eds.), *Demystifying crime and criminal justice*. Los Angeles, CA: Roxbury.

Worden, R. E., Pratte, M, Dorn, S., Harris, C. J., & Schlief, S. (2003). *Problem officers, problem behavior, and early warning systems*. Paper presented at the Academy of Criminal Justice Sciences.

Worden, R. E., Pratte, M, Dorn, S., Harris, C. J., & Schlief, S. (2005). *Intervening with problem officers: An evaluation of an early warning system intervention*. Paper presented at the American Society of Criminology, Toronto, Canada, November.

Zaworski, M. J. (2006). Automated information sharing: Does it help law enforcement officers work better? *NIJ Journal, 253*, 25-26.

8. THE COURTS AND HARD TECHNOLOGY: APPLYING TECHNOLOGICAL SOLUTIONS TO LEGAL ISSUES

by

Eric T. Bellone, Assistant Professor

Roxbury Community College

THE BEGINNINGS OF HARD TECHNOLOGY IN THE COURTS

The integration of hard technology in the American court system is presently altering many courtroom practices. Many new types of hard technologies – including, but not limited to, computers, laptops, video cameras, and video displays – are being used more and more. Unfortunately, it is difficult to define hard technology as it relates to the courts. "Courtroom technology," like the hard technology that goes into them, is itself a generic expression used to describe numerous forms of technology that may or may not be collectively present in any given courtroom (Lederer, 2005).

For the purposes of this chapter, hard technology (as opposed to soft technology), is defined as the technological devices and tangible objects created and used to meet a need. Computers, video conferencing cameras, and lab facilities are examples of hard technology. Courts that use hard technology are collectively called "wired courts" or "cyber courts." According to Exon (2002, p. 2): "Cyber courts, also known as virtual courts or cyber tribunals, assume a variety of appearances because they have no established definition. Some cybercourts are designed for educational purposes. Some courts may claim the status of cybercourt because they maintain Web sites for informational purposes and/or accept electronic filings. Other courts are coined 'cybercourts' because the courtrooms are set up with evidence presentation technology."

Courts have always used some type of hard technology. Until recently those hard technologies have been decidedly "low-tech," such as typewriters and word processors used for document preparation, photographic enlarge-ments used for the presentation of evidence or summation of data, or simply pencils and paper for a jury's trial notebooks.

In the late 1960s, the Federal Judicial Center (FJC) and the Administra-tive Office of the U.S. Courts (AO) shepherded hard technology into the federal courts, establishing early versions of electronic docketing and case management systems while evaluating their use and effectiveness. The FJC and AO continue to introduce, integrate, and evaluate hard technology in federal courts today (Bermant, 2005).

The birth of "high-tech" hard technologies occurred in the 1960s. Some experts pinpoint the exact location as the Court of Common Pleas in Sandusky, Ohio, with Judge James McCrystal presiding. Judge McCrystal sought to reduce his expanding docket of cases by taking depositions by video. The depositions were later edited under court guidance, and with proper stipulations by both parties that such edits were acceptable, then spliced together for the jury. These trials were later called Pre-Recorded Video Taped Trials (PRVTT), the first large-scale, well-documented use of modern hard technology in the American courts. Other courts soon fol-lowed suit. The Superior Court for San Francisco County, California permit-ted the use of PRVTT technology in the case of *Liggons v. Hanisko* (Bermant, 2005). This use of hard technology was well documented by social scientists from the Battelle Seattle Research Center and the University of Washington and presented to the National Center for State Courts (NCSC). To this day the NCSC is significantly involved with the testing and implementation of hard technological advancement in the courts (Bermant, 2005, pp. 2-3).

From the beginning of the information age it has been clear that hard technology has had and will continue to have a profound effect on the courts. Because of cutbacks in court budgets, the courts have been asked to be more efficient and effective with fewer resources. This has resulted in an even greater reliance on hard technology to improve the operation and presentation of information in the courtroom (Byrne and Buzawa, 2004). The need to do more with less has spurred interest and research in the application of hard technology and the courts. Such interest has also opened the way to discussions concerning the opportunities and chal-lenges that hard technology introduces to the administration of the courts on the federal, state, and local level (Byrne and Buzawa, 2004).

Opportunities, Challenges, and Controversy

The ever-changing face of hard technology offers the courts exciting prospects, opportunities and challenges. For example, it opens the possibilities for multi-jurisdictional/multi-courtroom hearings, allowing courts to use a more comprehensive array of hard technology than ever before. Pretrial matters of discovery, legal research, and case preparation are also being altered by hard technology. In addition, the presentation of evidence and remote testimony offer new avenues for courts to conduct business at trial.

The reception of hard technology is currently being tested in courtrooms across the country, and the reception has in the aggregate been favorable. According to anecdotal evidence, presenting evidence using hard technology to a judge or jury has met with substantial approval, and trials have moved quickly and efficiently (Lederer, 1997). Further, studies show that jurors retain only 15% of what they hear in the courtroom as compared to 85% of what they both see and hear on videotape in the jury room (Lederer, 1997).

Hard technology enables the storing and transporting of information, which liberates the courts from having to gather all parties in the same location to view, review, analyze, and/or utilize information relevant to a proceeding. Communications and information can be immediately transmitted and shared among all parties in the court system, who no longer have to be in the same courtroom, to make decisions in a constitutionally speedy manner. Hard technology eliminates of the need for concurrency of time and space, and changes courtroom practices and procedures at a fundamental level. To be effective, such hard technology must be available to all parties, and all parties must be well versed in their application and use.

Yet the introduction of science into the courtroom remains controversial. The admission and impact of fingerprint, DNA, and medical evidence in the courts remain contentious. As hard technological capabilities become more extensive, they will have growing impact on the very nature of the American court system. Courtrooms will become equipped with more and better hard technologies, and counsel will be able to present testimony and evidence with greater effectiveness to emphasize their points. The judge can then use such technology to assess any discrepancies between counsel's arguments and legal texts (Lederer, 1997). As these hard technological changes in the courts become more pervasive, not only will their impact on efficiency and effectiveness be researched, but their impact on the role of the courts as a branch of government and on constitutional rights will be assessed as well.

The Rise of the Cybercourts

The federal judiciary has recently embraced the technological revolution, and select courts are now equipped with state-of-the-art technology to aid in trial presentations. Before the judiciary made these improvements, litigants had to keep pace with the technological advances themselves, and often at a great cost. The installation of new technology into a courtroom serves to equalize what would otherwise be a "digital divide" if the parties provided their own systems (Heintz, 2002, p. 1). Two projects in particular are examples of some of the most comprehensive use to date of an integrated high-tech courtroom using hard technology. William and Mary School of Law and the National Center for State Courts have instituted the Courtroom 21 Project, which develops and tests the use of hard technology in the courtroom. The Ninth Judicial Circuit in Orlando, Florida has undertaken a similar project, the Courtroom 23+ Project, in the Orange County Courthouse. Using these projects as benchmarks, we can explore how significant areas of law will be altered by hard technology.

The Courtroom 21 Project (2006) is a showcase and test lab of hard technology in the court system that has received national and international attention. Started in September 1993, the Courtroom 21 Project is an ongoing research center adapting and integrating some of the newest hard technology as it becomes commercially available. One of its goals is to determine how hard technology can improve different aspects of the legal system.

The Courtroom 21 Project has been actively researching and testing how hard technology affects court procedures, prevailing law, and court custom. The primary evaluation technique has been mock trials augmented by hard technology. These lab trial cases are designed to test the use and effect of specific technologies on legal processes such as taking remote testimony, presentation of evidence, and jury deliberations. Such lab trial cases also test the efficiency and capabilities of the hard technology and the effects on judges, court personnel, attorneys, and juries (Courtroom 21 Project, 2006).

In its 13-year history, the Courtroom 21 Project has proven to be very successful: it has received a Foundation for the Improvement of Justice

Award for its work in the arena of technology and the court system. The project has also received attention from the American Bar Association, and judges, court administrators, attorneys, and law students across the country. Moreover, British, Australian, Canadian, and Mexican court researchers have also viewed the project as an intriguing marriage of jurisprudence and technology. Its state-of-the-art courtroom and conference center have hosted many legal and criminal justice groups, including the Department of Justice, the American Bar Association section of Criminal Justice and Litigation, and the International Working Conference on Technology Augmented Litigation. Not only does the Courtroom 21 Project test and showcase the possible uses and integration of hard technology in the courtroom, but it discusses the ability and desirability of altering the substantive, procedural, and evidentiary rules to accommodate such changes (Courtroom 21 Project, 2006).

Inspired by the Courtroom 21 Project, Orlando, Florida's Courtroom 23+ Project (2006) is a similar high-technology courtroom operated by the Ninth Judicial Circuit at the Orange County Courthouse. Officially opened in May 1999, the courtroom seeks to achieve an optimum combination of the most up-to-date hard technology with the legal process. Designed by a team including judges, court administrators, court clerks, county facilities management personnel, the State's Attorney's Office and public defenders, the courtroom offers a state-of-the-art evidence presentation system, video conferencing, Internet and remote broadcast capabilities, realtime and digital court reporting, audio and video monitors in an integrated format (Courtroom 23+, 2006). The Courtroom 23+ Project strives to parallel the Courtroom 21 Project as one of the country's most technologically advanced and integrated courtrooms.

While the Courtroom 21 and Courtroom 23+ Projects offer the most up-to-date and integrated courtrooms, other "high tech" courtrooms have sprung up across the country. One of the more significant experiments is the Michigan Cyber Court, which was launched in 2003 and which will become arguably the country's first completely "virtual" court. This cyber court is not yet operational: it is still a work in progress. When it does become operational, the court will not be limited to a "brick and mortar" location; it will operate completely in cyberspace using the Internet. All court documents will be filed on line, appearances and testimony will take place exclusively through videoconferencing and webcasts, and correspondence will be by e-mail. Judges, attorneys, witnesses, and all court personnel involved in a "traditional" trial will all participate via computer with no central location for the virtual court. The training of judges, attorneys, and court personnel has begun and the project will be phased in over time. Information on the progress of the cyber court may be obtained at the project web site (www.michigancybercourt.net). The Michigan Cyber Court experiment is arguably the most ambitious use of hard technology in the courts to date (Pointe, 2002).

Even with the bold high-tech courtroom experiments nationwide and the accolades they have received, technological change has come slowly to the courts. The courts, hidebound by tradition and custom, often resist innovations and change that is more readily accepted by other segments of the criminal justice system. Many court procedures have a pedigree going back over a thousand years. Further, American courts have a tradition of solemn dignity that many compare to organized religion. When Supreme Court Justice Stephen Breyer dedicated a new Boston courthouse, he argued that it should be "accessible to civic life, as intensely dramatic as theater, and as rich in liturgical significance as a cathedral. Nothing should be done in the design of courthouses to impoverish these aspirations" (Bermant, 1999, p. 3). As technology strives to streamline the court system by making it more efficient, traditionalists within the court system frequently argue that technology detracts from the essential dignity and formality of the court and its legal process.

Moreover, American courts are not merely an institution of government, but an actual branch of the government, and the very " . . . physical seat of judicial authority" (Bermant, 1999, p. 6). Traditionalists maintain that changes within the courts potentially alter the very nature of American government, and that the delicate checks and balances of its three branches must be carefully weighed and analyzed against changes brought by hard technology before they are introduced. The constitutional protections under the Bill of Rights, the rules of criminal procedure, and the rules of evidence are all affected by the introduction of hard technology into the courts. The right to face one's accuser(s), rather than a digital facsimile of that person transmitted from another location, is one issue. The right to handle actual evidence, and not digital reproductions of evidence, is another. As hard technology is introduced into the court system, many such issues, over and beyond its effectiveness and efficiency, will be considered.

This chapter focuses on the "nuts and bolts" of hard technology operations as they relate to legal issues. Because change comes slower to the court system than to other segments of the criminal justice system, there exist only fledgling studies to assess hard technology in the courts. Further, until recently such studies have been largely informal, empirically assessing if such technologies can be introduced and integrated successfully while the court conducts its business. Let us now focus on some of the major initiatives to introduce hard technology into the courts and the more prevalent legal issues that hard technology alleviates and challenges (see Table 1).

Pretrial Proceedings and Trial Preparation

Hard technology is changing the way attorneys prepare for court. In pretrial terms, the areas where hard technology has the biggest impact are client/witness contact meetings, depositions, and legal research. Having courts imbed hard technology into the courtroom itself, as in the Courtroom 21 and Courtroom 23+ projects, is beneficial for all. It allows a court trial to be more efficient and effective, and for the parties it levels the playing field since small firms and solo practitioners will not have to afford the hard technology necessary to compete with large firms or government agencies for a technological edge (Heintz, 2002).

Meeting with clients and witnesses as attorneys prepare for trial is often a logistical challenge. Hard technology has brought concurrency of time and space to this aspect of trial preparation. "Historically, the telephone served as a traditional alternative to face-to-face meetings. Up-to-date technology can provide the benefits of face-to-face meetings combined with the benefits of telephone and fax machine conferences" (Epstein, 2004, p. 3). Video conferences and the use of interactive streaming video over the Internet are improving attorney/client/witness contact. One technology survey revealed that most attorneys have not used most forms of hard technology, including videoconferencing, which was not available at their firms. For those attorneys who do use videoconferencing, the most popular use was for client contact rather than courtroom use (ABA, 2002).

Depositions are a method of pretrial discovery which consist of "a statement of a witness under oath, taken in question and answer form as it would be in court, with opportunity given to the adversary to be present and cross-examine, with all this reported and transcribed stenographically" (James and Hazard, 1977, sec. 6.3). Processing the raw information uncovered by lengthy, often multiple series of depositions is now made easier by hard technology.

> Discovery depositions are often a critical aspect of case investigations and case preparation. An ideal deposition provides counsel not only

Table 1: Types and Uses of Hard Technology

HARD TECHNOLOGY	DESCRIPTION	PRIMARY USES
CD-ROM	Compact disk on which a large amount of read-only memory data is stored.	Legal Research
Desktop Computer	Personal computer for use on a standard-size desk.	Legal Research
Laptop Computer	Small, portable personal computer that can operate for short periods of time on a battery.	Legal Research Evidence presentation
Internet Connection	Wired or wireless porthole for access to the World Wide Web (Internet).	Legal Research Evidence presentation
Real Time Transcription	Transcription of deposition or courtroom testimony that is virtually simultaneous. • Computer-Assisted Transcription (CAT). • Communication Access Realtime Translation (CART).	Depositions/ Witness testimony
Video Camera	Device for the transmission of visual images stored on magnetic tape.	Depositions/ Witness testimony Evidence presentation
Digital Video Camera	Device for the transmission of visual images via digital signal and storage.	Depositions/ Witness testimony Evidence presentation
Video Conferencing	Remote meeting via visual transmission.	Depositions/ Witness testimony Evidence presentation
Stored Testimony	• Video Tape-Video signals stored on magnetic tape. • Digital Storage-Video signals stored in a computer.	Evidence presentation

Table 1 *(continued)*

HARD TECHNOLOGY	DESCRIPTION	PRIMARY USES
Document Camera	A specialized camera for the projection and storage of a document or piece of evidence.	Evidence presentation
Video Monitor	A receiving device for the display and viewing of data. • Cathode Ray Tube • Plasma	Depositions/ Witness testimony Evidence presentation
Interpreting System	System for the translation of one language to another.	Depositions/ Witness testimony
Integrated Lectern	A lectern that serves as a control panel for multiple hard technology devices.	Evidence presentation
Annotation Equipment	Equipment that allows for the alteration and/or highlighting of data without permanently changing the data. • Touch Screen • Light Pen	Depositions/ Witness testimony Evidence presentation
Braille System	A system that translates written and spoken testimony into the Braille system for the blind.	Depositions/ Witness testimony Evidence presentation
Hearing Devices	Audio devices that enhance the hearing ability of court personnel, witnesses, or jurors. • Microphones • Headphones	Depositions/ Witness testimony Evidence presentation
Virtual Reality	A realistic simulation of reality using a computer via interactive hardware and software.	All types of presentation

with raw information which can be read and electronically searched for comprehensive discovery purposes, but which also can be used persuasively at trial. To accomplish all these goals, the wise deposing lawyer will use a court reporter who uses "CAT," Computer Assisted-Transcription at the deposition. CAT . . . yields an electronically searchable computerized transcript in addition to the traditional paper transcript. At the same time, a contemporaneous audio/video record should be made. In the event that the deposition is used at trial, whether on the merits or for impeachment, the more persuasive video deposition should be used. Further, there are an increasing number of firms, especially court reporting firms, which can create a unified CD-Rom disk containing the audio, video, and computerized transcript. At trial, counsel can use a TV – particularly a large screen projection television – to show the video taped deposition testimony as the synchronized transcript scrolls by. (Lederer, 1997, pp. 2-3)

Hard technology is an increasingly popular way for attorneys to conduct legal research, proving to be efficient and cost effective. CD-ROM libraries are available for nearly all legal specialties and state laws and regulations, and CD-ROM library products can be purchased and updated for a monthly maintenance or license fee. CD-ROM virtual libraries are most beneficial for small law firms, enabling them to gain access to library sources carried by large law firms and government agencies. CD-ROMs are small, inexpensive, and portable, which makes them financially and easy to use (Epstein, 2004).

The number of attorneys using hard technology during pretrial proceedings is relatively high. Attorneys who take their computers into court tend to use them in some form of "litigation support." Among lawyers who use laptops in the courtroom, 67.6% of small firm lawyers indicated a use for litigation support, compared to 87.7% of large firm lawyers (Heintz, 2002). As hard technology becomes more affordable and ever more user-friendly, this trend will undoubtedly continue.

Hard Technology in the Courtroom

Hard technology is changing the way business is conducted in the courtroom, as it offers alternatives for visual presentations as well as information in data-intensive cases. Court system personnel believe that jurors are more responsive to electronically presented material, and they seem to retain more information than in traditionally presented cases (Heintz, 2002). Presenting hard copies of documents, photographs, and enlargements will be used less and less as hard technology offers more effective and efficient ways of presenting data.

Hard technology is especially suited to viewing evidence more efficiently. Visual presentations that illustrate or demonstrate data and situations can be presented with more accuracy and impact. The evidence presented might include documents, photographs, x-rays, or 3-D representations of objects and situations relevant to the case. The evidence is centrally stored in a technology system accessed and operated by the attorney from a centralized podium. Monitors using touch-screen technology can be effective in highlighting images or events (by either the attorney or witness) depicted on the screen for closer scrutiny. Digitized video, DVD, or VHS cassette tapes can also be used to present evidence (Courtroom 23+, 2006).

Video monitors strategically placed around the courtroom can be directly connected to any outside site by fiber optic line or cable, which can then be connected to any ISDN site on the Internet or any remote location through digital camera. An ISDN is a circuit-switched telephone network system designed to allow digital transmission of voice and data over ordinary copper telephone lines, resulting in better quality and higher speeds. In videoconferencing, this provides simultaneous voice, video and text transmission between videoconferencing systems, which offers everyone in the courtroom the ability to simultaneously view the same evidence. For example, while a witness testifies and examines a piece of evidence, the judge, opposing counsel, the jury, the court reporter, and the courtroom observers can all view the evidence simultaneously rather than passing the evidence from hand to hand. Reproductions do not have to be made, and the original document can be viewed in an effective and efficient manner. Furthermore, it is likely that the court and the jurors will understand and retain more witness testimony if they can both hear the witness testimony and view the evidence at the same time (Courtroom 23+, 2006).

Hard technology is also making court proceedings more accessible to public viewing through the use of web cameras and streaming video. Unlike the traditional courtroom sketch artists or television cameras in the courtroom, which can contribute to a circus-like atmosphere (as during the O. J. Simpson murder trial in the 1990s), web cameras and streaming video offer a less disruptive way of having a large number of people view any legal proceeding. The U.S. Supreme Court currently allows the audio recording of its proceedings. The U.S. Congress has a bill pending that would allow for video recording as well, although many Supreme Court justices have voiced disapproval. It will be interesting to revisit this issue should the bill become law and then be subsequently reviewed by the Supreme Court.

The examination of witnesses from remote locations is also possible with video cameras and real-time streaming video through the Internet. This hard technology can "produce" previously unavailable witnesses in the traditional courtroom. This compression of the concurrency of time and space can allow a trial to take place in a more timely fashion, saving participants a tremendous amount of time and money spent on travel and preparation to be in a specific location at a specific time.

Strategically, attorneys will make a judgment call on whether to avail themselves of video technology in a case. The visual strength of a witness will be assessed before video is possibly used instead of the more traditional written deposition recorded only in a transcript. Video can be a double-edged sword. An inopportune expression, an extended pause, or an ill-conceived demonstration by the witness that would be undetectable in a transcript can prove devastating when captured on film. The very strengths sought through the use of video can turn into a liability for the party sponsoring the witness (Jones, 1996).

Of course, not all witnesses can or should avail themselves of such technology. As a general rule, the more important the witness, the more likely that witness will be required to appear in person. When technology is used to allow important (key, or expert) witnesses in the proceedings to "appear in court" via telephone or video technology (synchronous audio or audiovisual display), controversy could erupt (Bermant 1999). The defendant's constitutional right to confront witnesses and evidence may also become an issue when utilizing such technology.

Counsel can use hard technology to present evidence and information in their cases, or the court itself can introduce it to be used by all parties. The latter is the concept behind the Courtroom 21 Project and the Courtroom 23+ Project, initiatives that offer technology-based solutions to age-old problems of efficiency and time management in today's courts.

William and Mary School of Law's Courtroom 21 Project made the first use of immersive virtual reality for the jury in their 2002 lab trial *United States v. New Life MedTech*. This innovative use of hard technology allowed the jury, wearing special goggles, to "step into the shoes" of key witnesses and participants. This same lab trial used instant messaging and computer compression techniques to compile the most comprehensive court record available to be used by the jury during deliberations to arrive at a verdict (Courtroom 21 Project, 2006, Experiments and Research).

Having the court itself make available hard technology in the courtroom for the presentation of evidence can eliminate many of the obstacles that prevented the presentation of evidence through hard technology in the past. In traditional courtrooms where hard technology was not available, counsel would ask the judge's permission not only to use the technology, but also questions pertaining to the positioning of cables, wires, screens, etc., so they did not create a distraction or unsafe situation. Often, attorneys feared that hard technology and its technological glitches would make unavailable, delay, or lessen the impact of evidence presented at trial. Further, where technology was not made available by the court, counsel had to make allowances for the installation, operation, support, and removal of whatever technology was introduced into court for that trial. The logistics and expense of such preparations probably had a chilling effect on the use of hard technology in the courtroom. The Courtroom 21 Project and the Courtroom 23+ Project initiatives eliminate this kind of anxiety, logistical headache, and expense.

It is important to note that presenting evidence and exhibits through hard technology does not replace the evidence and exhibits, but merely offers a different way to observe such evidence during trial. The use of hard technology in presenting evidence promotes efficiency for the court and effectiveness for counsel, but it is never a replacement for the original evidence. The judge, opposing counsel, and the jurors will still be able to observe, handle, and/or inspect the actual physical/hard evidence in deciding the case.

The ultimate goal of hard technology in the courtroom, as envisioned by the Courtroom 21 Project and the Courtroom 23+ Project initiatives, is to have any attorney place a document or data set into evidence and have that evidence simultaneously viewed by all trial participants. This concurrency of time and space marks a revolution in courtroom procedure.

Hard Technology in Multi-jurisdictional and Multi-court Hearings

Black's Law Dictionary defines "jurisdiction" as, "the power to hear or determine a case." Hard technology offers parties the ability to be in multiple jurisdictions (locations) while one centralized court hears and decides a case. Courtroom trials are highly-focused events that have profound consequences for the litigants. They are uniquely formalized and stylized, relative to other public or private decision-making processes (Bermant, 1999). Multiple jurisdictions will call for the need of multiple courtrooms to bring together the different parties involved in multi-jurisdictional/multi-court hearings.

Hard technology offers the ability to enhance communication and joint resolution. The use of videoconferencing and exhibiting over the Internet present some of the best examples of testable technological solutions in the introduction of hard technology to the courtroom, though not without some flaws. The Courtroom 21 Project has researched and mock-trial tested many different trial issues and proceedings, bringing together many parties from different locations in order to assess the various difficulties and possibilities. For example, a mock trial of an al-Qaeda terrorist was designed to test the admissibility of a potential witness's testimony; a child abduction case involving parties from the United States and Mexico tested the multi-jurisdictional/multi-court concept of dispute resolution; an international construction contract mediation case involving four different nations tested the uniting of multiple parties/participants from several different nations; and an air piracy trial was also mock-tested (Courtroom 21 Project, 2006, Experiments and Research).

The strengths and weaknesses of the hard technology used were empirically assessed. "Mock virtual trials have shown that these new court technologies are subject to technological glitches that can weaken case presentation" (Pointe, 2002, p. 12). Not only are these technologies sometimes "quirky," but they must work together seamlessly in an adversarial environment where participants' constitutional liberties (or their lives) may be decided. The mock trials being conducted around the country, and particularly in the Courtroom 21 Project, are the most ambitious to date; they are invaluable to testing and improving hard technology in the courtroom.

Every proceeding has diverse issues that need to be addressed. The Courtroom 21 and Courtroom 23+ projects conduct annual experiments to test the innovative use of technology for use throughout the nation as hard technology becomes more available.

There are many advantages to using hard technology in multi-jurisdictional/multi-court situations, particularly the savings in time and expense. Assembling all parties, evidence, and witnesses in one location can take an inordinate amount of time in a complex case. Often, the necessity for witnesses to travel to a common location is the most time-consuming aspect of a trial or hearing (It is not the travel itself that takes the most time, but rather the preparation witnesses must make to attend to their private and professional business prior to an extended period away from home.) The expense of assembling all parties, evidence, and witnesses can be excessive. Expert witnesses require payment and expenses, and traditional witnesses who must leave their normal lives to give testimony far from home for an extended time period often pay high costs in lost opportunity.

The concurrency of time and space that hard technology provides in multi-jurisdictional/multi-court situations liberates courts and parties from the time and expense of travel. Also, the use of videoconferencing and the Internet with real-time web cameras and streaming video create an environment that allows parties to resolve issues and the court to make decisions on cases from remote locations.

Use of Hard Technology during Jury Deliberations

The use of hard technology is now permitted for jury deliberations. As technology becomes more pervasive, court administrators, legal scholars, and social scientists are looking into how hard technology can be used that is effective, judicially efficient, and constitutionally compliant (Marder, 2001). As part of the Courtroom 21 Project, William and Mary Law School and the National Center for State Courts recently funded a research study concerning the use of technology and jury room deliberation to enhance deliberations in both traditional trials and technology-augmented cases (*The use of technology in the jury room*, 2002). The research was a culmination of the surveys and experiments of the Courtroom 21 Project's empirical findings to date and field tested in Florida's Courtroom 23+ Project as well as the U.S. District Court for the District of Oregon. The data obtained strongly supports the use of hard technology in the courtroom. Jurors who have proper access to hard technology report a belief in the greater accuracy of their deliberations and shorter deliberation time. What is unknown, and possibly not measurable from the data is whether hard technology enhances the quality of the verdicts (*The use of technology in the jury room*, 2002).

The type of hard technology, and its level of use, differ under federal and individual state law. When jurors deliberate, not all evidence introduced at trial is made available in the jury room. Whether such evidence can be used is generally determined by two sources: the rules of evidence and the procedural rules concerning jury deliberation. In most circumstances, the jury can only receive evidence that has been introduced at trial and only if the judge sends it to the jury for use in deliberations. An important issue is raised when technology allows evidence to be "summarized" or "demonstrated." Strictly speaking, such representations are not evidence at all, and their use in the jury room depends on applications of the rules of evidence and of jury procedure, particularly in regard to the concepts of relevance and unfair prejudice.

Hard technology used in the jury deliberation room includes the following categories: (1) "input" technologies – those devices which provide information (exhibits) to the jury through electronic display; (2) display technology; (3) annotation technologies – the ability to write or make markings on exhibits; and, (4) assistive technologies – those that help jurors with sight or hearing difficulties (*The use of technology in the jury room*, 2002, p. 30). Like most hard technologies, these are primarily visual: cameras and computers display electronically most or all of the evidence.

Input technologies allow for the presentation in the jury room of most common types of evidence: witness testimony, documents, photographs, charts, etc. Types of input devices include DVD players, video tape players, or digital displays.

The most frequently used input technology in the Courtroom 21 Project is the document camera. The document camera consists of a vertically-mounted color television camera aimed down at a base on which a document or object is placed. This camera is then connected to some type of display device (laptop computer, monitor, or projection unit) so that a piece of evidence can be viewed by all members of the jury at the same time. Large screen television/computer monitors let all the jurors comfortably view the screen. Plasma screen monitors are large and have high resolution with diagonal measurements from 40 to 61 inches. They are flat, allowing them to be wall mounted for ease in viewing and space. Further, plasma screens can be connected to other types of hard technology allowing from document cameras, the Internet, DVD, or VCR tapes (*The use of technology in the jury room*, 2002).

Annotation technologies allow jurors to make notes, points and counterpoints and/or temporarily alter evidence or digital representations of evidence as an aid to deliberations. These hard technologies take the traditional concepts of "pencil and paper" one step further by allowing jurors to view the same piece of evidence simultaneously while the evidence is being altered (*The use of technology in the jury room*, 2002, p. 37).

Assistive technologies assist jurors with sight or hearing impairments. These hard technologies can enlarge small or obscure objects and text for examination. The resolution of plasma technologies as well as the accuracy of document cameras and video allow for unparalleled clarity. A Communication Access Realtime Translation (CART) service can also assist jurors by instantaneously recording every word transcribed by the court recorder, which allows for instant translation to a Braille reader (*The use of technology in the jury room*, 2002, p. 39). Hearing-impaired jurors can benefit from devices such as infrared headphones, which collect sound from strategically-placed microphones around the courtroom, which is then transmitted to headphones via infrared technology. The same technology can be used by jurors to translate foreign languages.

The Courtroom 21 Project has compiled all of its research, data, and findings to date concerning technology and jury deliberations in its *Manual for Jury Deliberation Room Technology,* a road map for the marriage of hard technology and the jury deliberation phase of the court process. The manual details the types of hard technology currently available at the Courtroom 21 Project, analyses possible ways that hard technology might be integrated and used, and discusses all the hard technologies detailed in this chapter. The manual can be viewed online at: www.courtroom21.net.

Hard Technology and Court Safety

Hard technology aids court security in ensuring a safe, orderly environment for court personnel. Courthouses have become susceptible to growing violence, with court personnel becoming prime targets. Proactive steps and preventive planning involving hard technology are being taken to provide safety. Weapon detection, the control of defendants and prisoners, and courthouse monitoring are now considered high priorities in many courts regardless of resources, size, or operational complexity (Faust and Raffo, 2001).

Weapon detection has always been a primary concern for the courts. Escalating attacks on judges, attorneys, and other court personnel have made this issue a top priority. Security personnel typically screen for weapons at the courthouse's point of entry. Electronic entry screening is becoming commonplace, with magnetometers (metal detectors) being the most common. Other devices offer a greater degree of detection and are not limited to finding magnetic metals. Detection systems using low doses of x-ray radiation (3-microRem doses) to detect both metal and non-metal objects on a person are being used at many courthouses. These hard technology devices can detect any metal weapon, as well as explosives including dynamite, plastique, semtex, and C-4; and black powder. Other weapon detection systems are designed to "sniff out" chemically-based weapons, such as explosives, by sampling the air around the person being checked. These units, which are used at the U.S. Capitol in Washington, D.C., can detect nitrate-based explosives with a sensitivity of one-part-per-trillion and are often integrated with the more traditional walk-through metal detectors (Geiger, 1994).

The issue of defendant and prisoner control at the courthouse is problematic because safety concerns often clash with issues of defendants' rights. Putting a defendant in shackles or restraints without cause is prejudicial in established law, but the security concern is to stop a potentially violent defendant from escaping or injuring someone. Hard technology could possibly solve this problem if a defendant, out of sight of the jury, could be secured with a device that would instantly incapacitate a defendant attempting a violent attack or escape. This device is along the lines of a stun gun, but fastened around a defendant's waist. In the appropriate situation a charge of 50,000 volts in the 3 to 4 milliamp range could be delivered within a range of 300 feet (Geiger, 1994).

Hard technology devices also address safety in the monitoring of the courthouse and its personnel. Video camera surveillance has long been a courthouse staple. Duress alarms (panic buttons) are also being used in courthouses nationwide. Duress alarms can be wired to a specific location, such as a judge's bench, or be wireless and mobile. These devices signal court security personnel in the anticipation of violence or a violent event (Greacen and Klein, 2001).

Hard Technology and Specialized Courts

Drug courts focus on the treatment of drug offenders, with reduced emphasis on punishment. The drug court is a "specialized court," that pursues alternatives to the prosecution approach of traditional criminal courts. Supervised by a drug court judge, the drug court is an intensive, community-based treatment, rehabilitation, and supervision program for drug defendants (Office of National Drug Control Policy [ONDCP], 1988-1998).

Specialized courts, especially drug courts, operate most effectively when the most current information is made available to the court in real time. Hard technologies offer a means to accumulate such information as well as offer a real time delivery system. Specialized courts continually work to improve such technologies. In an effort to improve and accelerate the development and implementation of such hard technologies, studies are now being conducted to address the practical requirements for more timely monitoring and reporting in specialized courts nationally.

The e-Court project, conducted under Criminal Justice-Drug Abuse Treatment Studies (CJDATS), with the support of the federal Office of Justice Programs (OJP), is a project whose objective is to increase the efficiency and effectiveness of hard technology in drug courts. Further, the project intends to aid in the transfer and implementation of hard technology among drug courts. The objectives of e-Court include: (1) the testing and development of hard technologies that can be readily adopted and implemented in drug courts; (2) assessment of how drug courts can use web-based hard technologies; and, (3) investigating the actual and potential impacts of hard technology in areas such as case management, compliance with treatment, and the effectiveness of services (CJDATS, 2005). Several hard technologies are now available for study in these areas.

Hard technology, in the form of a computer system, provides access to clinical and case information for all members of the drug court team. Different levels of access ensure that all information is made available only to proper authorized personnel. The computer system allows all users to contribute and have access to all relevant information concerning a case (Casey, 2004). This in turn allows the drug court judge to have real-time information concerning drug testing and compliance. Orders issued by the court can be immediately accessed by all members of the drug court team, allowing for a coordinated effort in enforcing any drug court plan (Hack, 2003).

A key part of the program is the supervision of a defendant over an extended period of time. This supervision always entails some type of drug testing to ensure compliance with the program's guidelines. There are several different ways to test an offender to ensure compliance. All testing involves hard technology (see Table 2).

Urinalysis is the most prevalent type of testing done at this time. It has been in use for many years and is one of the more accepted technologies in terms of accuracy and cost. It measures drug consumption over the last few days prior to the test, and results can be obtained quickly (NIDA/Drug Abuse, 1995). This type of testing is very useful to drug court judges, who often base rulings and sanctions on the most up-to-date information available (Miller, 2004).

Another example is testing a strand of the defendant's hair, which can indicate drug history going back three months. The testing of hair is limited in that it cannot detect as wide a range of drugs as urinalysis can, most notably the presence of alcohol (ONDCP, 2002).

Drugs and alcohol can also be tested through saliva. This test is not as invasive as a urinalysis test in terms of privacy and, as such, is easier to administer in a more public forum. Saliva tests only uncover relatively recent drug and alcohol use and cannot go as far back in time as the urinalysis test (ONDCP, 2002).

Table 2: Drug Testing Methods

Type of Test	Pros	Window of Detection
Urine	• Highest assurance of reliable results. • Least expensive. • Most flexibility in testing different drugs, including alcohol and nicotine. • Most likely of all drug-testing methods to withstand legal challenge.	• Typically 1 to 5 days.
Hair	• Longer window of detection. • Greater stability (does not deteriorate). • Can measure chronic drug use. • Convenient shipping and storage (no need to refrigerate). • Collection procedure not considered invasive or embarrassing. • More difficult to adulterate than urine. • Detects alcohol/cocaine combination use.	• Depends on the length of hair in the sample. Hair grows about a half-inch per month, so a $1^1/2$-inch specimen would show a 3-month history.
Saliva	• Sample obtained under direct observation. • Minimal risk of tampering. • Non-invasive. • Samples can be collected easily in virtually any environment. • Can detect alcohol use. • Reflects recent drug use.	• Approximately 10 to 24 hours.
Sweat Patch	• Non-invasive. • Variable removal date (generally 1 to 7 days). • Quick application and removal. • Longer window of detection than urine. • No sample substitution possible.	• Patch retains evidence of drug use for at least 7 days, and can detect even low levels of drugs 2 to 5 hours after last use.

Source: Office of National Drug Control Policy, 2002.

The sweat patch is another type of drug test which involves the offender wearing a patch on the skin over an extended period of time. The sweat sample collected from the offender is then tested to determine drug usage. This test is becoming more accepted as drug courts become more widespread and the concept of supervision and compliance becomes more accepted as a condition of the program (NIDA/Drug Abuse, 1995).

Unfortunately, the hard technology of drug testing cannot keep up with all the drugs currently used by offenders. New "designer" drugs are constantly being made that are undetectable by the tests described above. Further, no standard test is able to detect inhalant abuse (the sniffing of glue, spray paint, gasoline, etc.; ONDCP, 2002).

Specialized alternative courts seem to lend themselves more readily to hard technology than traditional courts. Perhaps the innovative, progressive approach of these alternative courts makes them more receptive to new technology than their more custom-bound counterparts in traditional courts.

Technology in Multi-jurisdictional Courts

To properly use such hard technology in multi-jurisdictional/multi-court situations, challenges involving choice-of-law questions, attorney strategy issues, and constitutional issues, among others, must be overcome.

When multi-jurisdictions/multi-courts situations apply, the judge and jury, being located in a single jurisdiction/court, must know what law to apply. The choice-of-law issue becomes even more pronounced in international cases where the very basis of the law may be radically different. Choice-of-law decisions in multi-jurisdictional/multi-court circumstances must be made prior to cases coming to trial, either through international treaty, federal legislation, or private contract.

Further, attorneys often use decisions on venue, jurisdiction, and choice of law as strategic issues. "Choice of law" is defined as the body of law that will be used in adjudicating a dispute. For example, if a legal disagreement takes place between a resident of Massachusetts and a resident of California for a dispute that takes place in Ohio, determining not only where the case will be heard but which state's law applies can be an issue. Some examples include forcing parties of a case to travel to a remote location to create a "chilling effect" on the opposing party's trial strategy. Creating a hardship based on time and/or space is another weapon used by counsel. Selecting a venue that may be perceived as more sympathetic to a party is another strategy. For example, the first trial of the Rodney King case in the early 1990s was conducted in Simi Valley, California, an area known to be a retirement community for many former police, fire, and military personnel. The defense in this case calculated that a jury selected from this population would be more sympathetic to the defendants, who were the police officers accused of beating Mr. King. The defense lawyers were right, and their clients were acquitted. (This verdict led to massive rioting in Los Angeles and the eventual retrial of the defendants on federal charges, in which they were found guilty of federal civil rights violations.)

Another issue attorneys may experience in multi-jurisdictional/multi-court settings is that assessing a defendant's or witness's demeanor on video during trial or while on the stand may be more difficult for counsel, the judge, and the jury. Defendants and witnesses may behave more like television actors when on camera than they would in a traditional court setting.

Lastly, there are many constitutional issues that must be resolved in order for multi-jurisdictional/multi-courts to be properly used. Perhaps the most glaring issue falls under the Sixth Amendment to the U.S. Constitution, which guarantees the right of the accused to face one's accusers and to be presented with any evidence against him or her. Does the constitutional requirement imply a physical face-to-face meeting, or can it be properly conducted through videoconferencing or interactive streaming video?

Until hard technology made reliable, interactive video available, it was assumed that facing one's accuser(s) was done literally, in person. The tradition of concurrency, and the corresponding rules of criminal procedure and evidence, also made that assumption. Hard technology, however, allows the accused to view a digital representation of the accuser(s). Seeing and hearing testimony is only part of the overall assessment that judges, juries, parties, attorneys, and courtroom observers make in rendering decisions concerning veracity, remorse, regret, and ultimately guilt or innocence. A person's actions or demeanor "off camera" often have impact. Reactions during another witness's testimony or during a lull in the proceedings are all potentially observed and assessed by the court's decision makers and taken into account when rendering judgment. A video camera only records what it is pointed at, thereby limiting a judge's, jury's, party's, attorney's, and/or courtroom observer's ability to obtain a clear, more accurate picture of a witness.

A similar challenge to hard technology in the courtroom concerns the examination of physical evidence and other actual documents, rather than a digital facsimile. Such concerns are not limited to the defense in a criminal case; both sides may have issues with hard technology's ability to render an image of evidence instead of presenting the actual evidence for maximum impact. For example, the display of an actual weapon, or genuine documents bearing signatures or distinguishing marks, or any object that would cause an emotional reaction requires a physical presence that would be of greater benefit to the prosecution.

CONCLUSION

Hard technology offers the courts many opportunities and challenges. The hidebound traditional attitudes and customs that are the benchmarks of the courts and its procedures will undoubtedly be modified by hard technology. The extent of that modification will be determined by the creative minds of hardware engineers, court administrators, and courtroom attorneys tempered by legal challenges and constitutional interpretation of basic rights.

The introduction of hard technology into the courts is a recent phenomenon. Most of its practitioners are self-taught with little or no formal training. Approximately 72% of attorneys in a recent survey (Epstein, 2004) had no training in courtroom technologies. Many attorneys were unaware of most of the technology available. Among the attorneys who used hard technology, the laptop was most used. Attorneys rarely used more advanced litigation tools, especially those available for annotation or evidence presentation, such as streaming video, the Internet, or video monitors. But little true social science research has been conducted to assess the impact of hard technology on the courts. William and Mary School of Law's Courtroom 21 Project is the most comprehensive and oldest experiment to date, but even this project has only been conducting its lab trials since 2000. A great deal of research still needs to be conducted.

Given the special significance of the courts, perhaps the slow pace of adopting hard technological is appropriate because it leaves room for social scientists and legal scholars to properly measure the impact and ramifications of such changes on the judiciary as a branch of government. The courts are notoriously slow in adapting technology for use in the courtroom. But, as technology has developed that is specifically targeted at the legal field, visionary projects like the Courtroom 21 and Courtroom 23+ initiatives have begun to show that it is possible to incorporate hard technology into daily court activities and make them more effective and efficient (Epstein, 2004).

With the introduction of hard technologies into the courts, it is clear that new laws, protocols, and rules of evidence and procedure must be introduced, or current laws adapted, to address the many issues highlighted by hard technology. What should a court do when a technical failure takes place? Do attorneys have an additional duty of competence due to the introduction of hard technology into the courts? Who will control this technology, both tactically at the time of trial and strategically in an overall sense (Lederer, 2005)?

Susan Nauss Exon believes that the hard technology of today will inevitably lead to a world cybercourt modeled after the Michigan cybercourt, where all proceedings take place in cyberspace but have a centralized location, like the Courtroom 21 Project. Participating countries would develop the rules and standards for this world cybercourt, and it would be backed by international treaty, along the lines of the International Court of Justice or the European Court of Human Rights. The hard technology would be futuristic indeed. Holograms, laser projections, and high-speed Internet connections and computing would be the order of the day (Exon, 2002). It is easy to let one's imagination run wild and conjure up all types of science fiction scenarios for hard technologies role in the courts. While the possibilities are infinite, the hard work of assessing the constitutional impact, the effectiveness, and efficiency of such technologies is left to the social scientists and legal scholars of today and the future.

◆ ◆ ◆ ◆

REFERENCES

American Bar Association, Legal Technology Research Center (2002). *Web and communication technology.* Retrieved from: www.abanet.org/tech/ltr6/commcoll.html.

Bermant, G. (1999). *Courting the virtual: Federal courts in an age of complete interconnectedness.* 25 Ohio Northern University Law Review, 527-562.

Bermant, G. (2005). The powers and pitfalls of technology: The development and significance of courtroom technology: A thirty year perspective in fast forward mode. *New York University Annual Survey of Law, 60,* 621-562.

Byrne, J., & Buzawa, E. (2004). Information, technology, and criminal justice education. In A. Pattavina (Ed.), *Information technology and the criminal justice system* (pp. 243-260). Thousand Oaks, CA: Sage Publications.

Casey, T. (2004). When good intentions are not enough: Problem solving courts and the impending crisis of legitimacy. *Southern Methodist University Law Review, 57,* 1459-1529.

Criminal Justice Drug Treatment Studies (CJDATS), (2005). Retrieved from: www.cjdats. org

Courtroom 21 Project Web Site. (2006). Retrieved from: http://www.courtroom 21.net/

Courtroom 23+ Website. (2006). Retrieved from: http://www.ninja9.org/court admin/mis/courtroom_23.htm

Crowell, J. (1997). The electronic courtroom. *Boston University Journal of Science & Technology Law, 4,* 10-15.

Epstein, L. A. (2004). The technology challenge: Lawyers have finally entered the race but will ethical hurdles slow the pace? *Nova Law Journal, 28,* 721-747.

Exon, S. N. (2002). The internet meets Obi-Wan in the court of next resort. *Boston University Journal of Science & Technology Law, 8,* 1-23.

Faust, T., & Raffo, M. (2001). Local trial court response to courthouse safety. *Annals of the American Society of Political and Social Science, 576*(1), 91-101.

Federal Judicial Center (2004). *Effective use of courtroom technology: A judge's guide to pretrial and trial.* Retrieved from: www.nicic.org/library/020405

Friedman, R.D. (2002). Remote testimony. *University of Michigan Journal of Law Reform, 35,* 695-717.

Geiger, F. A. (1994). *Security technology update.* Retrieved from: www.ncsconline.org/ D_Tech/ctc/showarticle.asp?id=126

German, H. (2005). Courthouse aftermath: Video conference an answer. *Security Magazine.* Retrieved from: www.ivci.com.international_videoconferencing_news_ 050105-2.html

Greacen, J. M., & Klein, R. J. (2001). Statewide planning for court security. *Annals of the American Society of Political and Social Science, 576*(1), 109-117.

Hack, D. (2003). *Data, delinquency, and drug treatment: How technology can aid a juvenile drug court.* New York: The Center for Court Innovation, New York State Unified Court System (www.courts.state.ny.us).

Heintz, M. E. (2002). The digital divide and courtroom technology: Can David keep up with Goliath? *Federal Communications Law Journal, 54,* 567-592.

Hillis, B. J. (2000). What is a wired court? Legal Intelligence Column. *The Jurist.* University of Pittsburgh School of Law (http://jurist.law.pitt.edu/court tech6.htm).

James, F., & Hazard, G. (1977). *Civil procedure.* New York: Thomson/Foundation Press.

Jones, G. T. (1996). Lex, lie & videotape. *University of Arkansas at Little Rock, 18,* 613-647.

Kamin, S. (1996). Law and technology: The case for a smart gun detector. *Law and Contemporary Problems, 59*(1), 221-262.

Lederer, F. I. (1997). *An introduction to technologically augmented litigation.* William and Mary School of Law. Retrieved from: www.courtroom21.net/about_us/articles/auglit.html (also available at: www.legaltechcenter.net).

Lederer, F. I. (1998). *Courtroom technology from a judge's perspective.* http://www.courtroom21.net/reference/articles/perspecti ve.pdf (also available at: www.legaltechcenter.net).

Lederer, F. I. (2003). *High-tech trial lawyers and the court: Responsibilities, problems, and opportunities: An Introduction.* 2003 Courtroom 21 Affiliate Conference. Retrieved from: www.legaltechcenter.net

Lederer, F. I. (2005). The powers and pitfalls of technology: Technology-augmented courtrooms: Progress amid a few complications, or the problematic interrelationship between court and counsel. *New York University Annual Survey of Law, 60,* 675-699.

Marder, N. S. (2001). Juries and technology: Equipping jurors for the twenty first century. *Brooklyn Law Review, 66,* 1257-1282.

Miller, E, J. (2004). Embracing addition: Drug courts and the false promise of judicial intervention *Ohio State Law Journal, 65,* 1479-1589.

National Institute of Drug Abuse (NIDA), (1995). Retrieved from: www.drugabuse.gov/NIDA_notes/NNvol20n5/dirrepvol20n5.html

National Institute of Drug Abuse/Drug Abuse (NIDA), (2003). Retrieved from: www.drugabuse.gov/pdf/monographs/162.pdf

Office of National Drug Control Policy (2002). *Drug testing in schools.* Retrieved from: www.whitehousedrugpolicy.gov

Office of National Drug Control Policy (1988-1998). *Drug treatment in the criminal justice system.* Retrieved from: www.whitehousedrugpolicy.gov.

Office of National Drug Control Policy (1995). *Sweat testing may prove useful in drug use surveillance.* Retrieved from: www.whitehousedrugpolicy.gov

Pointe, L. M. (2002). The Michigan Cyber Court: A bold experiment in the development of the first public virtual courthouse. *North Carolina Journal of Law & Technology, 4,* 51-93.

Susskind, R. (1999). *The challenge of the information society: Application of advanced technologies in civil litigation and other procedures.* Retrieved from: http://ruessmann.jura.uni-sb.de/grotius/english/Reports/england.htm

Technology Forecast for the Federal Judiciary, (2001). Washington, DC: Office of Information Technology Administrative Office of the U.S. Courts.

The use of technology in the jury room to enhance deliberations, (2002). Courtroom 21 Research Report. Retrieved from: www.courtroom21.net

Young, P. (2001). *An informed response: An overview of the domestic violence court technology application and resource link.* New York: The Center for Court Innovation, New York State Unified Court System (www.courts.state.ny.us).

9. THE COURTS AND SOFT TECHNOLOGY

by

Ronald P. Corbett, Jr.

Executive Director, Supreme Judicial Court of Massachusetts

INTRODUCTION: COURTS AND THE TECHNOLOGICAL IMPERATIVE

In August of 2005, the Conference of Chief Justices (CCJ) and the Council of State Court Administrators (COSCA) issued a joint resolution communicating the resolve of both organizations to giving their highest priority to the establishment of a clearinghouse of information on court-based technology (Hall et al., 2005). This action by the two leading court administrator organizations in the country is one of many recent indications that a revolution in the use of available computer-based technology is underway in our nation's courts.

Government agencies typically lag behind the private sector in the introduction of cutting-edge solutions to problems of efficiency and quality management, with courts often the most conservative and change-resistant public entities. Nonetheless, growing public expectations have put pressure on all of government to leverage technology in the service of greater access and productivity. Those conveniences, now widely available to consumers of private sector goods, are expected to be similarly available in the provision of public goods. All that the Internet provides by way of accessing information and transacting business, instantly and from a variety of locations, is looked for from government. As one example, now that many citizens are comfortable with and reliant on the availability of on-line filing of tax returns, they will expect other routine public sector transactions to offer comparable ease-of-use. In sum, there is a demonstrable and classic crisis of rising expectations, felt very acutely by public administrators.

In the face of these pressures for modernization, the signs of a sea change in the ways courts do business and particularly in a growing reliance on the latest technology are everywhere evident:

- David Rottman (2004), in his report on trends in state government, remarked that a new "consumer orientation" is taking hold that will place new demands on public administrators to streamline their practices.

- Jonathan Lippman (2005), chief administrative judge for the New York state courts, refers to the acceleration in use of technology in society as "The Emergence of E-Everything" and warns government officials to expect and increased demand for technology based services.

- Between 1980 and 2000, America's courts spent "billions" of dollars on the planning, design, implementation, and staff training related to automated applications (Cornell, 2001).

- In 2002, it is estimated that $500 million dollars was spent by courts nationally on technology (Collins et al., 2002).

In the midst of all the manifest commitment to technology and the related techo-boosterism sweeping through the professional organizations, a clear note of caution and some restraint on the rhetoric is justified. While much is in the works, there are, as well, countervailing pressures that will impede the ability of courts to realize the full potential of technology. In a report issued in September 2005, staff from the National Center of State Courts (NCSC) observed that "file drawers and paper reports are still the dominant means of storing and delivering information in many courts" (Hall et al., 2005, p. 5). Elsewhere in the report, court systems are described as swamped by accumulated data, mired in traditional practice, and lacking the managerial acumen and vision to accommodate and exploit emerging technology.

While the magnitude of the investment in technology now underway ought to provide hope for soon-to-be-realized improvements, the track record for most technology projects – whether public or private sector – would not leave an observer sanguine. In "Technology Projects: What Goes Wrong and Lessons Learned," Clark and his colleagues (2001) offer discouraging evidence:

- 31% of information technology (IT) projects are cancelled before completion;

- most projects cost nearly twice the initial projected costs; and,

- only 16% are completed on time and under budget.

While the IT movement continues full throttle, it is hampered by a very checkered record of implementation thus far.

MAIN FEATURES OF COURT-BASED "SOFT" TECHNOLOGY

Chapter 8 in this volume addresses the use of hard technology (equipment, devices, etc.). Complementing those developments are innovations in software and programming which affect public knowledge of and understanding about court operations, as well as the quality of court administration and sentencing and correctional practices within the judiciary. It is these latter "soft" developments that are the focus of this paper.

While the recent growth in the utilization of technology in courts has been dramatic, as has been the increase in the functionality of the applications, automation was first introduced into the court environments over 25 years ago. First generation automated systems could record case information, track payments made to the court, and assemble jury lists – and do little else. Utilizing data to improve efficiency, save resources, or provide greater access was not contemplated until more recent years. As a practical matter, courts in the early days of automation found themselves data rich and analysis poor, lacking the capacity for generating the kind of managerial reports that would serve organizational goals. Such performance reports as were generated had to be manually produced, with the consequence that weeks, if not months, would pass between the generation of the data and the publication of analyses. The labor involved in the production of such reports and their ultimate lack of timeliness discouraged their use.

By contrast, during the last decade or so, improvements in the available software along with the growth in the use and sophistication of the Internet, has translated into powerful new capabilities for courts. The major functional improvements serve the superordinate goals of *transparency, efficiency and effectiveness,* each of which will now be taken up in turn.

Transparency

Exploiting the power of the Internet has allowed courts to provide information to users and citizens both more broadly and more quickly. Lippman (2005) identifies three categories in this "explosion of court data." First, court web sites provide basic information about court operations, including rules and procedures, hours and locations, as well as collateral information such as job opportunities, public education programs, etc. One example of a growing area for Internet-based dissemination of information concerns self-represented litigants whose needs for basic information on the routine conduct of court proceedings is critical to their ability to navigate the system successfully.

A second area, more recently developed, provides for on-line access to case information, such as names of parties, attorneys, scheduled appearance dates, judges assigned, etc. Those who are involved in litigation or have an interest in particular proceedings can easily obtain information that might previously have required several calls to the courthouse to obtain. Depending on the sophistication of the database software employed, some systems allow web-site visitors to search by type of case, party, or other identifying information if there is interest in features of particular proceedings.

Lippman's third and final area concerns court documents – the various motions, briefs and affidavits that underlay litigation – and their electronic availability. This area is fraught with controversy since it creates the potential for obtaining confidential information concerning parties to legal proceedings, including financial data, medical and psychiatric records, domestic occurrences, etc. Later in this paper, the prospects for privacy violations heightened by developments in technology will be explored.

Illustrations of the potential for technology to promote *transparency* can be found at *www.NCSC.org*, the web site of the National Center for State Courts, where a list of the top ten court sites is maintained for viewing.

Efficiency

Courts are information-driven, paper-intensive enterprises. Accordingly, the typical measures of success for a court – particularly in the view of its major constituency, the legal profession – are how quickly and how nimbly it can maintain its files, organize, schedule, and complete its business, keep participants informed of its activities, and obtain, as well as disseminate, information to affiliated entities (e.g., police departments and correction agencies). In furtherance of satisfying these expectations, court administrators can be greatly aided by advances in database technology.

At the most basic level, newly automated court record systems allow judges and other court officials with a "click of the mouse" to access and manipulate data and information previously "dispersed in fragmented and often poorly designed electronic systems, libraries and paper records" (National Association of Court Management [NACM], 2003, p. 59).

Modern software-supported case management systems allow judges to easily and quickly connect case histories and related documents, exchange information with attorneys and social service personnel, and maintain close control of their calendars. A better grasp of the flow of business allows for better deployment of staff, courtrooms, and equipment. Automated financial record keeping and noticing systems allows for more accurate and timely dispersal of funds, including expedited restitution payments to needy victims. The result of reliance on these systems, in the view of NCSC, is that "the right people are more likely than not able to get the information they need, at the right time and in the right format" and that "same or better justice is achieved, sooner for many cases" (NACM, 2003, p. 59.)

This emerging cult of efficiency has manifested itself most strongly in the development of performance measures for courts, built onto existing case management systems. The central purpose of these *court performance measurement systems* is to generate reports that document the speed (average elapsed time to judgement) and the productivity (volume of work completed in an established time frame) of a court.

The application of performance measures to courts is simply a recent illustration of a growing trend for accountable government. Influenced by Gaebler and Osborne's (1992) seminal publication *Reinventing Government,* the use of performance measures and related instruments has grown exponentially in the last decade, throughout all branches of government. The assumption behind the reinventing movement is that for any organization – but most especially for those in the public sector where the discipline of the free market does not apply – improvement in the quality of operations will depend critically on the enunciation of objective criteria (or benchmarks for performance) against which the organization is routinely measured and to which administrators are held accountable.

Exemplar: NCSC's "CourTools"

In 2005, NCSC released its long awaited set of performance measures for courts, titled "CourTools" (Hall et al., 2005). Court administrators had been speaking about and making tentative efforts toward a comprehensive set of goals for some time prior to the NCSC release. This new comprehensive guide to excellence in court administration drew upon fledgling previous efforts as well as models in use in other parts of the public and private sector. The set includes 10 measures, the majority of which focus on the timeliness of movement of cases through the system, including as examples the following measures:

- *Time to disposition* – The percentage of cases disposed or otherwise resolved within established time frames.

- *Age of active pending caseload* – The age of the active cases pending before the court, measured as the number of days from filing until the time of measurement.

- *Trial date certainty* – The number of times cases disposed by trial are scheduled for trial.

- *Collection of monetary penalties* – Payments collected and distributed within established time lines.

With these measures as the new "gold standard" for assessing court performance, court administrators have relied on computer software products specifically designed to support performance management – products generically referred to as "business intelligence" (BI). These products, while still in first-generation use in courts, are offered by industry leaders such as Microsoft, Microstategy, SAS and SPSS. One company, ACS, has developed a court-specific application, still in prototype, titled "CourtMetrix" (Hall et al., 2005).

The software involved in this application focuses on "capturing, organizing, analyzing and displaying performance data to help organizations make decisions" (p. 6). BI products provide both for automatic generation and distribution of pre-designed management reports – aligned with measures such as those contained in CourTools – as well as the functionality that allows approved users to customize reports through the combination and manipulation of interrelated performance data (e.g., disaggregating results on a measure by geography or type of case.)

CourTools and its progeny are predicted to have staying power. In September 2005, staff from NCSC reported that a number of court systems had adopted CourTools, including systems in Arizona, California, and North Carolina (Hall et al., 2005). On the strength of the expression of interest by courts thus far, NCSC staff predicted that the development of performance guidance systems is likely to take "center stage in the field of judicial administration in the next few years" (p. 5).

Exemplar: DeKalb County Radio Frequency Identification Technology (RFID)

A rather unlikely but nonetheless intriguing attempt to harness technology in the service of efficiency was reported by Dale Phillips (2005) in the pages of *Court Manager*, the official publication of the National Association for Court Management (NACM). The DeKalb County Georgia Juvenile Court – the second largest in the state – recognized that its push to operate as efficiently as possible was highly dependent on the courts' capacity to maintain its files in a fashion that allowed for quick retrieval, allowing judges in a court that conducted some 17,000 hearings in 2004 to have the information needed readily on hand in order to make timely decisions. The urgency of the problem grew out of the recognition that "no activity (was) more disruptive to the normal flow of court and case management operations than a lost or misfiled court record" (p. 24) and from the reality that clerks in the court's record room were spending an average of 10 hours each week looking for lost files.

The answer was found in the world of radio frequency transmission. Radio Frequency Identification Technology (RFID) has been characterized as "bar-coding on steroids" (p. 25). It allows for the tagging of any product with a miniature computer chip or antenna that can then be read telemetrically be a computer or hand-held device by the insertion of an appropriate identifying number. At any time, through wireless communication from the base to the folder sought, a "read" can be made of the folder's current location within a limited area (easily encompassing the space occupied by even a large court complex). The underlying technology was developed first to track airline luggage and library books, and the system employed by the DeKalb Court was developed by 3-M Corp. Pilot implementation was underway at the time this article was written, so progress reports are not yet available.

Data Warehouses and the Courts

The disturbing events of September 11, 2001 brought to light many weaknesses in the security systems in place to prevent such tragedies and protect citizens form terrorist activities. As is often the case, much good can come from the worst of events. In the aftermath of 9/11, there has been a dramatic spike in interest in reviewing the criminal justice system's capacity for collecting, analyzing, and rapidly retrieving basic identifying and background data on suspect individuals. It is not as if the need for modernized, centralized data-bases have not been previously recognized – it just had not gotten the traction that many had hoped for. A report from 2002 captures these spotty efforts:

> Since the mid-1990's, state courts, law enforcement, and other entities involved in public safety and justice have acknowledged a need for electronic exchange of information among their various agencies – an integrated criminal justice information system (ICJIS). Most states have initiated efforts in this direction, but results have been less than satisfactory. (Walker, 2002, p. 1)

The accumulated weight of tradition, the fear of loss of control of one's own data, the mistrust among key players in the criminal justice system that arises whenever "sharing" anything is contemplated, coupled with the need for new funding in support of the architecture and installations required had all combined to frustrate progress.

But 9/11 changed everything. Turf wars have given way to a near universal call for interoperability and collaboration. A NCSC report of 2003 put the task this way:

> Over the next 20 years, courts will be required to develop information systems that take into account the fact that they are dependent upon others for the information they need to administer justice, and, in turn, are a major source of information for others. . . . The Internet has generated tools and system development procedures that promise, if used effectively, to make the 30-year-old vision of a seamless movement of information among courts, prosecutors, law enforcement, and corrections a reality instead of a chase after a will-o-the-wisp. (Henderson, 2003, pp. 1-2)

The accelerated movement to build an integrated criminal justice information system (ICJIS) in each state is a variation of a broader societal movement to construct what are referred to as data "warehouses." The original idea for such warehouses originated – as with most innovations – in the private sector. In the 1990s, large companies recognized the advantages of timely access to a variety of business information and also realized that the extant information systems technology was inadequate. The notion of a *data warehouse* emerged, conceived of as a single repository for information otherwise spread around the typical system in spreadsheets, databases, and files. This centralization of disparate data allows for easier retrieval and facilitates complex analysis through convenient combination of newly integrated databases. Strategic reports, the production of which had previously been labor-intensive even in companies of considerable size, often requiring weeks of efforts, could be developed within days with the advent of warehousing (Inmon and Hackathorn, 1994).

The concepts and programming underlying the ICJIS were derived from the early experiences with data warehousing. The ICJIS collects data from a variety of sources, including court case files, police files, motor vehicle records, correctional databases, and, increasingly, social service agencies. The notion is that from the point of initial contact with an offender – the moment of arrest – straight through to sentencing and ultimate release, data can be forwarded electronically to a central "warehouse" and be immediately available to all appropriate parties. Each participating agency controls its own dispersal of information and enters into a multi-agency agreement as to whom should be permitted access to the ICJIS data. The result is a range of efficiencies in locating case-related data for investigatory, prosecutorial, court management, and correctional purposes. Inquiries that previously would have relied upon returned calls and faxes or mail deliveries could now be answered immediately with a single inquiry (Walker, 2002).

How does the development of an ICJIS implicate courts? In many respects, the court systems are at the center of the criminal justice process, the hub of the production line. The central importance of the need for courts to be a participant in ICJIS was underscored in a recent study of criminal justice information sharing that found that "more than 80% of all exchanges involved the courts" (Collins et al., 2002, p. 18).

Exemplar: Pennsylvania's Justice Network (JNET)

Pennsylvania has been in the vanguard of states developing an ICJIS – its JNET system is generally regarded as one of the "success stories" in he field. (JNET's stature grew considerably after it was credited with playing a significant role in the assisting the FBI in gathering information on the suspects identified as responsible for hijacking and crashing United Flight 93 on 9/11.) JNET's origins trace to 1997, with the appropriation of $11 million to support its development, and its initial implementation occurred in 1998. The network involves the participation of municipal, county, state, bordering states, and federal agencies in the maintenance of a secure automated system for the sharing of justice information among authorized users. Drawing upon Internet-based technologies and standards, JNET provides an on-line functionality through which parties distributed around the state and elsewhere can, if authorized, access offender records and other justice information supplied by the participating agencies (Commonwealth of Pennsylvania, 2006).

The kind of isolationism alluded to above that had frustrated better coordination and collaboration in the past is overcome through procedures aimed at allowing the provider agencies to maintain control over their entry of their data. Governance structures facilitate collegial decision making and early detection of potential problems. A steering committee, comprising a representative from each participating agency, meets and collaboratively decides, by vote, how policy and process problems will be resolved.

As of 2004, the JNET user base had expanded to 18,500 users from 39 state agencies, 30 counties, 200 municipalities, 12 federal agencies, and over 500 district justice offices. Among the dividends in terms of increased efficiency reported by Pennsylvania state officials is faster identification of suspects, reduced costs associated with offender processing, reduced delays in the prosecution of cases through much more timely access to case information. Correctional agencies – probation and parole – report quicker location of absconders and more reliable detection of subsequent violations.

Effectiveness

Court officials are accustomed to talking of their ultimate objective as "justice," a notoriously difficult goal to measure easily and reliably. Consequently, conventional measures of the quality of courts have fallen back on more procedural variables, focused on what we have referred to as *efficiency*.

While the goal of efficiency addresses the speed and productivity manifested in justice operations, *effectiveness,* by contrast, refers to the record of the justice system in achieving identified goals and outcomes. It looks more at results and less at process. One area where courts have taken an increasingly ambitious, results-oriented approach relates to what have become known as *problem-solving courts* (Berman and Feinblatt, 2005), the most well known of which is the drug court. Here also technology has been a great boon to the courts.

Drug courts emerged in this country first in the late 1980s, most prominently in Miami, where they were encouraged by then-district attorney (later U.S. Attorney General) Janet Reno. These specialized courts are distinguished from conventional court processing of criminal defendants by three features – close involvement of judges in monitoring the offender's compliance with the drug court regimen, intensive treatment services, and active in-the-courtroom interagency teamwork. In exchange for the avoidance of a more onerous sentence, drug court participants agree to enter a highly structured, multifaceted program, including regular drug tests. The centerpiece of the intervention involves regular in-court status hearings before a judge who typically has in-depth specialized training in substance abuse and who receives detailed reports on the participant's activities in assigned treatment programs, in the community, and at work. As reported by the Office of National Drug Control Policy, independent research has repeatedly confirmed the effectiveness of drug court handling of defendants, as compared to more traditional responses, measured by reductions in drug use and criminal behavior (Bureau of Justice Assistance [BJA], 2003).

Drug courts – and problem-solving courts generally – are not a passing fad. The number of such courts reached 2,000 in 2005, with all 50 state Chief Justices endorsing further expansion. The first major publication on this innovation – *Good Courts* (Berman and Feinblatt, 2005) – projected continued growth and mainstreaming in the future.

Technology is critical to the successful operation of drug courts. The intensity and the frequency of involvement by the drug court in the life of the offender require the availability of information that is both *comprehensive* (drug testing results, police contacts, probation reports, treatment notes, financial and job related updates) and *timely* (focusing on week-to-week progress). In this respect, drug courts are very information reliant, requiring "a range of information . . . to be consistently effective (that) far exceeds that of a typical criminal court" (BJA, 2003, p. 3). In the view of a 2003 Bureau of Justice Assistance monograph on drug courts (BJA, 2003, p. 1): "The volume of information that needs to be recorded, processed, accessed, shared, and analyzed – often in a time-critical context – is a strong argument for developing a management information system." Indeed, the utilization of up-to-date management information systems (MIS) is growing among active drug courts. Courts have employed both public domain software applications, as well as commercial products, and some systems have developed their own customized program building off of standard database software.

Each stage of the drug court process – screening assessment, treatment, and supervision – is expedited and strengthened by the ready availability of relevant automated data. One important example of on-line processing facilitating decision making involves the various offender assessments that are part of the drug court regimen. Beginning at the point of arrest, where many systems will conduct initial screens for drug dependency, the related questionnaires are often completed by staff on-line so that the results are immediately available to the participants in the "assembly line" (court clerk, judge, treatment staff, etc.). The initial evaluation can, for example, be used by a treatment intake specialist to match an offender with an available and appropriate treatment slot, by matching the assessment data with an automated inventory of available programs (BJA, 2003).

Once admitted to a program, an offender will be counseled, supervised, and tested regularly and, in the most advanced systems, this data is recorded in real time and made available to the key decision maker, the drug court judge. The availability of information for judicial decisions is so immediate that, in the case of the New York City drug court, the computer screen next to the presiding judge "lights up" when a case is called involving a defendant who has been pre-screened as drug-dependent, in order to alert the judge that a drug court admission may be appropriate (Center for Court Innovation, 2006).

Unlike the technology featured above, which serves the goal of *efficiency,* the automation common to the most progressive drug courts has been developed to promote *effectiveness* – that is, the technology is designed to facilitate appropriate admissions and thereafter close monitoring of compliance with conditions, leading to the desired outcomes of reduced drug use and lessened criminal offending. In connection with the salience of concern for *effectiveness,* BJA (2003) reports a growing emphasis on building performance report capability directly into the drug court MIS and underscores the utility such outcome evaluation data has had in sustaining political support and funding. The collaboration between the Kentucky courts and the University of Kentucky's Center on Drug and Alcohol Research (www.cdar.uky.edu) in the construction of an automated system that both supported day-to-day operations and evaluation needs is considered a prominent example of this trend.

Exemplar: Multnomah County's Sentencing Support Tools

An additional and thus far unique use of technology to promote effectiveness has been developed in the last few years in Oregon. Michael Marcus (2005), in a presentation made to a court technology conference in September 2005, decried what he took to be the nearly exclusive emphasis in court-based technology on the goal of "speed" without regard to impact on the goal of public safety. He then proceeded to describe an application that does focus on the outcome of reduced crime through "smarter" sentencing. Since early 2005, Multnomah judges in criminal sessions have had available to them a computerized "sentencing support tool" (drawing extensively on the data-warehousing model described above) that allows them to obtain actuarial predictions of likely outcomes – in terms of future recidivism – of sentencing options applied to particular offenders. In essence, a judge enters the criminal charges in a particular case along with identifying data on the offender into the database. By searching for the data in the "warehouse" associated with a particular individual, and then matching that defendant with similar offenders (e.g., those who have comparable criminal records and demographic profiles) facing similar charges, the computer can then provide aggregate data on results for similar offenders facing similar charges, sorted by recidivism rates correlated with different sentencing packages. Put differently, the output that judges receive allows them to see which sentencing options have been the most effective in reducing subsequent recidivism. (Recidivism is measured as a repeat of a similar crime in the three years following release from correctional custody or supervision, though users can use a different definition of recidivism, such as "any" subsequent crime in similar cases adjudicated in the county.) It should be said that judges are not obliged to sentence based on the analysis but are encouraged to let the actuarial data inform their judgments.

This innovative approach to guided decision making was developed as a result of a variety of new statutes passed by the Oregon legislature, requiring increased attention to the public safety impact of sentencing practices. Unlike the usual hue-and-cry about lenient judges and the predicable related call for stiffened sentences, the legislature in the this case called for the development of "evidence based" sentencing practices, and required the development of a data warehouse to "permit analysis of correlation between sanctions, supervision, services and programs, and future criminal conduct" (Marcus, 2005, p. 6).

As of late 2005, Marcus reported that it was "too early" for any "rigorous analysis" of the impact of the use of these tools, though he did aver that there was no rush to embrace their use by attorneys and judges. He concludes his article with a statement echoing the themes of this present analysis:

> Sentencing support tools represent an ambitious application of technology as part of an attempt to change institutional culture to serve a function the courts have traditionally avoided. As such, they answer the least heeded but highest and most urgent calling of technology:

*not to increase our speed or to lower our costs, but to improve our performance
as measured against our public mission* (emphasis supplied). Nowhere
is the challenge or the promise more profound than in criminal
sentencing. (Marcus, 2005, p. 8)

COURT TECHNOLOGY AS A "TROJAN HORSE"

> *"Access to more information significantly improves decision-making
> and organizational efficiency but is creating new problems, particu-
> larly concerning privacy."*
>
> Rep. Roger Roy, Delaware
> (Council of State Governments, 2005, p. 23)

Progress almost always carries a price. Something can be lost or sacrificed
when we strive to be faster ("speed kills") and better in carrying out important public missions. Corbett and Marx (1991), in discussing the mixed
blessing of technological advances, refer to the "fallacy of the free lunch
or painless dentistry," in which it is too quickly assumed that innovations
will return only positive benefits without offsets or unintended, if not perverse, consequences.

It is clear that the electronic revolution in the storage and dissemination of court information makes heretofore personal information significantly more accessible. With respect to information that was always intended
to be public (names, charges, dispositions, etc.), this is positive as it serves
the public's "right to know." However, data elements such as Social Security
numbers, names of minor children, financial account numbers – previously
available but accessible only if the seeker was prepared to pour through
dockets and public files at the courthouse – are now available with a few
strokes of a keyboard and can easily be retrieved by those who may have
unscrupulous intentions. Unwanted intrusions could range from the merely
annoying in the form of focused marketing and sales inquiries to the
dishonest or sinister in the form of fraudulent schemes perpetrated against
unsuspecting but wealthy seniors or shock tabloid journalism. Whether
mild or severe, the "data mining" that follows from newly available personal
information is the dark side of court automation.

Jonathan Lippman (2005), the New York State court administrator,
reported that some states have statutes prohibiting the release to the public
of certain data in child welfare, domestic relations, and family violence
cases in order to protect the privacy of people involved in these cases. In
other instances, newly developed court rules provide guidance on which
information should be excluded from court documents, typically focusing

on sensitive information about children and financial data. More recently, courts have experimented with redaction software which automatically purges electronic records of information deemed inappropriate for public release.

The most likely future for the clash between public access and individual rights to privacy is contained in this NCSC (2005, p. 58) prediction: "The battle between institutional efforts to protect the personal information of their clientele and the ingenuity of those who seek the sensitive data for dishonest endeavors will continue to escalate."

What Future for Court Technology?

In the face of the technological juggernaut that seems, in the eyes of senior court officials, to be overtaking the courts, the themes of caution and lowered expectations warrant revisiting. A sober assessment: In late 2001, the Joint Technology Committee of the Council of State Court Administrators and the National Association of Court Managers observed ruefully that despite the billions of dollars invested, "any objective observer would have to conclude that the courts have not received the return they should have from the time, efforts, and dollars expended on court technology" (Cornell, 2001, p. 17). The report went on to describe the courts as "demonstrably behind-the-times" (p. 17) in automation compared to the private sector.

Why would this be so? The Joint Technology Committee traced this case of arrested development to "excessive parochialism" on the part of court administrators who insist on seeing the work of justice as *sui generis,* requiring only customized solutions that are very expensive and often beyond the means of the average system. The committee also decried the lack of vision among administrators who are unschooled in the art and science of mapping business processes and system re-engineering, of the sort required to leverage the added value of improved automation.

Despite the hand-wringing, the best guess is that courts will continue to yield to the riches of technology – the power and functionality of which will advance inexorably. Such is the power of the technological imperative.

◆ ◆ ◆ ◆

REFERENCES

Berman, G., & Feinblatt, J. (2005). *Good courts: The case for problem solving justice.* New York: New Press, 2005.

Bureau of Justice Assistance [BJA] (2003). *Supporting the drug court process: What you need to know for effective decision making and program evaluation.* Washington, DC: U.S. Bureau of Justice Assistance.

Bureau of Justice Assistance (2006). *Informed decisions.* Retrieved from: http://www.drugcourttech.org

Center for Court Innovation (2006). *Principle of technology: Informed decisions, accountability, and partnership.* New York: Center for Court Innovation (http://www.courtinnovation.org).

Clark, D., Crawford, C., Husa, C., Roggero, J., O'Leary, M., & Wyatt, J. (2001). *Technology projects: What goes wrong and lessons learned.* Retrieved from: http://www.ncsc.org

Collins, H., Wessels, R., & Henderson, T. (2002). Making technology work for state courts. *Court Manager, 17*(4), 17-20. Williamsburg, VA: National Association for Court Management.

Commonwealth of Pennsylvania (2005). *JNET project summary.* Retrieved from: http://www.pajnet.state.pa.us

Corbett, R., & Marx, G. (1991). No soul in the new machine: Technofallacies in the electronic monitoring movement. *Justice Quarterly, 8*(3), 399-414.

Cornell, J. (2001). The work towards standards. *Court Manager, 16*(1), 17-24. Williamsburg, VA: National Association for Court Management.

Council for State Government (2005). *Trends in America: Charting the course ahead.* Lexington, KY: Council for State Governments.

Hall, D., Keilitz, I., Ostrom, B., & Barret, J. (2005). *Court Performance Measurement Systems (CPMS): From vision to reality.* Retrieved from: http://www.ncsc.org

Henderson, T. (2003). *Integrated justice information systems: Trends in 2003.* Williamsburg, VA: National Center for State Courts.

Inmon, W., & Hackathorn, R. (1994). *Using the data warehouse.* New York: John Wiley and Sons.

Lippman, J. (2005). *The emergence of E-everything.* (White paper.) Williamsburg, VA: Council of State Court Administrators.

Marcus, M. (2005). *Sentencing support tools: Technology as strategy.* Retrieved from: http://www.smartsentencing.com

National Association for Court Management (NACM) (2003). Information technology management. *Court Manager, 18*(2), 59-64. Williamsburg, VA: National Association for Court Management.

National Center for State Courts (NCSC) (2005). *Trends report: Technology and science* (pp. 52-63). Williamsburg, VA: National Center for State Courts.

Osborne, D., & Gaebler, T. (1992). *Reinventing government: How the entrepreneurial spirit is transforming the public sector.* Reading, MA: Addison-Wesley.

Phillips, D. (2005). Strategic applications of technology: Radio-Frequency Identification (RFID) technology and the DeKalb County, Georgia, Juvenile Court. *Court Manager, 20*(2), 214-227. Williamsburg, VA: National Association for Court Management.

Rottman, D. (2004). Trends and issues in state courts: Challenges and achievements. In K. S. Chi (Ed.), *The book of the states* (pp. 235-260). Lexington, KY: The Council of State Governments.

Walker, L. (2002). *Integrated criminal justice systems trends in 2002: Communication, collaboration, and cooperation.* Retrieved from: www.ncsc.org

10. INSTITUTIONAL CORRECTIONS AND HARD TECHNOLOGY

by

Jacob I. Stowell

University of Massachusetts, Lowell

INTRODUCTION

A recent report issued by the Vera Institute of Justice paints a mixed picture regarding the state of American correctional institutions (Gibbons and Katzenbach, 2006). On the one hand, rates of homicides and suicides in correctional facilities have experienced dramatic and sustained declines over the past two decades. Indeed, as Mumola (2005, p. 2) argues, since 1980 "inmate mortality rates have displayed dynamic changes." For example, homicide rates in state prisons fell from 54 to 4 per 100,000 inmates between 1980 and 2002. During this same period, suicide rates were cut by more than half, falling from 34 to 16 incidents per 100,000 prisoners. The positive news has not come unalloyed, however. By all accounts, state and local correctional facilities tend to be characterized by high levels of interpersonal violence (i.e., gang violence, rape, brutalization of inmates by authorities), which endangers the welfare of both correctional officers and inmates. Additionally, Gibbons and Katzenbach (2006, p. 6) assert that facilities are often overcrowded and are unable to provide adequate mental health care. Coupled with the fact that the size of the incarcerated population in this country continues to rise, it is evident that criminal justice systems face new challenges in their efforts to effectively (and humanely) manage inmates (Harrison and Beck, 2005).

With increasing frequency, correctional institutions are adopting technologically based inmate management solutions to address these ongoing problems. Interestingly, as Turner (2001, p. 154) indicates, many of the technologies employed in correctional settings were "adapted effectively" from other fields. Although the technologies cater to a wide variety of correctional strategies, it is important to recognize that they share a common objective; that is, to maximize the ability of officers to maintain safety and order, while protecting the lives of inmates and corrections officers. An exhaustive review of hard correctional technologies is beyond the scope of this chapter. Rather, it is designed to provide an overview of the various types of technologies currently utilized in correctional settings, and to provide some insight into the specific issues they are designed to address. The primary focus of this chapter will be on the use of technology in three general substantive areas of corrections: (1) facility monitoring; (2) inmate/officer interaction; and (3) other hard technology applications.

FACILITY MONITORING

The monitoring of correctional facilities is of central importance in maintaining order in jails and prisons. Through the use of surveillance techniques, it is hoped that corrections officers will be able to identify and respond to inmate transgressions more readily. Traditionally, much of this work has been done by line officers observing inmates directly or remotely through the use of video cameras. While both methods are still commonly used to combat the distribution of weapons and other illicit items among the inmate population, correctional facilities have also introduced additional measures to aid in this task. The following discussion highlights a number of technologies introduced to elevate levels of safety and security in jails and prisons by enhancing the data about the inmate population that is available to officers. In particular, the technologies to be reviewed include systems designed for weapon and contraband detection, the tracking of inmates, the notification of officer duress, and perimeter security.

Weapon and Contraband Detection

Hand-held (HHMD) and Walk-through (WTMD) metal detectors are among the most frequently used Concealed Weapon and Contraband Imaging Detection Systems (CWCIDS). In part this is owing to the fact that these devices tend to be affordable, portable, and relatively easy to use (Paulter, 2001). Metal detectors operate by producing a magnetic field that can identify the "presence of any electronically conducive or magnetizable material" (Paulter, 2001, p. 36). Both WTMD and HHMD are used as an initial means of screening inmates and visitors to correctional facilities. Because of their portability, another benefit of HHMD is that they can also be used to locate items that have been hidden "in the yard of a correctional facility or in the quarters of an inmate" (Paulter, 2001, p. 53).

Metal detectors are classified as detection-only CWCIDS. As the name suggests, metal detectors are only able to identify the presence or absence of a magnetic material. Because they are unable to offer any additional information regarding the size or the shape of the detected item, metal detectors have a higher rate of "false positives" for weapons and/or contraband. Another limitation of WTMD and HHMD is that they are only sensitive to the presence of metallic items, and thus cannot be used as a means of locating a wide array of illicit objects. For example, research has shown that non-metallic weapons are often fashioned from items prisoners may find or purchase from a prison store (Lincoln et al., 2006). It is clear that such items would go unnoticed by metal detectors. This is also true for illicit drugs, which according to the U.S. National Institute of Justice represent a "big problem" in jails and prisons. The presence of drugs carries with it hazards for inmates and officers, as violence may result from competition for control over drug markets (NLECTC, 2002). Despite these limitations, metal detectors remain one of the most commonly used weapon and contraband detection devices in correctional facilities.

An approach to detecting drugs that research has shown to be effective is a process known as Ion Mobility Spectrometer (IMS) scanning (Wright and Butler, 2001). What makes the IMS systems unique is that they are able to detect drugs, even when only traces of the substances are present. Indeed, IMS systems are primarily employed in mailrooms, as this is the manner by which many illicit drugs enter jails and prisons. Empirical findings demonstrate that IMS devices had a high success rate for detecting cocaine (90%), and a somewhat lower (24%) rate for marijuana detection (Butler, 2002). Further, IMS systems outperformed other techniques of drug-detection, such as x-raying or spraying mail with chemicals that change color in the presence of drugs. Beyond their use in mailrooms, the possibility also exits that IMS technology, and particularly hand-held IMS systems, could be used by officers to locate drugs that have found their way into correctional facilities. Similar to HHMD, hand-held IMS devices may also be a valuable resource in finding illicit substances hidden by inmates in their cells or other locations to which they have access. These strengths, coupled with its moderate pricing, have contributed to IMS becoming "one of the most widely used techniques for the trace detection of illicit drugs and other contraband materials" in jails and prisons (Parmeter et al., 2000).

The backscatter x-ray is another contraband detection technique that is being utilized in the field of corrections. Similar to conventional x-ray machines, the use of backscatter x-rays requires inmates to be scanned and the resulting images to be reviewed by officers. The advantage of the backscatter x-rays is that they are able to detect contraband that is either metallic or non-metallic in nature. That is, unlike the detection systems described above, backscatter x-rays are able to detect a wider range of unauthorized material that is hidden on individual inmates. While it has been argued that the versatility of the backscatter x-ray systems has made them the "cornerstone" of contraband detection in jails and prisons, they have also been sharply criticized by those concerned with inmate rights (Cothran, 2001). Specifically, Paulter et al. (2001, pp. 43-44) acknowledge that because the x-ray images contain detailed anatomical information, many assert that they violate the inmate's right to privacy, even if the data are never displayed. Moreover, the process of x-ray scanning exposes inmates to radiation, which many believe may have a detrimental impact on the health of inmates. At the time of this writing, neither of these issues has been resolved in the legal system, but they are discussed here because they may have implications for the future use of backscatter x-ray detection systems in correctional institutions.

Remote Monitoring of Inmates

Monitoring the whereabouts of prisoners as they move throughout a jail or prison presents a nearly constant challenge for corrections officers. As Miles and Cohn (2006) assert, many correctional institutions continue to use rudimentary tools to track the movement of prisoners, and thus, are generally unable to obtain precise locational information about inmates. The authors discuss how inmates are typically monitored as well as a number of potential consequences associated with these techniques in the following passage:

> Monitoring [the movement of prisoners] requires corrections officers to accurately identify individual prisoners by sight as they pass through security posts. It also requires frequent telephone and radio communications between officers at two or more security posts, paper passes authorizing inmates' movements, and dry-erase or clip boards with handwritten records to note when prisoners left one area and entered another. Despite the best precautions and well-thought-out practices, mistakes can be made, officers' attention can be diverted, and late-arriving inmates not noticed or searched for promptly. Late-arriving,

> out-of-place prisoners can cause problems in correctional set-
> tings . . . [they] may be engaging in illegal activities. Assaults and even
> murders have been committed by inmates as they moved from one
> part of a prison or jail to another. (Miles and Cohn, 2006, p. 6)

Recognizing the liabilities associated with conventional systems of inmate
tracking, correctional facilities have begun adopting more technologically
advanced monitoring programs.

One such technique is the tracking of inmates using Radio Frequency
Identification (RFID) devices. As of 2005, RFID systems were already being
implemented in a number of states with large inmate populations (California, Illinois, Michigan, and Ohio; see NLECTC, 2005). RFID systems are
wireless, and inmates wear small transmitters (typically bracelets) which
communicate "real time" data regarding prisoner location to a central
information center. In addition to the continual counting of all inmates,
which ensures that all persons are accounted for, the RFID system also
notifies officers if inmates enter restricted areas of a jail or prison, or
if attempts are made to disable or destroy the transmitter. Because the
information transmitted via RFID is saved to electronic databases, these
data may also be used for administrative purposes to help cut down on
institutional costs. For example, rather than having to be compiled manually, it is possible to use RFID databases to gather information about inmates'
"medicine and meal distribution [and] adherence to time schedules"
(NLECTC, 2005, p. 2).

A number of more elaborate monitoring procedures exist, although
they have yet to be introduced into correctional institutions on a large
scale. Biometric and "smart card" monitoring systems are two such technologies that have characteristics that make them particularly attractive for
use in the field of corrections. Biometrics, broadly defined, refers to "the
automated recognition of a person based on unique physiological or behavioral characteristics, such as fingerprints, speech, face, retina, iris and hand
geometry" (Seymour et al., 2001, p. 75). According to a survey conducted by
the National Institute of Justice, hand geometry and fingerprint detections
devices are the most frequently used biometric devices in correctional
facilities (NLECTC, 2000). Because such characteristics are thought to be
unique for every individual, biometric identification provides a reliable
means of identification. Essentially, the use of biometric devices in correctional institutions is attractive because they closely regulate the movement
of inmates throughout facilities.

In jails and prisons with operational biometric systems, not only are
inmates prevented from entering unauthorized portions of the institution,

but the systems can also be configured to monitor the movement of inmates. If, for example, a prisoner exceeds the allotted time to travel between points, guards will be notified automatically. Corrections officers will also be alerted to attempts made by inmates to gain access to unauthorized locations or if inmates try to escape by posing as a visitor or staff member (NLECTC, 2000). As Seymour et al. (2001, p. 76) contend, the value of using biometric technology in jails and prisons is that "discrepancies are automated, therefore, unauthorized movements will be far easier to detect and validation of inmate locations will be faster and less staff-intensive." Because such measures will help to increase efficiency in diagnosing and responding to problems, they will contribute to increased levels of facility safety and security.

A second emerging correctional technology is the use of credit card-sized devices called smart cards. Smart cards are identification cards that contain the inmate's photograph and that are integrated with a circuit chip that stores pertinent information about each prisoner. Similar to the biometric readers, smart card identification systems can be used for the purposes of controlling inmate access and closely tracking their movements. In addition, the smart cards carried by inmates can be linked to other institutional record systems, which can save institutions both time and money. It is possible that other administrative information can be stored on the smart cards (i.e., personal account balance, phone privileges, medication history), allowing the inmates to use them to fulfill a number of routine tasks (Pilant, 1988; Seymour et al., 2001). One advantage that smart cards have over biometric identification techniques is that their use does not require the same extensive computing infrastructure. Specifically, because smart card systems do not require identification readers to be linked to a centralized database, a "time-consuming search of the entire database" is not necessary each time the system is engaged (Seymour et al., 2001, p. 75). To be sure, smart card systems have their own set of limitations, including how to limit the trading and/or destroying of cards by inmates, but their flexibility suggests that smart card monitoring systems may be more readily incorporated into correctional institutions.

Notification of Officer Duress

The threat of attack is one that correctional officers confront on a daily basis. The number of attacks on staff within jails and prisons is high and will continue to climb as the incarcerated population continues to grow.

According to Stephan and Karberg (2003, p. 9), between 1995 and 2000 the annual number of inmate assaults on staff in federal and state institutions rose by approximately 27% (from 14,200 to 18,000). Although the annual rates of inmate assaults on staff members have remained fairly stable, the sheer increase in the number of attacks points out the need for facilities to employ the most effective systems to help ensure the safety of the correctional officers.

Jails and prisons are equipped with alarm systems that can be triggered by officers at times when they are under duress. Such mechanisms, generally known as officer duress notification devices, are classified into one of three broad categories: (1) panic-button alarms; (2) identification alarms; and (3) identification/location alarms (SPAWAR, 2003; Baker et al., 2004). The characteristics of each type of alarm system currently in operation will be discussed below, including some of their limitations. Following this review will be a description of new directions in the development of duress systems with specific attention paid to their incorporation of new technology.

Panic-button alarms are the simplest type of duress notification system. The panic-button alarms are devices carried by officers that, when activated, send a distress signal to a central command center. The panic-button alarm systems are able to provide information about the location of the troubled officer(s); however, they are unable to identify which officer initiated the alarm. The effectiveness of panic-button alarms is also limited by the fact that it is possible for the button to be inaccessible during times of emergency. For example, if a guard is incapacitated by inmates (i.e., taken captive, knocked unconscious), s/he will be unable to send a call for help. Still, according to an evaluation of duress systems funded by the U.S. Department of Justice, panic-button alarms "are simple and effective for many types of emergencies" (SPAWAR, 2003, p. 4).

Identification alarms are typically small wireless transmitters worn by guards and staff members. As the name implies, identification alarms are able to identify the officer who activates the alarm when s/he encounters a duress situation. In addition to being able to identify officers in trouble, another advantage is that this identification technology is scaleable, meaning that correctional facilities do not have to introduce this system to the entire institution all at once; instead, they can increase the size of the coverage area as necessary. Identification alarm systems share with panic-button alarms the limitation that in extreme situations officers may be rendered incapable of registering a call for help. Another shortcoming of identification alarms is that the systems do not have the capacity to locate or track the officer or staff member in trouble. If an officer activates the alarm and then moves to another location (either voluntarily or involuntarily), finding that officer may be complicated by the fact that those movements will go undetected by identification alarm systems.

The third type of officer duress system combines the strengths of the two aforementioned notification techniques. Specifically, once activated, identification/location alarms are able to identify the officer in need, locate the area from which the call originated, and track any movements of the transmitter. Such elaborate duress notification systems may help to reduce the numbers of deaths and severe injuries sustained by correctional officers because they will allow for officers in close proximity to converge on the problem area more quickly (SPAWAR, 2003). As with any technologically sophisticated program, correctional facilities will incur large costs to purchase and to integrate identification/location alarms into existing systems. Despite the clear advantages to comprehensive identification/location systems, it is likely that the cost of acquiring them will be too steep for many facilities.

According to the review conducted by SPAWAR (2003), duress notification systems that will be more widely available in the years to come are likely to capitalize on several emerging technologies. For instance, Global Positioning Systems (GPS), which determine precise geographic location by transmitting information to satellites, may be utilized to locate and track the position of officers under duress. Currently, GPS systems are best suited for use in outdoor settings, which precludes their use inside prisons and jails. Once this issue is resolved, however, GPS-based duress systems may be a more viable alternative for jails and prisons with smaller operating budgets because they would not require the same heavy acquisition costs.

Notification and tracking systems that transmit radio frequencies may have a more immediate impact on the development of enhanced guard and staff security systems. As described above, due to its versatility and ability to communicate in both indoor and outdoor environments, duress notification systems based on radio frequency identification (RFID) may be forthcoming. Devices that communicate via ultra wideband (UWB) ranges represent another technological advance with the prospect of being adapted for use in duress systems. UWB devices can be used for identification and tracking purposes. Part of what sets UWB technologies apart from other monitoring techniques is that they can be programmed, or "coded," to operate using very specific frequencies, thus increasing the likelihood that the system will be activated by only legitimate distress calls (SPAWAR, 2003).

Perimeter Security

In the strictest sense, perimeter security measures are a means of monitoring prisoners. However, they have a slightly different objective from many of the techniques described above. Specifically, whereas the biometric, RFID, and smart card systems are concerned with inmate access, or keeping inmates *from entering* particular areas, the primary goal of perimeter security techniques is to keep inmates *from leaving* facility grounds. Because the risk of escape is low relative to attacks on corrections staff or attempts to smuggle contraband, the technologies used for the purposes of perimeter security are somewhat less sophisticated than many of the devices used for other purposes. Nevertheless, advances in technology have influenced efforts to ensure that detained individuals remain in corrective custody.

One method undertaken by jails and prisons to enhance perimeter security is the installation of additional video cameras accompanied by an increase in the amount of external lighting (Horn, 2000). With the cameras and lighting structures mounted in plain view, inmates are aware of the increased surveillance, which may help to thwart escape attempts. The relatively low cost to acquire and maintain video surveillance systems certainly adds to their attractiveness. It is worth mentioning that the increased use of video surveillance, both within correctional facilities and for the purposes of perimeter security, also helps to serve some of the broader objectives of correctional institutions. Namely, the use of video surveillance is cited as an effective way to help reduce levels of violence (perpetrated by inmates and guards) in jails and prisons. As the Commission on Safety and Abuse in America's Prisons (Gibbons and Katzenbach, 2006, p. 23) argues, "the ability of a correctional facility to protect prisoners and staff from physical harm is a fundamental measure of the success or failure of that institution – day to day within the walls, and over time as men and women carry their prison experience home to their families and neighborhoods." Moreover, video surveillance is recognized as a necessary precursor to the realization of this goal.

The creation of sensor fences, the process of adding weight and intrusion detectors to the fences surrounding jails and prisons, is one of the more technologically advanced perimeter security devices. Sensor fences were developed by the Institute of Emerging Defense Technologies (IEDT), an organization that is committed to maximizing the use of technology in correctional settings (Mazzara et al., 2003). This monitoring technique works by essentially "converting the entire fence into a detector, similar to a spider web," which is linked to a computer that is able to detect when attempts are made to climb over or cut through the fence (Mazzara et al., 2003, p. 1). Interestingly, the sensor fences are able to differentiate with surprising accuracy between actual ingress and/or egress efforts and shifting in the fences caused by naturally occurring phenomena (i.e., wind, rain, or wildlife sitting on the fence). Although this technology is under active development, Mazzara et al. (2003, p. 2) argue that the "low cost, low maintenance, and low false-alarm rate" are likely to lead to the wide-scale adoption of this technology.

INMATE/OFFICER INTERACTION

The daily contact between inmates and correctional staff members can range from respectful to contentious, unremarkable to extremely dangerous. Due to the increasing diversity among the inmate population, the job of corrections officers can be complicated by an inability to communicate effectively with prisoners (Harrison and Beck, 2006; see also NLECTC, 2003). More importantly, the daily experience of guards working inside the walls of a correctional facility is characterized by an element of unpredictability. Although they will be called on to settle any instances of unrest that occur within jails and prisons, corrections officers are generally not kept apprised of when such disturbances will take place. Faced with uncertain and dangerous circumstances, responding with an appropriate use of force is an added challenge. With increasing frequency, correctional institutions have looked to technology to ease some of the difficulties experienced by corrections officers.

Language Translation Devices

To overcome language barriers, a number of new devices are being developed that may allow officers to communicate with inmates in their native languages without the presence of human translators. Currently, the language assistance technologies are more commonly used by police officers, although their adaptation for corrections settings is underway. One such device, the Voice Response Translator (VRT), operates by translating key phrases spoken into the machine by an officer into one of 50 different languages (NLECTC, 2003). The VRT is not a dynamic language translator, meaning that it cannot be used for the purposes of carrying on a direct conversation with an inmate. Rather, the VRT stores thousands of pre-recorded phrases in the various languages, which can be used to obtain "basic information" during the questioning of non-English-speaking inmates (NLECTC, 2003, p. 1).

While the use of VRTs is able to overcome many of the challenges associated with communicating with inmates not proficient in English, they are limited in that their use does not permit in-depth questioning of detainees. However, devices imbedded with language translation software have been created to promote a more fluid exchange between participants. One such product, called CopTrans, is a two-way translation mechanism that allows individuals to speak directly to one another. The development of the software used in CopTrans devices has focused extensively on translating between English and Spanish. Recognizing the need for more versatile translators, the creators of the software are in the process of designing programs that are capable of communicating in several additional languages (NLECTC, 2003).

There is also the need for corrections staff to be able to review material written by and to inmates to ensure the content is consistent with institutional mandates. Similarly, any documents that need to be read and signed by prisoners will also have to be made available to them in their native languages. One software product that has been designed for just such tasks is called SYSTRAN (NLECTC, 2003). A strength of SYSTRAN is that its conversion algorithm takes into consideration the grammatical structure of the target language, providing a more authentic translation. Further, SYSTRAN may be a particularly attractive tool for use in diverse correctional settings, as it is able to translate content into 36 different languages. A limitation of SYSTRAN is that it is only able to work with electronic files. In other words, SYSTRAN can only translate documents saved in a digitally editable format (i.e., webpage, text file, etc.). Despite these positive attributes, it is clear that developers will need to devise a systematic method of converting paper copies into digital documents before such software can be used to review the large amount of non-digital communication (i.e.,

mail) processed by correctional facilities. More generally, while the technological advances in language translation will not replace the need for human
interpreters, they do provide valuable tools for corrections officers.

Less-than-Lethal Force

Over a decade ago, the U.S. National Institute of Justice convened a conference to discuss the role that technology would play in all aspects of criminal
justice in the 21st century (Travis, 1995). At that conference, which brought
together leading academics and practitioners in the field, calls were made
for the increased use of weapons that promote "the compliance of an
offender or control an incident without the substantial risk of permanent
injury or death to the subject(s)" (Travis, 1995, p. 7). Departments of
corrections around the country responded to this suggestion, and over
the past decade, have adopted a variety of less-than-lethal (LTL) weapon
technologies. Three LTL mechanisms commonly used in jails and prisons
will be discussed in more detail below; namely, oleoresin capsicum (pepper
spray), diversionary (flash-bang) devices, and impact munitions.

Oleoresin capsicum (OC), or pepper spray, is designed to help subdue
unruly inmates by temporarily incapacitating them. In fact, Chan et al.
(2001) contend that while pepper spray has been used in by law enforcement in the United States for 30 years, the caustic effects of exposure to
pepper extract have been used for centuries in other cultures. Pepper spray
operates by irritating "the skin, eyes, and mucous membranes of the upper
respiratory tract," rendering the individual on which it is used incapable
of physically resisting officers (Chan et al., 2001, p. 1). Further, research
has shown that the use of pepper spray to be linked to reductions in assaults
on law enforcement personnel (NIJ, 2003).

Yet, there is concern that pepper spray may have negative health
consequences for inmates, or may even be fatal. Although there have been
a number of instances where individuals died after being exposed to pepper
spray, medical examiners have been unable to find conclusive evidence
that OC was the cause of death (Chan et al., 2001; NIJ, 2003). Indeed, in
all but a two of the deaths reviewed, preconditions such as drug use and/
or diseases were cited as the causes of death. In the two cases where pepper
spray was found to be a contributing factor, both of the victims suffered
from asthma. Despite these unforeseen complications, research supports

the continued use of pepper spray because "solid scientific evidence" confirms its value as a safe and effective LTL method of restraint (Chan et al., 2001, p. 7).

The National Institute of Justice has also provided partial funding for the development of a LTL weapon referred to as the flash-bang round. The flash-bang round is a device that, when detonated, produces an extremely loud burst and overwhelmingly bright explosion. The combination of effects, designed to disorient and terrify the target, carry with them no long-term negative consequences. In the short term, however, the experience is likely to cause the unruly or combative inmate(s) to become "less aggressive, or retreat in full flight" (Lewis, 2003, p. 1). Similar to pepper spray, flash-bang rounds can be deployed at close range to gain control over an individual who fails to yield to officer instructions. It is also possible to detonate these rounds from a distance, which is particularly useful when corrections officers need to disperse groups of inmates. This long-range capability also benefits staff members by allowing them to restore order in the facility while maintaining a safe distance from potentially dangerous situations. That is, the flash-bang rounds represent an effective means of reducing unnecessary fatalities, while making the job of the officers easier and safer (Lewis, 2003, p. 2).

Impact munitions are an array of LTL projectiles that are also used in jail and prison settings to minimize the number of inmate deaths. Many of these munitions are fired from guns (i.e., bean bags, plastic or rubber bullets), but they dispense a blunt-trauma that is certainly painful, but far less injurious than conventional ammunition. Because impact munitions are designed for use with conventional firearms, they are particularly useful for the purposes of crowd control. However, unlike the other methods of LTL force, such as those described previously, the use of impact munitions carries a higher likelihood of serious injury or death. In their study of the impacts of LTL munitions, Hubbs and Klinger (2004) reveal the conditions under which fatalities resulted from the use of impact munitions. More specifically, the data indicate that when the rounds are fired at close proximity, or when individuals are fired upon multiple times, there is an elevated risk that they will sustain severe internal injuries that may be fatal. The authors recognize the continued need to seek mechanisms that will lower the number of deaths resulting from the use of impact munitions even further. However, because the "likelihood of death from being shot by impact munitions is extremely low," Hubbs and Klinger (2004, p. 22) conclude that these devices remain a relatively safe and effective tool for use in all aspects of law enforcement.

OTHER HARD TECHNOLOGY APPLICATIONS

Nowhere is the increased reliance on technology in the field of corrections more evident than in the systems designed to control inmates defined as high-risk, or those who require careful management. Although this group of inmates represents a relatively small portion of the total incarcerated population (between 10-15%), they warrant special treatment because they are violent, disruptive, or fail to abide by prison rules (Austin and McGinnis 2004). Moreover, as Austin and McGinnis (2004, p. 3) suggest, the differential treatment of high-risk inmates has practical implications because "a disproportionate amount of staff and agency resources must be allocated to them to maintain prisoner safety and institutional security." The current trend in handling this group of high-risk inmates – approximately 20,000 inmates nationally – has been to remove them from the general prison population and to place them in ultra-secure housing units (Mears, 2005). Inmates confined to the super maximum-security, or supermax, settings are very restricted in their contact with others, as they remain isolated in their cells for up to 23 hours each day.

Despite the long periods of isolation, the confinement experiences in supermax prisons are uniquely different from traditional methods of segregating inmates (i.e., solitary confinement). As Pettigrew (2002, p. 194) argues: "advanced technology distinguishes supermax prisons from their conventional counterparts and allows for the isolation of prisoners . . . [in ways that were] previously impossible." Namely, a key objective in the design of supermax facilities is to minimize the need for interpersonal contact between inmates and corrections officers. For example, cells are constructed with audio and video monitoring devices, meaning that officers have the ability to observe prisoners and to issue commands remotely. Similarly, because inmates are required to eat in their cells, guards do not escort them to and from the dining facilities. Person-to-person contact is further limited by the fact that meetings between the inmates and persons outside of the institution (i.e., lawyers, family, friends) are conducted via closed-circuit television (Pettigrew, 2002).

In principle, the removal of inmates prone to commit acts of violence against corrections staff or fellow inmates is thought to yield positive results for correctional facilities. Based on a survey of state prison wardens, Mears (2005, p. 47) concludes that supermax prisons "hold considerable promise for improving many dimensions of correctional management, especially in the areas of creating greater order, safety, and control." Yet in practice, these encouraging findings do not come without cost. Critics of supermax prisons argue that the extreme social isolation inmates in these units are forced to endure is inhumane and perhaps unconstitutional (Toch, 2001; see also Pettigrew, 2002). Toch (2001) argues that the lack of human interaction is likely to damage inmates psychologically. The words of the inmates themselves may provide some insight into the levels of despair that accompanies a lack of human contact. In a recent *New York Times* article, an inmate currently confined in a supermax prison in California underscores his struggles with isolation by saying that he would "cut off his right arm to be able to hold his mother" (Liptak, 2006). Further, Toch (2001, p. 383) contends that the depravation experienced in supermax prisons "impairs the mental health of prisoners . . . [making] violent men more dangerous." While the courts will ultimately decide if supermax prisons represent a cruel and unusual form of punishment, it is interesting to note that critics of this confinement strategy charge that they perpetuate the very behavior they are trying to control.

Issues to Consider

In the preceding review, the role that technology plays in three key areas of corrections was discussed in detail. Generally, the extant literature presents the technologies used in jails and prisons in a positive light and confirms their effectiveness. In addition, it is evident from this research that the field of corrections relies heavily on technology and that practitioners endorse the continued use of technologically innovative solutions to help maintain order and safety within correctional institutions. These are certainly important objectives, and ones that cannot be realized without the aid of technology. Still, if we turn a more critical eye to these results, they may provide us with a slightly different impression.

One topic that was discussed only indirectly was the fact that the companies developing many of the devices described above stand to profit from the adoption of their product(s). It stands to reason, then, that these companies have a vested interest in presenting their products in the most favorable light possible. Further, because government agencies often partner with these companies, this may further complicate the ability to objectively evaluate a given technology. For example, each year the Office of Law Enforcement Technology Commercialization (OLETC) and the National Institute of Justice stage a mock prison riot in Moundsville, West Virginia. At this event, newly developed proprietary technologies are showcased and officers are able to use them in "real world" scenarios. Therefore, as a co-sponsor of the mock riot, the NIJ is perhaps indirectly advocating the use of certain items before their effectiveness has been independently validated by a disinterested party.

A more pragmatic concern has to do with the cost associated with the use of technology, both in terms of acquisition and staff training. With the size of the incarcerated population increasing and jail and prison budgets shrinking, the ability to effectively manage prisoners has never been more difficult. One challenge that the field of corrections faces is how to strike a balance between the amount of resources dedicated to inmate control (i.e., technological upgrades) compared to that devoted to the treatment (i.e., mental health services, programming) of inmates. Although both are fundamentally important components of the correctional process, unfortunately, these factors are inversely related. In other words, the more resources that are earmarked for the former, the less the latter receives.

Therefore, the issue at hand is not simply whether technology should continue to play an important role in correctional institutions. The weight of the evidence clearly documents that correctional officers and inmates both enjoy the benefits of technological innovations. Rather, the more pressing concern is how much should be invested in technologically-based initiatives. Although the balance of control versus treatment is likely to vary across institutions, everywhere this decision must be made with careful consideration. To be sure, technology will continue to advance at an exponential rate, but it will be critical not to let the desire for technological solutions outpace the need to treat individuals under the care and supervision of America's correctional systems.

◆ ◆ ◆ ◆

REFERENCES

Austin, J., & McGinnis, K. (2004). *Classification of high-risk and special management prisoners: a national assessment of current practices.* Washington, DC: U.S. Department of Justice, National Institute of Corrections (NIC-194468; http://www.nicic.org/downloads/pdf/video/04_classif_participguide.pdf).

Baker, R., Broyles, E., & Pomerada, J. (2004). Navy provides input to DOJ's officer duress system guide. *Corrections Today, 66*, 85-86 (http://www.ncjrs.gov/pdffiles1/nij/02_04.pdf).

Butler, R. F. (2002). *Mailroom evaluation scenario, Final Report*. Washington, DC: U.S. Department of Justice, National Institute of Justice, Washington, D.C (NIJ-199048; http://www.ncjrs.gov/pdffiles1/nij/grants/199048.pdf)

Chan, T. C., Vilke, G M., Clausen, J., Clark, R., Schmidt, P., Snowden, T., & Neuman, T. (2001). *Pepper spray's effects on a suspect's ability to breathe*. Washington, DC: U.S. Department of Justice, National Institute of Justice (NIJ-188069; http://www.ncjrs.gov/pdffiles1/nij/188069.pdf).

Cothran, L. (2001, Winter). Technology for corrections: California style. *TechBeat*, 1-3 (see: http://www.nlectc.org/techbeat/winter2001/TechCalifWint01.pdf).

Gibbons, J. J., & de B. Katzenbach, N. (2006). *Confronting confinement: A report of the Commission on Safety and Abuse in America's prisons*. New York: Vera Institute of Justice (http://www.prisoncommission.org/pdfs/Confronting_Confinement.pdf).

Harrison, P. M., & Beck, A. J. (2005). *Prisoners in 2004*. Washington, DC: U.S. Department of Justice, Bureau of Justice Statistics (NCJ-210667; http://www.ojp.usdoj.gov/bjs/pub/pdf/p04.pdf).

Harrison, P. M., & Beck, A. J. (2006). *Prison and jail inmates at midyear 2005*. Washington, DC: U.S. Department of Justice, Bureau of Justice Statistics (NCJ-213133; http://www.ojp.usdoj.gov/bjs/pub/pdf/pjim05.pdf).

Horn, M. (2000, Winter). Keeping bad guys behind bars. *TechBeat* 1-2 (http://www.nlectc.org/techbeat/winter2000/BadGuysWint2000.pdf).

Hubbs, K., & Klinger, D. (2004). *Impact munitions data base of use and effects*. Washington, DC: U.S. Department of Justice, National Institute of Justice (NCJ-195739; http://www.ncjrs.gov/pdffiles1/nij/grants/204433.pdf).

Lewis, B. (2003). NIJ's less-than-lethal flash-bang round project. *Corrections Today, 65*, 117-118 (http://www.ncjrs.gov/pdffiles1/nij/08_03.pdf).

Lincoln, J. M., Chen, L-H., Mair, J.S., Biermann, P. J., & Baker, S. P. (2006). Inmate-made weapons in prison facilities: Assessing the injury risk. *Injury Prevention, 12*, 195-198.

Liptak, A. (2006). Behind bars, he turns M&M's into an art form. *New York Times*, July 22 (online edition).

Mazzara, A. F., Swanson, D. C., & Nicholas, N. C. (2003). Sensor fence: A new approach to large-perimeter security. *Corrections Today, 65*, 1-2 (http://www.ncjrs.gov/pdffiles1/nij/02_03.pdf).

Mears, D. P. (2005). A critical look at supermax prisons. *Corrections Compendium, 30*, 43-49.

Miles, C. A., & Cohn, J. P. (2006). Tracking prisoners in jail with biometrics: An experiment in a Navy brig. *National Institute of Justice Journal, 253*, 6-9. (http://www.ojp.usdoj.gov/nij/journals/253/tracking.html).

Mumola, C. J. (2005). *Suicide and homicide in state prisons and local jails*. Washington, DC: U.S. Department of Justice, Bureau of Justice Statistics (NCJ-210036; http://www.ojp.usdoj.gov/bjs/pub/pdf/shsplj.pdf).

National Institute of Justice (NIJ) (2003). *Research for practice: The effectiveness and safety of pepper spray*. Washington, DC: U.S. Department of Justice, National Institute of Justice, (NCJ-195739; http://www.ojp.usdoj.gov/nij/pubs-sum/195739.htm).

National Law Enforcement and Corrections Technology Center (NLECTC) (2000). Biometrics in corrections. *TechBeat* (Fall), 1-3. (http://www.nlectc.org/techbeat/fall2000/BiometricsFall 2000.pdf).

National Law Enforcement and Corrections Technology Center (NLECTC) (2002). The check is in the mail. *TechBeat* (Summer), 1-3 (http://www.justnet.org/techbeat/summer2002/CheckMailSum02.pdf).

National Law Enforcement and Corrections Technology Center (NLECTC) (2003). Nothing lost in translation. *TechBeat* (Fall), 1-3 (http://www.nlectc.org/techbeat/fall2003/NothlostFall03.pdf).

National Law Enforcement and Corrections Technology Center (NLECTC) (2005). Technology primer: Radio frequency identification. *TechBeat* (Summer), 1 (http://www.justnet.org/techbeat/summer2005/Technology_Primer.pdf).

Parmeter, J. E., Murray, D. W., & Hannum, D. W. (2000). *Guide for the selection of drug detectors for law enforcement applications.* Washington, DC: U.S. Department of Justice, National Institute of Justice (NIJ Guide 601-00; http://www.ncjrs.gov/pdffiles1/nij/183260.pdf).

Paulter, N. G. (2001). *Guide to the technologies of concealed weapon and contraband detection.* Washington, DC: U.S. Department of Justice, National Institute of Justice (NIJ Guide 602-00; http://www.ncjrs.gov/pdffiles1/nij/184432.pdf).

Pettigrew, C. A. (2002). Comment: Technology and the eighth amendment: The problem with supermax prisons. *North Carolina Journal of Law and Technology, 4,* 191-215.

Pilant, L. (1998). Smart cards: An information tool for the future. *National Institute of Justice Journal,* 23-25 (http://www.ojp.usdoj.gov/nij/journals/jr000236.htm).

Quinn, D. (2001). Mock prison riot 2001 – A technology showcase. *Corrections Today, 63,* 178-179 (http://www.ncjrs.gov/pdffiles1/nij/04_01.pdf).

Seymour, S., Baker, R., & Besco, M. (2001). Inmate tracking with biometric and smart card technology. *Corrections Today, 63,* 75-77 (http://www.ncjrs.gov/pdffiles1/nij/biometrics_smartcard.pdf).

SPAWAR Systems Center (2003). *Correctional officers duress systems: Selection guide.* North Charleston, SC: (http://www.ncjrs.gov/pdffiles1/nij/grants/202947.pdf).

Stephan, J. J., & Karberg, J. C. (2003). *Census of state and federal correctional facilities, 2000.* Washington, DC: U.S. Department of Justice, Bureau of Justice Statistics (NCJ-198272; http://www.ojp.usdoj.gov/bjs/pub/pdf/csfcf00.pdf).

Toch, H. (2001). The future of supermax confinement. *The Prison Journal, 3,* 376-388.

Travis, J. (1995). *Second Annual Conference on Law Enforcement Technology for the 21st Century: Conference Report, May 15-17, 1995.* Washington, DC: U.S. Department of Justice, National Institute of Justice (NCJ-158024; http://www.nlectc.org/pdffiles/confrep.pdf).

Turner, A. (2001). Corrections technology committee: A valuable resource for practitioners. *Corrections Today, 63,* 154-155; http://www.ncjrs.gov/pdffiles1/nij/08_01.pdf).

Wright, S., & Butler, R. F. (2001). Technology takes on drug smugglers: Can drug detection technology stop drugs from entering prisons? *Corrections Today, 63,* 66-68; http://www.ncjrs.gov/pdffiles1/nij/drug_detection.pdf).

11. INSTITUTIONAL CORRECTIONS AND SOFT TECHNOLOGY

by

James M. Byrne

and

April Pattavina

University of Massachusetts, Lowell

INTRODUCTION

The term *soft technology* has been defined elsewhere in this text as "the various forms of information technology used to administer criminal justice programs and manage and control criminal justice populations" (Byrne and Rebovich, this volume), including management information system (MIS)-based software programs, offender classification instruments, crime analysis programs/hot spot identification capabilities, and new information sharing protocols and expanded information system networks. There are a variety of current and potential soft technology applications used in problem solving in *institutional* settings, focusing on a wide range of inmate-related (e.g., classification, treatment and control) and staff-related (management and protection) activities, including: the initial classification of inmates; subsequent offender location decisions; ongoing offender monitoring and management and behavior change strategies (both health- and behavior-related); crime analysis within prison and jail; and information sharing with police, courts, corrections, public health, and public/private sector treatment providers during offender reentry.

In this chapter, recent soft technology advances in three areas of prison management are described in detail: (1) initial inmate classification; (2) in-prison inmate management; and (3) inmate release from prison and reentry to the community. Evidence of the effectiveness of each innovation is reviewed, and the key issues and controversies related to the ongoing technological transformation of institutional corrections are discussed.

THE NEW TECHNOLOGY OF
INMATE CLASSIFICATION

One of the underlying assumptions of the U.S. prison system is that prison violence and disorder is affected by decisions made each day, not only about *who* should be in prison and for *how long*, but also about *where* offenders will be housed within the prison system and *when* they should be moved from one level of security to the next. With over two million inmates currently under institutional control in the U.S., it is clear that imprisonment is viewed as an appropriate sanction for individuals convicted of a variety of crimes (violent, drug, property, public order). To efficiently impose this sanction, the U.S. currently has over 5,000 adult prisons and jails, each with its own unique design features, staffing ratios, design and operational capacity, offender population characteristics and resource level. In each of these facilities, classification decisions are made that directly affect the level of violence and disorder in prison. According to the Commission on Safety and Abuse in America's Prisons (Gibbons and Katzenbach, 2006, p. 29):

> Reducing violence among prisoners depends on the decisions corrections administrators make about where to house prisoners and how to supervise them. Perhaps most important are the classification decisions managers make to ensure that housing units do not contain incompatible individuals or groups of people: informants and those they informed about, repeat and violent offenders and vulnerable potential victims, and others who might clash with violent consequences. And these classifications should not be made on the basis of race or ethnicity, or their proxies (*Johnson v. California*, 2005)

In the following section, we highlight the recent developments in the classification and reclassification of offenders sent to prison, focusing on the impact of new advances in information technology generally, and new automated MIS system development in particular, on decisions made regarding the classification, control and treatment of inmates in prison settings.

External and Internal Classification Systems

At the outset of any review of prison classification technology, it is important to distinguish *external* from *internal* classification decisions. In a recent nationwide review of prison classification systems, Austin (2003, p. 2) highlighted the difference between external and internal classification:

External classification places a prisoner at a custody level that will determine where the prisoner will be housed. Once the prisoner arrives at a facility, internal classification determines which cell or housing unit, as well as which facility programs (e.g. education, vocational, counseling, and work assignments) [to which] the prisoner will be assigned.

We highlight the key features of both external and internal classification systems in the following section. Figure 1 provides an overview of external and internal classification systems.

External Classification Systems

Objective *external* classification systems are currently used by all federal and state prison systems in the U.S. to determine the initial level of security/control needed over the incoming prisoner population. Utilizing data such as the seriousness of the commitment offense, sentence length, the offender's criminal history, his/her escape history and prior incarceration history and special monitoring needs (due to security threat assessment, gang affiliation, potential victimization, etc.), each offender is assessed using an objective risk classification system. Based on the offender's overall assessment "score," he/she is assigned to a minimum, medium, maximum, or super-max prison facility. An example of one such objective scoring system is included in Table 1.

In relation to inmate management, The initial inmate location decision can be viewed as an example of the critical link between organizational structure (e.g., the number and type of prisons available in a particular prison system) and organizational purpose (e.g., offender punishment and control versus offender change). We can learn a great deal about a prison system by closely examining how and why inmate location decisions are made. Consider the following: according to a recent nationwide review of prison classification systems conducted by Austin and McGinnis (2004), approximately 80% of the current federal and state prison population has been identified as being appropriate for location in the *general* prison population: these inmates are placed in minimum (35%), medium (35%) and maximum security facilities (10%) and in super-max facilities (about 1%). Approximately 15% of all inmates are classified (or reclassified) as *special* populations requiring separate housing away from the general population of prisoners: they are placed in administrative segregation (6%), protective custody (2%), and facilities designed specifically for inmates with severe mental health (2%) or medical problems (2%). The remaining

Figure 1: Overview of External and Internal Classification Systems

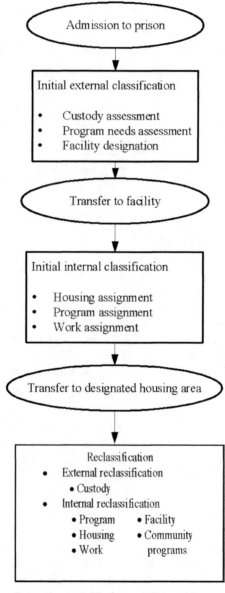

Source: Austin & Hardyman (2004, p. 10).

Table 1: Virginia Department of Corrections Initial Inmate Classification Score Sheet

Inmate Name._____ Number._____ Date._____

1. HISTORY OF INSTITUTIONAL VIOLENCE (Jail or prison, score most serious within last 5 years.)

None	.0	_____
Assault not involving use of a weapon and not resulting in serious injury	.8	
Assault involving use of a weapon and/or resulting in serious injury or death	.20	

2. SEVERITY OF CURRENT OFFENSE (Refer to the Severity of Offense Scale. Score most serious offense if there are multiple convictions.)

Low	.0	_____
Low moderate	.1	
Moderate	.3	
High	.8	
Highest	.15	

3. PRIOR OFFENSE HISTORY SEVERITY (Refer to the Severity of Offense Scale. Score most serious felony conviction in inmate's history.)

None	.0	_____
Low or low moderate	.1	
Moderate	.2	
High	.7	
Highest	.10	

4. ESCAPE HISTORY (Last 5 years)

None	.0	_____
An escape or attempt from outside security perimeter	.4	
An escape or attempt from within security perimeter and/or from custody or direct supervision	.8	

5. LENGTH OF TIME REMAINING TO SERVE

5 years or less	.2	_____
5 years 1 day – 10 years	.4	
10 years 1 day – 20 years	.10	
20 years 1 day – 80 years	.15	
80 years 1 day – LIFE/LIFE +	.20	

6. CURRENT DETAINER

None	0	_____
Felony and/or INS detainer	10	

7. CURRENT AGE

Under age 21	2	_____
21–26	0	
27–34	-4	
36 and above	-6	

8. PRIOR FELONY CONVICTIONS

None	0	_____
One	2	
Two or more	4	

9. OTHER STABILITY FACTORS (Score all appropriate factors.)

High school diploma or GED.	-1	
Employed or attending school (full- or part-time) for 6 months or longer	-1	
Prior successful confinement in Security Level I	-2	

TOTAL POINTS _____

Table 1 *(continued)*

INMATE NAME:_____ NUMBER:_____ UNIT:_____

DATE:_____ CIRC:_____ MED. LOC:_____ MH: _____

ANNUAL REVIEW:_____ ADMINISTRATIVE REVIEW:_____ TOTAL SCORE:_____

SCORED SECURITY LEVEL

to +6 pts................LEVEL 1   14 – 20 pts................LEVEL 3   28 – 33pts................LEVEL 5

7 – 13 pts ....LEVEL 2   21 – 27 pts................LEVEL 4   34+ pts................LEVEL 6

MANDATORY RESTRICTORS

- ☐ R1 More than 20 years remaining to serve (must be assigned to Level III or higher)
- ☐ R2 Current violent sex offense (must be assigned to Level III or higher)
- ☐ R3 1st degree murder (must be assigned to Level II or higher)
- ☐ R4 Enemy at scored level

DISCRETIONARY OVERRIDES

High — Increases Security Level
- ☐ H1 Assaultive prior institutional conduct
- ☐ H2 Serious prior criminal record indicates caution
- ☐ H3 Severity of current offense
- ☐ H4 Serious escape history/risk
- ☐ H5 Recent pattern of poor institutional adjustment
- ☐ H6 Needs to establish stable adjustment
- ☐ H7 Other _____

Low — Decreases Security Level
- ☐ L1 Exceptional institutional conduct
- ☐ L2 Singular nature of incident
- ☐ L3 Prior success at lower level
- ☐ L4 Other _____

ICA RECOMMENDATIONS

TOTAL SCORE:_____ RESTRICTOR:_____ OVERRIDE:_____ RECOMMENDED LEVEL:_____

PRIMARY TREATMENT(S) NEEDED:_____

RECOMMENDED ASSIGNMENTS:_____ COMMENTS:_____

SIGNATURE:_____ DATE:_____

WARDEN/SUPERINTENDENT ACTION

APPROVE ICA ☐ DISAPPROVE ICA ☐ RESTRICTOR____ OVERRIDE_____ SECURITY LEVEL_____

ASSIGNMENTS:_____ COMMENTS:_____

SIGNATURE:_____ DATE:_____

CENTRAL CLASSIFICATION BOARD

APPROVE ☐ DISAPPROVE ☐ RESTRICTOR:_____ OVERRIDE:_____ SECURITY LEVEL:_____

COMMENTS:_____

SIGNATURE:_____ DATE:_____

DISTRIBUTION: CCR – WHITE   ICR – YELLOW   INMATE – PINK

Table 1 *(continued)*

Exhibit A.4. Virginia Department of Corrections — Security Levels

Levels	Restrictions
Level 1 — Low	No Murder I or II, robbery, sex-related crime, kidnap/abduction, felonious assault (current or prior), flight/escape, carjacking, malicious wounding, and assault/flight/FTA pattern, no escape risks, no felony detainers, and no disruptive behaviors.
Level 1 — High	No Murder I or II, sex-related crime, kidnap/abduction, and flight/escape history, and no disruptive behaviors in last 24 months.
Level 2	For Initial Assignment only: No escape history within past 5 years. Single life sentences must have reached parole eligibility date. No disruptive behavior in last 24 months prior to consideration for a transfer to any less secure facility.
Level 3	Single, multiple, and life+ sentences—must have served 20 consecutive years of sentence. No disruptive behavior in last 24 months prior to consideration for a transfer to any less secure facility.
Level 4	Long Term: Single, multiple, and life+ sentences. No disruptive behavior in last 24 months prior to consideration for a transfer to any less secure facility.
Level 5	Long Term: Single, multiple, and life+ sentences. No disruptive behavior in last 24 months prior to consideration for a transfer to any less secure facility.
Level 6	Long Term: Single, multiple, and life+ sentences. Profile: Disruptive, assaultive, severe behavior problems, predatory-type behavior, and/or escape risk. No disruptive behavior in last 24 months prior to consideration for a transfer to any less secure facility.

Source: Hardyman, Austin and Tulloch, 2002, pp. 7-8.

5% of inmates were not classified at the time of this review (Austin and McGinnis, 2004).

There was considerable variation across states on the utilization of options for housing *special populations*, which suggests that this classification is being used for different purposes in different state prison systems. For example, the percentage of inmates placed in administrative and disciplinary segregation increased 40% nationally between 1995 and 2000; by comparison, the total prison population increased by 28% during this same period (Gibbons and Katzenbach, 2006). However, a recent study of special population units by Austin and McGinnis (2004) noted that several states reported using segregation for less than 1% of the male and female inmate populations (Maryland, New Hampshire, Ohio, and Vermont), while a few states placed a much larger percentage of inmates in segregation: e.g., West

Virginia (16%), New Mexico (13%), and Colorado (8%). Similarly, there was also variation in the percentage of inmates assigned to mental health units: while several states housed less than 1% of their male and female inmate populations in mental health units (Florida, Indiana, Missouri, New York, Oregon, Pennsylvania, Vermont), two states (Georgia – 12 %, and Alaska – 5%) took a very different approach to the housing of mentally ill inmates.

The decision on which offenders will be placed in general verses special populations is affected by the size of the available special population system, as well as the outcome of the external classification process. In some prison systems (e.g., Rhode Island), only a small proportion (fewer than 5%) of all inmates are housed in one of these special population units; in other systems (e.g., Massachusetts), a much larger proportion (close to 40%) of all inmates is placed in these locations. It should be emphasized that the size of a particular state's special population system is not driven entirely by inmate characteristics and classification criteria; it represents a policy choice by corrections managers in each system. Since it costs much more to house offenders in special population groupings than in general population groupings, it is not surprising that some corrections systems limit the size of the special population system by narrowly defining the criteria used to make this initial classification decision.

Similarly, the designation of security levels within the general population also affects correctional costs, with maximum security being significantly more expensive to operate than either medium or minimum security facilities. It probably doesn't come as a surprise that an inmate placed in a maximum security facility in one state (or federal) system, may be placed in a different security level facility somewhere else. In fact, Austin and McGinnis (2004, p. 36) argue that: "many general population prisoners classified as maximum custody do not present management problems and are so classified because of the crime they committed, their prison sentence, or a violent event that occurred many years in the past." If their assessment is correct, then factors (e.g., punishment) other than risk control (or risk reduction) are driving the initial assignment process in many state and federal prisons today.

We should emphasize that the success of an objective external classification system is not measured primarily in terms of cost containment: it is also measured in terms of its contribution to prison safety. Table 2 below highlights the types of screening currently completed in state prisons, according to a recent national survey of the management of high risk

Table 2: Typology of High-Risk and Special Management Inmates

Category and Assessment Method	Placement
Security threat group Subjective assessment based on at least three sources of independent objective data as applied to well-defined agency criteria.	Administrative segregation or general population – high custody.
Likely victim Subjective assessment based on at least three sources of independent objective data as applied to well-defined agency criteria.	Protective custody or restricted general population facilities.
Mentally ill Standardized psychometric tests and clinical judgment by mental health staff.	Mental health unit and/or administrative segregation.
Chronic misbehavior – assaultive Objective external classification.	General population – high custody, administrative segregation, or mental health unit.
Chronic misbehavior – nonassaultive Objective external classification.	General population – high custody, administrative segregation, or mental health unit.
Nonsexual predator Subjective assessment based on at least three sources of independent objective data as applied to well-defined agency criteria.	General population – high custody, administrative segregation, or mental health unit.
Sexual predator Subjective assessment based on at least three sources of independent objective data as applied to well-defined agency criteria.	General population – high custody, administrative segregation, or mental health unit.
Developmentally disabled Standardized psychometric tests and clinical judgment by mental health staff.	General population – high custody, administrative segregation, or mental health unit.

Source: Austin and McGinnis, 2004, p. 2.

inmates completed for the U.S. National Institute of Corrections. In order to make prisons safer, a variety of assessment instruments are used to classify inmates in each of the following areas: (1) threat/dangerousness, (2) mental health/potential for victimization and self-injury, (3) physical health, (4) treatment/programming needs, and (5) escape/flight risk. In the following section, we highlight the types of assessment instruments currently employed in each classification area.

Area 1: Dangerousness and Threat Assessment

Once an inmate is sent to prison, a determination must be made regarding the danger this particular inmate poses to others while in prison. This assessment examines both individual offender characteristics (i.e., individual dangerousness) and the inmate's affiliation with groups designated as threats to institutional security (i.e., group dangerousness), including gangs and terrorist/radical groups.

Dangerousness Assessment Technology

Once an offender is sentenced to a period of incarceration in a federal or state prison, he/she is sent to a central classification unit and the offender assessment process begins. One of the first assessments made at this point is a dangerousness assessment. *Dangerousness* refers to the likelihood that an inmate will be violent during his/her period of incarceration. Although prison – and prisoner – safety is an important stated goal for all corrections systems in the U.S., the prediction of dangerousness is not an easy task and there is much debate on the reliability and validity of current dangerousness classification procedures (Austin and McGinnis, 2004). Nonetheless, objective assessment instruments are widely viewed as an improvement over past practice, which relied on subjective assessments by intake staff of the likelihood of inmate violence while in prison (Gottfredson and Moriarty, 2006).

There are a number of different risk assessment instruments currently in use across the country. Some instruments focus on specific forms of violence (e.g., the Rapid Risk Assessment for Sexual Offense Recidivism [RRASOR], the Sexual Violence Risk-20 [SVR-20], and the Static-99 all target sex offending), while other instruments assess an individual's general propensity for violent/assaultive behavior (e.g., the Hare Psychopathy Checklist-Revised (PCL-R; see chapters by Andrew Harris and Lurigio and by Pattavina and Taxman chapter, this volume). The main problem associated with using the latest generation of risk assessment tools in prison settings is that these instruments were developed and validated using subsequent offender behavior in the *community* as the outcome measure of interest; they have not been developed and tested using institutional violence as the criterion/outcome measure.

A related problem associated with use of the current generation of risk instruments is that rates of violence – at least officially reported rates – are lower in prison than in the inmates' home communities. Because the base rate of various forms of institutional violence is very low, it is likely that current risk instruments – when validated – will have difficulty distinguishing dangerous from non-dangerous inmates (Hardyman et al., 2002). This creates two potential problems for corrections managers: (1) false positives, i.e., individuals predicted to be violent who actually do not become violent while in prison; and (2) false negatives, i.e., individuals predicted to be non-dangerous who do in fact commit a violent act while in prison. And finally, given the fact that these classification instruments were developed and tested on populations consisting almost entirely of male offenders, it is possible that their application to the classification of *female* inmates results in even higher levels of misclassification.

Threat Assessment Technology

In addition to individual risk assessment instruments targeting inmate violence, intake classification units are also expected to conduct a threat assessment, focusing on the gang affiliation – if any – of incoming inmates, as well as the inmate's connection with known radical/terrorist groups. Focusing first on gang classification and security threat group (STG) membership, a recent review by Austin and McGinnis (2004) revealed that while almost 90% of all prisons screen for gang/security threat group membership, there was significant variation in the percentage of the inmate population (male and female) actually identified as gang/STG members. In some states, such as Wisconsin (43%), New Mexico (36%), and Minnesota (30%), a large proportion of the incoming inmate population was identified as gang/STG affiliated; but in several other prison systems the initial screening resulted in the identification of a much smaller proportion of the inmate population. In California and Michigan, for example, only 1% of the inmates were classified as gang/STG members (Austin and McGinnis, 2004). While it is likely that gang/STG group membership varies from jurisdiction to jurisdiction, we agree with Austin and McGinnis that, "this variation may be the result of differences in classification methods or definitions of gang/STG membership used by the responding states" (2004, p. 44).

Gang/STG membership can be determined from a range of sources, including inmate interviews, official police and court records, and evidence of inmate tattoos identifying gang affiliation. In Florida's department of corrections, for example, an inmate would be classified as a gang member if he/she met any two of the following criteria:

- Admits to criminal street gang membership

- Is identified as a gang member by a parent/guardian

- Is identified as a gang member by a documented reliable informant

- Reside/frequents a gang's area, adopts their style of dress, hand signs, or tattoos, and associates with known gang members

- Is identified as a gang member by an informant of previously untested reliability and such identification is corroborated by independent information

- Was arrested more than once in the company of identified gang member for offenses which are consistent with usual criminal street gang activity

- Is identified as a criminal street gang member by physical evidence such as photographs or other documentation

- Was stopped in the company of known criminal street gang members four or more times.

Prison systems classify the gang affiliation and/or STG membership of incoming inmates based on the notion that the prison violence – and disorder – can be directly linked to gang/STG involvement. However, a number of recent reviews have indicated that the influence of *gangs* on both community *and* institutional violence and disorder has been exaggerated (Byrne and Hummer, in press; Byrne, 2006). In addition, there is no current empirical evidence identifying a link between *security threat group* membership and prison violence (Cilluffo and Saathoff, 2006). Despite this research shortfall, gang/STG status will likely continue to result in placement of inmates in administrative segregation and/or location in a high security facility (maximum security or supermax prison). In some prison systems, it may even affect offender location during the initial prison classification process or upon transfer to a new institution.

In California, for example, until recently corrections authorities were assigning inmates to racially segregated cells in order to "prevent members of race-based gangs from turning on one another in two-man cells" (Lane, 2005, p. A04). However, in *Johnson v. California*, the U.S. Supreme Court declared this practice unconstitutional. According to Justice Sandra Day O'Connor's opinion in the case : "When government officers are permitted to use race as a proxy for gang membership and violence without demonstrating a compelling government interest and proving that their means are narrowly tailored, society as a whole suffers" (as quoted in Lane, 2005, p. A04). While only a few other state prison systems (such as Texas and Oklahoma) consider race explicitly in determining initial inmate location, the Supreme Court's decision in this case reinforced the need for an objective risk classification system that has been constructed and validated using prison violence as the outcome measure.

We suspect that as new methods for identifying gang membership and/or security threat group status and then placing inmates in general or special population units are introduced in response to this decision, the Supreme Court will be involved once again. One area of potential controversy is an upcoming initiative to improve data collection (and information sharing) on both religious preferences and religious conversion in prison; this approach is based on the belief that prisoner radicalization may result in increased levels of domestic terrorism in this country over the next few years. Since it is estimated that over 70% of religious conversions in prison involve conversion to Islam, it appears that the identification and tracking of this group of converted inmates that will be the primary focus of this strategy, although radicalized right-wing Christian extremist groups (e.g., the Aryan Nation) are also identified (Cilluffo and Saathoff, 2006). To the extent that religion – like race in California – is explicitly used to classify inmates and place them in either the general or special populations, we anticipate a similar response by the Supreme Court, in large part because "there is insufficient information about prisoner radicalization to qualify the threat" (Cilluffo and Saathoff, 2006, 15). However, it is certainly possible that religion (and religious conversion) will be included in the next wave of threat assessment instruments developed for use in the federal and state prison systems. It is also likely that we will begin tracking the movements of radicalized inmates, both while inside prison and upon return to the community.

Area 2: Mental Health Assessment

A number of recent reviews of federal, state, and local prisons and jails in the United States have identified the classification, treatment, and control of the mentally ill offender as one of the most serious management problems facing prison officials today (Gibbons and Katzenbach, 2006; American Correctional Association, 2003; National Commission on Correctional Health Care [NCCHC], 2002). While estimates of the size of the mentally ill prison and jail populations vary by the type of assessment completed and the definition of mental illness used, there is general agreement that – at minimum – about one in five offenders entering our prison system today has a serious mental disorder (Gibbons and Katzenbach, 2006; NCCHC, 2002). According to the results of a recent NCCHC review of correctional health care, for example, the rate of schizophrenia or other psychotic disorders is three to five times greater among prisoners than in the U.S. population as whole, while the rate of bipolar disorder is 1.5 to 3 times greater (NCCHC, 2002). Conservatively, it is estimated that "there are at least 350,000 mentally ill people in prison and jail on any given day" (Ditton, 1999, as cited in Gibbons and Katzenbach, 2006, p. 43), which means that there are *three times* as many severely mentally ill individuals in prison as there are in psychiatric hospitals (Lurigio and Snowden, in press). We agree with the conclusion of the National Commission on Safety and Abuse in America's Prisons that: (1) it certainly appears that we have replaced yesterday's asylums with today's prisons; and that (2) "the result is not only needless suffering by the individuals who are under treated but safety problems those prisoners cause staff and other prisoners" (Gibbons and Katzenbach, 2006, p. 43).

While at least some assessment of serious mental illness (schizophrenia, bipolar disorder, major depression) is now – in the aftermath of *Ruiz v. Estelle* (1980) – a requirement of any prison admission screening process (ACA, 2003), it appears that current mental health screening protocol results in a significant number of false negatives, i.e., individuals classified as not having a serious mental health problem at intake who actually do have a serious mental illness (Lurigio and Swartz, 2006). New brief mental health screening devices represent the latest attempt to improve our assessment of the inmate's mental health status upon arrival at prison or jail. According to a recent review by Lurigio and Swartz (2006), two new risk screening devices, the K6/K10 scales and the Brief Jail Mental Health Screen (BJMHS), have just recently been validated on correctional inmate populations. Both devices reduce the false negative rates without yielding corresponding increases in false positives (i.e., individuals classified with serious mental illness who are not actually seriously mentally ill). Lurigio and Swartz (2006, p. 32) found that "[these] screening tools can be implemented by lay interviewers to identify individuals with the most severe psychiatric disorders, regardless of diagnosis. This approach conserves limited resources for only those mentally ill persons most in need of services . . . such tools can avoid false positive [and] a low false positive rate is especially important in criminal justice settings, in which scarce mental health resources must be used sparingly." Lurigio and Swartz (2006) conclude by recommending further research on gender-specific screening protocol, as well as continued research on the identification of inmates with co-occurring disorders, particularly substance abuse.

Area 3: Physical Health Assessment

A number of recent studies have examined the health problems of prison and jail inmates (Gibbons and Katzenbach, 2006; National Commission on Correctional Health Care, 2002). The results of these reviews are highlighted in Table 3. When compared to the U.S. population, the prevalence of infectious disease (active tuberculosis, hepatitis C, AIDS, HIV infection), chronic diseases (asthma, diabetes/hypertension), serious mental illness (schizophrenia, major depression, bipolar disorder), and substance abuse/dependence (alcohol, drug abuse) is significantly higher among both prison and jail inmates. New classification systems are being developed to identify the health status of inmates in prison, but it is clear that we simply do not have the resources to isolate and treat inmates for the myriad of health problems present at admission to prison (Gibbons and Katzenbach, 2006; NCHCC, 2002). The problem is even more pronounced among jail inmates, many of whom have a myriad of health problems related to ongoing substance abuse problems that jails are ill equipped to handle (Maruschak, 2006).

As the average length of prison terms has increased and our prison population has grown older (and sicker) in prison, the cost of correctional health care has increased as well. To reduce correctional costs, some prison systems have *privatized* their health care functions, while others have experimented with the use of *telemedicine* to reduce the costs associated with sending inmates to specialists for further diagnosis and treatment.[1] While these strategies may result in marginal cost reduction, there is no evidence that they improve the quality of health care provided in prison.

Table 3: The Health Status of Prisoners

Category	Condition	Prevalence Compared to U.S. Population
Infectious Diseases	Active tuberculosis	4 times greater
	Hepatitis C	9–10 times greater
	AIDS	5 times greater
	HIV infection	8–9 times greater
Chronic Diseases	Asthma	Higher
	Diabetes/hypertension	Lower
Mental Illness	Schizophrenia or other psychotic disorder	3–5 times greater
	Bipolar (depression) disorder	1.5–3 times greater
	Major depression	Roughly equivalent
Substance Abuse and Dependence	Alcohol dependence	25% fit CAGE profile
	Drug use	83% prior to offense; 33% at time of offense

Sources: NCCHC, "Prevalence of Communicable Disease, Chronic Disease, and Mental Illness Among the Inmate Population," *The Health Status of Soon-To-Be-Released Prisoners, A Report to Congress*, 2002; *BJS Special Report: Substance Abuse and Treatment, State and Federal Prisoners, 1997*, NCJ 172871, 1999.

Focusing on the problem of infectious disease, it is clear that "proper screening and treatment of infectious disease in prisons and jails would improve public health" Gibbons and Katzenbach, 2006, p. 47), because the vast majority of inmates in our federal, state, and local prisons and jails eventually leave prison and reenter the community. Of course, some neighborhoods have much higher concentrations of reentering offenders than others; and in the high risk poverty-pocket areas, the problems of poverty, inequality, homelessness, and crime are compounded by the spread of infectious disease. According to a recent report from the National Commission on Correctional Health Care (2002), it was estimated that 1.3 to 1.4 million people were released from prison and jail in 1996 with hepatitis C; in the same year, it was estimated that as many as 145,000 people with HIV, 39,000 with AIDS, 566,000 with latent tuberculosis, and 12,000 with active tuberculosis were released from prison.

New initiatives designed to provide proper screening of inmates for infectious disease at intake, the ongoing tracking of prisoners' health status as they move through the prison system, and new MOUs (memorandums of understanding) for information sharing with federal, state, and local public health agencies, are the basic features of an automated inmate health tracking system. However, the development of an automated health tracking system, by itself, does not address the much larger issue: how can prison and jail systems afford to provide treatment while developing inmate location strategies that minimize the spread of infectious disease among the general inmate population? Since the number of inmates with infectious diseases far exceeds the current capacity of special population medical units in prison, complete relocation/segregation is not possible. One possible solution would be to extend Medicaid and Medicare benefits to eligible prisoners, but for this to occur current restrictions on eligibility for those medical benefits would first have to be rewritten by Congress (Gibbons and Katzenbach, 2006, p. 49). Absent new funding mechanisms, we face the grim prospect of the continued spread of a number of infectious diseases among inmates in prisons and jails, and upon their release, among residents of a small number of high risk, poverty-pocket neighborhoods where returning inmates will reside.

Area 4: Treatment Assessment

During the initial external classification process, the treatment/programming needs of each inmate are assessed, using a variety of assessment instruments. Review areas include: (1) education (and learning disabilities); (2) skill level/work history and experience; and, perhaps most importantly, (3) individual problem areas to be addressed during confinement (e.g., the need for sex offender treatment, substance abuse treatment, and various forms of mental health treatment for individual and/or family problems). In each of these areas, the trend has been to replace subjective, clinical (and non-clinical) assessments with objective, standardized assessment instruments.

However, it is one thing to classify an individual inmate's treatment needs; it is quite another to place inmates in appropriate treatment programs while in prison. An inevitable consequence of an overcrowded, understaffed prison system is that both the *availability* and *access* to treatment programming must be limited, in order to maximize inmate control. One of the paradoxes of our federal and state prison system, for example, is that despite the serious substance abuse problems of inmates, and the fact that the majority of inmates classified as needing drug treatment do not receive it while in prison, many prison drug treatment programs actually operate at less than capacity (about 70%).

As we noted at the outset, there is now a fairly sizable research base from which to evaluate the evidence on the link between in-prison programming and post-release offender behavior (for detailed evidence-based reviews, see, for example, Wilson et al., 2005 and Welsh and Farrington, 2001). Based on recent research reviews, it has been estimated that provision of various forms of treatment in prison settings (for mental health, drug/alcohol problems, educational deficits, etc.) will have a significant, but modest (10% reduction), impact on subsequent offender criminal behavior (Welsh and Farrington, 2001). However, given the movement of offenders back and forth between institutional and community control, even modest reductions in return-to-prison rates can – over time – have a major impact on the size of the corrections population (Jacobsen, 2005). Clearly, a strong argument can be made that based on an evidence-based review of the research, the provision of treatment – in both institutional and community settings – is the most effective crime control strategy currently available in this country (Byrne and Taxman, 2006). It appears that while many legislators, governors, and corrections administrators have been preoccupied with the latest innovations in the technology of control, the real cost savings and crime reduction effects are to be found in the technology of offender change, both at the individual and community level.

An argument can also be made that the provision of treatment – and programming generally – will reduce the level of violence and disorder *in prison*. While this makes sense intuitively, some have argued that expensive, high quality, in-prison treatment programs are too costly too and too difficult to implement, and that the same prison violence and disorder reduction effects will result from putting offenders in recreation programs (Farabee, 2005). While a recent evidence-based research review (Byrne and Hummer, in press) identified only one study (Wormith, 1984) comparing the relative effects of various types of programming (including recreation) on prison violence and disorder, this review did identify 18 separate research studies conducted during the review period (1984-2006) that evaluated the impact of specific types of programming on institutional behavior. Included among the 18 studies were 4 randomized field experiments, 3 quasi-experiments, and 11 level 1 or 2 studies using non-experimental research designs.[2] Using the Campbell Collaborative (and University of Maryland) review criteria (at least two level 3 or above quality research studies are needed), Byrne and Hummer (in press) offer an assessment of "what works" in the area of offender programming as a prison violence and disorder reduction strategy.

Three of the four randomized field experiments reviewed by Byrne and Hummer (in press) found that program participation resulted in significant improvements in institutional behavior (experimental versus control group comparisons of disciplinary infraction rates). All three quasi-experiments reported similar, statistically significant reductions in confrontations and disciplinary infractions for program participants (treatment versus comparison group). These positive findings were supported by the findings from the 11 additional non-experimental research studies conducted on the same topic area, i.e., the link between program participation and institutional behavior. Over all, Byrne and Hummer (in press) found that the provision of treatment in prison is an effective, evidence-based, prison violence and disorder reduction strategy. Since the type of treatment varied across the 18 studies reviewed, it appears that there is a wide range of treatment programs that may be effective in a particular prison setting. And the key finding is that inmates' involvement in some aspect of the change process (e.g., cognitive behavioral programs focusing on drug treatment, group discussions on self-control and lifestyle change, therapeutic communities, etc.) improves their institutional behavior.

Byrne and Hummer's (in press) research review revealed that one proven strategy for reducing prison violence and disorder is to expand and improve in-prison programming. However, we recognize that given the system's current emphasis on the technology of control, this recommendation is "easier said than done." The management culture that exists today does not value individual offender change because many corrections leaders simply do not believe that offender change is possible, given the educational, economic, and social deficits the inmates must overcome. The research summarized here suggests a different approach to the correctional control of offenders, one that emphasizes the importance of prison-based programming for education, vocational training, mental health, substance abuse, and a variety of other problems (including health) as an offender control mechanism.

Area 5: Escape/Flight Risk

One of the problems with classifying the escape risk of incoming inmates is that the *base rate* (the number of escapes divided by the number of inmates) of escapes is very low. With such a low base rate, the identification of individual escape risk characteristics among incoming inmates becomes exceedingly difficult. The problem of classifying the escape risk of incoming inmates is compounded by the lack of consistent operational definitions of attempted/completed escapes, incomplete information on the escape incident (e.g., within facility versus outside facility) and characteristics of escapees, and the lack of an automated record of escapes in many state prison systems (Wright et al., 2003).

Despite the data collection shortfalls we have highlighted, it seems safe to conclude that there are very few attempted escapes from prison and jail and that most attempted escapes – including the most common, walkaways from minimum security facilities – are unsuccessful (about 75% of escapees are captured and returned to prison). According to a recent review by Culp (2005, p. 279), "Although prison population in the United States grew exponentially over the study period – nearly tripling from 627,600 inmates in 1988 to 1,816,931 in 1998 (Beck, 2000) – the prison escape rate declined considerably during the period, from 1.4 escapes per 100 inmates in 1988 to 0.4 in 1998." Since one of the performance measures usually identified with a successful prison system is the prevention of escapes, it certainly appears that prisons achieve this important public safety goal. However, we need to collect better data on escapes and escapees before we can offer an accurate assessment of (1) the escape risk of newly incarcerated inmates, and (2) the effectiveness of current inmate location strategies in terms of escape risk reduction.

Internal Classification Systems

Comprehensive *internal* prison classification systems have also been developed and implemented in federal and state prison systems across the U.S. Internal classification systems focus on those decisions affecting inmates *after* they have been placed in a specific prison. For example, custody/cell assignment decisions will be made based on a review of each inmate's case file; this review may include dangerousness assessments along with a number of other types of assessments (mental health, physical health, programming needs, gang affiliation, flight/escape risk, etc.). Once living in a particular prison, decisions will be made about how and when each inmate will participate in various prison activities and programs, while individual inmates' progress in treatment can also be monitored. In addition, inmate rule infractions, grievances, institutional sanctions, and reclassification decisions can also be included in these automated systems. Given the amount of information collected on inmates, advances in information technology provide the promise of more efficient and effective case management in prisons and jails.

Indeed, comprehensive, automated, on-line management information systems represent the future of prison classification and offender management. According to a recent review by Brennan et al. (2004, p. xix), "Valid, effective classification is fundamentally dependent on accurate, timely, and relevant information. As prison information technology evolves and as prison databases become 'smarter,' these developments have the potential to improve profoundly the quality of offender classification. Conversely, if prison MIS software and related databases are poorly designed, poorly implemented, or ineffectively used, the quality of classification decisions may be substantially undermined."

While there are a number of comprehensive internal classifications systems currently in use, perhaps the best known system is the Adult Internal Management System (AIMS), often referred to as the Quay system because it was designed and tested in several prison systems by Dr. Herbert Quay (Quay, 2004). According to a recent review by Austin and McGinnis (2004, p. 16), "As of 2002, AIMS was being used by several facilities in the Federal Bureau of Prisons" and in all or part of several state prison systems (Ohio, South Dakota, Missouri, and South Carolina). Austin and McGinnis (2004, pp. 15-16) observe that: "AIMS relies on two instruments to classify inmates according to a personality typology: the Life History Checklist and the Correctional Adjustment Checklist. The *Life History* Checklist focuses on the inmate's adjustment and stability in the community. It includes 27 items designed to assess a number of personality dimensions known to be related to an individual's potential to be housed successfully with other types of inmates. The *Correctional Adjustment* Checklist is designed to create a profile of an inmate's likely behavior in a correctional setting. Its 41 items focus on the inmate's record of misconduct, ability to follow staff directions, and level of aggression toward other inmates."

Another well known internal classification system is the Prisoner Management Classification (PMC) System, which was first implemented in the state of Washington in the early 1990s. "The PMC system attempts to identify potential predators and victims and inmates who require special programming or supervision, and it requires significant staff training for inmate assessment, supervision, and interaction. To classify inmates, the PMC system uses a semi structured interview supplemented by ratings of 11 objective background factors that assess the inmate's social status and offense history. . . . Inmates are then assigned to one of four groups: Limit Setting (LS), Casework Control (CC), Selective Intervention (SI) and Environmental Structure (ES). LS and CC inmates are expected to be more aggressive and difficult to control, whereas SI and ES inmates require minimal supervision but should be separated from LS and CC inmates" (Austin and McGinnis, 2004, p. 17). Regardless of which classification system is selected in a particular federal or state prison, automation of key features of this classification process appears to be inevitable.

External and Internal Classification Systems: Issues to Consider

Austin (2003) points out that we currently are further along in the development of external than internal classification systems, but a review of the research on the effectiveness of current classification schemes reveals limitations for both external and internal classification systems. Byrne and Hummer (in press) recently completed an evidence-based review of the research on the impact of classification decisions on the level of violence and disorder in prison. Only seven research studies were completed on the relationship between classification decisions and inmate behavior in prison during the study review period (1984-2006), including three randomized field experiments and four non-experimental, level 1 and level 2 studies.

Focusing first on external classification, Byrne and Hummer (in press) looked at two randomized field experiments that asked deceptively simple questions: what would happen if we placed a high risk, maximum security inmate in a medium security housing unit? And similarly, what would happen if we placed a medium risk inmate in a low risk environment? If *where* we place inmates affects their behavior – and more specifically, if such placement has a mediating effect on their behavior – we would expect higher rates of inmate misbehavior in lower risk settings.

Camp and Gaes (2005) randomly assigned medium security inmates to minimum security facilities, while Bench and Allen (2003) randomly assigned maximum security inmates (based on the external risk classification) to medium security facilities; both studies found no significant differences in either overall misconduct or serious misconduct violations across experimental and control groups. The implications of these findings for external classification systems are straightforward: (1) contrary to expectations, placement of higher risk offenders in more restrictive prison settings does not lower their rate of institutional misconduct, while placement of higher risk offenders in lower risk settings does not raise their rate of misconduct; and, (2) alternatives to control-based placements should be field-tested to determine their effect on inmate misconduct. Unfortunately, we currently know very little about the link between inmate classification level and prison classification level (minimum, medium, maximum, supermax) outside these two well-designed, but narrowly focused, studies.

In addition to the initial external classification decision, a second soft technology application involves the facility-specific internal classification decision. Once the results of external classification determine where an offender should be located within a federal or state system, an internal classification system is employed to determine where in that prison each new offender should be housed and, equally important, which programs they will have access to while in that prison. Essentially, these internal classification systems focus on three separate, but related, issues: (1) risk (of escape), (2) treatment (for mental health, physical health, educational/vocational deficits, substance abuse, multiple problems, etc.), and (3) control (of intra-personal, inter-personal, and collective violence and disorder).

Byrne and Hummer's (in press) evidence-based review revealed that very little quality research has been conducted over the past two decades on: (1) how to identify the potential high risk (or high rate) offenders (i.e., those at high risk for institutional violence and/or disorder) at the internal classification stage (Berk et al., 2006); and (2) how to respond proactively (and programmatically) to offenders with identified risk factors associated with institutional misconduct. For example, age (younger), gender (male), history of violence (known), history of mental illness (known), gang membership (known), program participation (low), and recent disciplinary action (known) have been identified by Austin (2003) as variables included in risk classification systems because of their known correlation with inmate misconduct. The question is: once these risk factors have been identified, how should prison managers respond programmatically? It is the linkage between risk and specific placement decisions that is critical to the development of an effective internal classification system.

Berk et al. (2006) offers one possible model for predicting "dangerous" inmate misconduct (defined as assault, drug trafficking, and robbery), based on data from 9,662 inmates assigned and classified (between November 1, 1998 and April 30, 1999) by the California Department of Corrections and Rehabilitation, with prison misconduct monitored during a 24-month follow-up after intake. While Berk et al. caution that predicting a rare event (only 3% of inmates had one serious misconduct during the review period) such as serious prison misconduct will necessarily involve selecting 10 false positives for every 1 true positive, this is a cost they are willing to pay, because "false positives have a configuration of background characteristics that make them almost sure bets to engage in one of the less serious forms of misconduct" (2006, p. ii). According to Berk and his colleagues, "The high risk inmates tend to be young individuals with long criminal records, active participants in street and prison gangs, and sentenced to long prison terms" (2006, p. 9). Given the researchers' questionable decision regarding the "acceptable" level of false positives (10:1), the very low base rate for serious misconduct (3%), and the 50% accuracy rate for the forecasting model, it appears that discussion of the application of this technique to inmate classification levels is premature.

For the most part, classification decision makers focus on offender control; much less attention has been focused on how to change the risk level of offenders placed in institutional settings. As Byrne and Hummer (in press) highlight in their review, it is disappointing that few quality research studies have been conducted that focused on how effective current internal classification systems have been at classifying offenders for appropriate treatment while in prison. Are drug-dependent inmates getting into appropriate drug treatment programs? Are mentally ill inmates getting the mental health care they need? What about the offenders with deficits in education/vocational skills and the multiple-problem inmates? Research linking classification, prison program placement, and inmate in-prison behavior has simply not been conducted.

Although a few high quality research studies on *external* prison classification systems have been conducted on the link between classification and control (the link appears tenuous at best), we have to conclude that we "don't know" whether classification, treatment/programming, and control decisions made in conjunction with *internal* classification systems are effective. Given recent reviews highlighting the over-classification of female inmates (Austin, 2003), and the expansion of protective custody, administrative and disciplinary segregation (Gibbons and Katzenbach, 2006), it appears that the primary purpose of current external and internal classification systems is the short-term control of the inmate population. There is no evidence that the current emphasis on control-based classification systems makes prisons any safer; but there is a mounting body of evidence that we can reduce violence and disorder in prison by increasing inmate program participation rates (Byrne and Hummer, in press).

THE NEW TECHNOLOGY OF PRISON MANAGEMENT

There are a variety of ways that information technology can be applied to the administration and management of prisons. We have already highlighted the role of new technology innovations in the area of external and internal classification/reclassification. In the following section, we consider three additional soft technology applications in prison settings: (1) problem solving and hot spot analysis; (2) staff training and development; and, (3) performance measurement.

Problem Solving and Hot Spot Analysis

As state and local corrections managers consider the lessons learned by police, court, and community corrections managers in the area of information technology, they will find a number of ways many of the soft technology applications discussed by both Chris Harris (this volume) in the area of policing (e.g., Compstat programs), and April Pattavina and Faye Taxman (this volume) in their chapter on community corrections (e.g., crime mapping) can certainly be applied in institutional settings once automated management information systems are fully operational. Byrne et al. (2005), for example, highlighted how the simple identification of high rate, multiple incident inmates can be used as the first step in applying a proactive, problem-solving strategy to reduce violence and disorder in prison. Their analysis of incidents during a six-month review period identified a small number of individuals (15 inmates, 1% of the inmate population) who were involved in over 20% of the incidents in one facility. Rather than continue to respond to these inmates using existing sanctioning policies and practices, the authors recommended that this subgroup of "problem" inmates be targeted for further analysis and review. For many disruptive inmates, the problem may be solved by the provision of mental heath treatment, transfer to a special population unit, or some other response that moves beyond the enforcement of sanctions.

A similar analytic approach using crime mapping technology can be used to identify incident "hot spot" locations within prison and then develop problem-solving strategies (e.g., increased officer presence at hot spots, changes in inmate movement patterns, etc.) in targeted areas. Wortley (2002) has identified a number of promising situational prison control strategies that would appear to flow logically from this type of analysis, including changes in environmental design, prison size, crowding levels, staffing ratios, access to treatment, and the use of special population housing to protect vulnerable prisoners (Byrne, 2006). While any discussion of the effectiveness of specific "hot spot" problem-solving strategies is premature, there appear to many potential benefits to enhanced within-prison crime analysis.

Staff Training and Development

There are a number of soft technology applications in the area of staff development and training, including the use of standardized assessment tools to examine both individual staff attitudes (toward work, management, and inmates, for example) and overall staff culture (e.g., the Organizational Culture Inventory). In addition, the same analytic strategies that Chris Harris (this volume) describes to identify police misconduct and problem employees (early warning or early identification systems) can also be applied to the problem of correctional officer misconduct. Finally, the use of simulations to introduce new technology and/or programs has been used recently by the National Institute of Corrections (e.g., mock prison riots).

Performance Measurement

Institutional corrections lags behind both police and community corrections in basic research and evaluation. With the exception of the work of researchers at the Federal Bureau of Prisons (Gaes et al., 2004), there are simply not many good examples of quality research studies available for review in the area of institutional corrections (Byrne and Hummer, in press). However, the recent emphasis on evidence-based practice in other parts of the criminal justice system will eventually lead to a new emphasis on research and evaluation in institutional corrections. In addition to conducting quality, external evaluation research on the effectiveness of current prison management and control strategies, we also need to standardize our criteria for reviewing prison and jail performance. By fully implementing the national performance measurement system recommended by the Association of State Correctional Administrators (Wright, 2003), we would be taking an important first step in this direction. According to a recent review, "The underlying assumption of this strategy is simple to articulate: *what gets measured gets done*. Corrections administrators will know that the performance of their prison will be assessed based on these outcome measures and they will respond to this public performance review by developing strategies to address problem areas in their prison's performance review" (Byrne, 2006, p. 10).

INFORMATION TECHNOLOGY AND OFFENDER REENTRY

There are a number of ways that new information technology can be applied to the problem of how best to manage the transition of inmates from prisons and jails back to their home communities, including: (1) the development of new information sharing protocols among corrections, police, public health, and treatment providers in the public and private sector; (2) the use of crime analysis technology to map offender locations, treatment/ service delivery networks, and to identify high risk neighborhoods; and, (3) the development of comprehensive information systems that bridge the gap between prison and community.[3]

Although prisoner reentry is not a new criminal justice issue, recent research has focused on the ongoing movement of a significant number of offenders back and forth between institutional and community control (a practice called *churning*). Each year for the past decade, approximately 600,000 inmates were released from prison in the U.S. And in the same years, about 600,000 new offenders were sent to prison; one-half of these new admissions were individuals that had been convicted of new crimes, while the other half were being returned to prison for technical violations of probation or parole (Byrne, 2004). It appears that this *churning* problem is exacerbated by sentencing and correctional control policies that have resulted in the incarceration of large numbers of persons, longer periods of time served, the exposure of prisoners to institutional violence, release of prisoners who had not received treatment, and the failure to provide adequate services, support and surveillance in the communities once they are released (Burke and Tonry, 2006; Petersilia, 2001; Travis et al., 2001).

The "new" reentry perspective emphasizes a holistic approach to the issue of offender reintegration. The approach is broad-based and calls for the consideration of the circumstances facing the prisoners as they prepare to leave prison and return to society as well as the impact of inmates' release on their families, victims and the communities in which they live. Current reentry models are grounded in a comprehensive theoretical framework that often draws upon restorative justice ideals, social disorganization theory, and specific treatment modalities that emphasize the importance of the individual and community for successful outcomes (see, e.g., Byrne and Taxman, 2005; Petersilia, 2004).

To fully support individuals released from prisons, reentry initiatives call for a reorientation of how incarcerated individuals are treated that spans the criminal justice system and involves prison, treatment programs, the police and the community. Under this model, agencies share the responsibility for the successful integration of offenders back into the community. Participating agencies collaborate with each other and with offenders (or clients) in ways that serve to monitor progress. Byrne et al. (2002) describe this process of reentry using a systems perspective, where the focus is not on one agency per se, but on sharing roles and responsibilities that best support individuals as they progress through the various stages of reentry.

There are formidable challenges presented by such a comprehensive view of offender treatment, surveillance, services and control. One significant challenge that comes from the call for agencies to collaborate involves the need to make informed decisions about offenders using data from agencies responsible for offender reintegration. Advances in information technology (IT) over the past few decades have made it easier for criminal justice agencies to collect, process, analyze, and share information. More importantly, the information that is maintained in computer systems can be used to provide decision making support for reentry programs.

Most criminal justice agencies are using some form of IT to manage information. IT can be used to promote effective planning, management and evaluation of reentry initiatives in ways that address the individual, agency and community levels. To highlight the role that IT can play in the reentry process, we will now consider the information needs of reentry initiatives; examine the current state of information technology as it pertains to each need; and describe the opportunities and current challenges of IT for reentry.

The New Technology of Reentry

Table 4 summarizes the potential application of information technology to support reentry decision making by monitoring offender progress in prison and the community. The discussion of IT support for reentry will start from a statement of goals and objectives and move toward the specifics of how IT can support their realization through performance-based measurement. Performance-based measurement involves quantifying organizational indicators that can be used to gauge how well an organization is meeting its goals (Wright, 2003).

There are three goals of reentry initiatives. The first is to maximize offender (client) readiness for release from prison. Second is to maintain individual success in the community once offenders are released. The third

Table 4: Information Technology and Decision Support for Reentry Initiatives

Goals	Objectives	Information Needs	IT Support	Performance Measures
Individual readiness for prison release	Treatment	Program specific progress & Classification	Prison-based RMS	Individual and program-based performance indicators (i.e., attendance, completion)
	Surveillance	Incident reports	Incident reporting system	Rule violations
Individual success in the community	Treatment	Program specific progress & Classification	Community Corrections RMS	Individual and program based performance indicators (i.e., attendance, completion)
		Program Inventory	Computerized phone and other service directories / GIS software	Needs/Availability assessment of services for individuals and communities
	Supervision	Condition Compliance	Community Corrections RMS	Violation types/ sanctions
	Surveillance	Monitoring capabilities	Electronic tracking devices (EM, GPS)	Violations of space/mobility restrictions
Community Safety	Control	Offender profiles	Local Police RMS / Biometric systems (AFIS) / Criminal History Systems	Arrests/incidents involving offenders
	Community support	Community based information	GIS software / Statistical software	Community crime rates, Social capital indicators

Source: Pattavina, 2004, p. 44.

goal is to protect and support the communities to which these persons return. Each of these goals has different objectives and therefore different information needs. Some of the more specific questions to consider at this point include: what information is needed? is it currently collected? how is it collected and shared? and how can it be used to the support the program?

At the individual level, the objectives for in-prison reentry goals are treatment and surveillance. To some extent the information technology needs of treatment providers in prison and communities are similar. Both need classification and treatment information about individuals on a program-specific basis. Records management systems (RMS) should include classification information on those participating in reentry programs along with indicators of program involvement. A recent national review conducted by the U.S. National Institute of Corrections found that management information systems for intake and classification were being used by correctional facilities in some states (Hardyman et al., 2004). The authors of that report also emphasized the need for increased data sharing among intake facilities, courts and other correctional agencies as well as linked management information systems that would allow for more accurate and up-to-date assessments.

Those responsible for administering treatment programs should also be responsible for automated record keeping. The users of this information (and therefore those who would need access to it) would be case managers and parole and probation officers who must monitor the progress of offenders through treatment. The opportunities presented by this information include the development of performance measures regarding individual treatment, such as participation, completion, and other progress indicators. These indicators would also be available at the agency level to determine program-level performance measures, such as completion and participation rates.

There are additional information needs for offender treatment that takes place in the community. Once offenders are out of prison, programs and services that may be needed (such as those that deal with employment, housing, etc.) are available in the community at large. Case managers, parole and probation officers need to identify where these services are and determine the availability of these programs to service their clients. These data sources may also be used to identify services available for victims. Many phone directories and yellow pages are now computerized and have search capabilities based on business classifications that include social services or program inventory databases may be developed especially for this purpose.

Moreover, many of these data sources can also be mapped using Geographic Information System (GIS) software.

The opportunities presented by these program inventory sources include more efficient planning for offenders as well as the increased capacity to determine service or program needs for a particular area. This approach was used in research by Harris et al. (1998). They used GIS software to map the proximity of recently released inmates to social services including unemployment offices, mental health services and substance abuse treatment centers. They found that offenders living in rural areas had limited access to these facilities, and the information was used to justify the need for drug rehabilitation services for offenders as they reintegrate into their communities.

An example of a sophisticated integrated offender case management system is the University of Maryland High Intensity Drug Trafficking Area Automated Tracking System (HATS). HATS is an automated information system that is used in by the Maryland Division of Probation and Parole, drug courts, community-based treatment programs, and other agencies serving offenders in Maryland. This system integrates data from many sources relating to offender treatment and supervision. Information is available for offenders regarding intake, referrals and appointments, program inventory, offender confidentiality and releases, supervision, graduated sanctions and treatment tracking (Taxman and Sherman, 1998).

Community supervision and surveillance are additional objectives for ensuring individual offenders' success in the community. Offender compliance with release conditions is essential for anticipating recidivism risk. Violations of release conditions and any imposed sanctions would be useful performance measures. To meet the surveillance objective, electronic tracking devices such as electronic monitoring equipment or global positioning systems can be used for continuous geo-based monitoring of offenders in the community. The performance measures that can be generated from such systems include violations of space or mobility restrictions (see Patricia Harris and James Byrne, this volume).

The impact of incarceration and reentry on the community has been well documented in the literature (Rose and Clear, 2003; Cadora, 2003; Clear et al., 2003). It can be argued that this research has been instrumental in helping to promote the philosophy underlying current reentry initiatives. Community safety is always an important objective of any crime control strategy, and reentry is no exception. To promote community safety, the police are being asked to contribute to the reentry process by offering support in the form of crime control. In many jurisdictions, departments inform patrol officers about offenders being released in their communities and this intelligence can be used by police to help monitor offenders and inform parole/probation about an offender's involvement in criminal activity.

This is a central feature of the Lowell, Massachusetts reentry program (Byrne and Hummer, 2004). The crime analysis unit in the Lowell Police Department is responsible for creating these profiles. Crime analysis units, which are largely responsible for data-driven identification of crime patterns, are well suited to provide this information. These research units are typically found in large, urban police departments.

The information used to create offender profiles may include photos, fingerprints and other biometric information, behavioral histories, supervision plans, etc. Physical descriptors such as photos or fingerprints may be available in local, state and federal databases such as the FBI's Automated Fingerprint Identification System (AFIS). Criminal history information may be available from state and federal criminal history databases. To monitor potential criminal activity in the community, many police departments maintain records management information systems (RMS) that include arrests and incidents that can be routinely searched. The discovery of an arrest or investigation involving offenders can be forwarded to probation or parole officers in a timely manner. In addition, offender progress in treatment can be mandated by treatment providers, and any change in offender participation/progress could potentially be "shared" with local police as well as community supervision personnel.

The second community level reentry objective is to gain the support of community residents for ongoing reentry initiatives. The information needed to assess the condition of communities includes measures of social and economic conditions and crime rates that can be used as indicators of community health. These measures may include but are not limited to crime rates, incarceration rates, employment, public assistance and family support, and public expenditures. For example, Eric Cadora (2003) used computer mapping to demonstrate the geographic relationship between rates of incarcerated individuals and those receiving public aid. This information can be used to provide community-based assessments of reentry initiatives.

There are some programs in place that gather this type of neighborhood-based information. One example is the National Neighborhood Indicators Project (NNIP). Funded by the Annie E. Casey and Rockefeller

Foundations, the NNIP goal is to provide operational and development support to projects in major cities that merge agency data from many sources to create neighborhood level social and economic indicator databases (Kingsley and Petit, 2000; Pattavina et al., 2002).

These "ready made" neighborhood indicator databases, developed at universities and research organizations, are available in many cities. They are very useful for area-based analysis because they are comprehensive in content and cover communities for entire cities over long periods of time. Moreover, neither the police nor any other participating criminal justice agency is solely responsible for the considerable effort needed to build and maintain and distribute such databases. This model is currently serving as the basis for the Urban Institute's Reentry Mapping Network project, which will examine neighborhood level data on incarceration, community supervision, and indicators of community social and economic well-being to support reentry programs (Urban Institute, 2003).

Information Technology, Decision Making and Reentry

There is little doubt that an infrastructure of information gathering can significantly support reentry operations. Of course, simply identifying relevant information needs and technology available provides only part of the reentry decision support picture. Those with experience in building information technology capacity in any criminal justice agency understand that it is not enough to put the technology in place, although that alone can be a considerable feat. It is also necessary to incorporate this new technology into day-to-day decision making, problem analysis and strategic planning initiatives. The technical aspects of making the hardware and software IT components work lie beyond the scope of this chapter. There are, however, organizational and policy issue that are appropriate for discussion because of their relevance to making the most of information technology for reentry programs.

Organizational Challenges

The first issue involves building and maintaining the commitment to develop IT capacity. Organizational support is crucial at this stage. Support efforts may include the steady funding for IT projects and updates, the direct involvement of agency personnel in building IT capacity and the support for IT skill development among the staff. If there is no organizational commitment to IT development, it is unlikely that changes in work processes that would maximize the use of IT for internal (i.e., information gathering and processing) and external functions (i.e., information sharing and indicator measures) would be successfully implemented.

A parallel issue involves organizational culture and resistance to change. Reentry initiatives call for the reconsideration of the roles and responsibilities of participating agencies in dealing with offenders. This approach may challenge the cultural embeddedness of existing organizational functions of the police and corrections. The result may be that participating agencies simply adapt information technology to support current functions rather than to support new or evolving ones (Manning, 2004). This concern has echoed in other agencies as well. In a meeting of the National Institute of Justice's Mapping in Corrections Resource Group, a major factor impeding the adoption and use of mapping technology was the reluctance of corrections personnel to change the ideology of corrections from one that is institution- or "fortress-"based to one that is more community-based and willing to take advantage of mapping technologies (Crime Mapping Research Center, 1999).

Legal and Political Considerations

The second issue involves the challenges of creating information sharing protocols. Not only must IT be well designed to support internal functions of an agency, but in the case of reentry, it should also be flexible enough to support external functions, such as information sharing. Such a capability is necessary to support the collaborative and evaluative aspects of reentry. Agencies must buy in to the collaboration and perhaps even be willing to alter their approach to dealing with offenders. Collaboration sounds good in theory, but sustaining it over time is usually much more difficult (Sridharan and Gillespie, 2004).

Central issues to be addressed with respect to information sharing include who should have access to the information, how should access be supported and how will the information be used. These questions are technical, legal and political in nature. The technical aspects will depend upon the type of the information systems maintained by each agency. In an integrated system, each participating agency would own its own data, but would share critical information with other agencies in one of several ways, possibly including sophisticated methods such as Web-based technologies to access agency information, remote access capabilities or other data transfer processes among agencies.

Although fully integrated systems – where all participating agencies have the technological capacity and organizational support to effectively collect, manage and share information for reentry functions – do not currently exist, it is not too soon to address the issues that may affect their development and contemplate interim information sharing solutions that may not be the most technologically advanced, but nonetheless promote the process of information sharing. For example, the establishment of information sharing protocols must take place against a backdrop of legal and political considerations. There are federal and state legal restrictions that govern the sharing and use of information on those involved in the criminal justice system. The intent of this legislation is to protect the privacy of individuals (see Snavely et al. [2005] for a discussion).

The political culture of information sharing among criminal justices agencies is not a popular topic for discussion among proponents of collaboration and information sharing because criminal justice agencies are notorious for resisting cooperative efforts. In a recent report, Byrne et al. (2002) emphasize leadership as one of three essential characteristics of a successful reentry program. They argue that there must be strong leadership within the organization and within the partnership. This person(s) should serve as project director and should have the ability and authority to develop a programmatic strategy that transcends the boundaries of traditional organizations.

Performance Measurement and Evaluation Opportunities

The other two characteristics Byrne et al. (2002) identify as necessary for a successful reentry program are partnership and ownership. These characteristics relate directly to the third challenge of using IT for reentry, which is the establishment of performance measures. Indeed, strong leadership will depend on being informed about the progress of individuals as well the success of participating agencies in the collaboration. Informing this process should be performance measures that can be used for decision making. Partnerships can be created and strengthened with a collaborative approach to creating performance measures and determining how information from their agency will be shared, with whom and for what purposes.

All stakeholders, including community groups and victims can partake in the process of determining desired outcomes, selecting meaningful outcome indicators, and developing data collection procedures. Wright (2003) refers to this type of collaboration across agencies as performance partnerships. This process can be used to determine responsibilities, ownership, and accountability for program planning and evaluation. The challenges would be the establishment of standards for determining individual and agency success (i.e., who gets to decide, what data should be collected, how should performance measures be calculated). Other issues include the development of information sharing procedures.

The impact of reentry initiatives on the community will eventually be an important consideration when the politics of crime control comes once again to focus on "what works" in corrections according to evidence-based review criteria (MacKenzie, 2006). The success or failure of agency collaborations, along with their individual and collective roles in successfully reintegrating offenders, will be judged by the evidence. For comprehensive initiatives like reentry, program evaluation should measure indicators of success or failure across individual, program and community levels. Moreover, process evaluations are necessary to understand how the reentry process operates, if it works, and how it can be improved.

Information technology can support both process and outcome evaluations at individual, program and community levels. Performance measures that can be generated with the use of IT will help to promote accountability because they can be used to determine if public resources are being spent wisely (Wright, 2003). This is especially important in light of recent studies showing that criminal justice system expenditures were relatively high in communities with high rates of incarceration (Cadora, 2003). Moreover, the use of performance measures is consistent with the trend toward using evidence-based research to determine best practices in corrections (Sherman et al., 1998).

IT Resources and Support for Reentry

There is a growing network of IT support resources available to the criminal justice community designed to help those interested in building IT capacity. During the past few decades, the financial resources devoted to IT development in criminal justice have been substantial (Davis and Jackson, 2004). Many agencies have taken on the challenge of building IT capacity and have shared their experiences and lessons learned with the criminal justice community.

Lessons learned have been shared with the criminal justice community in a variety of ways. There have been agencies created to provide technical support for technology development, such as the National Law Enforcement Corrections Technology Center (NLECTC) sponsored by the U.S. National Institute of Justice (NIJ). IT acquisition and implementation guides have been published and made available through a technology publications archive supported by NIJ. Forums for discussing and sharing IT experiences across agencies have been organized. Courses that emphasize IT are being offered in criminal justice programs at colleges and universities. All of these resources support a growing commitment in the field to building IT capacity that is coming to fruition in innovative and useful ways that can be incorporated into reentry programs.

CONCLUSION

Our review of soft technology applications in prison and jail settings described how various forms of information technology are currently being used at three key decision points: (1) initial external and internal classification of inmates; (2) subsequent inmate management; and, (3) inmate preparation for release/reentry. As a result of these new soft technology applications, corrections managers anticipate the following positive outcomes:

1. improved inmate classifications systems (external and internal) that integrate risk, treatment, and control;

2. improved within-prison crime analysis and response capabilities (examination of incident/sanctioning patterns, including transfer, segregation, loss of privileges, etc. identification of high rate offenders and/ or prison hot spot locations);

3. improved information sharing with community corrections, police, treatment providers (continuity/seamless system), and the public health system, which should result in a more efficient and effective reentry process;

4. improved identification, monitoring, and control of inmate health problems (e.g., mental and physical); and,

5. improved training and development of line corrections officers, due to the use of soft technology applications in prison and jails (e.g., testing new technologies in a simulated "mock" riot).

Ultimately, the performance of prisons will be evaluated using a number of different outcome measures, covering areas such as public safety, institutional safety, cost effectiveness, and various indicators of treatment provision and individual offender change. As we improve our information systems, we also need to provide the public with *access* to these measures of prison performance, because it is only by demanding transparency that we will begin to change the negative prison culture that exists in many prison systems today (Byrne, 2006; Gibbons and Katzenbach, 2006). In the new era of information technology, the old adage, *"What happens in prison stays in prison,"* no longer applies.

◆ ◆ ◆ ◆

NOTES

1. Privatization refers to the subcontracting of certain corrections functions (e.g., health care) to a private for-profit company (Camp and Gaes, 2005). Telemedicine is a new strategy to reduce the cost of sending inmates to medical specialists by using videoconferencing and off-site review of test results (see Joseph, 2005).
2. For a detailed discussion of the scoring procedures that lead to the levels assigned to various studies, see Mackenzie (2006) or Sherman et al. (1988). In general, randomized field experiments (random assignment to treatment and control groups) will score a 4 or 5; quasi-experiments (using some form of matched group design) will score a 2 or 3; while non-experimental designs (no comparison group) will score 1.
3. Adapted from Pattavina (2004).

REFERENCES

American Correctional Association (ACA) (2004). *Performance-based standards for adult local detention facilities* (4th ed.). Lanham, MD: ACA.

Austin, J. (2003). *Findings in prison classification and risk assessment.* Washington, DC: U.S. National Institute of Corrections.

Austin, J., & McGinnis, K. (2004). *Classification of high risk and special management prisoners: A national assessment of current practices.* Washington, DC: U.S. National Institute of Corrections.

Austin, J., & Hardyman, P. (2004). *Objective prison classification: A guide for correctional agencies.* Washington, DC: National Institute of Corrections.

Beck, A. J. (2000). *Prisoners in 1999.* Washington, DC: U.S. Bureau of Justice Statistics.

Beck, A., & Maruschak, L. (2001). *Mental health treatment in state prisons, 2000.* Special Report series. Washington, DC: U.S. Department of Justice, Bureau of Justice Statistics.

Berk, R. A., Kriegler, B., & Baek, J. (2006). *Forecasting dangerous inmate misconduct.* Berkeley, CA: California Policy Research Center, University of California, Berkeley.

Brennan, T., Wells, D., & Alexander, J. (2004). *Enhancing prison classification systems: The emerging role of management information systems.* Washington, DC: U.S. Department of Justice, National Institute of Corrections.

Bureau of Justice Statistics (BJS) (2003). *BJS Special Report: Substantice abuse and treatment, state and federal prisoners, 1997.* Report # NCJ-172871. Washington, DC: BJS.

Burke, P., & Tonry, M. (2006). *Successful transition and reentry for safer communities: A call to action for parole.* Silver Springs, MD: Center for Effective Public Policy.

Byrne, J. (2006, February 8). *Gang affiliation and drug trafficking in prison.* Presented to the Commission on Safety and Abuse in America's Prisons, Los Angeles, CA.

Byrne, J., & Hummer, D. (in press). Examining the impact of institutional culture (and culture change) on prison violence and disorder: An evidence-based review. In J. Byrne, F. Taxman, & D. Hummer (Eds.), *The culture of prison violence.* Boston, MA: Allyn and Bacon.

Byrne, J. M., & Hummer, D. (2004). The role of the police in reentry partnership initiatives. *Federal Probation, 68*(2), 62-69.

Byrne, J., & Pattavina, A. (2006, September). Assessing the role of clinical and actuarial risk assessment in an evidence-based community corrections system: Issues to consider. *Federal Probation,* 64-67.

Byrne, J. M., & Taxman, F. S. (2006, June). Crime control strategies and community change: Reframing the surveillance vs. treatment debate. *Federal Probation,* 3-12.

Byrne, J. M., Taxman, F. S., & Hummer, D. (2005). *An evaluation of the implementation and impact of NIC's Institutional Culture Initiative: Year 2 update.* Prepared for the National Institute of Corrections (Project # S10002750000006). Washington, DC: U.S. Bureau of Prisons.

Byrne, J., Taxman, F., & Hummer, D. (in press). *The culture of prison violence.* Boston, MA: Allyn and Bacon.

Byrne, J., Taxman, F., & Hummer, D. (in press). The National Institute of Corrections' Institutional Culture (Change) Initiative: A multi-site evaluation. In J. Byrne, F. Taxman, & D. Hummer (Eds.), *The culture of prison violence.* Boston, MA: Allyn and Bacon.

Byrne, J. M., Taxman, F. S., & Young, D. (2002). *Emerging roles and responsibilities in the reentry partnership initiative: New ways of doing business.* Washington, DC: U.S. National Institute of Justice.

Cadora, E. (2003). Criminal justice and health and human services: An exploration of overlapping needs, resources and interests in Brooklyn neighborhoods. In J. Travis & M. Waul (Eds.), *Prisoners once removed.* Washington, DC: Urban Institute Press.

Camp, S., & Gaes, G. (2005). The criminogenic effects of the prison environment on inmate behavior: Some experimental evidence. *Crime & Delinquency, 51,* 425-442.

Clear, T. R., Rose, D. R., Waring, E., & Scully, K. (2003). Coercive mobility and crime: A preliminary examination of concentrated incarceration and social disorganization. *Justice Quarterly, 20*(1), 33-64.

Cilluffo, F., & Saathoff, G. (2006). *Out of the shadows: Getting ahead of prisoner radicalization.* Washington, DC: Homeland Security Policy Initiative.

Crime Mapping Research Center (1999). *Mapping in corrections.* National Institute Justice Mapping in Corrections Resource Group meeting summary. Washington, DC: U.S. National Institute of Justice.

Culp, R. (2005). Frequency and characteristics of prison escapes in the United States: An analysis of national data. *Prison Journal, 85*(3), 270-291.

Davis, L., & Jackson, B. (2004). IT acquisition and implementation in criminal justice agencies. In A. Pattavina (Ed.), *Information technology and the criminal justice system.* Thousand Oaks, CA: Sage Publications.

Farabee, D. (2005). *Rethinking rehabilitation: Why can't we reform our criminals?* Washington, DC: AEI Press.

Gaes, G., Camp, S., Nelson, J., & Saylor, W. (2004). *Measuring prison performance.* Walnut Creek, CA: Alta Mira Press.

Gibbons, J. J., & Katzenbach, N. *Confronting confinement: A report of the Commission on Safety and Abuse in America's Prisons.* New York: Vera Institute of Justice.

Goldberg, A., & Higgins, B. (2006, August). Brief mental health screening for corrections intake. *Corrections Today,* 82-84.

Gottfredson, S., & Moriarty, L. (2006, September). Clinical versus actuarial judgments in criminal justice decisions: Should one replace the other? *Federal Probation,* 15-18.

Hardyman, P. L., Austin, J., & Peyton, J. (2004). *Prisoner intake systems: Assessing needs and classifying prisoners.* Washington, DC: U.S. National Institute of Corrections.

Hardyman, P., Austin, J., & Tulloch, O. C. (2000). *Revalidating external classification systems: The experience of seven states and model for classification reform.* Report submitted to the National Institute of Corrections. Washington, DC: Institute on Crime, Justice and Corrections, George Washington University (available at http://www.nicic.org).

Hardyman, P., Austin, J., Alexander, J., Johnson, K., & Tulloch, O. (2002). Internal prison classification systems: Case studies in their development and implementation. In J. Austin & P. Hardyman (2004) (Eds.), *Objective prison classification: A guide for correctional agencies.* Washington, DC: U.S. National Institute of Corrections.

Harris, R., Huenke, C., & O'Connell, J. P. (1998). Using mapping to increase released offenders' access to services. In N. La Vigne & J. Wartell (Eds.), *Crime mapping case studies: Successes in the field.* Washington, DC: Police Executive Research Forum.

Hilton, N. Z., Harris, G., & Rice, M. (2006). Sixty-six years of research on the clinical versus actuarial prediction of violence. *Counseling Psychologist, 34*(3), 400-409.

Jacobsen, M. (2005). *Downsizing prisons.* New York: New York University Press.

James, D., & Glaze, L. (2006). *Mental health problems of prison and jail inmates.* Special Report series. Washington, DC: U.S. Department of Justice, Bureau of Justice Statistics.

Joseph, J. (2005). Technoprison: Technology and prisons. In R. Muraskin & A. Roberts (Eds.), *Visions for change: Crime and justice in the twenty-first century.* Upper Saddle River, NJ: Prentice-Hall.

Kingsley, T. G., & Petit, K. L. S. (2000). Getting to know neighborhoods. 2000. *National Institute of Justice Journal,* 10-17.

Lane, C. (2005). *Justices rule against prisoner segregation.* Thursday, February 24, p. A04 (retrieved from: www.washingtonpost.com).

Lawrence, S., Mears, D., Dubin, G., & Travis, J. (2002). *The practice and promise of prison programming.* Washington, DC: The Urban Institute.

Liebling, A., & Maruna, S. (Eds.). (2005). *The effects of imprisonment.* Portland, OR: Willan Publishing.

Lurigio, A., & Snowden, J. (in press). The impact of prison culture on the treatment and control of mentally ill offenders. In J. Byrne, F. Taxman, & D. Hummer (Eds.), *The culture of prison violence.* Boston, MA: Allyn and Bacon.

Lurigio, A., & Swartz, J. (2006, September). Mental illness in correctional populations: The use of standardized screening tools for further evaluation and treatment. *Federal Probation,* 29-35.

MacKenzie, D. (2006). *What works in corrections: Reducing the criminal activities of offenders and delinquents.* New York: Cambridge University Press.

Manning, P. K. (2004). Environment, technology and organizational change: Notes from the police world. In A. Pattavina (Ed.), *Information technology and the criminal justice system.* Thousand Oaks, CA: Sage Publications.

Maruschak, L. (2006). *Medical problems of jail inmates.* Special Report series. Washington, DC: U.S. Department of Justice, Bureau of Justice Statistics.

National Commission on Correctional Health Care (NCCHC), (2002). *The health status of soon-to-be-released inmates: A Report to Congress* (vol. 2). Washington, DC: U.S. National Institute of Justice.

Pattavina, A. (2004). The emerging role of information technology in prison reentry initiatives. *Federal Probation, 68*(2), 40-44.

Pattavina, A. P., Pierce, G., & Saiz, A. (2002). Urban neighborhood information systems: crime prevention and control applications. *Journal of Urban Technology, 9*(2), 37-56.

Petersilia, J. (2004). What works in prisoner reentry? Reviewing and questioning the evidence. *Federal Probation, 68*(2), 4-8.

Petersilia, J. (2001). Prisoner reentry: Public safety and reintegration challenges. *Prison Journal, 81*(3), 360-375.

Quay, H. (1984). *Managiong adult inmates: Classification for housing and program assignments.* College Park, MD: American Correctional Association.

Rose, D. R., & Clear, T. R. (2003). Incarceration, reentry and social capital: Social networks in the balance. In J. Travis & M. Waul (Eds.), *Prisoners once removed.* Washington, DC: Urban Institute Press.

Sampson, R. J., Morenoff, J., & Raudenbush, S. (2005). Social anatomy of racial and ethnic disparities in violence. *American Journal of Public Health, 95*(2), 224-232.

Sherman, L. W., Gottfredson, D. L., MacKenzie, D. L. Eck, J., Reuter, P., & Bushway, S. D. (1998). *Preventing crime: What works, what doesn't and what's promising.* Washington, DC: U.S. National Institute of Justice.

Snavely, K., Taxman, F. S., & Gordon, S. (2005). Offender-based information sharing: Using a consent driven system to promote integrated service delivery. In A. Pattavina (Ed.), *Information technology and the criminal justice system*. Thousand Oaks, CA: Sage Publications.

Sridharan, S., & Gillespie, D. (2004). Sustaining problem-solving capacity in collaborative networks. *Criminology & Public Policy, 3*(2), 259-264.

Stowell, J. I., & Byrne, J. (in press). Does what happens in prison stay in prison? Examining the reciprocal relationship between community and prison culture. In J. Byrne, F. Taxman, & D. Hummer (Eds.), *The new culture of prison violence*. Boston, MA: Allyn and Bacon.

Taxman, F. S., & Sherman, S. (1998). Seamless system of care: Using automation to improve service delivery and outcomes of offenders in treatment. In L. Moriarty & D. Carter (Eds.), *Criminal justice technology in the 21st century*. Springfield, IL: Charles C Thomas.

Travis, J., Solomon, A. L., & Waul, M. (2001). *From prison to home: The dimensions and consequences of prisoner reentry*. Washington, DC: Urban Institute.

Urban Institute (2003, April, 15). *New initiative aims to strengthen community strategies for prisoners returning to society*. Press Release. Washington, DC.

Veysey, B., & Bichler-Robertson, G. (2002). Prevalence estimates of psychiatric disorders in correctional settings. In National Commission on Correctional Health Care (Ed.), *The health status of soon-to-be-released inmates: A report to congress* (vol. 2). Washington, DC: U.S. National Institute of Justice.

Wilson, D., Bouffard, L. A., & MacKenzie, D. (2005). A quantitative review of structured, group-oriented, cognitive-behavioral programs for offenders. *Criminal Justice and Behavior, 32*(2), 172-204.

Wormith, J. S. (1984). Attitude and behavior change of corrections clientele: A three year follow-up. *Criminology, 22*, 595-618.

Welsh, B. C., & Farrington, D. P. (2001). Toward an evidence-based approach to preventing crime. *Annals of the American Academy of Political and Social Science, 578*, 158-173.

Wortley, R. (2002). *Situational prison control: Crime prevention in correctional institutions*. Cambridge, UK: Cambridge University Press.

Wright, K. (2005). Designing a national performance measurement system. *Prison Journal, 85*(3), 368-393.

Wright, K. (2003). *Defining and measuring correctional performance*. Middletown CT: Association of State Correctional Administrators.

Wright, K., Brisbee, J., & Hardyman, P. (2003). *Defining and measuring performance*. Washington, DC: U.S. Department of Justice.

12. COMMUNITY CORRECTIONS AND HARD TECHNOLOGY

by

Patricia M. Harris

University of Texas at San Antonio

and

James M. Byrne

University of Massachusetts, Lowell

INTRODUCTION

The following chapter focuses on the application of a wide range of new *hard* technologies to the community control of offenders, including the latest generation of electronic monitoring (EM) devices and drug testing equipment, new technologies to manage alcohol-involved offenders (ignition interlock systems, remote alcohol monitoring), new technologies for managing sex offenders (polygraph testing, penile plethysmograph, computer monitoring devices), new automated reporting systems (telephone, kiosks), and new technologies for communicating with offenders (language translation devices). For each of these technological innovations, we provide a description of the device and its application to community corrections, while also reviewing the available research on both implementation and impact.

1. ELECTRONIC MONITORING

We begin our examination of the application of new hard technologies in the area of community corrections by focusing on the design, development, and implementation of EM programs in a variety of community corrections settings, including probation, parole, and day reporting centers operated out of county jails. In addition, we review the empirical evidence on the impact of EM systems on the community control of offenders. We conclude this section by highlighting the major issues and controversies surrounding current and proposed EM systems.

1a. Types of Monitoring Systems

At the outset of any review of EM, a distinction needs to be made between EM *devices* and/or EM systems versus EM *programs*. As Corbett and Marx (1991) observed over 15 years ago, "electronic monitoring is a technology in search of a program." We begin our review by describing the latest innovations in EM technology, but we recognize that the success of this technology will depend largely on the design and implementation of the programs established by community corrections managers across the country that include an EM component. Stated in its simplest form: it is one thing to collect information about offenders, it is quite another to use this information as an offender management and control tool. With this caveat in mind, we can now focus on the various EM devices available to the community corrections field.

There are currently two categories of EM systems being used in this country: devices that rely on radio frequency (RF) monitoring, using either continuous signaling (CS) or random calling (RC) technology; and devices that use global positional systems (GPS) and cell phone technology (Lilly, 2006; Renzema & Mayo-Wilson, 2005). While radio frequency technology was the primary form of EM in the 1980s and 90s, it is being challenged (in terms of market share) by the newer, more advanced GPS technology (Lilly, 2006). Unlike the RF monitoring systems, which allow the identification of an individual at a specific geographic location, the GPS-based monitoring systems allow "real time" tracking of offender movements across wider areas (home, work, neighborhood). Figures 1a and 1b provide a graphic comparison of the key features of both types of EM technology.

1b. Extent of Monitoring System Usage

Despite the post-9/11 surveillance technology explosion in the U.S. (Lilly, 2006), it appears that relatively few of the nearly five million persons on probation or parole in 2004 were supervised using EM technology (Glaze & Palla, 2005). In 1998, the most recent year for which national data are available on the use of EM as a condition of community supervision, individuals supervised with EM in the United States comprised fewer than 1% (.06%) of the 3,417,613 offenders on probation supervision in federal and

Figure 1a: A Comparison of GPS-Based and RF-Based Electronic Monitoring Technology

GPS Systems

(1) **Design**: GPS systems can be used for either active, real-time supervision, or passive, recording-mode supervision. They can also be combined with GIS technology to link offender and crime locations.

Active GPS devices:
- Offender wears a tracking device.
- 24-hour, continuous monitoring of the offender's location (using GPS satellites and cell phone technology).
- Device can be programmed to restrict offender's movement and to prevent his/her entry into "restricted" areas (e.g., school zones, playgrounds, victim residence).
- Any tampering, GPS signal failure, and/or violation of location restriction triggers an alarm to monitoring station.

Passive GPS devices:
- Offender wears a tracking device
- 24-hour, continuous recording of the offender movements; this information is downloaded periodically during the day to the tracking station.
- Periodic review by tracking station personnel; breaches identified and reported to supervisory agent, but after the fact (several hours).

(2) **Reliability of GPS Technology**:
- Battery-Powered units last 15-30 hours and require a 4-6 hour recharge.
- GPS satellite location affected by weather, tall buildings, and other geographical factors.

(3) **Cost Estimates**: $15-25 per day, not including the cost of violation notifications; Active GPS are more costly and labor-intensive than passive GPS units

Radio Frequency Systems

(1) **Design**: utilizes radio-frequency transmission to monitor the offender at a specific location (home).

- Offender wears a transmitter, typically on his/her ankle.

- Receiver unit placed at the location and attached to a landline telephone.

- Unit transmits a signal to a monitoring center.

- Monitoring center has the capability to either immediately notify the supervising agent if a violation occurs, or to record the violation and report violations periodically.

- Mobile monitoring capacity by PO's.

- Some units use intermittent voice-verification, other may include alcohol-sensors.

(2) **Reliability of RF Technology**:
- Radio-frequency may be affected by building design and location (e.g., high-rise buildings).
- Improved reliability in latest-generation of RF devices.

(3) **Cost Estimates**: $5-10 per day, depending on the cost of add-ons (e.g., alco-sensors), and not including cost of violation notifications.

Figure 1b: A Comparison of Continuously Signaling (RF) Devices and Location Tracking Systems (GPS)

Continuously Signaling Devices

 Transmitting device

 Radio transmission

 Receiving device

 Telephone communication between receiver and computer

 Computer detects when transmissions begin or end: Monitoring staff notify supervision officers

 Supervision officers follow up on violations

Location Tracking Systems--GPS

 Offender wears transmitter and carries receiver

 Signals from four satellites are received by the receiver

 Cellular phone communicates between receiver and monitoring computer

 Supervisor follows up on violations

Source: Crowe et al., (2002). *Offender Supervision with Electronic Technology: A User's Guide.*

state jurisdictions, and just 1.4% of the 704,964 offenders on federal or state parole (Bureau of Justice Statistics, 2002). However, a somewhat higher estimate was included in a report by the National Law Enforcement and Corrections Technology Center (NLECTC; 1999), which indicated that, "As of January 1998, approximately 1,500 programs existed and 95,000 electronic monitoring units were in use, including those being used by individuals on pretrial status, home detention, probation, and parole as well as in juvenile detention" (NLECTC, 1999, p. 1). Using the combined 1%-2% figures, we estimate that there are between 50,000 to 100,000 offenders being supervised today with some type of RFD or GPS monitoring system. Unfortunately, we have no data available that provide a more recent (post-9/11) estimate.

Without these data, it is inevitable that there would be some disagreement on the extent of EM usage in the U.S. For example, one recent "rough" estimate did assert that "20 percent of community supervision ... now involves EM" (Gable & Gable, 2005, p. 21), which would translate to almost *one million* offenders on EM. We are skeptical of such claims; a careful review of the research reveals that the actual prevalence of EM is still very modest. For example, the Florida Legislature reported that, at the end of 2004, only 705 or 0.6% of the 116,277 offenders under community supervision in that state were being electronically monitored (Office of Program Policy Analysis . . . , 2005). Similar estimates can be found in reviews conducted in several other states, including California (Jannetta, 2006) and Maryland (Tewey, 2005). However, the EM industry appears to be expanding post-9/11 (Lilly, 2006), and there is a renewed interest in the use of EM for specific subgroups of offenders, such as drunk drivers and sex offenders. Jannetta (2006, p. 4) has reported that, "At least 17 states are in some stage of development or implementation of GPS monitoring systems for sex offenders under community supervision," while a total of 25 states now have statutory provisions regarding GPS tracking of sex offenders (National Conference of State Legislatures, 2006). These developments certainly bode well for the EM industry.

1c. Effectiveness of Electronic Monitoring Programs

Given the recent emphasis on evidence-based practice in community corrections, it is surprising that a comprehensive evidence-based review of the research on the effectiveness (cost, diversionary impact, recidivism reduction, offender change) of EM programs has yet to be completed and its results used to guide policy and practice in community corrections. When one considers the ongoing debate between advocates of deterrence-based community corrections (e.g., Farabee, 2005) and advocates of a rehabilitation-based community corrections system (Byrne & Taxman, 2005), it is evident that such an evidence-based review is sorely needed.

Just recently, an evidence-based review of all EM studies (n = 154) conducted between 1986 and 2002 has become available under the auspices of the Campbell Collaboration (Renzema & Mayo-Wilson, 2005). As we find in many other areas of criminal justice (particularly institutional corrections), the quality of the EM evaluations conducted during this review period was remarkably low, while the few quality research studies conducted to date offer little empirical support for the continuation of EM programs. Of the 154 studies initially reviewed, only 19 met basic methodological review criteria and only 3 were included in the final group of studies reviewed by the authors, who targeted studies focusing on moderate- to high-risk offenders (Finn & Muirhead-Steves, 2002; Bonta et al., 2000; Sugg et al., 2001). A review of these three studies underscored a simple point: there is no empirical evidence that EM works as a recidivism reduction strategy. According to the authors of this review, "It is hardly surprising that recidivism has not been reliably reduced by an intervention that is typically quite short, applied in a standard fashion, and applied to a diverse group of offenders for whom it may or may not have any relevance to their motives for offending" (Renzema & Mayo-Wilson, 2005, p. 232).

Renzema and Mayo-Wilson believe that their review underscores the need to move in a different direction: "If E.M. continues to be used as it has been used, shortsighted governments will continue to waste taxpayer dollars for ideological reasons and political gain. Governments that choose to use EM in the future ought to use it to enhance other services that have a known effect on crime reduction. Those governments *must* test the marginal effects of EM, publish the results, and discontinue use of EM if it fails to provide quantifiable public benefits. Money spent on E.M. could be spent on empirically-tested programs that demonstrably protect our communities" (2005, p. 233).

The problem with the above review is that only three studies were identified as meeting the authors' study inclusion criteria, which tells the public much more about the sorry state of evaluation research than it does about the effectiveness of EM programs. Besides the Renzema and Mayo-Wilson review, the closest we could come to identifying a *comprehensive* evidence-based review in this area was a research review of EM programs recently completed by MacKenzie (2006), which examined the recidivism reduction effects reported in nine studies conducted between 1990 and 2000 (see Table 1 below). Using a ranking system developed by MacKenzie and other researchers at the University of Maryland (Sherman et al., 1997), the quality (or methodological rigor) of each study was rated on a scale of 1 to 5, with 1 representing the lowest and 5 representing the highest quality research design. A review of Table 1 reveals three level-5 studies, four level-4 studies, one level-3 study, and one level-2 study.

According to MacKenzie (2006, p. 321), "The three studies using experimental designs [the level 5 studies] found no significant difference in recidivism when the behavior of offenders who are electronically monitored on home confinement was compared with those being manually supervised." Based on this review, MacKenzie – like Renzema and Mayo-Wilson – offers a bleak assessment of the impact of EM: "Restraining offenders in

– 292 –

Table 1: Electronic Monitoring Studies Showing Recidivism Rates and Length of Follow-up

Study (Methods Score)	Measure of Recidivism	Recidivism				Follow-up Period (in months)
		Experimental (%)	N	Control (%) #1/#2/#3	N	
Austin and Hardyman, 1993 (5)	Rearrest	13.9	175	11.2	575	3.6
	Technical Violation	14.7		10.1		
Baumer and Mendelsohn, 1991 (5)	New Rearrest	0.01	78	0.08	76	6
Roy and Brown	Rearrest	16.9	72	25.9	72	12
Bonta et al., 2000a (4)	Reconviction	26.7	262	37.9*/33.3*	30/240	12
Bonta et al., 2000b (4)	Reconviction	31.5	54	35.3/31.0	17/100	12
Courtright, Berg, and Mutchnick, 1997 (4)	Rearrest[a]	19.3	57	33.3	57	14.8
	New Arrest/M(SD)	0.197 (0.553)		0.333 (0.988)		
Jolin and Stipack, 1991 (4)	Rearrest	32.0	98	47.0/33.0	64/96	24
	Reconviction	15.0		30.0/18.0		
	# of Arrests/M[b]	0.58		0.92/0.59		
	# of Convictions/M	0.20		0.66		
Brown and Roy, 1995 (3)	Program Failure	22.0	392	18.0	139	30
Glaser and Watts, 1992 92 (3)	New Arrest	0.05	124	0.06	200	6

[a]Percentages reflect the total number of rearrests in groups, including multiple arrests for an individual offender.
[b]No standard deviation was reported.
[c]Significantly different from experimental groups, $p < 0.05$.
Source: Mackenzie (2006, p. 320).

the community by increasing surveillance and control over their activities does not reduce their criminal activities. In general, program participants' recidivate as often as their counterparts who receive less surveillance. The increased surveillance may actually increase the probability of detection and, thus, result in more technical violations" (2006, p. 322). MacKenzie does note, however, that researchers have not fully explored how the surveillance component of an EM program has been integrated with the *treatment* component of the program. In fact, treatment was not adequately defined and measured in the small number of studies she reviewed. Without much more rigorous examination of both the control and treatment components of current EM programs, we simply cannot offer an assessment of the effectiveness of the latest generation of EM programs.

1d. Electronic Monitoring Issues and Controversies

The application of surveillance technology in community corrections has raised a number of issues, which we can only briefly highlight in this review. Fifteen years ago, Corbett and Marx (1991) provided one of the most often cited reviews of the potential "techno-fallacies" associated with the initial development of surveillance-driven EM programs in the U.S. While the technology of EM has certainly improved during this period, many of the *programmatic* issues associated with the first wave of EM programs (e.g., the role of treatment, offender targeting, the technical violation sanction policy, and privatization) have not been resolved. We highlight the key techno-fallacies identified in the Corbett and Marx (1991) review in Table 2, identifying ten key areas where the "perception" of EM technology does not appear to fit the "reality" of what we can actually expect from a surveillance-oriented community supervision program.

One area of particular concern is the extent to which the expansion of privately operated EM programs reduces our reliance on public sector surveillance and control programs. If we privatize both the treatment component of community corrections agencies and the surveillance component of community corrections, then what exactly do we leave in the hands of probation and parole officers? Inevitably, such role restriction and redefinition will result in the downsizing of personnel in federal, state, and local community corrections systems, because the money previously spent to hire probation and parole officers will be needed to fund contracts for both treatment providers and surveillance providers.

How will increased private sector control over offender movements and treatment/service provision affect line community corrections officers?

Table 2: The Use of Electronic Monitoring (EM) in Criminal Justice*

Perception	Reality
1. There is widespread use of EM devices through-out the criminal justice system.	1. There are between 50,000 and 100,000 EM devices currently in place for a correctional system of over 6 *million* offenders.
2. EM transcends distance, darkness, and physical barriers.	2. RF and GPS technology have a number of specific limitations which reduce the span of control they can actually deliver.
3. EM can transcend time.	3. EM offers a technology which *records* rather than transcends time.
4. EM is capital- rather than labor-intensive.	4. There are a number of management decisions that must be reviewed before it can be determined whether EM is capital- rather than labor-intensive.
5. EM triggers a shift from targeting a specific suspect to categorical suspicion.	5. EM is being used by criminal justice managers as a "bait and switch" tactic to induce the public to "buy" home confinement for certain offenders.
6. One of the major concerns of EM is the *prevention* of violations.	6. We don't know if the claim is true: a comparison of "person" versus "thing" technologies is long overdue. Moreover, EM is also being marketed as an intermediate punishment.
7. EM is decentralized and triggers self-policing.	7. EM is actually a centralized system of monitoring and control, often operated by a private (for-profit) vendor.
8. EM has low visibility or is invisible.	8. However, punishment advocates have suggested that "high" visibility EM units are an integral part of the punishment process.
9. The EM technology is ever more intensive – probing beneath surfaces, discovering inaccessible information.	9. The intensity of electronic surveillance will vary by the *actual* degree and type of monitoring by agency personnel.
10. The new technology grows ever more extensive, covering not only deeper, but larger areas.	10. Post 9/11, the EM surveillance net is certainly widening. EM programs are now found at key decision points throughout the criminal justice system.

*The identification of techno-fallacies has been adapted from Corbett and Marx (1991), and it originally appeared in a review by Byrne, Kelly, and Guarino-Ghezzi (1988).

Corbett and Marx (1991) argued that it would lead to the "dummying down" of community corrections because we would not need to hire line staff with specialized skills and training. While this is certainly a possibility, we suspect that a greater danger lies in strategies that result in less contact between line probation officers and offenders under their supervision: specifically, we're referring to the diminished opportunity for line proba-tion and parole officers to develop relationships with offenders that result in higher levels of informal social control. As a number of observers have noted, the key to offender control (and change) in both institutional and community settings is the identification of the appropriate "tipping point" between the use of formal and informal control strategies (Byrne & Taxman, 2006). Probation and parole officers play a critical role in the offender supervision process, not only in their *formal* social control functions (e.g., monitoring compliance with conditions of community supervision), but also in terms of *informal* social control, due to the relationship that develops between officers and offenders under community supervision (Byrne et al., 2002). It is unclear how the expanded use of private sector EM programs will affect the line probation or parole officer, but change in roles, responsi-bilities, and relationships appears inevitable.

2. DRUG TESTING TECHNOLOGY

The second "hard" technology we review in this chapter is drug testing. We begin by reviewing the range of drug testing procedures available in community corrections, including urinalysis, collection of oral fluids, hair analysis, and even the use of sweat patches. We then provide a review of the frequency of various forms of drug testing in community corrections, and examine the evidence of the effectiveness of drug testing – both as a technology and as a component of a comprehensive case management plan for offenders under some form of community supervision and/or in a specialized court program (e.g., drug court, reentry court). We conclude by highlighting the major issues and controversies surrounding the use of drug testing technology in community corrections.

2a. Types/Methods of Drug Testing

Different testing methods provide different sensitivities to the type as well as the timing of drug use. Various methods may be distinguished by whether they are: a) incremental (assessing recent use) or cumulative (assessing any use over a prolonged period); b) more versus less invasive to the individual being tested; and, c) apt to generate high versus low rates of "false hits" (Swan, 1995). Though urinalysis is the most popular measure of drug abuse in community corrections (Vito, 1999), it has several important limitations. First, urine tests do not detect drug use immediately after consumption. An offender who reports to his or her officer "high" may yield a negative test. Second, urine tests cannot detect drug use longer than two or three days after use (Swan, 1995; Harrell & Kleiman, 2000). Consequently, agencies would need to conduct frequent urinalysis (at least twice a week) to more accurately capture drug use by clients. Third, urinalysis is especially susceptible to adulteration leading to false negative results (Government Accounting Office, 1997). On the other hand, urinalysis yields a lower rate of false positives than sweat patches and hair analysis (Swan, 1995).

A second drug testing procedure involves the testing of oral fluid taken from the offender. Collection of oral fluid is a recent drug testing technology that has advantages over other methods. Oral fluids can capture a wide variety of drugs. Certain drugs, such as amphetamines and heroin, display higher concentrations in saliva specimens than blood and plasma for the first 48 hours following use (Crouch et al., 2004). A drawback to this method it that measurements taken from oral samples do not separate concentrations due to residual drugs remaining in the mouth versus drugs that have entered the bloodstream which can elevate results (Crouch et al., 2004).

Finally, two additional drug testing procedures have been tested on community corrections populations: hair analysis and sweat patches. Hair analysis can provide information about an offender's drug use over extended periods of time, but is controversial. The hair of a non-drug using individuals who keep company with drug users who smoke illicit substances or who have handled certain drugs but not used them, is subject to contamination and false results (Crouch et al., 2004). The reliability of sweat patches rests on a less established consensus regarding the interpretation of drug concentrations that they accumulate (Crouch et al., 2004).

2b. Extent of Drug Testing in Community Corrections

Drug testing is currently the most prevalent kind of hard technology in community corrections. A nationally representative survey of adult probationers found that 45% of probationers (with prior drug use) were subject to drug tests in their first year of supervision, a figure that rose to 63% for those with greater than one year of supervision (Mumola, 1998). The need for drug testing in community corrections is linked to research on the drug use patterns of offenders. In one recent study, 70% of the probationers sampled reported prior drug use (Mumola, 1998). Similar findings are reported for those offenders sent to prison and then released under mandatory or discretionary parole supervision (Mumola and Karberg, 2006; Burke and Tonry, 2006). The underlying assumption of drug testing strategies is that if offenders are using illegal drugs, they are not only breaking the law but also increasing the likelihood that they will commit other criminal acts in the near future.

Adele Harrell and Mark Kleiman (2000) recently provided perhaps the clearest description of the drugs-crime connection we have seen: "Drug testing of offenders reflects the widespread recognition among criminal justice professionals that reductions in some forms of drug use among certain offenders result in reductions in crime. The relationship of crime and chronic hard-drug use has been well documented in research literature. . . . Chronically hard-drug-involved offenders have high rates of criminal activity, with the frequency and severity of criminal behavior rising and falling with the level of drug usage. . . . Drug addicts commit more crimes while they are addicted – some four to six times more than when they are not abusing narcotics, a pattern that is even more pronounced among habitual offenders" (Harrell & Kleiman, 2000, p. 2). Of course, most of the offenders who are drug tested are not the chronic, hard-core drug users the authors describe; thus, the assumption is that we "test the many to identify the few."

There is no set protocol on who should be drug tested, the number and timing of the tests, and how to respond to positive tests for marijuana (the most frequently identified drug) and other drugs. In many respects, these programmatic decisions are actually more important to the success of a drug testing program than the decision about which drug testing technology to employ. For this reason, we will address each of these drug testing program elements.

Focusing on the issue of who should be tested, it could certainly be argued that *every* offender under community supervision should be drug tested, not just the subgroup of offenders either convicted of a drug offense (about 1 in every 4 under community supervision at the state level) or those (70%) with a documented history of drug abuse (Glaze & Palla, 2005). Support for this broad testing strategy can be found in a recent evaluation of an attempt to drug test – at the pretrial stage – every offender arrested in 24 separate federal judicial districts across the U.S. (Longshore et al., 2001, p. v): "Roughly 13% of defendants who tested positive on the initial test were 'hidden users.' They represent 4% of all defendants tested. Because hidden users were not identifiable on the basis of any other information available, the initial test was, for them, the sole indicator of a possible need to require drug testing as a condition of pretrial release. Without the initial test, these defendants might not have been placed on a test condition and monitored for drug use while on release." Of course, since the most likely drug to be detected was marijuana, there are many who would argue that our federal and state court and correctional systems have more important things to do than search for the hidden marijuana users among the arrestee population.

The second programmatic decision related to drug testing is the determination of when to test and how often to test. Most jurisdictions allow community corrections officers the opportunity to conduct both proactive (random) and reactive tests (based on the officer's subjective assessment that an offender may be using drugs). However, existing research has yet to determine the optimal number of tests (weekly, biweekly, monthly) needed to identify drug use and/or to induce an individual offender to abstain from drug use due to the increased probability of detection (Haapanen et al., 1998). In many jurisdictions, both the number and timing of drug tests are determined by cost and budgetary restrictions, which could limit the level and/or type of testing conducted.

The third programmatic decision related to drug testing is how to respond to a positive drug test. To some, failure to comply with the conditions of community supervision is a reason to terminate community supervision and incarcerate the offender in the name of community protection. Florida, for example, has recently embarked on a short-lived and highly controversial *zero tolerance* strategy for drug test failures, which led to an immediate jump in the number of new prison admissions in that state. In many other jurisdictions it has been reported that unsatisfactory drug test results and the failure of offenders to report for drug tests has contributed to increases in prison populations. In 1997 alone, these two factors accounted for 7.9 and 2.3%, respectively, of parole violators revoked and returned to prison (Hughes et al., 2001).

However, there appears to be an emerging perspective on technical violations generally, and drug test failures in particular, with direct consequences for offenders under community supervision. This perspective is that we need to stop incarcerating technical violators of probation, parole, and other forms of community supervision and focus our energies on alternative strategies for improving offender compliance (Taxman, 2006). As an example, in Washington State the legislature passed a law in 1999 that essentially prohibits the use of prison as a sanction for offenders who violate the technical conditions of community supervision (Jetzer, 2004). Other states, including California and Michigan (Petersilia, 2006), are considering similar strategies for reducing the flow of technical violators into the prison system. While public support for community-based treatment – rather than incarceration – appears much higher than it was a decade ago (Travis, 2006), state legislators have been reluctant to move decisively in reaffirming the notion that offender treatment – as opposed to offender surveillance – is perhaps the most effective crime control strategy currently available. Despite these shifts in legislative policy and public opinion, drug testing is still viewed as a critical feature of community supervision. The question is not whether to test; it is how to respond to evidence of continued drug use by offenders under community supervision *without using the threat of incarceration* (National Institute on Drug Abuse, 2006).

2c. Effectiveness of Drug Tests

As we observed in our review of EM technology, it is important to distinguish the effectiveness of the *device* used to detect various forms of drug use from the *programs* that incorporate drug testing technology into their case management procedures. Harrell and Kleiman (2000, p. 7) recently reviewed the research on the accuracy of various drug testing devices and offered the following assessment: "Biochemical testing of urine is, by far, the dominant technology within criminal justice agencies. Compared to other approaches, it is highly accurate and inexpensive. Its greatest limitation is its relatively narrow 'detection window': heroin, cocaine, and methamphetamine use remains detectable in urine for only 48 to 72 hours. Hair and sweat testing offer longer detection periods at higher costs and with much longer lags between test administration and results; the accuracy of hair testing remains in doubt."

It is much easier to assess the accuracy of drug testing *technology* than it is to assess the effectiveness of community corrections *programs* that incorporate some form of drug testing. The effectiveness of drug testing – as a stand-alone surveillance technology – in curbing new drug use is currently unknown. This is partly because drug testing may be only one of several conditions imposed on offenders under community supervision. For example, drug tests are a key component of drug court sentences, but so are treatment services and a non-adversarial approach to the offender (Huddleston et al., 2005). Moreover, drug testing frequency and conditions vary from program to program and within programs, as well as between offender and offender, making it difficult to measure the independent effects of this technology and/or its administration (Harrell & Kleiman, 2000).

However, the results of one fairly recent experimental study of the impact of varying the number of drug tests administered to parolees in the California Youth Authority are revealing for what they didn't reveal – that the actual level of drug testing does matter greatly. According to Haapanen et al., (1998, p. xxviii): "This study showed that routine drug testing by parole agents beyond a minimum level did not seem to have a positive impact on the criminal behavior of parolees. . . . In fact, all observed differences were in favor of lower levels of drug testing." According to Haapanen et al. (1998), the critical decision facing program managers in community corrections is not when – or how often – to test; it is what to do with drug tests results indicating that offenders continue to use drugs even though they know they will be tested. Since the typical response by offenders in this study who tested positive more than once was to go AWOL, it seems obvious that the offender's *perception* of the likely punitive response of community corrections officers did *not* deter them from using drugs; it deterred them from continuing in treatment/supervision. This certainly poses a dilemma for community corrections program developers, because they don't want to establish drug testing policies that scare offenders out of treatment, but they do believe that offenders need to be drug-free while in treatment. Despite this caveat, most recent reviews suggest that drug testing, in conjunction with appropriate treatment and a structured hierarchy of sanctions for noncompliance/drug test failures, is a key component of successful community supervision strategies for drug-involved offenders (Taxman et al., 2004).

2d. Drug Testing Issues and Controversies

There are a number of critical issues related to the use of drug testing in community corrections. Questions have been raised about the *purpose* of drug testing at key decision points in the criminal justice process (e.g., at the pretrial, sentencing, and community supervision phases), as well as the *consequences* of drug test failures for both offenders and communities, due to subsequent incarceration (Byrne & Taxman, 2006; Jacobson, 2005). In addition, others have raised the issue of racial disparities inherent in our response to various forms of criminal behavior generally, and particularly in our response to noncompliance by minority offenders under community supervision. Given shortfalls in treatment availability, treatment quality, and treatment funding in communities with high concentrations of minorities, it is not surprising that poor, minority residents living in poverty-pocket areas are significantly overrepresented in our correctional population (Taxman et al., 2005). To the extent that drug testing contributes to racial disparity (due in large part to the incarceration of probationers and parolees for technical violations involving positive drug tests), its widespread use in community corrections will be challenged.

And finally, it has been argued that money spent on this type of surveillance technology is money that could have been used to expand residential treatment capacity instead. If the real target of drug testing is the hard-core drug user, then we need to identify these individuals and place them in the appropriate treatment program. As Harrell and Kleiman contend, "[Drug] test results can also be used for assessment and treatment planning for offenders. Compared to alternative approaches for monitoring drug use including self-reports, observation of symptoms, or informant reports, testing greatly increases the probability of detecting offenders' drug use and reduces the lag between the beginning of a relapse and its detection. Insofar as test results help break through the denial often characteristic of substance abuse disorder, they can have a direct therapeutic benefit" (2000, p. 3). For those offenders who continue to test positive while in outpatient treatment or voluntary residential treatment, an alternative to incarceration will be needed. One possible strategy would be to place non-compliant, chronic drug users in mandatory, long-term residential treatment programs, and to keep them in treatment (utilizing involuntary civil commitment or some other mechanism) until they demonstrate an ability to abstain from chronic drug use. If we are serious about changing the behavior of chronic drug users, then it may be time to move in this direction.

3. TECHNOLOGIES FOR MANAGING ALCOHOL-INVOLVED OFFENDERS

It is common knowledge that alcohol is the "drug of choice" among both young and older adults in this country. We also know that alcohol consumption has been consistently linked to various forms of violent behavior and that a majority of those arrested each year report that they were under the influence of alcohol (either alone or in combination with some other drug) at the time of their arrest. While drinking is legal in the U.S. for individuals 21 and over, drunkenness is not, due to the negative consequences of excessive alcohol consumption for the individual drinker (e.g., alcohol poisoning, victimization, and other injury risk) and the people he/she harms as a consequence of drinking to excess (murder, rape, robbery, and assault have all been linked to individual offender alcohol consumption). In this section we will examine two new technologies for monitoring the alcohol consumption of offenders while under community supervision: ignition interlock devices targeting offenders who drink and drive, and remote monitoring of alcohol consumption by offenders whose conditions of supervision include restrictions on alcohol consumption.

3a. Ignition Interlock Devices

Nowhere is the harm associated with alcohol more apparent than in the case of the drunk driver. According to the latest research from the National Center for Injury Prevention and Control (NCIPC, 2007), 16,885 people died in alcohol-related motor vehicle crashes in 2005. In total, 39% of all traffic-related deaths in 2005 can be linked to individuals who drove while impaired. Police arrested 1.4 million individuals for drunk driving in 2005; about half of these arrests resulted in conviction. While these totals suggest that the criminal justice system responds aggressively to this problem, the general public seems to take a different view. According to a recent review by the NCIPC (2007, p. 1), "[drunk driving arrests represent] less than one percent of the 159 million self-reported episodes of alcohol-impaired driving among U.S. adults each year (Quinlan et al., 2005)." Clearly, a significant number of people drink and drive, but an argument can be made that the subgroup of arrested and convicted drunk drivers (mostly first timers based on official records) may actually represent individuals with a chronic drunk driving problem. In 2004, 15% of the 4.15 million offenders on probation were convicted of driving while intoxicated. Whether first time or multiple drunken driving offenders, these individuals pose a significant public health hazard when they drink and drive.

A variety of new technologies have recently been applied to the problem of controlling the drunk driver, including the use of ignition interlock devices. *Ignition interlock* refers to devices installed in motor vehicles that help prevent alcohol-impaired driving by requiring the driver to pass a breathalyzer test for the vehicle to start. The breathalyzer is an alcohol sensor unit pre-set to prevent vehicle operation whenever the operator blows a breath sample with a blood alcohol content (BAC) exceeding a predetermined threshold. The threshold used in ignition interlock devices is generally very low (under .025), especially relative to various states' "legal" BAC limits, which permit moderate alcohol consumption. Use of the interlock device as a condition of community supervision provides an alternative to license suspension for first time and repeat driving under the influence (DUI) of alcohol or drugs offenders, thereby enhancing the offender's ability to retain employment and remain financially stable (Crowe et al., 2002; Voas et al., 1999).

In addition to its role in preventing drunk driving, the ignition interlock device functions as a surveillance tool for community supervision officers. A memory chip in the mechanism can store data that can be retrieved each time the vehicle is serviced. Examples of data that can be downloaded include the number and outcome of vehicle starts, the driver's blood alcohol content per test and retest, tampering attempts, and the total number of hours of operation (Crowe et al., 2002). Offenders who do not log sufficient number of starts and hours of operation may raise suspicion that they have driven alternate vehicles, possibly while under the influence of dangerous substances. The data logs also provide an avenue to collateral benefits of ignition interlock programs; for example, using very large samples of interlock users and breath test results from Canadian provinces, researchers have demonstrated a link between rate of test failure and DUI recidivism in post-interlock periods (Marques et al., 2001; Marques et al., 2003). Such results suggest that ignition interlock data can be used to predict the offender's behavior and well as monitor it.

Extent of Use

Several states have recently passed legislation allowing judges to require installation of ignition interlock devices as a condition of probation supervision. In addition, the annual drunk driving "Rating the States" survey published by MADD (Mothers Against Drunk Driving) each year identifies ignition interlock systems as one of several effective control strategies; states that allow the installation of these devices score better on their annual report cards. However, reliable estimates of the extent of current usage of ignition interlock devices are difficult to find (Voas et al., 2002).

Effectiveness of Ignition Interlock Systems

Evaluations of ignition interlock programs are generally favorable, but the findings have some important limitations. First, it should be emphasized that the quality of the evaluation research on drunken driving control strategies is too weak to offer definitive statements of "what works" in this area (Byrne, 2002). According to Byrne (2002, p. 26), "There is no sound body of recent empirical research on which to base an assessment of which (if any) control-oriented drunk driver intervention strategies are effective, either as a general or specific deterrent to drunk driving." The best judgment that can be offered about the ignition interlock device is that it represents one of several promising drunk driver control strategies, along with license suspension/revocation (DeYoung, 1999; DeYoung, 2000), and vehicle impoundment/forfeiture (Voas & DeYoung, 2002).

While nearly all of the published North American studies reveal lower rates of DUI among offenders during the period their vehicle use is restricted to ignition interlock use, as compared to DUI offenders not subject to required interlock use, the same studies show more modest and sometimes statistically non-significant differences in rates of recidivism for the two groups once interlock restrictions have been lifted (see, e.g., Beck et al., 1999; Voas et al., 1999; Weinrath, 1997). For example, in the study by Beck et al. (1999), subjects randomly assigned to the interlock and comparison group experienced failure rates of 2.4% and 6.7%, respectively, while the former group was restricted to interlock use, but rates of 3.5% and 2.6% once the restriction was lifted.

In addition, research studies on the effectiveness of ignition interlock devices either employ non-experimental research designs or rely on questionable comparison groups. For example, Beck et al. (1999), Weinrath (1997), and Morse and Elliot (1992) all evaluated interlock programs using groups of offenders whose driving licenses had been suspended. While use of a suspended license group is common in this area of research, inasmuch as suspension typically attaches to offenders who refuse to participate in interlock programs, a troubling implication from the standpoint of program evaluation is that this condition necessitates comparisons of volunteers with non-volunteers. Even efforts to match the groups on other characteristics cannot overcome the fact that offenders who have had their licenses suspended face dual disincentives (i.e., potential punishment for driving while one's license is suspended plus sanctions for impaired driving). This particular feature of studies of ignition interlock use may be instrumental in suppressing evidence of the device's actual impact in deterring drunk driving.

Research on the *technology* used in ignition interlock systems highlights the various technical limitations of these systems; stated simply, they are not invulnerable. Offenders who are intent on defeating the ignition interlock could, of course, simply operate a different vehicle. However, it is at least possible to reduce the probability that the offender will circumvent the device when he or she is limited to driving the vehicle in which an ignition interlock has been installed. For example, when paired with a biometric identification device such as "hum-tones" (requiring the operator to hum while blowing into the sensor) and breath pulse codes (which involves submitting a combination of short and long breath pulses to identify the driver; see Beirness, 2001), it is more difficult for someone other than the offender to start the automobile. Compulsory and random breath testing ("running retests") of the driver while the vehicle is in transit help to reduce the opportunity to drive once the vehicle is engaged. Incorporation of temperature sensors into the devices causes stored breath samples, such as from a balloon, to be rejected (Beirness, 2001).

Another threat to the integrity of the ignition interlock technology is that accuracy can vary according to the type of alcohol detection method that is built into the device. Frequent recalibration is required for alcohol sensing units that rely on semiconductor as compared to electrochemical (fuel cell) sensing, because the former, albeit less expensive, offers less stable measurements over time (Beirness, 2001). As a result, conditions of supervision should include a stipulation to require offenders to have the ignition interlock device recalibrated for optimal performance in order to avoid equipment malfunction (Crowe et al., 2002). An additional drawback to the semiconductor technology is that its sensitivity is not limited to alcohol only; other vapors, such as cigarette smoke and vehicle exhaust fumes, may trigger false positive readings and thereby prevent legitimate vehicle use. In contrast, sensors based on fuel cell technology respond to alcohol alone (Beirness, 2001).

Finally, it is important to keep in mind that nothing about the interlock device bars offenders from abusing alcohol when not driving. It is certainly possible that these offenders will continue to drink excessively, resulting in a higher likelihood of both offending and victimization. In those instances where abstinence is a goal of supervision, it would be wiser to pair interlock restrictions with other conditions, such as continuous monitoring by remote alcohol sensors and/or participation in a treatment program of some kind.

3b. Remote Alcohol Monitoring

According to a recent study by Phillips (2001) approximately 10% of all offenders placed on probation after a driving while intoxicated (DWI) conviction are ordered to abstain from alcohol consumption while under community supervision. Similar restrictions are placed on offenders convicted of other crimes who also appear to have a serious alcohol problem. Recently, traditional office-based alcohol testing strategies have been supplemented (and/or replaced) by remote monitoring systems. Breathalyzers located in the home allow for random testing of the offender's compliance with alcohol-related terms of community supervision. Phone calls or beepers alert subjects when it is time to take the breathalyzer test, the results of which are conveyed by phone line to a computer at a central monitoring center. Systems are programmed to trigger additional tests upon detection of positive results, to rule out competing explanations (e.g., mouthwash or foods with alcohol content) for the initial reading. Some agencies follow receipt of positive breathalyzer results with immediate home visits, if feasible, so that a field sobriety test can be administered to the offender in person. Like the equipment used in ignition interlocks, home breathalyzers incorporate identity verification features to circumvent the possibility that individuals other than the offender are blowing into the device. Transmission of the offender's image at time of testing and voice matching are examples of security measures that may be used (Crowe et al., 2002).

One drawback of home breathalyzers is the obvious requirement that the offender be periodically present in the residence for testing to occur. Consequently, these devices are more suitable for offenders who are subject to home detention than those who are employed or otherwise lawfully engaged outside of the home. More recent technology to monitor compliance with alcohol-related conditions of community supervision couples a transdermal alcohol sensor – a device worn within an ankle bracelet that captures excretion of sweat through the skin – with radio frequency communications. In contrast to breathalyzer technology, remote sensors provide 24-hour monitoring in addition to giving offenders the freedom to maintain employment and other aspects of successful reintegration (*Corrections Forum*, 2004).

The Secure Continuous Remote Alcohol Monitor (SCRAM) comprises waterproof and tamper-resistant ankle bracelets that automatically measure the offender's alcohol level according to a schedule established by the subject's supervising officer. Types of data transmitted by the bracelet to a central monitoring station include alcohol readings, tamper alerts, and attempts to remove the devices (Phillips, 2001). Though transmission of data to the central monitoring system occurs only when the subject comes within range of a modem located in his or her home, SCRAM can create and store many readings throughout the day or over a longer period if necessary.

Extent of Use

Unfortunately, no data are currently available on the extent to which transdermal alcohol sensors are used in probation. However, it seems logical to assume that as community corrections systems expand the use of EM, they will consider adopting EM systems that also provide remote monitoring of alcohol use by offenders.

Effectiveness of Remote Alcohol Sensors

As was true for both drug testing and EM, it is important to distinguish the evaluation research on the *technology* from the evaluation research on the *programs* using the technology. Research on transdermal alcohol sensors centers on their reliability and validity as vehicles for measuring alcohol use, in comparison to the status quo, the breathalyzer. In laboratory conditions using a variety of subjects (e.g., sober individuals, nonalcoholic drinkers, and intoxicated alcoholics) whose blood alcohol contents were measured by both breathalyzers and transdermal sensors, the sensors have been found to produce reliable indicators of alcohol consumption with no false positive readings, though breathalyzer and transdermal measures do not produce equivalent readings (Sakai et al., 2006; Swift et al., 1992). Unfortunately, quality evaluation research on the effectiveness of community corrections programs using the SCRAM technology has yet to be completed. In the interim, we are left with the following caveat to consider: "Developers of the SCRAM transdermal technology are careful not to position their EM program as a complete solution. Instead, SCRAM is designed to work in conjunction with other program elements, including offender assessment and on-going client evaluation, substance abuse treatment, home arrest, definitive consequences for violations, and graduated sanctions" (Phillips, 2001, p. 44).

As to cost-effectiveness, one recent estimate of $12 per day (*Corrections Forum*, 2003) seems to place the per diem cost of these devices in the same cost category as other types of EM. If correct, such costs appear to be modest when compared to the costs of an incarceration alternative, but expensive when compared to traditional methods of detecting alcohol use among probationers. However, the real cost of these devices cannot be determined until we examine the impact of programs that utilize remote alcohol detection technology on subsequent offender compliance and/or revocation from probation and incarceration. In addition, it is possible that in some programs an offender's ability to pay for this new technology may limit the number (and background) of offenders who participate.

4. TECHNOLOGIES FOR MANAGING SEX OFFENDERS

Sex offenders represent a significant challenge for community corrections officials: 60% of all convicted sex offenders are placed under some form of community supervision with special conditions restricting offender location, movement, employment, interactions with children, and even computer access (Terry, 2006). In addition, 90% of these offenders are required to participate in some form of sex offender treatment, although both treatment availability and quality are a constant problem, particularly in areas where many offenders are not fluent in English (Terry, 2006). Faced with the unenviable task of supervising offenders convicted of a wide variety of sex crimes (rape, child pornography, child molestation, pedophilia, hebophilia, etc.) in communities where residents are fearful that they will repeat their behavior, many community corrections managers have turned to the legislature and requested funding for a variety of hard technology control strategies, including EM, polygraph testing, penile plethysmographs, and new computer technology designed to monitor the computer use of sex offenders. In addition, federal and state community corrections managers have requested new personnel and training as they move to manage these offenders using specialized caseloads, particularly in response to recent legislative initiatives (e.g., Proposition 83 in California) to keep known sex offenders away from schools, parks, and other public areas.

The paradox inherent in this control-based sex offender supervision strategy is that: (1) very few sex offenders will actually recidivate by committing a new sex crime, and (2) the subgroup who do recidivate are much more likely to commit their crimes in private (homes) than in public (schools, parks) settings (Sample & Bray, 2003; Sample & Bray, 2006; Miethe et al., 2006; Terry, 2006). Nonetheless, it appears that the public generally – and state legislatures in particular – are less interested in *risks* (sex offenders as a group have the lowest recidivism risk of all offender groups) than they are with *stakes* (the serious types of crimes these offenders will commit in the rare instances they do reoffend). When viewed in this context, sex offenders represent a group of high-stakes, but low-risk offenders that the public wants controlled. According to a recent report from the National Conference of State Legislatures (2006), 25 states now have statutory provisions authorizing the GPS tracking of sex offenders. In addition to EM, which we cover separately, there are three other hard technology innovations that are currently being used to control sex offenders: (1) polygraph testing, (2) the penile plethysmograph, and (3) new computer monitoring devices. We examine each of these applications below.

4a. Polygraph Testing

The polygraph is an instrument that measures and compares changes in such physiologic activities as heart rate, respiration, blood pressure, and galvanic skin reactions in a subject during his or her responses to specific questions (Pullen et al., 1996). The most frequent target of the polygraph in community corrections is the sex offender. According to a telephone survey of over 700 probation and parole agencies nationwide, the most common uses for the polygraph include identification of the offender's sexual history and offense patterns, verification of the offender's account of events in the conviction offense, and monitoring of the offender's compliance with conditions of supervision. With respect to monitoring, an officer may resort to polygraph testing to determine whether the offender has access to potential victims and engages in deviant fantasies or other high-risk triggers to reoffending (English et al., 2000).

The polygraph is regarded as an essential component of the "containment approach" to managing sex offenders in the community (English et al., 1997). However, we should point out that until polygraph testing is found to meet the standard of reliability that would allow the results to be admissible in court, the use of this technology will continue to be challenged. Current emphasis on the polygraph in community supervision stems from general recognition by criminal justice practitioners and sex offender treatment providers of the inadequacy of both official information about a sex offender's sex crime activity and the offender's self-reports (English et al., 2000). The polygraph is viewed as a means to overcome sex offenders' finely honed social skills and manipulative abilities that have served them so well in their commission and concealment of sexual offending (Pullen et al., 1996).

What exactly the offender should be questioned about and how his responses should be evaluated are best determined by the team of professionals involved in the offender's management: the probation officer, the treatment provider, and the polygraph examiner (Blasingame, 1998; Pullen et al., 1996). Preferred examiners are those who have completed training on the use of the polygraph with sex offenders, have extensive experience carrying out polygraph examinations, and comply with professional standards for polygraph testing (Pullen et al., 1996; Cross & Saxe, 2001).

Polygraph examiners should incorporate both test and control questions as a means for better distinguishing respondents who have engaged in the target activity of interest from those who have not. Test questions are those that inquire about a specific target activity of interest to the sex offender management team; control questions inquire about broader activities. When control questions are used, individuals who have not engaged in the target activity produce greater reactions to the control questions, relative to those who have participated in the target activity (Blasingame, 1998; Pullen et al., 1996).

Unfortunately, polygraph examination is not yet subject to uniform regulation and licensing from state to state. Variability in examiner expertise and lack of standardized polygraph testing are concerns to community corrections practitioners. For this reason, the video and audiotaping of polygraph examinations are recommended practices for enhancing objectivity and quality control (Pullen et al., 1996).

Extent of Use

No recent statistics on the prevalence of the polygraph in community supervision are available; English et al. (2000) report that 16% of probation and parole agencies employed the polygraph in sex offender supervision in 1998. However, this does not mean that all sex offenders under supervision by those agencies were subjected to polygraph testing, and its use may be especially limited in jurisdictions where examination costs are passed on the offender. Though current estimates of actual prevalence are unavailable, there is emerging recognition that the polygraph may become an indispensable tool for managing sex offenders in community corrections (Lane Council of Governments, 2003; Pullen et al., 1996).

Evidence of Effectiveness

To date, no published research has directly evaluated the impact of polygraph examinations on the recidivism of sex offenders under community supervision, though research is available on other aspects of polygraph testing using this population. For example, Kokish et al. (2005) examined the reactions of 95 sex offenders to polygraph experiences in an outpatient treatment program. Seventy-two percent of the offenders stated that the polygraph had aided their successful treatment by compelling them to be more truthful in therapy. However, 19% of subjects claimed to have been incorrectly rated deceptive, and another 6% claimed to have been incorrectly rated as truthful when they had provided deceitful responses. Whether test results actually produced such false positives and negatives is subject to speculation.

Grubin et al. (2004) studied the impact of polygraph testing on the high-risk behaviors of 32 sex offenders participating in community treatment programs. Subjects were divided into two groups: a "polygraph aware group" whose members were told to expect a polygraph test after three months, and a "polygraph unaware" group. All subjects were tested after a 3 month period. Contrary to expectation, there was no significant difference between the two groups in average number of high-risk behaviors reported. In light of the low number of subjects tested, it would be best to interpret these results cautiously.

The polygraph remains a controversial tool, despite the enthusiastic support it receives from some community corrections practitioners. Cross and Saxe (2001) raised several objections to the use of the polygraph in sex offender supervision. First, the polygraph's level of accuracy in detecting deceit is actually unknown – without a confession or corroborating evidence, there is no definitive way to determine if those who "beat" the polygraph are really being truthful. This is because there is no known physiological response that is unique to lying. Second, reliance on the device may lead to a false sense of security about offenders who have successfully deceived the examiner. Third, polygraph use may be contrary to treatment-centered ideology, because the treatment provider is not forthright with the client regarding the accuracy of the polygraph.

4b. The Penile Plethysmograph

The plethysmograph is a device used to measure changes in a subject's penile circumference or volume, in response to video and audio stimuli.

The plethysmograph is the most common means of assessing the nature and extent of the offender's deviant sexual arousal, a practice known as phallometric assessment (Dutton & Emerick, 1996).

The main purpose of plethysmograph-based phallometric assessment in community corrections is to identify sexual preferences. These include the age and sex of partners as well as preference for nonconsensual sexual acts and violence. In community corrections, the plethysmograph has four uses. First, it provides data that can be used to confront and overcome an offender's denial about his behaviors. Second, it captures a baseline, pre-treatment record of the offender's arousal patterns. Third, when coupled with behavioral interventions such as aversion therapy or covert sensitization,[1] the plethysmograph can provide the offender with feedback regarding his or her ability to control sexual arousal. Fourth, it measures the offender's arousal patterns post-treatment, and as such is one means to evaluate treatment success (Dutton & Emerick, 1996). Moreover, though it has not received the endorsement of the community corrections field as such, phallometric measurement is also valued for its contribution to the prediction of violent recidivism in sex offenders (Lally, 2003; Lalumiere & Harris, 1998; Quinsey et al., 2006).

Extent of Use

Data regarding the extent to which community corrections agencies resort to the plethysmograph in sex offender supervision are not available. However, it is certainly an example of a new technology being applied to a target population (sex offenders) that we are attempting to treat and control in the community.

Evidence of Effectiveness

While there is ample research on plethysmograph-based phallometric assessment (for a recent review, see Kalmus & Beech, 2005), the focus of this research is not on the efficacy of the plethysmograph in the management of sex offenders in the community. Rather, scholars have been especially interested in the role played by different stimuli (e.g., video, audio, pictures, text) and other procedural variations on penile response. A second focus of research is on the discriminant validity of phallometric assessment: i.e., the extent to which plethysmographic responses correctly distinguish sex offender types, such as rapists from pedophiles, violent child-sex offenders from nonviolent ones, incest offenders from extrafamilial offenders, and so forth (Harris et al., 1992; Kalmus & Beech, 2005; Launay, 1999). A third research area centers on the validity of phallometric assessment in predicting recidivism (e.g., Rice et al., 1990; Rice et al., 1991).

The phallometric assessment of sexual arousal is an extremely contentious pursuit, even among academics. As Harris et al. point out, "Physiological changes are easier to measure than to interpret" (1992, p. 502). Disagreement persists over phallometric scoring methods, eligibility criteria (whether subjects who cannot obtain full erections can be assessed), and which type (video, slide or aural) and content of assessment stimuli are most effective (Harris et al., 1992; Kalmus & Beech, 2005). There is also longstanding debate regarding the extent to which the plethysmograph reliably distinguishes rapists from non-offenders, as well as sex offender sub-types (Launay, 1999; Marshall & Fernandez, 2000). Contributing to the controversies surrounding phallometric assessment are studies attesting to the relative ease with which subjects can suppress penile responses to deviant stimuli (Launay, 1999), though procedures to detect and interfere with faking may be successful in addressing this problem (Lalumiere & Harris, 1998). Finally, there is reluctance in some quarters to using phallometric assessment on juvenile sex offenders, due both to apprehension about the potential for exposing young offenders to what may be new deviance and to recognition that relatively little research on the plethysmograph has been conducted using samples of juveniles in comparison to samples of adults (Dutton & Emerick, 1996).

4c. Management and Monitoring of Computer Use by Sex Offenders

A third hard technology, sex offender surveillance strategy involves the installation of a simple computer program – Field Search – by the community corrections officer, which will then allow the officer to monitor the use of an offender's home computer. This free software tool was developed by the National Law Enforcement and Corrections Technology Center and is available on the Center's website (www.justnet.org/fieldsearch/). Since it is estimated that "about 70 percent of all sex offenders supervised in the community have access to the internet" (Russo, 2006, p. 1), it certainly appears to make sense to examine computer use by these offenders during visits to the offender's home, while also looking for other items that have been linked to sex offender "relapse," such as video games, magazines, children's food, videos, animals, cable television, cameras, and sporting equipment (Terry, 2006, p. 174).

According to a recent review by Russo (2006, p. 1), "The Field Search software can be downloaded onto a CD or flash drive that the officer can bring into the field. At the offender's home, the software is run on the target computer. In about 20 minutes, it performs four major functions: Internet history search, image search, multimedia file search, and keyword search." Because it was just recently developed by NLECTC, no data are available either on the extent of its use or its effectiveness as a monitoring technology for sex offenders. However, it is currently being field tested by the Boston federal probation office and at several other locations. One federal probation officer we interviewed noted that for many offenders, fear of detection on home computers has led some sex offenders to visit Internet cafes, suggesting that surveillance of home computers will have to be supplemented with an "old school" monitoring strategy: field surveillance by federal probation officers at these locations (personal communication).

5. AUTOMATED REPORTING SYSTEMS

One recent assessment of the newest generation of risk classification devices is that they result in the oversupervision of low-risk offenders and the under-supervision of high-risk offenders (Austin, 2006). Given the resource shortfalls in many state probation systems, one strategy that has gained greater acceptance in recent years is to reduce or eliminate the active supervision requirement for certain categories of low risk (and low stakes) offenders, leaving community corrections officers with smaller active supervision caseloads. New technological advances in automated reporting systems, pagers, and the use of reporting kiosks offer an attractive alternative to supervision without requiring a significant personnel allocation.

According to a recent description of the kiosk system used in the District of Utah Probation and Pre-Trial Office (Ogden and Horrocks, 2001, p. 2), "With a kiosk, officers enroll an offender/defendant and capture their fingerprints digitally with scanners from Index. A user identification number is created based upon the PACTS number, and the fingerprint becomes the password to the system. An e-mail account is also created. They will be entered—with case-specific information—into the database. When defendants/offenders use the kiosk, a biometric sample is taken (via scanner) and compared to the one collected during enrollment. Once a match is established, the offender/defendant can interact with the kiosk by pressing buttons on the touch screen." With over four million offenders currently under probation supervision, kiosks appear to offer a new technological solution to an enduring problem: how to triage a large proportion of offenders from active supervision without ignoring ongoing monitoring responsibilities. To date, however, neither the implementation nor the impact of this new generation of reporting systems has been evaluated.

6. LANGUAGE TRANSLATORS

Corrections practitioners are called upon to supervise growing numbers of offenders who do not speak English. Languages spoken by non-English speaking clients include not just Spanish and its various dialects but an increasingly heterogeneous array of Asian, Pacific Islander, Eastern European, East Indian, and African tongues, to name a few (National Institute of Justice . . . , 2000). To help bridge the language divide, corrections and law enforcement agencies are turning to technological solutions called language translators.

Language translators are portable electronic devices that play mainly pre-recorded phrases in the offender's language. Several electronic translator products are now available on the market, and each differs in the features it offers. For example, CopTrans offers two-way translation of live speech as well as pre-recorded dialogues for typical justice system events (such as booking into jail or relaying court dates), whereas Phraselater carries out one-way translation only. The Voice Response Translator (VRT), on the other hand, emits pre-recorded phrases in the language of choice in response to a brief prompt in English for its operator. Each prompt triggers whole statements of questions in the offender's language. The VRT device has the advantage of producing audible phrases recorded by fluent speakers instead of a machine-synthesized voice (National Law Enforcement and Corrections Technology Center, 2003). Moreover, VRT now supports at least 125 languages, with the potential for up to 125,000 phrases per language, though typical use by agencies may call for no greater than 500 phrases (Cohen, 2005).

Available research on voice translators centers on field evaluations by law enforcement officers and physical testing of various translator units (Gelb & Marshall, 2003; Naval Air Systems Command . . . , 2003). Evaluations of VRT language translator use by police officers have noted such problems as the failure of the unit's microphone to pick up the officer's voice and its unreliability in noisy situations. In addition, officers have noted a need for additional commands to cover routine situations (e.g., reciting the Miranda warnings and requesting permission to search for weapons) beyond the unit's pre-programmed capacity. Further, because the VRT is user-specific (i.e., officers must train the unit to their specific voice patterns before they can begin to issue commands), its effectiveness depends on the extent to which the user relays the trigger commands with the same inflection and volume as in the initial training (Gelb & Marshall, 2003). This particular deficit may be alleviated if the unit is reprogrammed to accept single-word phrases (Naval Air Systems Command . . . , 2003). Review of the relative merits of different units concludes that adding a mechanism to abort phrases that have been triggered unintentionally (due either to operator or unit failure) would be a positive enhancement to language translators, as would the capacity to use a stylus to pick out desired phrases when voice commands are unreliable, such as in noisy situations (Gelb & Marshall, 2003).

To date, no literature has reported on the diffusion of language translator technology in the field of community corrections, nor are there any field evaluations of these devices by community corrections personnel. It is clear, however, that language translators can play an important role in a variety of community corrections settings, such as in probation and parole intake, and routine office contacts.

CONCLUSIONS

Technological advances have transformed the nature of community corrections, not in terms of what specific *types* of information is collected, but rather in the techniques and *technologies* used to collect this information. Probation and parole agencies now have access to unprecedented scope and quantity of information about their clients' whereabouts and illicit activities. Yet, important questions and issues emerge from an examination of the most recent fascination with the new technology of offender surveillance and control, particularly concerning: (1) how this information is used to change offender behavior; (2) the effect of new technology on the interplay between formal and informal social control mechanisms; and, (3) the integration of treatment and control mechanisms in the latest wave of "new" community corrections programs (Byrne & Taxman, 2006, Kleiman, 2005).

Our review of the available research on various hard technology innovations in community corrections was revealing. Three key findings bear careful consideration as we expand our reliance on new technologies of surveillance and control. First, it is indisputable that hard technology innovations in community corrections are under-evaluated. Few innovations have been examined with respect to their capacity to affect recidivism; those studies that have been conducted are too poorly designed to be included in an evidence-based research review. While the uses of EM and drug testing technology have attracted the interest of many researchers, we know remarkably little about the effectiveness of EM and drug testing *programs*. Until this research is completed we need to be cautious, and to resist the impulse to embrace the notion that newer is better.

Second, it is also apparent that despite the publicity, most offenders under community supervision will not be placed under EM, nor are they likely to be supervised using the other new technology innovations we highlight in this chapter. With the exception of drug testing (and the use of reporting kiosks in New York City and a few other large probation systems), the technological innovations discussed here are probably not among the supervision measures that will be imposed upon most offenders. The availability of technology will be further limited in jurisdictions that choose to pass costs along to offenders. The public may place unrealistic expectations on community corrections, based on the perception that community corrections agencies already have a wide variety of technological tools at their disposal when, in reality, most jurisdictions today are technology poor; out of necessity, "triage" is the management strategy being used by community corrections managers today. (Triage has been described as a strategy used in "MASH" medical units where decisions have to be made quickly about who will receive – and benefit most from – immediate treatment. Some people are too sick; others do not have life-threatening illnesses. Applied to community corrections, the triage strategy focuses limited treatment and control resources on those who need it – and will benefit most from it.)

Third, it is important to consider carefully the consequences of using available technological innovations to monitor the actions of offenders under community supervision. We have the technology to monitor where offenders go, what they really feel, how truthful they are, and which substances they consume. Greatly expanded access to information regarding clients' misbehaviors (e.g., curfew violations, drug test failures) carries with it increased "burdens," both to community corrections departments and other system components. For agencies that have adopted coherent procedures for graduated sanctions, earnest application of those procedures inevitably diverts resources away from treatment and other client services. In the absence of graduated sanctions, or at their end, lies revocation and increased demand for costly institutional resources. On the other hand, community corrections agencies face the burden of diminished accountability and credibility when no actions follow discovery of repeated violations by the individuals under their supervision. Ultimately, the effectiveness of the new technological innovations we describe will be determined by where we draw the line between tolerance and intolerance of various forms of offender misbehavior (Kleiman, 2005).

NOTE

1. According to a review by Blanchette (1996), "Aversion therapy, like covert sensitization, uses the tenets of classical conditioning to reduce inappropriate arousal patterns. Generally, aversion therapy pairs the deviant object/event of arousal with an unpleasant stimulus, such as mild electric shock or a foul odor. Many aversion techniques follow by presenting a more appropriate object/event of arousal (e.g., a slide of a naked adult woman for pedophiles) with no aversive rejoinder." Blanchette goes on to describe covert desensitization: "With covert sensitization, the offender is first asked to identify the sequence of events or behaviors that leads to his or her sexual offending. Next, these events or behaviours are systematically paired with highly negative consequences, such as being apprehended and going to prison. It is hoped that through this repetitive imagery, the offender will associate the precursors to his/her offending with these negative consequences." For a more recent discussion, see Terry (2006).

REFERENCES

Austin, J. (2006). How much risk can we take? The misuse of risk assessment in corrections. *Federal Probation, 70*(3), 58-63.

Beck, K. H., Rauch, W. J., Baker, E. A., & Williams, A. F. (1999). Effects of ignition interlock license restrictions on drivers with multiple alcohol offenses: A randomized trial in Maryland. *American Journal of Public Health, 89*(11), 1696-1700.

Beirness, D. J. (2001). *Best practices for alcohol interlock programs.* Ottawa, Ontario: Traffic Injury Research Foundation.

Blanchette, K. (1996). *Sex offender assessment, treatment, and recidivism: A literature review.* Ottawa: Correctional Services of Canada. Available at: http://www.csc-scc.gc.ca/text/rsrch/reports/r48/r48e_e. shtml

Blasingame, G. D. (1998). Suggested uses of polygraphy in community-based sexual offender treatment programs. *Sexual Abuse: A Journal of Research and Treatment, 10*(1), 37-45.

Bonta, J., Wallace-Capretta, S., & Rooney, J. (2000). Can electronic monitoring make a difference? An evaluation of three Canadian programs. *Crime & Delinquency, 46*(2), 61-75.

Bureau of Justice Statistics (2002). *Correctional populations in the United States, 1998.* Washington, DC: Author. Available at: http://www.ojp.usdoj.gov/bjs/abstract/cpusst.htm

Burke, P., & Tonry, M. (2006). *Successful transition and reentry for safer communities: A call to action for parole.* Silver Springs, MD: Center for Effective Public Policy.

Byrne, J. (2002). *Drunk driving: An assessment of "what works" in the areas of classification, treatment, prevention, and control.* Final report. Baltimore: State of Maryland, Council on Productivity and Management, Department of Parole and Probation.

Byrne, J., Kelly, L., & Guarino-Ghezzi, S. (1988, Spring). Understanding the limits of technology: An examination of the use of electronic monitoring in the criminal justice system. *Perspectives,* 14-24.

Byrne J., & Taxman, F. (2006). Crime control strategies and community change. *Federal Probation, 70*(3), 3-12.

Byrne, J., & Taxman, F. (2005). Crime (control) is a choice: Divergent perspectives on the role of treatment in the adult corrections system. *Criminology & Public Policy, 4*(2), 291-310.

Byrne, J., Taxman, F., & Young, D. (2002). *Emerging roles and relationships in the reentry partnership initiative: New ways of doing business.* Washington, DC: U.S. Department of Justice, Office of Justice Programs.

Cohen, M. P. (2005). The voice response translator: A valuable police tool. *NIJ Journal, July 2005*(252), 8-13.

Corbett, R., & Marx, G. (1991) Critique: No soul in the new machine: Technofallacies in the electronic monitoring movement. *Justice Quarterly, 8*(3), 399-414.

Corrections Forum (2003). Putting the clamp on boozers. *Corrections Forum, 12*(6), 6-8.

Corrections Forum (2004). Some Michigan courts using alcohol-detection anklets. *Corrections Forum, 13*(6), 8-10.

Cross, T. P., & Saxe, L. (2001). Polygraph testing and sexual abuse: The lure of the magic lasso. *Child Maltreatment, 6*(3), 195-206.

Crouch, D. J., Day, J., Baudys, J., & Fatah, A. A. (2004). *Evaluation of saliva/oral fluid as an alternate drug testing specimen.* NIJ Report 605-03. Washington, DC: National Institute of Justice.

Crowe, A. H., Sydney, L., Bancroft, P., & Lawrence, B. (2002). *Offender supervision with electronic technology: A user's guide.* Lexington, KY: American Probation and Parole Association.

DeYoung, D. (2000). An evaluation of the general deterrent effect of vehicle impoundment on suspended and revoked drivers in California. *Journal of Safety Research, 31*(2), 51-59.

DeYoung, D. (1999). An evaluation of the specific deterrent effects of vehicle impoundment on suspended, revoked, and unlicensed drivers in California. *Accident Analysis and Prevention, 31*(1-2), 45-53.

Dutton, W., & Emerick, R. (1996). Plethysmography assessment. In K. English, S. Pullen, & L. Jones (Eds.), *Managing adult sex offenders: A containment approach* (pp. 14.1-14.16). Lexington, KY: American Probation and Parole Association.

English, K., Jones, L., Pasini-Hill, D., Patricia, D., & Cooley-Towell, S. (2000). *The value of polygraph testing in sex offender management.* Denver, CO: Colorado Division of Criminal Justice.

English, K., Pullen, S., & Jones, L. (1997). *Managing adult sex offenders in the community – A containment approach.* Washington, DC: National Institute of Justice.

Farabee, D. (2005). *Rethinking rehabilitation: Why can't we reform our criminals?* Washington, DC: AEI Press.

Finn, M. A., & Muirhead-Steves, S. (2002). The effectiveness of electronic monitoring with violent male parolees. *Justice Quarterly, 19*(2), 293-312.

Gable, R. K., & Gable, R. S. (2005). Electronic monitoring: Positive intervention strategies. *Federal Probation, 69*(1), 21-24.

Gelb, K., & Marshall, L. (2003). *Voice recognition evaluation report.* Orlando, FL: Naval Air Systems Command Training Systems Division.

Glaze, L., & Palla, S. (2005). Probation and parole in the United States, 2004. *Bureau of Justice Statistics Bulletin,* November. Washington, DC: U.S. Department of Justice.

Government Accounting Office (1997). *Drug courts: Overview of growth, characteristics, and results.* Washington, DC: Author.

Grubin, D., Madsen, L., Parsons, S., Sosnowski, D., & Warberg, B. (2004). A prospective study of the impact of polygraphy on high-risk behaviors in adult sex offenders. *Sexual Abuse: A Journal of Research and Treatment, 16*(3), 209-222.

Haapanen, R., Boyken, G., Henderson, S., & Britton, L. (1998). *Drug testing for youthful offenders on parole: An experimental study.* Final report to the National Institute of Justice, U.S. Department of Justice, prepared under grant number 91-IJ-CX-K023. Sacramento: State of California, Department of the Youth Authority.

Harrell, A., & Kleiman, M. (2002). *Drug testing in criminal justice settings.* Washington, DC: The Urban Institute.

Harris, G. T., Rice, M. E., Quinsey, V. L., Chaplin, T. C., & Earls, C. (1992). Maximizing the discriminant validity of phallometric assessment data. *Psychological Assessment, 4*(4), 502-511.

Huddleston, C. W., Freeman-Wilson, K., Marlowe, D. B., & Roussell, A. (2005). *Painting the current picture: A national report card on drug courts and other problem solving court programs in the United States* (volume 1, No. 2). Washington, DC: Bureau of Justice Assistance and National Drug Court Institute.

Hughes, T. A., Wilson, D. J., & Beck, A. J. (2001). *Trends in state parole, 1990-2000.* Washington, DC: Bureau of Justice Statistics.

Jacobson, M. (2005). *Downsizing prisons.* New York: New York University Press.

Jannetta, J. (2006). *GPS monitoring of high-risk sex offenders: description of the California department of corrections and rehabilitation's San Diego county pilot program.* Working paper. Irvine, CA: Center for Evidence-Based Corrections, University of California, Irvine.

Jetzer, K. (2004). *The effects of OAA (Offender Accountability Act) on community custody violations.* Olympia, WA: Washington State Department of Corrections.

Kalmus, E., & Beech, A. R. (2005). Forensic assessment of sexual interest: A review. *Aggression and Violent Behavior, 10*(2), 193-217.

Kleiman, M. (2005). *When brute force fails: Strategic thinking for crime control.* Washington, DC: U.S. Department of Justice, National Institute of Justice.

Kokish, R., Levenson, J. S., & Blasingame, G. D. (2005). Post conviction sex offender polygraph examination: Client-reported perceptions of utility and accuracy. *Sexual Abuse: A Journal of Research and Treatment, 17*(2), 211-221.

Lally, S. J. (2003). What tests are acceptable for use in forensic evaluations? A survey of experts. *Professional Psychology: Research and Practice, 34*(5), 491-494.

Lalumiere, M. L., & Harris, G. T. (1998). Common questions regarding the use of phallometric testing with sexual offenders. *Sexual Abuse: A Journal of Research and Treatment, 10*(3), 227-237.

Lane Council of Governments (2003). *Managing sex offenders in the community: A national overview.* Eugene, OR: Author.

Launay, G. (1999). The phallometric assessment of sex offenders: An update. *Criminal Behaviour and Mental Health, 9*(3), 254-274.

Lilly, R. (2006). Issues beyond empirical EM reports. *Criminology & Public Policy, 5*(1), 93-102.

Longshore, D., Taxman, F., Turner, S., Harrell, A., Fain, T., & Byrne, J. (2001). *Operation Drug Test Evaluation.* Washington, DC: National Institute of Justice.

MacKenzie, D. L. (2006). *What works in corrections: Reducing the criminal activities of offenders and delinquents.* New York: Cambridge University Press.

Marshall, W. L., & Fernandez, Y. M. (2000). Phallometric testing with sexual offenders: Limits to its value. *Clinical Psychology Review, 20*(7), 807-822.

Marques, P. R., Tippetts, A. S., Voas, R. B., & Beirness, D. J. (2001). Predicting repeat DUI offenses with the alcohol interlock recorder. *Accident Analysis and Prevention, 33*(5), 609-619.

Marques, P. R., Voas, R. B., & Tippetts, A. S. (2003). Behavioral measures of drinking: Patterns from the Alcohol Interlock Record. *Addiction, 98*(Suppl. 2), 13-19.

Miethe, T., Olson, J., & Mitchell, O. (2006). Specialization and persistence in the arrest histories of sex offenders: A comparative analysis of alternative measures and offense types. *Journal of Research in Crime and Delinquency, 4*(3), 204-229.

Morse, B. J., & Elliott, D. S. (1992). Effects of ignition interlock devices on DUI recidivism: Findings from a longitudinal study in Hamilton County, Ohio. *Crime & Delinquency, 38*(2), 131-157.

Mumola, C. J. (1998). *Substance abuse and treatment of adults on probation, 1995.* Washington, DC: Bureau of Justice Statistics.

Mumola, C., & Karberg, J. (2006). *Drug use and dependence, state and federal prisoners, 2004.* Bureau of Justice Statistics Special Report, October. Washington, DC: U.S. Department of Justice.

National Center for Injury Prevention and Control (2007). *Impaired driving: Fact sheet.* Atlanta, GA: Centers for Disease Control. Available at http://www.cdc.gov/ncipc/factsheets/drving.htm

National Conference of State Legislatures (2006). *Preliminary information on the enactment of statutory provisions regarding GPS tracking of sex offenders.* Available at: http://www.npr.org/programs/morning/features/2006/oct/prop83/ncsl_gps.pdf

National Institute on Drug Abuse (2006). *Principles of effective drug abuse treatment for criminal populations: A research guide.* National Institute of Health Publication no. 06-5316. Washington, DC: NIDA.

National Institute of Justice, Office of Science and Technology Staff (2000). Do you speak English? *Corrections Today, 62*(7), 164-167.

National Law Enforcement and Corrections Technology Center (2003). Nothing lost in the translation. *Techbeat,* Fall 2003.

National Law Enforcement and Corrections Technology Center (1999, October). Keeping track of electronic monitoring. *National Law Enforcement and Corrections Technology Center Bulletin,* 1-7.

Naval Air Systems Command (2003). *Voice response translator (VRT): Support for prototype development and results of initial field testing.* Orlando, FL: Naval Air Systems Command Training Systems Division.

Ogden, T., & Horrocks, C. (2001). Pagers, digital audio, and kiosk: officer assistants. *Federal Probation, 65*(3), 35-37.

Office of Program Policy Analysis and Government Accountability (2005). *Electronic monitoring should be better targeted to the most dangerous offenders.* Report no. 05-19 (April 2005, 1-7). Available at: http://www.oppaga.state.fl.us/reports/pdf/0519rpt.pdf

Petersilia, J. (2006). Understanding California corrections. California Policy Research Center. *CPRC Brief, 18*(1), 1-3.

Phillips, K. (2001). Reducing alcohol-related crime electronically. *Federal Probation, 65*(2), 42-44.

Pullen, S., Olsen, S., Brown, G., & Amich, D. (1996). Using the polygraph. In K. English, S. Pullen, & L. Jones (Eds.), *Managing adult sex offenders: A containment approach* (pp. 15.1-15.17). Lexington, KY: American Probation and Parole Association.

Quinlan, K., Brewer, R., Siegel, P., Sleet, D., Mokdad, A., Shults, R., & Flowers, N. (2005). Alcohol-impaired driving among U.S. adults, 1993-2002. *American Journal of Preventive Medicine, 28*(4), 345-350.

Quinsey, V. L., Harris, G. T., Rice, M. E., & Cormier, C. A. (2006). *Violent offenders: Appraising and managing risk* (2nd ed.). Washington, DC: American Psychological Association.

Renzema, M., & Mayo-Wilson, E. (2005). Can electronic monitoring reduce crime for moderate to high-risk offenders? *Journal of Experimental Criminology, 1*(2), 215-237.

Rice M. E., Harris G. T., & Quinsey, V. L. (1990). A follow-up of rapists assessed in a maximum-security psychiatric facility. *Journal of Interpersonal Violence, 5*(4), 435-448.

Rice M. E., Quinsey, V. L., & Harris, G. T. (1991). Sexual recidivism among child molesters released from a maximum security psychiatric institution. *Journal of Consulting and Clinical Psychology, 59*(3), 381-386.

Russo, J. (2006). Emerging technologies for community corrections. *CT Feature,* 1-3.

Sakai, J. T., Mikulich-Gilbertson, S. K., Long, R. J., & Crowley, T. J. (2006). Validity of transdermal alcohol monitoring: Fixed and self-regulated dosing. *Alcoholism: Clinical and Experimental Research, 30*(1), 26-33.

Sample, L., & Bray, T. (2003). Are sex offenders dangerous? *Criminology & Public Policy, 3*(1), 59-82.

Sample, L., & Bray, T. (2006). Are sex offenders different? An examination of rearrest patterns. *Criminal Justice Policy Review, 17*(1), 83-102.

Sherman, L. W., Gottfredson, D., MacKenzie, D. L., Eck, J., Reuter, P., & Bushway, S. (1997). *Preventing crime: What works, what doesn't, what's promising.* Washington, DC: National Institute of Justice.

Swan, N. (1995). Sweat testing may prove useful in drug-use surveillance. *NIDA Notes,* 10(5). Available at: http://www.drugabuse.gov/NIDA_Notes/NNVol10N5/Sweat.html

Sugg, D., Moore, L., & Howard, P. (2001). *Electronic monitoring and offending behavior reconviction results for the second year of trials of curfew orders.* Research Findings No. 41. London: Home Office Research, Development and Statistics Directorate.

Swift, R. M., Martin, C. S., Swette, L., LaConti, A., & Kackley, N. (1992). Studies on a wearable, electronic, transdermal alcohol sensor. *Alcoholism: Clinical and Experimental Research, 16*(4), 721-725.

Taxman, F. (2006). Assessment with a flair: Offender accountability in supervision plans. *Federal Probation, 70*(3), 2-7.

Taxman, F., Byrne, J., & Pattavina, A. (2005). Racial disparity and the legitimacy of the criminal justice system: Exploring consequences for deterrence. *Journal of Health Care for the Poor and Underserved, 16*(4), 57-77 (Supplement B).

Taxman, F., Sheperdson, E., & Byrne, J. (2004). *Tools of the trade: A guide to incorporating science into practice.* Washington, DC: National Institute of Corrections.

Terry, K. (2006). *Sexual offenses and offenders: Theory, practice, and policy.* Belmont, CA: Wadsworth Contemporary Issues in Crime and Justice Series.

Tewey, J. (2005). *Task force to study criminal offender monitoring by global positioning systems.* Final report to the governor and the general assembly (December, 31). Baltimore.

Travis III, L. (2006) Public preference for rehabilitation. *Criminology & Public Policy, 5*(4), 623-626.

Vito, G. F. (1999). What works in drug testing and monitoring. In E. J. Latessa (Ed.), *Strategic solutions: International Community Corrections Association examines substance abuse.* Lanham, MD: American Correctional Association.

Voas, R., Blackman, K., Tippetts, A., & Marques, P. (2002). Evaluation of a program to motivate impaired driving offenders to install ignition interlocks. *Accident Analysis and Prevention, 34*(4), 449-455.

Voas, R. B., Marques, P. R., Tippetts, A. S., & Beirness, D. J. (1999). The Alberta Interlock Program: The evaluation of a province-wide program on DUI recidivism. *Addiction, 94*(12), 1849-1859.

Voas, R., & DeYoung, D. (2002). Vehicle action: Effective policy for controlling drunk and other high-risk drivers? *Accident Analysis and Prevention, 34*(3), 263-270.

Weinrath, M. (1997). The ignition interlock program for drunk drivers: A multivariate test. *Crime & Delinquency, 43*(1), 42-59.

13. COMMUNITY CORRECTIONS AND SOFT TECHNOLOGY

by

April Pattavina
University of Massachusetts, Lowell

and

Faye S. Taxman
Virginia Commonwealth University

INTRODUCTION

According to recent estimates from the U.S. Bureau of Justice Statistics (2005), over 4.9 million adult men and women were under community supervision at the end of 2004. Many of these persons (4,141,100) were serving a probation sentence, where offenders are placed on community supervision by the courts. The remaining 765,000 persons were on parole, released to community supervision through a parole board decision or by mandatory conditional release after serving a prison term. The need to balance the goals of public safety with managing large caseloads in ways that promote equitable and meaningful treatment of offenders supervised in the community has been a driving force behind the development of soft technology in community corrections.

There are many questions to consider when making decisions about how to effectively and efficiently supervise offenders in the community. One important question is how to identify offenders who are most likely to re-offend or recidivate. If we are able to identify those most likely to re-offend, then those persons can be targeted for increased supervision and may be eligible for more intensive forms of treatment. Classification and assessment technologies have emerged in community corrections for this very purpose. These technologies attempt to promote system efficiency by sorting offenders into subgroups for purposes of allocating discrete supervisory and treatment resources in ways that promote public safety. Effectiveness is also enhanced because creating systems of classifying or grouping offenders helps to standardize criteria applied to all offenders. This is a desirable goal to many because it reduces discretionary decision making by professionals and may result in a more equitable correctional system.

Technology has played a central role in the development of the classification procedures used by many correctional agencies today. In fact, the development of classification tools has expanded considerably in the past 25 years. As Gottfredson and Tonry (1987, p. vii) observed in the late 1980s: "both the literature and practical application of science-based prediction and classification will continue to expand as institutions evolve to become more rational, more efficient, and more just." This quote relates to soft technology in that it addresses the movement in current correctional strategies to use information in systematic and scientific ways when planning for the release of offenders in the community.

Supporting this movement have been advances in computer technology that allow more efficient processing and sharing of information both within correctional agencies and with other criminal justice agencies. This is especially relevant for treatment planning, case management and public safety. The purpose of this chapter will be to chronicle these soft technology developments and describe their role in advancing the goals of community corrections that progress from prediction and understanding to treatment, case management and control (Clements, 1996).

Prediction

Every day, criminal justice officials must make decisions about how to deal with the future of people who have violated the criminal law. Examples include determining the length of sentence for a particular offender or offense and whether a person should be incarcerated or released into the community. An important consideration involves the calculation of risk. Officials must ask themselves the following: what are the chances that a person may re-offend based on the list of adjudicatory or correctional options from which they have to choose?

According to Clements (1996, p. 123), a basic premise of correctional classification is that offenders can be grouped into meaningful categories: " . . . somewhere between all offenders are alike and each offender is unique lies a system (or systems) of categorization along pertinent dimensions that will prove to be of value in reaching correctional goals." Classification systems serve this purpose by sorting individuals into subgroups that share similar traits, etiology, behavioral and psychological attributes or other pertinent characteristics.

Andrews et al. (2006) have developed an organizational typology of the evolution of classification technology that spans four generations. In the first generation of classification technology, often referred to as intuitive or clinical decision making, a psychologist or correctional manager simply considers the factors that are indicative of risk, based on his or her opinion and on past experience. A supervision and treatment plan is then developed accordingly. Little attempt is made to systematically include certain factors or weight their relevance in determining risk (Glaser, 1987).

In the late 1970s, the Wisconsin Department of Corrections began to standardize the process of risk assessment. The department moved away from a subjective risk assessment based on narrative reports and toward a more formal process that translated report information into a set of scoring instruments that would be used to determine the necessary level of staff supervision. The process was more efficient because using standardized forms on which most items simply can be checked required much less work from agencies than working with the narrative reports. This process of establishing an actuarial approach is the defining characteristic of the second generation of classification technology identified by Andrews et al. (2006). According to Bonta (2002), actuarial measures are structured, quantitative, and empirically linked to a relevant criterion. Often that relevant criterion is recidivism. Recidivism may be measured in several ways such as re-arrest, new conviction, drug use, technical violation, and probation or parole revocation.

Wisconsin's assessment of client risk form included a set of characteristics, historical in nature (i.e., prior criminal history), for which offenders were given scores. Higher scores were given for greater risk potential. The concept of risk was largely based on behavior in the past, the assumption being that past behavior will weigh heavily in the ability of offenders to function in a pro-social manner in the future (Taxman and Thanner, 2006). Some characteristics believed to be more important were weighted more heavily, and the items were added together for a total score. The total risk scores were found to predict revocation among parole and probationers. This system was implemented in other jurisdictions as well, but with mixed success. For example, the scores predicted revocation rates for probationers and parolees in California jurisdictions, but not in New York (Glaser, 1987).

The Wisconsin system also incorporated a needs assessment form which was created using input from correctional agents on the relative importance of various types of assistance clients need. Need was considered as the extent to which daily functioning is impaired in ways that may lead to greater involvement in criminal behavior (Taxman and Thanner, 2006). Each client was scored on 11 needs – for employment, education or vocational training, financial management, family relationships, companions, emotional stability, alcohol usage, other drug usage, mental ability, health, and sexual behavior – with higher scores for a category indicating greater assistance needs. The needs scores showed moderate reliability but virtually no utility for predicting revocation of probation or parole (Glaser, 1987). Clearly, risk assessment instruments and needs assessment devices were designed for different purposes (i.e., risk classification versus need classification) and produced different outcomes (risk prediction versus needs assessment).

Understanding

Classification instruments that place an emphasis on offender needs are useful because they can be used to assist in the development of at treatment plan. Criminogenic needs are traits of a person or his or her situation that when changed, lead to changes in criminal behavior (Andrews et al., 1990). In this respect, criminogenic needs are considered to be dynamic risk factors. This group is separate from static risk factors which do not change or change only in one direction (i.e., age, prior arrests). Bonta (2002) argues that criminogenic need or dynamic risk factors are important for managing risk, not just predicting recidivism. The assessment of dynamic factors can be used to identify targets for treatment services that facilitate offender change.

Advancing these tools even further was the argument that the utility of classification instruments would be considerably improved if the selection of dynamic factors included were better informed by theories of criminal behavior. This was the premise behind the development of Andrews et al.'s (2006) third generation of classification instruments. There are a variety of criminological theories that may be useful in guiding the development of classification, but general personality and social learning perspectives have emerged as dominant theories informing current correctional classification (Andrews et al., 2006).

Social learning theory was appropriate for this purpose because theoretical constructs could be empirically linked to offender behaviors, and cognitive behavior skill development could be used as a strategy to mediate risk. Andrews et al. (2006) use social learning theory and general personality theory in ways that have practical applications and empirical support. According to Bonta (2002, p. 363) these theories suggest that "criminal behavior is learned through complex interactions between cognitive, emotional, personality and biological factors and environmental reward-cost contingencies." This theory serves as the basis for identifying criminogenic needs included in the more current risk assessment instruments.

Drawing upon social learning and personality theory, Andrews et al. (2006) identify what they refer to as the "big eight" factors that are important for classification: (1) history of antisocial behavior; (2) antisocial personality; (3) antisocial cognition; (4) antisocial associates; (5) family and or marital; (6) school and or work; (7) leisure and/or recreation; and (8) substance abuse. For each of these factors a risk is determined and a dynamic need identified. For example, for the factor of history of antisocial behavior, the associated risk is early and continuing involvement in a number and variety of antisocial acts in a variety of settings, and the dynamic need is to build non-criminal alternative behavior in risky situations (Andrews et al., 2006, p. 11).

There have been a number of classification instruments that have been developed along these lines. Information collected for classification instruments may come from interviews with offenders, surveys of offenders or file extraction methods where records are used to measure the factors. Some common classification instruments (Kroner and Mills, 2001, p. 476) include the following:

PCL-R: The Psychopathy Checklist-Revised
The PCL-R is a 20-item instrument scored on a 3 point scale: 0 = does not apply; 1 = maybe in some respect; and 2 = does apply. The total score is the sum of all 20 items. Detailed criteria for the judgments are provided in the manual.

LSI-R: The Level of Service Inventory-Revised
The LSI-R has 54 items that are rationally grouped into 10 subscales: Criminal History, Education/Employment, Finances, Family/Marital, Accommodations, Leisure/Recreation, Companions, Alcohol/Drug, Emotional/Personal and Attitude/Orientation. The items are scored in a 0/1 format indicating the presence or absence of the item, and the total score is the sum of all 54 items.

HCR-20: The Historical, Clinical and Risk Management Violence Risk Assessment Scheme
The HCR 20 has 20 items scored on a 3-point scale: 0 = contraindicates; 1 = suggests; and 2 = clearly indicates. The total score is the sum of all 20 items.

VRAG: The Violence Risk Appraisal Guide
The VRAG is a 12-variable rating scale. Each variable is weighted, with the PCL-R having the greatest range. The total score is the sum of the weighted scores of the 12 items. As with the HCR-20, 1 of the 12 items uses the PCL-R total score.

LCSF: The Lifestyle Criminality Screening Form
The LCSF is a 14-item scale with 4 sections: (1) Irresponsibility: (a) nonsupport of a child, (b) termination of formal education prior to completing the 12th grade, (c) longest job ever held, and (d) quitting or being terminated from a job; (2) Self-indulgence: (a) history of alcohol/drug abuse, (b) marital background, and (c) tattoos; (3) Interpersonal intrusiveness: (a) intrusive confining offense, (b) prior intrusive offenses, (c) use of weapon during confining offense, and (d) physical abuse of family member; and (4) Social rule breaking: (a) prior arrests, (b) age at first arrest, and (c) history of school disciplinary problem Each section has a possible score of 5 or 6, and the total score is the sum of these items.

Other classification instruments have been developed for specific populations such as sex offenders (Austin and McGinnis, [2004], p. xiv). Examples include:

RRASOR: Rapid Risk Assessment for Sexual Offense Recidivism
The instrument assigns a score based on items found in inmates' case files: prior sex offenses, age at release, victim gender, and relationship to victim.

Static-99
Similar to the RRASOR, the Static 99 is an inventory of 10 items found in inmate case files that reflect attributes of convicted sex offenders and that were shown to be associated with recidivism.

MnSOST-R: Minnesota Sex Offender Screening Tool-Revised
This inventory scores 16 items drawn from inmate files: 12 static variables related to the offender's criminal record and relationship to his victims,

and 4 dynamic components that measure factors associated with age and behavior while incarcerated.

SVR-20: Sexual Violence Risk-20
Developed for use as a topical guideline for risk assessments linked with studying violent sexual offenders, the SVR-20 incorporates information pertaining to an offender's psychosocial adjustment and future plans. It also includes factors specifically related to the offender's attitude toward and history of committing sexual offenses.

Treatment

The inclusion of theory-based measures of offenders' psychological and social functioning in classification systems, although not necessarily useful in creating better predictive modeling, has presented new opportunities for treatment services and delivery. Especially promising is the opportunity for creating more individualized forms of treatment to match offender needs rather than abiding by a one-size-fits-all treatment program. This concept has resulted in the acknowledgment of a third dimension, responsivity, to the risk/need lexicon (Andrews et al., 1990). "The corrections terms risk and need were transformed into principles addressing the major clinical issues of who receives treatment (higher risk cases), what intermediate targets are set (reduce criminogenic needs) and what treatment strategies are employed (match strategies to learning style and motivation of cases: the principles of specific and general responsivity)" (Andrews et al., 2006, p. 7).

In promoting the Risk Need Responsivity (RNR) approach to offender treatment, Andrews et al. (1990) argue that the effectiveness of treatment modalities appears to depend upon certain offender characteristics, and they support this logic with several hypotheses. One example is the motivation hypothesis. Persons who are narcissistic and antisocial are not highly motivated to participate in treatment. Thus, with high-risk but low-motivation cases, treatment should be readily accessible and outreach-based. This group of offenders may also benefit by incorporating legal contingencies within a therapeutic context.

The RNR approach to classification guides the fourth generation of classification systems (Andrews et al., 2006). The fourth generation adheres to the RNR model within a case-management framework. In these systems, the RNR principle not only guides the development of service plans according to risks and needs, but also supervises the delivery of services, monitors offender progress through reassessment of needs, and links progress with outcomes such as recidivism and well being. This generation of classification system emphasizes the development of information systems with a focus on human service assessment and treatment systems.

According to Andrews et al. (2006), only a few of these types of systems exist. One example of this type of classification system is the Correctional Offender Management Profiling for Alternative Sanctions (COMPAS). This is a privately owned automated risk and needs assessment system. The COMPAS system assesses over 20 validated criminogenic factors, including criminal history, violence history, early onset of delinquency, substance abuse, criminal associates, criminal attitudes, criminal personality and criminal opportunity. Also included are measures of psychosocial stress that may be used in designing case plans. Examples include residence in a high-crime community, poverty, vocational problems, social isolation, and scarcity of social supports. The COMPAS software program also maintains a database of information that allows for the quick generation of reports and case outcomes. The COMPAS system has not been independently evaluated, but its creators' own research shows predictive validity (Austin and McGinnis, 2004).

The RNR principle requires that correctional agencies use a valid risk tool, have the ability to identify dynamic factors to address in treatment, and have suitable treatment programs that include clinical and control programmatic components. Taxman and Thanner (2006) conducted a test of the RNR principle where the treatment included a seamless system of care for offenders who were involved in drugs. The seamless model was developed by Taxman and her colleagues (Taxman and Sherman, 1998) to support the Washington-Baltimore High Intensity Drug Trafficking Area (HIDTA). It is an automated, inter-agency case-management system that involves providing intensive drug treatment services to hard-core offenders, drug testing on a routine basis, using graduated sanctions for offenders who were involved in drugs, and making sure that offenders are involved in treatment for a minimum of six months.

The Taxman and Thanner (2006) study involved randomly assigning offenders to two groups: treatment (seamless system) and control (traditional referral to treatment in the community). Their study found that the seamless model increased the treatment participation rate over the traditional referral model. Offenders in the seamless system were also able to access treatment sooner than those in the control group. They also found that effect sizes varied by risk level. High-risk treatment groups had higher treatment completion rates than the high-risk controls, and offenders in high-risk treatment groups had fewer overall arrests.

The development of classification systems is clearly evolving to become more comprehensive in terms of risk/need classification and management. To guide the development of classification systems with respect to effectiveness and efficiency, Clements (1996) argues that a classification system should have the following characteristics:

1. sufficient completeness so that most offenders can be classified;

2. provision of clear operational definitions to avoid ambiguity;

3. adequate reliability across raters and decision makers;

4. sufficient validity with respect to the attributes and behaviors predicted by the classification system;

5. sufficient dynamic properties so that changes in attributes, behavior or status would be reflected by a change in classification status;

6. implications for treatment and intervention; and,

7. economical classification of large number of offenders.

How do classification methods measure up to these criteria? A major concern among corrections officials and researchers is the validity of the instruments. Validity measures the degree to which a risk factor is associated with the behavior to be predicted. In the classification research, the behavior of major interest is recidivism, which can be measured a number of ways including arrest, positive drug tests, probation or parole violations, etc. The literature on this topic suggests that clinical assessment (or first-generation classification procedures) do not perform as well in predicting recidivism as the second-generation actuarial tools (Andrews et al., 2006). This also appears to be true for special populations such as mentally disordered offenders and sex offenders (Bonta, 2002). A summary of research by Andrews et al. (2006) also found that the predictive validity of third- and fourth-generation classification instruments was not convincingly superior to that of the best constructed second-generation instrument.

Some of the more common classification tools have also been found to be reliable, meaning that they are consistent across independent raters. For the PCL-R, LSI-R, HCR-20 and the VRAG, reliability estimates were in the vicinity of .80, which is an accepted standard (on a scale of 0 to 1.00, with 1.00 being highest; Kroner and Mills, 2001). Factual criminal history questions have been found to have the highest reliability scores (Austin et al., 2003).

The superior predictive validity and reliability of actuarial instruments compared to clinical assessments has led many corrections agencies to voice a preference for actuarial models. Hubbard et al. (2001) found that 75% of the correctional agencies they surveyed were using standardized, objective instruments. Recent estimates, however, also reveal that clinical assessments continue to be widely used (Bonta, 2002). Many actuarial instruments are proprietary and therefore cost money to implement. There also those who remain skeptical about the utility of the tools for their own offender populations. Recall the earlier research on the inability of the Wisconsin model to show consistent validity across different agencies. This underscores the issue raised by Young et al. (2006) concerning the need to validate models for each unique agency and offender population (i.e., juveniles, females). Such a process requires resources, dedication and commitment that many agencies may be unwilling or unable to support.

The fact that many second and later generations of instruments have been found similar in predictive ability may be because the field is reaching a point where the range of accumulated risk factors is not likely to change greatly. Dow et al. (2005) argue that even though minor predictors of recidivism will continue to emerge, some essential risk factors have been firmly established. Supporting their assertion is the observation of overlap in many of the risk factors included in various classification instruments. Kroner and Mills (2001) found a lack of variation in predictive accuracy among the PCL-R, LSI-R, HCR-20, VRAG and LCSF, which they believe may be due to content overlap. For example, The HCR-20, VRAG and the Sex Offender Risk Assessment Guide (SORAG) all include the PCL-R in deriving final scores.

Even if minor additional predictors of recidivism emerge, to include an increasing number of factors in classification tools without validating them on the targeted populations runs the risk of overclassification. Over-classification may occur when factors that may have an indirect or interactive effect on recidivism are included in deriving final scores. The result is a higher overall score that would place some offenders into more intensive treatment than is necessary, which may lead to an overly prescriptive supervision plan that may not be in the offender's best interest and would waste treatment resources. Overclassification of female offenders was found by Hardyman and Van Voorhis (2004). Young et al. (2006) observed that some practitioners were against the use of any factors that are treatable for juveniles such as substance abuse or failure in school, arguing that service needs may lead youth deeper into the system.

Related to the overclassification issue is the problem of low base rates. A base rate is the overall rate of recidivism for a group of offenders. If the base rate for a group is known, then without any other information practitioners would use that rate as the probability of recidivating for each offender in that group. If factors relating to recidivism are identified, then prediction can be improved and prediction error reduced. Problems arise, however, if the base rate is at one extreme or the other. If, for example, the base rate for recidivating was low for a group say 10%, we could then predict that 10% of these offenders would be arrested and we would be correct 90% of the time. This predictive accuracy is difficult to improve upon and may lead to high rates of false positives. The low base rate has been a particular problem for sex offenders. A recent review by Bynum (2001) found that base rates for sex offenders vary, and those that use general sex offender categorization tend to be the lowest, varying from 4 to 13%.

Despite all of the research support for actuarial classification tools, the door is not entirely closed on the importance of clinical judgment. For example, most discussions and guidelines for the implementation of classification methods recognize the need to provide professional overrides of classification results. These overrides may rely on some form of clinical input not captured in actuarial scores. Moreover, many classification schemes that include behavioral and personality assessments can be subjective, and practitioners that score them should have some form of clinical training. A recent study by Austin et al. (2003) revealed that reliability of LSI-R was improved with training. Taxman and Thanner (2006) recognize the need to have clinical expertise in assessing scores for a drug dependency score, the Addiction Severity Index. The need for clinical judgment is especially true if more individualized treatment plans are to be designed that match personality and behavioral traits of offenders.

Case Management

Advances in information technology have created opportunities to develop systems that are capable of incorporating more comprehensive classification information systems along with supervision and treatment planning and management (fourth generation). Some of these systems share information with other criminal justice agencies as well. Such a system has been developed by the Court Services and Offender Supervision Agency (CSOSA) for the District of Columbia, which has created the Supervision and Management Automated Record Tracking (SMART) system (Lu and Wolfe, 2004). It is a Web-based case management and information retrieval system custom designed to meet agency needs. SMART provides tracking and monitoring capabilities not found in off-the-shelf community supervision applications.

Modules for this system include client intake, reports, offender demographics, drug testing results, detailed supervision information, and tracking capabilities for treatment, community service, employment and education. Other agencies also contribute to and use the system. For example, the police can upload re-arrest notifications and treatment providers can enter offender attendance at sessions.

The same agency also developed a classification system, the AUTO screener. This system establishes the level of supervision for an offender and suggests treatment and support services based on the offender's needs. The AUTO screener assessment takes place when an offender enters community supervision. A structured interview is performed by a community corrections officer when an offender enters community supervision. The offender answers a series of questions about education level, functional literacy, employment, residence, social networking, and originating offense. Each question contributes to determining the offender's criminal risk level, recidivism probability and supervision needs. Information is routinely updated every six months. From the data obtained in the interview, AUTO screener generates a prescriptive supervision plan that contains support service recommendations to guide correctional staff throughout the reentry process. An officer can override the recommended plan with approval from a supervisor. The offender signs a printed version of the plan and a contract specifying sanctions.

Fortunately, correctional planners and researchers may be well prepared to harness the benefits of information technology in ways that support their organizational objectives. For example, computer companies are designing proprietary systems specifically for case management in correctional populations. One example is a system under development by Syscon Justice Systems, an offender case management software company and Aradyme Corporation, a data management company (http://www.aradyme.com). In support of the development and implementation of these systems, the American Probation and Parole Association (2003) recently published a very detailed, technologically-oriented set of guidelines for agencies considering an automated case management system (CMS). The report (Brown, 2001) identifies two core functional groups that must be included in any case management system. One is a Case Processing Functional Group that supports case initiation, case planning, scheduling, monitoring and compliance, document generation and case closure. The second is the Management Functional Group that supports management and statistical reporting and security and data functions. The report also identifies three ancillary functional groups: file and document management; financial management, and Integrated Criminal Justice Information Systems (ICJIS).

Standards for CMS participation in an ICJIS describe what is necessary for the exchange/sharing of information between the CMS and other databases maintained by the courts, court support units, criminal justice (CJ) and non-CJ agencies. A central challenge to proper data integration across agencies involves the adoption of common personal identifiers allowing an offender to be accurately tracked across these systems. A valid system would allow for an individual with more than one personal identifier to be recognized as the same individual where criminal justice actions can be followed from arrest through completion of the sentence.

Electronic information sharing improves communication across agencies that previously had to rely on manual transfer of information through traditional means such as mail, fax, phone, and courier. Snavely et al. (2005, p. 198) identify additional benefits that support decision making at the client (services), management (efficiency) and system (effectiveness) levels:

> Through integration, agencies are equipped to determine the types of services necessary and to coordinate their efforts. Integrated information sharing can improve decision-making and feedback concerning offenders; this can lead to a reduction in the service redundancy that is often overwhelming to offenders trying to meet the requirements of several agencies simultaneously. Greater agency cooperation also creates increased offender accountability, reducing the amount of time that the client is under supervision and treatment. This reduced time may in turn reduce client recidivism.

Not only can technological aspects of developing comprehensive classification and case management systems be challenging, but as automated offender information becomes increasingly available, legal issues such as privacy come into play, especially with regard to treatment. The federal Drug Abuse Prevention, Treatment and Rehabilitation act of 1972 and the Comprehensive Alcohol Abuse and Alcoholism Prevention, Treatment and Rehabilitation Act of 1970 restrict the disclosure and use of substance abuse treatment records maintained by federally supported alcohol and drug abuse programs (Snavely et al., 2005). These laws are intended to ensure that patients in a government-sponsored treatment program are not made more vulnerable by the existence of patient records than persons who have not sought treatment. Disclosure is permitted when there is written authorization by the patient or under a court order.

The substance abuse patient records regulations will allow a program or facility to disclose information about a patient to entities within the criminal justice system when participation in the program is a condition of the disposition of any criminal proceedings or of the patient's parole or release from custody. However, the patient must sign a written consent to the disclosure, and the disclosure may be made only to those individuals in the system who have need for the information in connection with their duty to monitor the patient.

The privacy provisions of the federal Health Insurance Portability and Accountability Act of 1996 (HIPPA) govern the disclosure of patient identifiable electronic health care information maintained by providers. It was enacted with the recognition by the government that advances in electronic technology could erode the privacy of health information (Snavely et al., 2005). The law requires the U.S. Department of Health and Human Services to adopt privacy protections for individually identifiable health information.

There are no restrictions on the use or disclosure of information unless personal identifiers exist in the records. To make sure no personal identifiers are included in electronic records, the regulations specifically require the removal of all personal identifiers, including name, Social Security number, geographic identifiers smaller than a state, medical records, birth dates, telephone numbers, etc. Exceptions allow disclosure of patient identifiable health information to the individual, for treatment, payment and health care operations, for public interest and benefit activities and in limited data sets for research, public health, or health care operations (Snavely et al., 2005).

There are indeed many aspects to the development of classification tools and the management of offenders in the community. Thus far we have discussed soft technology and community corrections with a focus on how classification systems have evolved. The technical aspects and benefits of integrating these systems in comprehensive case management systems that promote efficient information sharing and offender management have also been covered. To support correctional agencies as they adapt to these advances, the government has sponsored the development of recent publications designed to inform correctional agencies on the most recent science-based best practices in offender management (Taxman et al., 2004).

Evaluations of Case Management Models

In addition to the establishment of resources and guidelines for case management systems, it is important that these systems be subject to process and outcome evaluations. A recent review of case management strategies by Vanderplasschen et al. (2004) for substance-use disorders found them to be associated with positive effects, including increased participation in treatment and retention and greater use of services. A process evaluation of the Proactive Community Supervision case management model in Maryland was recently conducted by Taxman et al. (2006). The PCS strategy is relevant for this review because it reflects the behavioral management theoretical model introduced earlier in this chapter. The PCS model incorporates the following steps (Taxman et al., p.1):

1. Identify criminogenic traits using a valid risk and need tool (LSI-R).

2. Develop a supervision plan that addresses criminogenic traits employing effective external controls and treatment interventions.

3. Hold the offender accountable for the progress on the supervision plan.

4. Use a place-based strategy wherein individual probation/parole office environments are engaged in implementing the strategy.

5. Develop partnerships with community organizations that will provide ancillary services to supervisees.

The PCS strategy focuses on the contacts between the offender and his/her probation agent. The nature and intent of contacts are necessary for the agent to facilitate change in three ways: (1) to promote the development of pro-social skills; (2) to use supervision tools and treatment interventions to address criminogenic traits; and (3) to assist the offender in sustaining change through positive involvement with community support networks like family. This strategy called for training probation and parole officers to change their offender management strategy from the traditional surveillance orientation to one where they are required to promote offender change though behavioral management strategies. To assist in developing and implementing the case plan, agents were provided with the Offender

Case Planning Software for Empowerment (MOSCE). This software integrates a series of offender performance indicators to be used by supervisors to monitor outcomes.

The purpose of the evaluation was to determine whether the implementation of the PCS core concepts had an impact on offender outcomes, particularly on rates of re-arrest and warrants for violation of probation and parole. Taxman et al. (2006) compared PCS offenders with those on traditional probation. They found that PCS offenders tend to have more responsibilities in their case plans than those on traditional probation. PCS offenders also had more contact with their agents than those on traditional probation. Additionally, the PCS probationers were more compliant with conditions than the traditional supervision group, with the exception of drug offenders. Being in the PCS group did not have an effect on the drug consumption patterns of offenders. The PCS group was significantly less likely to be arrested than the non-PCS group and had fewer technical violations resulting in a warrant. This study confirms that comprehensive case management strategies have positive outcomes for offenders.

Control

In addition to the development of classification technology that supports the identification of offender risks and needs, advances in other forms of information technologies have created new opportunities for monitoring offenders in the community. Important among these advances has been the development and use of Geographic Information Systems (GIS). For purposes of community corrections, these systems have the capacity to map the location of offender addresses, criminal incident locations, transportation routes, and treatment services, such as employment services, mental health services and substance abuse treatment centers, etc.

These systems may be used to develop more efficient treatment plans by matching offenders with services closest to their homes. Case managers, parole or probation officers need to identify where relevant services are and determine the availability of these programs to service their clients. These services must exist in offender communities if we are to expect them to sustain a pro-social life after probation or parole supervision ends. There are computerized directories either maintained by cities or private companies like Yellow Pages that contain the geographic locations of relevant services that can be mapped. These maps can be used to determine which services are closest to the offender's address (Pattavina, 2005).

The opportunities presented by these information sources include more efficient planning for offenders as well as the increased capacity to determine service or program needs for a particular area. This approach was used in research by Harris et al. (1998). They mapped the proximity of recently released inmates to social services, including unemployment offices, mental health services and substance abuse treatment centers. They found that offenders living in rural areas had limited access to these facilities and the information was used to justify the need for drug rehabilitation services for offenders as they reintegrate into their communities.

Public safety is a major objective of community corrections and surveillance is a necessary component of any community corrections program. Probation and parole officers must keep tabs on offenders in the community to ensure they are not violating the conditions of their release. GIS can be used for the continuous mapping of offender locations in the community. For example, this type of monitoring may be used for sex or drug offenders who have geographic restrictions around schools.

Some programs have integrated Global Positioning Systems (GPS) with crime mapping. GPS is a technology that uses satellite communication to identify geographic location. Offenders carry tracking devices that communicate their locations at given time intervals. In Florida, the Department of Law Enforcement, the Department of Corrections and the Tallahassee Police Department collaborated to create the CrimeTrax system. CrimeTrax uses GPS offender tracking data and combines them with crime data extracted from law enforcement agencies. The tracked offender movements are then examined in relation to mapped locations and times of reported crime incidents to check for possible connections (Frost, 2002). This program demonstrates the capabilities of combined geo-based technologies along with cross-agency and cross-jurisdictional collaboration in dealing with crime problems.

Cross-agency collaboration has been central to the development of prisoner reentry initiatives. These initiatives call for a reorientation of how incarcerated individuals are treated that spans the criminal justice system and involves prison, treatment programs, the police and the community. Under this model, a broad range of criminal justice agencies share the responsibility for the successful integration of offenders back into the community. Participating agencies collaborate with each other and with offenders (or clients) in ways that serve to monitor progress. The focus is not on one agency per se, but on sharing roles and responsibilities that best support individuals as they progress through the reentry process (Byrne et al., 2001).

Sharing offender information across agencies is crucial to the successful implementation of reentry initiatives and advances in information technology are providing the building blocks for creating fully integrated systems where all participating agencies have the technological capacity to effectively collect, manage, and share information pertinent to reentry functions (Pattavina, 2004).

Although well intended, advances in soft technology in community corrections have resulted in more control over offenders. We collect more information about them, use that information to shape their future behavior and then closely monitor and control that behavior in the community. We premise these advances on the hope of reducing recidivism. In face of high recidivism rates in general, even small reductions may seem worth it. Soft technology in community corrections results in more emphasis on changing and monitoring individuals, and less emphasis on dealing with the social and economic problems in the communities where many offenders reside.

CONCLUSION

The agents of control in community corrections have expanded and are increasingly connected. As this chapter has demonstrated, soft technology has served to promote this process. Not only are probation officers and case managers the main personnel responsible for offenders in the community, but new models have enlisted the support of courts with treatment mandates (such as drug courts) and the police, who have constant access to information on the whereabouts offenders. Best practices in community corrections, informed by social science have emerged to guide the future of community corrections. As we move toward a society that gathers significant amounts of information about individuals, we must always challenge ourselves to use these rapidly growing information sources in ways that are not only scientifically sound, but ethically and socially responsible as well.

◆ ◆ ◆ ◆

REFERENCES

American Probation and Parole Association (2003). *Functional standards development for automated case management systems.* Washington, DC: U.S. Department of Justice.

Andrews, D. A., Bonta, J., & Hoge, R. D. (1990). Classification for effective rehabilitation: Rediscovering psychology. *Criminal Justice and Behavior, 17,* 19-52.

Andrews, D. A., Bonta, J., & Wormith, J. S. (2006). The recent past and near future of risk and/or need assessment. *Crime & Delinquency, 52,* 7-27.

Aradyme Corporation (Feb. 6, 2006). *Syscon, Aradyme team to provide states with comprehensive solution for modernizing corrections systems, managing offender data* (http://www.aradyme.com).

Austin, J., Coleman, D., Peyton, J., & Johnson, K. D. (2003). *Reliability and validity study of the LSI-R instrument.* Washington, DC: George Washington University, Institute on Crime, Justice and Corrections.

Austin, J., & McGinnis, K. (2004). *Classification of high risk and special management prisoners: A national assessment of current practices.* Washington, DC: U.S. National Institute of Corrections.

Bonta, J. (2002). Offender risk assessment: guidelines for selection and use. *Criminal Justice and Behavior, 29,* 355-379.

Brown, T. (2001). *Functional standards development for automated case management systems for probation.* Lexington, KY and Washington, DC: American Probation and Parole Association and U.S. Bureau of Justice Assistance.

Bureau of Justice Statistics (2005). *Probation and parole in the United States, 2004.* Washington, DC: U.S. Department of Justice.

Bynum, T. (2001). *Recidivism of sex offenders.* Silver Spring, MD: Center for Sex Offender Management.

Byrne, J. M., Taxman, F. S., & Young, D. (2001). *Emerging roles and responsibilities in the reentry partnership initiative: New ways of doing business.* Washington, DC: U.S. National Institute of Justice.

Clements, C. (1996). Offender classification: Two decades of progress. *Criminal Justice and Behavior, 23*(1), 121-143.

Dow, E., Jones, C., & Mott, J. (2005). An empirical modeling approach to recidivism classification. *Criminal Justice and Behavior, 32*(2), 223-247.

Frost, G. (2002). Florida's innovative use of GPS for community corrections. *Journal of Offender Monitoring, 15*(2), 6-8.

Glaser, D. (1987). Classification for risk. In D. Gottfredson & M. Tonry (Eds.), *Prediction and classification: Criminal justice decision making* (pp. 249-252). University of Chicago Press.

Gottfredson, D. M., & Tonry, M. (1987). Preface. In D. Gottfredson & M. Tonry (Eds.), *Prediction and classification: Criminal justice decision making.* Chicago, IL. University of Chicago Press

Hardyman, P. L., & Van Voorhis, P. (2004). *Developing gender-specific classification systems for women offenders.* Washington, DC: U.S. National Institute of Corrections.

Harris, R., Huenke, C., & O'Connell, J. P. (1998). Using mapping to increase released offenders' access to services. In *Crime mapping case studies: Successes in the field* (Vol. 1, pp. 61-68). Washington, DC: Police Executive Research Forum.

Hubbad, D. J., Travis, L. F., & Latessa, E. J. (2001). *Case classification in community corrections: A national survey of the state of the art.* Washington, DC: U.S. National Institute of Justice.

Kroner, D. G., & Mills, J. F. (2001). The accuracy of five risk appraisal instruments in predicting institutional misconduct and new convictions. *Criminal Justice and Behavior, 28*(4), 471-489.

Lu, F., & Wolfe, L. (2004). Technology that works: An overview of the Supervision and Management Automated Record Tracking (SMART) application. *Corrections Today*, 66(4), 79-82.

Pattavina, A. (2005). Geographic information systems and crime mapping in criminal justice agencies. In A. Pattavina (Ed.), *Information technology and the criminal justice system* (pp. 147-167). Thousand Oaks, CA: Sage Publications.

Pattavina, A. (2004). The emerging role of technology for prisoner reentry initiatives. *Federal Probation*, 68(2), 20-25.

Snavely, K., Taxman, F., & Gordon, S. (2005). Offender-based information sharing: Using a consent driven system to promote integrated service delivery. In A. Pattavina (Ed.), *Information technology and the criminal justice system* (pp. 195-235). Thousand Oaks, CA: Sage Publications.

Taxman, F., Shepardson, E., & Byrne, J. (2004). *Tools of the trade*. College Park, MD: Bureau of Governmental Research, University of Maryland.

Taxman, F., & Sherman, E. (1998). What is the status of my client?: Automation in a seamless case management system for substance abusing offenders. *Journal of Offender Monitoring*, 2(4), 25-31.

Taxman, F., & Thanner, M. (2006). Risk, need, responsivity (RNR): It all depends. *Crime & Delinquency*, 52, 28-51.

Taxman, F., Yancey, C., & Bilanin, J. (2006). *Proactive community supervision in Maryland: Changing offender outcomes*. Report to the Maryland Division of Probation and Parole. Baltimore.

Techbeat. (2005). *Smart offenders*. Washington, DC: National Law Enforcement and Corrections Technology Center, U.S. National Institute of Justice.

Vanderplasschen, W., Rapp, R., Wolf, J., & Broekaert, E. (2004). The development and implementation of case management for substance abuse disorders in North America and Europe. *Psychiatric Services*, 5, 913-922.

Young, D., Moline, K., Farrell, J., & Bierie, D. (2006). Best implementation practices: Disseminating new assessment technologies in a juvenile justice agency. *Crime & Delinquency*, 52(1), 135-158.

For more information, we recommend the following websites:

National Institute of Corrections: www.nicic.org

National Correction & Law Enforcement Training and Technology Center: www.nclettc.org

Mapping and Analysis for Public Safety (MAPS): www.ojp.usdoj.gov/nij/maps

National Sex Offender Public Website: www.nsopr.gov

U.S. Department of Justice, Office of Justice Programs (Reentry): www.reentry.gov

14. THE ENGINEERING OF SOCIAL CONTROL: INTENDED AND UNINTENDED CONSEQUENCES

by

Gary T. Marx

Massachusetts Institute of Technology

The study of social control is a central element of sociological understanding. By social control I refer to the multi-faceted study of norms and rule enforcement. This can involve studying the creation of norms, processes of adjudication and sanctioning, and also the broad societal guidance, integration and ordering which were of concern to early theorists of industrialization and urbanization.[1]

Social control also centrally involves efforts to enforce norms. As the chapters in this volume suggest, an important part of contemporary enforcement efforts involves using science and technology to strategically structure normative environments to reduce rule breaking and increase the identification of offenders and offenses and the minimization of harm.

Rather than focusing on a particular crime control problem or an institutional setting such as courts or prisons, I will look more broadly at some of the issues involved in technology and social control. I emphasize norms, rather than other goals related to technology (e.g., its use in the courts for greater speed and efficiency noted by Corbett in this volume) and I am particularly interested in surveillance technologies.

I have also examined engineering efforts as applied to settings where there is a conflict of interest between agents and subjects of social control.[2] While all technological control efforts have elements in common, those involving dissensus show some distinctive characteristics such as the dynamics of control and counter-control and the centrality of human rights issues.[3]

The increased prominence of social control via engineering is related to concerns over issues such as crime, terrorism, drug abuse, border controls, AIDS and economic competitiveness, and to technical developments in electronics, computerization, artificial intelligence, biochemistry, architecture and materials science. The scale, mobility and anonymity of mass society, and ironically, the increased expectations of and protections for privacy, have furthered reliance on external, impersonal, distance-mediated, secondary technical means and database memories that locate, identify, register, record, classify and validate or generate grounds for suspicion. The perception of catastrophic risks in an interdependent world relying on complex technologies and the entrepreneurial efforts of the security industry and governments such as the United States, have helped spread the technologies internationally.

Of course the inventors and builders of the first locks, safes, moats and castles, and the developers of early biometric identification systems (e.g., the Italian criminologist Cesare Lombroso who lived in the years 1835-1909), were engaged in the engineering of social control. What is new is the scale and relatively greater scientific precision of this engineering, its continual invention and experimentation and rapid global diffusion. Technical means of control saturate modern society, colonizing and documenting ever more areas of life. The roots of contemporary social control lie in the development of large organizations and standardized control technologies (Beniger, 1986). They are one strand of broad processes of rationalization, professionalization and specialization occurring with modernization (Weber, 1964; Rule, 1973; Foucault, 1977; Cohen, 1985; Laudon, 1986; Gandy, 1993; Zuboff, 1988; Lyon, 1994; and Shenhav, 1999).

The use of contemporary technologies contrasts with traditional approaches in which environments were not strategically designed with rule enforcement in mind. Nor was there much probing beneath informational borders *before* untoward incidents occurred.[4] Current preventive and anticipatory control contrasts with traditional reactive control in which authorities become involved only after a violation occurs and in which the use of potentially escalating, lethal force pursuant to an arrest may be found. Social control through environmental actions contrasts with control sought through direct coercion, interpersonal influences, or more subtly through the creation and manipulation of culture and socialization, or the redistributive rewards of the welfare state.

The engineering emphasis may be on the offender (actual or potential), the control agent or broader environmental conditions. Consistent with the classical deterrence ideas implied in the work of nineteenth century social theorist Emile Durkheim and Michel Foucault in the twentieth century, strategic efforts may aim to create self-control and rational calculation on the subject's part.

An alternative (or complementary) emphasis found in the work of Karl Marx and Max Weber may be seen in rational organizational approaches to manage persons and environments.[5] Central here is the behavior of managers and supervisors with respect to factors in the material environment, the organization of work and the categorization and treatment of subjects. Rather than attention to the offender's consciousness or will, the emphasis may involve literally restricting or lessening the subject's ability to deviate by engineering away that choice.

The engineering of social control is one of the defining characteristics of modern society. It is so prominent, ubiquitous and transparent in daily life that it tends to be taken for granted. Our personal spatial, communication, social, cultural and psychological environments and borders are increasingly subject to technological strategies related to rules, as well as to other forms of influence.[6]

New forms of surveillance play an important role in much of this. An enhanced, medieval fortification ethos remains, but this increasingly coexists with decentralized, remote low visibility forms of management and manipulation. The *new surveillance* is a central factor in discovering and communicating (often silently and remotely) previously unseen personal information and merging this with additional sources of data for social control and other purposes (Marx, 1988).

In Jeremy Bentham's eighteenth century *Panopticon* (an ideal prison), the guards in a central control area were invisible to the inmates. Prisoners never knew when they were being observed. In the twenty-first century this is supplemented by the invisibility of remote transmissions from, and to, the individual – whether as suspect, consumer or citizen.

In our engineered society a major goal is to eliminate or limit violations by control of the physical and social environment. There is a strong emphasis on softer forms of control, and, as in other areas of social intervention such as public health, an emphasis on prevention.[7]

Foucault (1977) studied soft control in the nineteenth century as this involved appeals to the mind of the offender and the transformation of the soul (through isolation of the prisoner). This has its contemporary counterpart in appeals to the offender's reason and conscience through increasing the costs of violation, and the marketing of pro-social ideas, as well as efforts to build community, create positive peer relations and apply various types of therapy. Related forms are also seen in social influence, e.g., as expressed in efforts to affect consumer behavior.

These forms focusing on the subjectivity of the actor are distinct from soft control involving alterations to the physical environment, which are intended to make particular violations difficult or impossible to carry out, and those that involve various exclusionary and early identification preventive efforts. The historically important and uncertain reliance on the will and choices of the violator are sidestepped with many contemporary efforts.

Messing with the human will can be a messy business. Apart from the ethical issues, it's expensive and outcomes are uncertain. As the continuing presence of violations suggests, the endeavor always fails to some degree. From the control perspective, finding technical means for making the violation impossible may seem preferable.

In addition, the goal is often to eliminate or reduce the role of human agents. As a federal official responsible for airline security said, "We want to get the human out of the loop." Humans are prone to inattention, fatigue, error, and corruption. They can work only for limited time periods, under severely restricted environmental conditions, and they may talk back to the bosses and organize.

This book is divided into hard and soft technologies depending on whether they involve physical elements or computer-related data. My meaning is a bit different. By "soft" here I emphasize situations in which control tends to be of low visibility or invisible and is often built into the environment, not being perceived as a form of control. It may be part of the process as when a cell phone sends its location when turned on, software that sends a message and shuts down if it is misused or that monitors work – such as the number of keystrokes entered or black boxes that automatically record driving behavior.

Appeals to actors for a particular kind of behavior – such as volunteering to be searched or offer a Social Security number or other personal information, whether as a sign of good citizenship or for some reward – also reflect soft control.

Some engineering efforts involve traditional notions of target/victim hardening. But as considered here, the engineering of control may also involve the idea of suspect softening/weakening.

Below I consider six ways of controlling environments. These emphasize either protection/alteration of the victim or of what is desired in the violation, or an emphasis on making it impossible or more difficult for the offender to act.

We can identify *primary* direct prevention efforts (strategies #1 and 4 below), which are designed to make the offense impossible, or very difficult to carry out. With primary engineering strategies, it is not necessary to affect the will or calculation of the potential rule breaker. The subjective orientations of the actor (whether based on calculation, a content-filled socialization, or a contentless discipline) are simply ignored. The emphasis is on altering opportunity structures, and the actor's rational, conscious choice is ignored. The social engineering example of castration as a device to control sexuality (whether literal or as currently may be done chemically) clearly contrasts with appeals to virtue to accomplish the same end.

But primary strategies are not always available and sometimes fail. Hence we see a series of *secondary* engineering strategies (2, 3, 5 and 6 below) where concern with the will of the violator can be a factor. The more traditional goal of deterrence may be sought by affecting the calculations of potential violators through devaluing and insulating targets and increasing the likelihood that violations and violators will be discovered and that evidence can be traced. What cannot literally be prevented may nonetheless be deterred, by eliminating the gain or by enhancing the chances for identification and apprehension.

SIX SOCIAL ENGINEERING STRATEGIES

1. Target removal – The logic of prevention is clearest and most effective here. Something that is not there cannot be taken. The move toward a cashless society is one example. Merchants who only accept credit or debit cards, or whose registers never have more than a modest amount of cash are unlikely to be conventionally robbed. Furniture built into the wall cannot be stolen. Subway and bus exteriors built with graffiti resistant metals are hard to draw upon. Requiring methadone to be consumed in front of an observer prevents it being resold. Through software programming, computers and telephones can be blocked from sending or receiving messages to, or from, selected locations.

2. Target devaluation – The goal is to reduce or eliminate the value of a potential target of predation to anyone but authorized users. The target remains, but its uselessness (or greater risks and challenges involved in carrying out the violation) makes it unattractive to predators. Examples include products which self-destruct, as with some car radios when stolen, or which leave clear proof of theft, as with exploding red dye packs that stain money taken in bank robberies. Encrypted messages can often be easily intercepted; however, absent the decryption code, the data are useless. Telephones, computers, automobiles and even guns are increasingly available which can only be used with access devices such as a unique biometric identifier (e.g., retinal, voice or geometric hand pattern), card or access code. Throwaway "pin" numbers created and useable only one time would permit secure use in public or web settings.

Related examples reduce the desirability (or at least identifiability) of a victim or an environment. Consider advice to women to dress in a non-provocative fashion, to wear baggy clothes or to not show their faces in public, or note the tactic adopted by some mall shopkeepers as an anti-teenage congregating tool – the playing of classical music in front of their stores.

3. Target insulation – With this ancient technique the object of desire remains, but it is protected. Perimeter maintaining strategies such as fences, walls, moats, guards, and guards dogs can be separated from more specific protections surrounding an object, such as safes, chastity belts, goods that are in locked cases or chained to an immovable object and the hiding or disguising of valuables. High-security gated communities in which access and egress are carefully controlled, and the use of networked sensors, alarms and Internet video and bulletproof teller booths, are becoming more common. The architectural development of "skywalks" linking downtown private buildings creates "sanitary zones" more subject to control than the potentially disorderly public streets below.

Another kind of insulation lies in our childhood fantasies of invisibility and in adult realities of "Stealth" airplanes. Harry Potter's magic cloud of invisibility might someday cease to be magic, as scientists learn to divert light around an object in a thick shell of transparent material. Under these conditions light does not reflect back on the object. An observer would thus only see what was behind it (Boston Globe, 5/29/06).

4. Offender weakening or incapacitation – This classic strategy seeks to render potential offenders harmless with respect to the will, or ability, to violate the norm in question or to escape. The means may act directly on the body by permanently altering it and making certain offenses impossible

– e.g., literal or chemical castration for sex offenders, or cutting off the hands of thieves. Passivity, disorientation or the inability to flee may be created by sensory weapons, tranquilizers and other medications such as Depo-Provera or psycho-surgery for the violent. A variety of non-lethal disorienting, stopping, restraining or blocking devices are available, ranging from electrical, chemical and acoustical (percussive weaponry), immobilizers to sensory deprivation (e.g., Tasers, pepper spray, loud music, flash bang devices, sticky foam released on a floor, straight jackets and a net fired over a disruptive person). As means of influence these can be related to subliminal environmental efforts involving smells, architecture design, wall color, furniture shape and music in work and shopping settings.[8]

Related efforts deal not with the body of the offender but with the instrumentalities and/or environments involved in the offense. The goal is to render useless or unavailable something that is essential for the violation. Examples include anti-drunk driving interlock systems which require passing a breath analyzer test attached to the automobile ignition system before a car will start; limiting gun purchases to those who have undergone computer checks for purchase eligibility (e.g., no felony conviction); not permitting adolescents to purchase magic markers that can be used for graffiti; and removing phone booths from areas frequented by drug dealers. In the case of fleeing cars, devices include spikes in the road to stop a vehicle, and remote means of stopping the engine or a transmitter (whether attached beforehand or fired at the vehicle) that permit tracking its location. An anti-paparazzi device that remotely identifies the presence of a digital camera can also disable it by projecting a three-inch beam of light at the camera.

Consider also efforts that combine mechanical with discretionary control. One suggestion to regulate the Internet or television would require content providers to label their material and provide an electronic filter that could be activated at the user's discretion to block objectionable material.

5. Exclusion – Potential offenders and unwanted actors have traditionally been kept away from targets or tempting environments by exile, prison, curfew and place or activity exclusions (e.g., places where alcohol is sold for juveniles, the home of an ex-spouse for an abusing husband, or giving demonstrators a permit to march but only for an area removed from the location of the target of the group's protest).

The availability of massive personal databases on so many aspects of an individual's life – whether involving arrest or credit records, or magazines subscribed to and charities donated to – offers a rich potential for background checks and categorization. A variety of risk-classification systems are available (e.g., see Harris and Lurigio chapter, this volume). Vetting may be legally mandated, as in requiring a checking for criminal records among those working with children and those seeking various kinds of licenses.

The ultimate form of exclusion is not denial of access to a job, credit, an apartment or an entry visa based on one's prior record based or on comparisons to a general statistical model: it is capital punishment. At the other end, DNA via eugenics, may lead to exclusion as well, and will likely become more controversial. For example the belief (which ignores interactions with the environment and the socially crafted character of most rules) that DNA is linked to violence and other anti-social behavior could generate another ultimate form of elimination – requiring a license indicating an "acceptable" genetic pattern before a child could be born. Or it might lead to a caste system in which persons were selectively bred for mandatory occupations such as warrior or servant. The film *Gattaca* suggests some possibilities in the genetic division of the population into "Valids" and "In-Valids."

A related form is the visible warning offered by a stigma such as the brand or clipped ear of offenders in medieval Europe, which encouraged others to stay away and may have voluntarily kept the stigmatized away. Electronic monitoring or location devices based on Global Positioning Satellites are contemporary examples. In one form alarms go off and messages are sent to authorities if an adjudicated person wearing a transmitter gets too close to a prohibited person or area or leaves an area s/he is restricted to. This banning from access or a protected environment is the functional equivalent of the exclusion found in other perimeter- or border-maintaining means such as walls, fences, and moats. It may be applied either externally, as at a national border, or internally as at a gated community, a locked door or location of a potential victim.

Determining *exclusion* and *inclusion* and entrance and egress requires criteria against which individuals are to be judged. This surveillance can involve checking for required eligibility tokens, symbols and characteristics. Or it can involve tests, measurements and monitoring to create a data-based characterization of the individual which can be compared to broad statistical models that claim to predict behavior, at least in the aggregate. In the case of exclusion, the opportunity structure for rule breaking is simply denied. In the film *Minority Report*, for example, potential violators were identified and segregated before they could act.

Even when the above forms are unsuccessful because the surveillance may not be seen, understood, believed, or cared about, or the model may be faulty, the access tokens offered are fraudulent or there are no prior red flag indicators in an individual's profile, recording information can be helpful. The surveillance goal of documentation may result in evidence and can permit identifying and apprehending the violators and strategically allocating resources, crime mapping suggesting where to place video cameras and police patrols. Early warning here is linked (often in automated fashion) to preventive actions. An alarm is sent and this triggers defensive actions to stop or limit damage such as closing a gate.

6. Offense/offender/target identification – Where it is not actually possible to prevent the violation physically, or where that is too expensive, it may be possible to at least deter it because of the increased likelihood of apprehension. When that doesn't happen, authorities may know that a violation is occurring or has occurred, who is responsible and where they are to be found. Alarms can send a message to the perpetrator who may desist, as well as to authorities who may be able to intervene to minimize harm or apprehend a suspect. For perimeter security, virtual fences use radar sensors to identify and track the movement of outsiders meter by meter, sending images and locational information.

Major goals for an identification strategy are to increase visibility for (and often of) control agents, to document the occurrence of an event and identify the violator or goods taken. A central concern of nineteenth century forensic science was to develop reliable biometric measures of identity based on the analysis of fingerprints, facial measurements, and chemical properties (Thorwald, 1965). One technique used by the former East Germany involved identifying individuals by their unique olifactors (smells). Architectural design emphasizing visibility as a deterrent fits here (Newman, 1972), as do improved street and building lighting. Video, audio, motion, and heat detection means and access codes that are presumed to document who enters an area, or who is using a resource such as a computer, also are here. Hand-activated personal alarm systems, or a luggage alarm that goes off if a purse or suitcase is illegitimately moved or opened, and the electronic tagging of consumer items or expensive tools at work which give off an alarm if wrongly removed, are other examples. Items with indelible markings are a related example, as are devices pinpointing the time and place of a gunshot sound and cameras recording speeders and red light violations.

The ability to use mechanical means of identification may be required by law. Thus, consider the federal Communications Assistance for Law Enforcement Act ("CALEA"), which requires high-tech industries and organizations involved in telephone and Internet communication to use equipment that must be manufactured so it is readily amenable to wiretapping.[9]

New information technologies have made it possible not only to watch everyone, but for everyone to be a watcher. This greater ease of mobilizing the law by involving citizens in social control is one characteristic of the Anglo-American police tradition, although not in the rest of Europe. Citizens are encouraged to use hot lines to report infractions (e.g., erratic highway drivers, drug dealing, poaching or "whistle-blowing" regarding organizational malfeasance) via cell and traditional telephones and e-mail.

Adjudicated persons may also be required to participate by identifying themselves: e.g., "Megan's laws require convicted sex offenders to register their current addresses with local police. This is equivalent to historical visible stigma examples such as the scarlet letter of the adulterer. The police use mass communications media to help identify and locate wanted persons via information on web cites and crime reenactments on television.

SOME SOCIAL AND ETHICAL IMPLICATIONS

The reasons for using science and technology in criminal justice contexts are obvious. It would be irresponsible not seek to benefit from technical developments. There are many successful applications in specific contexts such as in parking lots and in traffic enforcement (Clarke, 1997). Yet such applications must be accompanied by careful analysis and attention to social and ethical implications that may be overlooked, given the sense of urgency about a problem and what is often the self-justifying tunnel rhetoric of those offering solutions. I next consider some less desirable aspects that may appear. Awareness of such factors calls for caution and sometimes midterm corrections, limitations or suspension of a tactic. But it is certainly not a call to cease innovation or the search for better solutions

However ideal a technical control system may appear in the abstract from the viewpoint of those advocating it, or successful in the short run, the world of application is often much messier and more complicated than the public relations efforts in initially selling it suggest. Tradeoffs, negative externalities and unanticipated outcomes are often present.[10] There is rarely a perfect, nor cost-free, technical fix (if nothing else, a given choice is likely to involve using resources that might have gone elsewhere). The technology's narrowing of focus on a given problem may come at a cost of failing to see larger systemic contexts, alternatives and longer-range consequences. The complexity and fluidity of human situations makes this a rich area for the study of tradeoffs, irony and paradox. In some cases there are parallels to iatrogenic medical practices in which one problem is cured, but at a cost of creating another.

Technical efforts to insure conformity may be hindered by many factors, including the following.

Goal Conflicts

At a more abstract level consider the possible tension between values. In the case of the new super-maximum security prisons there is the enduring tension between values of custody and punishment as against care and some form of rehabilitation (Rhodes, 2004). When more intensive mechanical control, whether within the prison or the community, comes (as it often does) with a diminution of human contact and help at efforts to overcome the social and personal deficits that contribute to violations, short-term gains in control may come at a cost of longer-term losses[11] (Byrne et al., forthcoming).

The broad universalistic treatment citizens expect may conflict with the efficiency-driven, specific treatment made possible by fine-honed personal surveillance data. At the same time, the expectation that one should be judged as an individual and in context may conflict with the greater rationality and predictive success believed to be found in responding to aggregates and creating models divorced from the richness of particular situations.[12] An automatic process that eliminates the misuse of authority can conflict with the need to respond to the uniqueness of particular contexts. The latter requires discretion to override the rule and human review of machine decisions that can significantly affect life chances.

We want both liberty and order. We value the right to know, but also the right to control personal information. We seek privacy and often anonymity, but we also know that secrecy can hide dastardly deeds and that visibility can bring accountability. But too much visibility may inhibit experimentation, creativity and risk taking and can lead to permanent stigmatization and the wrongful denial of opportunity. In our media-saturated societies we want to be seen and to see, yet also to be left alone.

But we can also look more concretely at goal conflicts in the immediate situation. Thus, barriers need to keep out those who are uninvited, while making it easy for those contained within to leave in the case of an emergency. Consider the case of metal bars bolted over windows to keep out thieves. These may also prevent occupants from escaping through the window in the event of a fire. Conversely, barriers intended to keep persons or animals contained within a facility may also lead to their being unable to get out when there is a fire (e.g., in a prison or a horse stall).

In commercial settings where access to merchandise is important, attaching expensive clothes (e.g., leather jackets) to a rack with a locked cable reduces the likelihood that an item will be stolen, but also complicates trying on clothes and impulse buying. Encryption of information offers security, but at a cost of increased expense and slowing down the time required for a transaction.

Unintended Consequences

Situations involving unexpected and unwanted results offer a rich area for analysis. (Merton, 1957; Sieber, 1982; Marx, 1981). From one standpoint, any of the negative or unwanted outcomes discussed in this section could be seen as unintended in an ideal environment. Of course the real world is not like the ideal environment of the laboratory setting. Once there is awareness of such consequences it may be difficult to say that they are unintended (although they may be unwanted) since if the technology continues to be used, intentionality is present. The side effect may be viewed as a necessary price to pay for obtaining a more important goal, and there may be means of ameliorating the new problems created. But here I refer to immediate consequences of an intervention that are not immediately anticipated.

It may be difficult to limit the impact of a technology. Terms such as blowback, collateral damage, backfire and overshooting the target capture this. Thus, some techniques that immobilize suspects may do the same for control agents. That was the case with an early sound wave technology intended to cause suspects to lose control of their bowels, as well as a slippery banana peel substance that made it difficult to walk and the playing of loud music. Uncontrollable wind patterns may send tear gas to places where it is not directed (including back on controllers who need to be protected). Consider the fact that enhanced lighting and lines of visibility can help perpetrators identify victims or control agents, as well as the reverse. The roads used by the ancient Roman legions as they ventured forth to conquer became equally available to other conquerors who later marched on Rome. President Nixon, in secretly taping others, also taped himself leading to his downfall. Conversely, a protective device can lock everyone out if the keys or encryption codes are lost. The removal of benches from public areas denies the homeless, as well as others, a place to sit.

Automatic processes can result in punishment without trial. For example, a thief in Mobile, Alabama, was killed in a trap set by a homeowner. The trap consisted of two hunting rifles in separate locations. One pointed down a staircase. The rifle fired when the thief stepped on a wire rigged to the trigger. A neighbor called police when he heard a shot fired and then entered himself (*New York Times*, Dec. 28, 1989). It is easy to imagine Good Samaritan scenarios that end disastrously (e.g., a passerby who is shot by a homemade burglar alarm after seeing a fire and rushing in to help).

There may be second-order effects. Thus, in their initial use, barrier strips intended to stop fleeing cars almost instantly released the air in the tire, sometimes causing high-speed crashes. Changes to tires and the strips resulting in slower air release have reduced this (see Hummer chapter, this volume). Those publicly identified as sex offenders may face vigilante attacks. The death of 30 persons in a fire in the London King's Cross subway station was attributed to fumes from anti-graffiti paint. Enhanced technical enforcement along the U.S.-Mexico border has led to a funnel effect in which immigrants seek to enter through more dangerous desert areas, resulting in an increase in mortality (Cornelius, 2001).

An intervention may interact with other conditions to produce an undesired outcome. Thus pepper spray, intended as a non-lethal alternative, is that for most persons. But that may not be the case for those with severe asthma or other respiratory problems (see Hummer chapter, this volume). Consider also the warnings to those with pacemakers that electronic sensors are in operation in retail settings. In the same vein, one wonders whether an antitheft device that delivers a 50,000-volt shock to the driver of a stolen car could be lethal to a person with a weak heart.

There may be longer-term health consequences that are not immediately visible. Questions have been raised, for example, about the effect of repeated exposure to radiation from x-ray search machines. Some evidence suggests that traffic officers using radar detection devices have higher rates of testicular cancer.

Awareness that a technology is in use is necessary to create deterrence, but this knowledge can also be a strategic support for clever rule breakers who know what they have to do to deal with it.[13]

Displacement

Several forms of displacement can be noted involving place, time, type of offence and offender (Reppetto, 1976; Norris, 1998). Issues of displacement are central to many control settings where there are conflicts of interest and where rule breakers, having some resources, find ways to beat control efforts. This can involve issues of equity as well. If relatively effective technical solutions are commercialized (as with embedding hidden transmitters in cars, which permits locating them by remotely activating the transmitter) or gated communities to keep out would-be thieves, predators may focus greater attention on those unable to afford enhanced levels of security. Lower income communities or individuals may be unable to afford an effective innovation and hence experience and increase in predation.

Another form of displacement involves the appearance of derivative offenses. The discovery that a target has been rendered useless to an offender may increase violence, whether as a resource to gain the needed access, or out of frustration. For example, the appearance of "car-jacking" is related to more sophisticated anti-theft devices on cars. The use of access codes to activate autos and appliances may mean that the crime of burglary is converted to robbery or kidnapping, as thieves confront property owners and demand not only the property, but the code to make it work. A frustrated thief may respond to a self-destruct automobile radio by fire-bombing the car.

We also see new kinds of violation related to the technology. Authorities may respond with new laws that criminalize the possession of artifacts or activities designed to thwart enforcement. These are forms of secondary deviance involving procedural violations having nothing directly to do with the primary social control goal. These artifactual legal accretions are a rarely studied contributor to the expansion of law seen in recent decades.

The new rules are intended to deter and punish. As of 2003, nine U.S. states had laws prohibiting the production, distribution, and use of products intended to falsify drug tests (Washington Post, Feb. 18, 2003). In Texas there have been arrests for using the "whizzinator." The offense consists of possessing this phallic-like device to provide a false urine sample. In many jurisdictions it is a crime to possess a radar detector that identifies police use of radar in traffic enforcement. The guilty face charges for the secondary offense of possession, even if they were not speeding.

Or consider the new secondary violation that can be called BUS (behavior unbecoming a shopper). In the less than brave world of the shopping mall, BUS can involve walking a dog or lounging. In research by McCahill (2002), the video observation of such activities mobilized corrective action by guards. Or note a new violation that might be termed LUC (lying under camera). Thus, a worker, unaware that he or she has been caught on a hidden camera, who denies a violation such as being in an unauthorized area, is now guilty of being a liar as well as a trespasser. Without the camera the individual would have been less likely to be caught and, if suspected, not given the chance to so easily fail the morality test regarding telling the truth. As with some violations resulting from undercover police practices, this aspect of the infraction is an artifact of the means of control.

Neutralization and Escalation

In a free market economy new controls create incentives to develop means of neutralization – either legally or available through the black market. Such new markets offering greater profits may draw in a more skilled class of violator. Whether out of self-interested rule breaking, principled rebellion or human contrariness, individuals can be very creative in neutralizing systems of control. This may lead to a higher level of play but not fundamentally alter the conflict between rule breakers and rule enforcers.

That locks open with keys and borders require access points means they are eternally vulnerable. A number of *behavioral techniques of neutralization* – strategic moves by which subjects of surveillance seek to subvert the collection of personal information – can be noted.[14]

The initial anti-drunk driving car interlock systems could be beaten either by saving air in a balloon or by having someone else blow into the device to start the car. A variety of means are available for beating drug tests – from contaminating the urine with bleach on one's hand to using a catheter to insert drug-free urine into the body (Tunnell, 2004). Dogs in heat have been used as antidotes to male guard dogs and debugging devices help discover hidden surveillance. Not long after anti-theft ignition protection systems appeared on automobiles, a device that permitted bypassing the lock appeared. Police use of radar detectors against speeders was soon followed by anti-radar detectors, and subsequently by a means for police to identify the latter.

When systems cannot be technically defeated, as with very sophisticated encryption, then their human context may be compromised, whether through coercion or deception. For example, a thief who could not break a manufacturer's sophisticated encryption code, nevertheless managed to embezzle millions of dollars through generating fake invoices. He did this by having an affair with the individual who had the decryption codes.

New control techniques may be turned against control agents. While authorities may have an initial advantage, this is often short-lived. Thus, more powerful armor, bulletproof vests and sophisticated communication systems are no longer the sole property of police. There may be something of an escalating domestic arms race in which the interaction becomes more sophisticated, but the fundamental dynamic does not change.

Meaning

Evaluation research is important to assess the validity and reliability of technical solutions. Given the expense and the importance of the problems, there is relatively little research on many of the techniques.[15]

Results may be invalid for many reasons – a less than perfect technique (e.g., the polygraph), poor implementation, improper application, distorting environmental factors (e.g., diet or prescription drugs or neutralization means that can interfere with accurate drug tests).[16]

Yet even in the best of cases, an *empirically valid* result does not guarantee a *socially meaningful* result. Thus, a DNA match between material from a crime scene and a suspect cannot reveal if a death resulted from a homicide or self-defense. The sample might have been planted or a secure chain-of-evidence custody not maintained. A computer match between persons on welfare and those with bank accounts may reveal a person over the savings limits, but that is not proof of cheating since funds may be held in trust for a funeral – something legally permitted, but not built into the computer program. Audio and video recordings may reflect what was done and said, but will not necessarily reveal why, or what a suspect intended. Seeing should not automatically mean believing. Thus a suspect in an undercover scheme may have been threatened or entrapped off-camera. A threat or seeming admission of a crime may have been said in jest or as boasting. Nor is a drug test, even if it is "valid" in indicating the presence of drugs within a person's system, a necessary indication of a violation. Depending on the assessment used, if the standard is set low enough it is possible to have a positive reading as a result of just being in a room where marijuana is being smoked (false positive).

SOME ADDITIONAL FACTORS

The overselling of technical solutions may exaggerate the risks, thereby engendering immobilizing fear and an unduly suspicious and untrusting society. Or we may see the opposite. An unexamined faith in a tactic's fail-safe nature can lead to complacency and a false sense of security in which individuals are lulled into not taking other necessary precautions. Consider a Los Angeles case in which a man sentenced to house arrest and required to wear an electronic surveillance bracelet shot and killed his estranged wife. She had not reported his threats to police because she thought she was safe as long as he had the bracelet on.

Documentation of all infractions may overload the control system. This may lower morale among enforcers who feel overwhelmed, or offer corruptible officials a resource (non-enforcement) to market. Since resources for acting on all the information may not be available, authorities may also face charges of discriminatory enforcement. This again touches the issue of discretion, and in broadening the documented pool of violations/violators authorities may feel compelled to take action in cases they feel it would be best to ignore.

Even if adequate resources for full enforcement action were available, organizational effectiveness could be harmed. Automatic technical solutions developed without adequate appreciation of complexity and contingency run the risk of eliminating the discretion, negotiation, compromise and informal understandings that are often central to morale and the effective working of organizations (Dalton, 1959; Goffman, 1961). The rigidity of the machine and limited possibilities for immediate innovations, while advantages for some purposes, may be severe limitations in others. One strand of humor involves this automatic, unthinking and repetitive quality of many mechanical devices (note the classic Charley Chaplin film *Modern Times*).

If technical solutions could some how be effective at eliminating all rule breaking (holding apart the conflict between, and ambiguity, and lack of consensus on, many rules), there could be some unexpected costs. Systems might become too rigid and unable to change. Much innovation is initially seen as deviance. Experimentation and risk taking can be aided by anonymity and secrecy. A socially transparent, engineered society would be more orderly, but likely less creative, dynamic and free.

If order depended only on technical means of blocking infractions, rather than on legitimacy, how would people behave when the means failed, as at some points they invariably would? A social order based primarily on technical fixes is likely to be as fragile over time as one based primarily on overt repression. Note the rapidity in which Eastern European countries replaced their communist governments once Soviet support disappeared. There are clearly natural balance points between popular attitudes and repression. The former do not disappear, although they may be less likely to be directly expressed as overt repression or mechanical means of control intensify.

Even if systems could somehow be made fool- and fail-proof with ever more and more advanced technology, there is a danger of viewing humans as robots, rather than as creative beings with a conscience capable of making choices about how they behave. The former image is inconsistent with belief in the dignity of the autonomous individual in a democratic society. Whatever a technology is capable of, the view of humans as volitional (and hence responsible for their behavior) and beliefs about the inviolability (absent clear justification) of the borders that protect private personal zones around one's body, mind, relationships, communications, physical space and past history, are central to ideas of respect for personhood. The tools we use to communicate say something about how we see human beings and what kind of a society we are and seek to become. Symbolism matters, as do precedents.

With a new and seemingly effective technique applied to important goals, we must nonetheless ask, "where might this lead and what kind of a society are we creating?" In the United States, a future radically at odds with the nation's higher ideals is not likely to come by cataclysmic change, but gradually in a thousand little ways, each perhaps understandable, but in totality, creating a very different world – a world arrived at by accretion under the radar, rather than through public dialogue.

For a variety of historical and legitimacy creating reasons, "soft" ways have become more prominent since the appearance of the modern democratic nation state and this trend has accelerated in recent decades.[17] However attractive, the tendency toward softer means can be beguiling. It is hard to say "no" if you are unaware of what is going on. Just because behavior can be guided or personal data can be collected relatively silently, non-invasively and often seductively, does not justify it, apart from the goals and the procedure used to develop the policy. Supreme Court justice Louis Brandeis noted that vigilance was most needed when purposes were benign. The same might be said for the softer means. Their very soft, non-problematic nature may take attention away from other aspects.[18]

In considering less invasive technical means, we need to be mindful that these come with the potential of vastly expanding the pool of those subject to social control. Of course, as the Texas judge reportedly said, "if you hang them all you will certainly get the guilty." Expanded nets and thinned meshes are a function of perceived threats and degrees of risk, as well as ease of application. The seemingly ever-greater ease and efficiency offered by technological means are on a collision course with traditional liberty protecting ideas of reasonable suspicion, minimization and impracticality.

As Byrne notes in his introduction, and several chapters in this book imply, the increased use of sophisticated information (and other) kinds of technology often requires government to turn to the private sector. This has resulted in unprecedented levels of the privatization or hybridization of forms of social control that traditionally were more exclusively in the public domain, which risks lessened public accountability.

Note the vast expansion in companies offering homeland security products. In 2003 there were 3,512 companies with homeland security contracts; by 2006, the number was 33,890. The government has provided over $130 billion in contracts just in this area, let alone those for the privatization of other services such as prisons and electronic monitoring.

Former U.S. Attorney General John Ashcroft, who was central to passage of the USA Patriot Act, now lobbies in support of technology companies, as does Tom Ridge, the first director of the Department of Homeland Security (along with 90 of the department's former officials). In 2001, there were 2 registered homeland security lobbying firms and by 2005 there were 543 (Harris, 2006). What are the implications of this for the public interest and for careful analysis of risks and the effectiveness of the solutions sold? The public goal of justice and the private goal of profit are uneasy bedfellows, requiring a high degree of transparency and accountability.

The search for stand-alone mechanical solutions also avoids the need to ask why some individuals break the rules, and points away from examining the social conditions which may contribute to violations and the possibility of changing those conditions, rather than changing the individual. Technical solutions seek to bypass the need to create consensus and a community in which individuals act responsibly as a result of voluntary commitment to the rules, rather than because they either have no choice or act only out of fear of reprisals. This emphasis can further social neglect and subsequent problems, leading to calls for more intensive and extensive reliance on technology in a seemingly endless self-reinforcing spiral.

There is a magisterial, legitimacy-granting aura around both law and science (Ericson and Shearing, 1986). This legitimacy is strengthened in free market societies where the tactics can often be used by citizens (e.g., video cameras to record police behavior or DNA analysis offered by a criminal defendant) and internally by police managers for guarding the guards.

Technological controls, presumably being science-based, are justified as valid, objective, neutral, universal, consensual and fair. They certainly can be. Yet we need to be mindful of the fact that tools and results are socially created and interpreted (and thus potentially disputable), and they exist in dynamic interdependent systems where interests may conflict, inequality is often present and where full impacts may be difficult to envision. Critical inquiry and humility are as needed as is innovation and experimentation.

Elsewhere (Marx, forthcoming) I identify a number of beliefs that need to be avoided, or at least questioned if we are to maximize the benefits from applying technology and avoid having the solution become a new problem.[19] I suggest that beliefs may be fallacious either logically, empirically or ethically.

A well known, if often naïve expression (given that individuals and groups do not start with equivalent resources), holds that "where there is a will there is a way." This speaks to the role of human effort in obtaining goals. With the control possibilities made available by science and technology, this may be reversed to "where there is a way there is a will." As the myth of Frankenstein implies, we must be ever vigilant to be sure that we control the technology rather than the reverse. As Jacques Ellul (1964) argues, there is a danger of self-amplifying technical means silently coming to determine the ends or even becoming ends in themselves, divorced from a vision of, and the continual search for, the good society.

NOTES

1. There are two social control traditions, one involving broader concerns with social ordering and the other focusing on particular rules. See, for example, Janowitz, 1975; Gibbs, 1989 and Horowitz, 1990.
2. This chapter draws from and builds upon Marx, 1995 and 2001. These and related articles are at garymarx.net.

3. An important factor here is whether the disagreement is viewed by the society as legitimate or illegitimate. Thus, employers and employees or buyers and sellers have distinct interests, even as they may have interests in common. These have a different status than the conflicting interests of bank robbers and banks, and will be more likely to involve less severe forms of social engineering.

4. In its broadest sense, engineering of control is not restricted just to material factors. Thus efforts to educate citizens (e.g., billboards about drinking and driving, signs indicating one's speed on the roadway) or to enhance a sense of social responsibility through neighborhood community policing activities can be seen as forms of social engineering. Any logical effort guided by some rational and strategic application of means to ends (from the view of the actor) can be so characterized (including magic). This could also include failing to act as part of a strategy to avoid seeing a situation escalate, although benign neglect needs to be differentiated from neglect via incompetence, incapability or malevolence.

   Whether a strategy works is of course a different issue, as is what it means "to work." My emphasis in this chapter is primarily on technologies involving action not inaction and on those involving some mechanical or physical elements. These often involve computerization but are not restricted to it.

5. Simon (2005) notes that this theme can also be found in Foucault even as most persons emphasize only the gaze. Foucault's emphasis on a broad governmentality under the presumed guise of rationality can apply to efforts to administer or manage the behavior of others – whether this involves crime prevention or discovery or traffic or consumption. It may focus directly on the environment, the governors or a person's subjectivity or body and can implicate rules or discretionary choices.

6. Efforts at social influence in contexts where rules mandating or prohibiting the desired behavior are not present can also be seen as a form of social control. In such settings the goal is to guide the person toward a particular choice as with consumer products and voting preferences, or to alter some legal but undesirable (from a standpoint of the agent and sometimes the subject) behavior, e.g., smoking or overeating. In such cases the subject has legitimate discretion about what choices to make. From a normative standpoint, that morally sanctioned discretion is absent in the rule contexts considered in this

chapter. The social engineering of playing fields goes far beyond rules per se. It would be useful to contrast types of social control and influence in greater detail in normative and non-normative settings. Consider as well engineered efforts to encourage (rather than discourage) a given behavior – such as a cigarette company gradually increased nicotine content or the increased sweetening of food.

7. In Marx (1988) I consider the engineered society along with other characteristics of a maximum security society. These involve a dossier, actuarial, transparent, suspicious and self-monitored society.

8. These efforts share the soft emphasis of modern direct appeals which play to the presumed rational choice and consciousness of subjects in gaining cooperation. Yet as with traditional hard, coercive means they are involuntary. The moral manipulation relies on the unnoticeable (or taken for granted) elements of the environment to influence the person's behavior, bypassing self-aware cooperation.

9. In the private sector, compliance is generally compelled not through legislation, but by the threat of service denial. Consider for example requirements that condition receiving insurance on meeting carefully defined physical security, licensing and bonding standards. Note also the lower premiums offered to car and homeowners who have various security devices.

10. In considering crime prevention and means beyond just technology, Grabosky (1996) offers a useful conceptualization involving crime escalation, displacement, overdeterrence and perverse incentives. The failure of programs is explained by bad science and planning and deficiencies in implementation that can involve lack of resources or co-ordination.

11. Even in the most extreme settings control may be limited. Note Rhodes's (2004) consideration of feces flinging by those maximally excluded from human interaction, let alone rehabilitative efforts, in maximum security settings. She writes, " . . . the tighter control becomes, the more problematic are the effects it precipitates" (p. 4).

12. The issue here is not only the appropriateness of the criteria used in the model, but what is good as a statistical prediction for an aggregate may not apply to a given individual. Criteria of efficiency need not correspond to justice in individual cases.

13. In Marx (1988, ch. 9) I identify this and 23 other operational paradoxes of social control.

14. Among forms noted in Marx (2003) are: direct refusal, discovery, avoidance, switching, distorting, counter-surveillance, cooperation, blocking and masking.
15. In the case of surveillance technologies such as drug testing, little is known about their effectiveness. The paucity of independent studies of drug testing is noteworthy. Much of the federally mandated testing has a ritual quality in simply being in response to a requirement for contracts and other funding (American Management Association, 1999; Tunnell, 2004).
16. This of course applies to non-humans as well. Accurate drug tests for race horses for example can be distorted by poppy seeds, alfalfa, jimson weed and human sweat among other factors (Tobin, n.d.).
17. With the Enlightenment and the rise of the democratic nation-state with social and economic rights and a consumer economy, legitimacy and social order are in principle based on the consent and choices of the citizen, rather than the sheer coercive power of elites.
18. In *Olmstead v. United States*, 277 U.S. 438 (1928), Brandeis wrote: "Experience should teach us to be most on our guard when the government's purposes are beneficent. Men born to freedom are naturally alert to repel invasion of their liberty by evil-minded rulers. The greatest dangers to liberty lurk in insidious encroachment by men of zeal, well-meaning, but without understanding." The same sentiment can be applied to means that are soft and seemingly non-invasive. These issues are considered in more detail in Marx (2006).
19. An earlier version applied to electronic location monitoring is in Corbett and Marx, 1991.

REFERENCES

American Management Association (1999). *U.S. corporations reduce levels of medical, drug and psychological testing of employees.* New York: American Management Association.

Beniger J., (1986). *The control revolution: The technological and economic origins of the Information Society.* Cambridge, MA: Harvard University Press.

Byrne, J, Taxman, F., & Hummer D. (forthcoming). *The culture of prison violence.* Boston: Allyn and Bacon.

Clarke, R. (Ed.). (1997). *Situational crime prevention: Successful case studies* (2nd ed.). Monsey, NY: Criminal Justice Press.

Cohen, S. (1985). *Visions of social control.* Cambridge, UK: Polity Press.

Corbett R., & Marx, G. T. (1991). No soul in the new machine: Technofallacies in the electronic monitoring movement. *Justice Quarterly, 8*(3), 399-414.

Cornelius, W. (2001). Death at the border: Efficacy and unintended consequences of US immigration control policy. *Population and Development Review, 27*(4), 661-685.

Dalton M. (1959). *Men who manage.* New York: Wiley.

Ellul, J. (1964). *The technological society.* New York: Vintage Books.

Ericson, R., & Shearing, C. (1986). The scientification of police work. In G. Bohme & N. Stehr (Eds.), *The knowledge society: The growing impact of scientific knowledge on social relations.* Dordrecht, Netherlands: Reidel.

Gandy, O. (1993). *The Panoptic Sort: Towards a political economy of information.* Boulder, CO: Westview Press.

Gibbs J. (1989). *Control: Sociology's central notion.* Urbana, IL: University of Illinois Press.

Goffman, E. (1961). *Asylums.* Garden City, NY: Anchor Books.

Grabosky, P. (1996). Unintended consequences of crime prevention. In R. Homel (Ed.), *Crime prevention studies* (Vol. 5). Monsey, NY: Criminal Justice Press.

Foucault, M. (1977). *Discipline and punish: The birth of the prison.* New York: Vintage.

Harris, P. (2006). How US merchants of fear sparked a $130bn bonanza. *Guardian,* Sept. 10.

Horowitz, A. (1990). *The logic of social control.* New York: Plenum.

Janowitz, M. (1975). Sociological theory and social control. *American Journal of Sociology, 81,* 82-108.

Laudon, K. (1986). *The dossier society: Value choices in the design of national information systems.* New York: Columbia University Press.

Lyon, D. (1994). *The electronic eye.* Cambridge, UK: Polity Press.

Marx, G. T. (1988). *Undercover: Police surveillance in America.* Berkeley: University of California Press.

Marx, G. T. (1981). Ironies of social control: Authorities as contributors to deviance through escalation, nonenforcement, and covert facilitation. *Social Problems, 28*(3), 221-246.

Marx, G. T. (1995). The engineering of social control: The search for the silver bullet. In J. Hagan & R. Peterson (Eds.), *Crime and inequality.* Stanford, CA: Stanford University Press.

Marx, G. T. (2001). Technology and social control: The search for a silver bullet. In N. Smelser & P. Baltes (Eds.), *International encyclopedia of the social and behavioral sciences.* St. Louis, MO and Oxford, UK: Elsevier.

Marx, G. T. (2003). A tack in the shoe: Neutralizing and resisting the new surveillance. *Journal of Social Issues, 59*(2), 369-390.

Marx, G. T. (2006). Surveillance: The growth of mandatory volunteerism in collecting personal information. "Hey buddy can you spare a DNA?" In T. Monahan (Ed.), *Surveillance and security.* Cullompton, UK and Portland, OR: Willan.

Marx, G. T. (forthcoming). Rocky bottoms and some Information Age technofallacies. *Journal of International Political Sociology.*

McCahill, M. (2002). *The surveillance web.* Devon, UK: Willan.

Merton, R. (1957). *Social theory and social structure.* Glencoe, IL: Free Press.

Newman, O. (1972). *Defensible space.* New York: MacMillan.

Norris, O., Moran, J., & Armstrong, G. (1998). *Surveillance, closed circuit television and social control*. Aldershot, UK: Ashgate.

Reppetto, T. A. (1976). Crime prevention and the displacement phenomenon. *Crime & Delinquency, 13*, 66-77.

Rhodes, L. (2004). *Total confinement: Madness and reason in the maximum security prison*. Berkeley: University of California Press.

Rule, J. (1973). *Private lives, public surveillance*. London: Allen-Lane.

Sherman, L. (1992). Attacking crime: Policing and crime control. In M. Tonry & N. Morris (Eds.), *Modern policing*. Chicago: University of Chicago Press.

Shenhav, Y. (1999). *Manufacturing rationality: The engineering foundations of the modern managerial revolution*. New York: Oxford University Press.

Sieber, S. (1982). *Fatal remedies: The solution as the problem*. New York: Plenum.

Simon, B. (2005). The return of the panopticon: Supervision, subjection and the new surveillance. *Surveillance and Society, 3*(1), 1-20.

Snyder, E., & Blakely, M. (1997). *Fortress America: Gated communities in the United States*. Washington, DC: Brookings Institution.

Tenner, E. (1997). *Why things bite back: Technology and the revenge of unintended consequences*. New York: Vintage Books

Thorwald, J. (1965). *The century of the detective*. New York: Harcourt Brace & World.

Tobin, T. (no date). *"Guilty Until Proven Innocent": Preventing inadvertent chemical identification in athletic horses* (htm//netpet).

Tunnell, K. (2004). *Pissing on demand*. New York: New York University Press.

Weber, M. (1964). *From Max Weber: Essays in sociology*. (Translated and edited by H.H. Gerth and C. W. Mills.). New York: Oxford University Press.

Zuboff, S. (1988). *In the age of the smart machine*. New York: Basic Books.

WEB LINKS FOR THE NEW TECHNOLOGY OF CRIME, LAW AND SOCIAL CONTROL

A) Technology Resources

Computerensics
http://www.computerensics.com/

Global Justice Information Sharing Initiatives (GLOBAL)
http://it.ojp.gov/topic.jsp?topic_id=8

High Technology Crime Investigation Association
http://www.htcia.org/

International Association of Computer Investigative Specialists
http://www.cops.org/

National Center for Missing & Exploited Children
http://www.ncmec.org/

National Criminal Justice Associations
http://www.ncja.org/web_resources.html

National Law Enforcement & Corrections Technology Center
http://www.nlectc.org/

National White-Collar Crime Center
http://www.llr.com/nwccc/nwccc.htm

Office of Justice Programs' Information Technology Initiatives
http://www.it.ojp.gov/index.jsp

Predicting a Criminal's Journey to Crime
http://www.ojp.usdoj.gov/nij/journals/253/predicting.html

SEARCH—The National Consortium for Justice Information & Statistics
http://www.search.org/

Soft Surveillance: The Growth of Mandatory Volunteerism in Collecting Personal Information
http://web.mit.edu/gtmarx/www/softsurveillance.html

Special Technologies for Law Enforcement and Corrections
http://www.ojp.usdoj.gov/nij/journals/jr000252.htm

Technologies of Crime
www.aic.gov.au/conferences/outlook4/Montano.pdf

The Engineering of Social Control: The Search for the Silver Bullet
http://web.mit.edu/gtmarx/www/bullet.html

U.S. Department of Justice Cybercrime website
http://www.cybercrime.gov

Workshop on Spyware
http://itpolicy.princeton.edu/spywareworkshop

B) New Technology of Crime

Check and Credit Card Fraud
http://www.popcenter.org/Problems/problem-check-card-fraud.htm

Clandestine Drug Labs
http://www.popcenter.org/Problems/problem-druglabs.htm

Common Fraud Schemes
http://www.fbi.gov/majcases/fraud/fraudschemes.htm

Identity Theft
http://www.popcenter.org/Problems/problem-identity_theft.htm

Identity Theft
http://www.ncjrs.gov/spotlight/identity_theft/summary.html

Misuse and Abuse of 9/11
http://www.popcenter.org/Problems/problem-misuse-911.htm

Old-fashioned land scams go high-tech
http://www.usatoday.com/tech/news/2006-09-26-land-scams_x.htm

Prescription Fraud
http://www.popcenter.org/Problems/problem-prescription-fraud.htm

Rave Parties
http://www.popcenter.org/Problems/problem-rave_parties.htm

Telemarketing Fraud
http://www.ojp.usdoj.gov/nij/journals/jr000252.htm

C) Police Technology

Automated Data Sharing
http://www.ojp.usdoj.gov/nij/journals/253/automated.html

Cruiser Technology
http://www.project54.unh.edu/overvie

Federal Bureau of Investigation Strategic Plan 2004-2009
http://www.fbi.gov/publications/strategicplan/stategicplantext.htm#recruit

Information Technology Initiatives
http://it.ojp.gov/index.jsp

International Association of Chiefs of Police Technology Website
http://www.iacptechnology.org

Law Enforcement Technology Guide
http://www.search.org/files/pdf/TECHGUIDE.pdf

Patrol Car Armor Systems
http://www.protecharmored.com/systems/special/leva.asp

NLECTC Video Resource Center
http://www.nlectc.org/videos/justnet.html

Non-Lethal Technology
http://www.unidir.org/pdf/articles/pdf-art2217.pdf

Non-Lethal Weapons - Pepperball Guns
http://www.non-lethal.com/?google-non_lethal

Office of Law Enforcement Standards (OLES)
http://www.eeel.nist.gov/oles/index.html

Officer and Cruiser Technology
http://policevehicletech.com/

Police One
http://www.policeone.com/police-technology/

Prediction and Control of Organized Crime
http://www.ojp.usdoj.gov/nij/international/programs/ukr_pred.html

Radar Cameras
http://www.cbsnews.com/stories/2004/08/16/earlys how/living/
main636197.shtml

The Death of Victoria Snelgrove
http://www.cityofboston.gov/police/pdfs/report.pdf

Urban Crime Statistics
http://www.onpointradio.org/shows/2006/02/20060220_a_main.asp

D) Court Technology

An Informed Response: An overview of the domestic violence court technology application and resource link
http://www.communityjustice.org/_uploads/documents/
Informed%20Response1.pdf

Center for Court Innovation
http://www.courtinnovation.org

Courtroom 21 Project
http://www.courtroom21.net/

Court-Technology: A Status Report
http://www.legaltechcenter.net/publications/articles/status.pdf

Internet Crimes Against Children Task Force Program
http://ojjdp.ncjrs.gov/programs/ProgSummary.asp?pi=3

Jurist Legal Intelligence
http://jurist.law.pitt.edu/courttech.htm

National Center for State Courts (NCSC)
http://www.ncsconline.org/D_Tech/

Preventing Targeted Violence Against Judicial Officials and Courts
http://www.secretservice.gov/ntac_aapss.shtml

Wired Courts
http://jurist.law.pitt.edu/courttech6.htm

E) Corrections Technology

Applied Physics Laboratory: Development of Safe Prison Materials
http://www.jhuapl.edu/newscenter/aplnews/2005/saferazor.asp

Classification of High-Risk and Special Management Prisoners
http://www.nicic.org/pubs/2004/019468.pdf

Corrections.com
http://www.corrections.com/technetwork/technews.aspx

Federal Probation: A Journal of Correctional Philosophy and Practice
http://www.uscourts.gov/fedprob/2001septfp.pdf

Massachusetts Prisoner Reentry
http://www.urban.org/UploadedPDF/411167_Prisoner_Reentry_MA.pdf

Mock Prison Riot Training Video
http://www.oletc.org/riot/riot_video.html

National Institute of Justice: Corrections Technology
http://www.ojp.usdoj.gov/nij/topics/corrections/technology.htm

National Institute of Justice: Corrections Technology
http://www.ojp.usdoj.gov/nij/topics/corrections/pubs.htm

National Institute of Corrections: Technology Year in Review, 2005
http://nicic.org/Library/021096

National Law Enforcement and Corrections Technology Center
(NLECTC) Library
http://www.nlectc.org/virlib/default.asp

New Location-Based Solution Precisely Monitors Offenders and Generates Revenue
http://www.bi.com/pdfs/BI_CS_MPRoanoke.pdf

Office of Law Enforcement Technology Commercialization (OLETC)
Mock Riot Homepage
http://www.oletc.org/riot/

Report on Prisoner Radicalization
http://hsgac.senate.gov/_files/091906Report.pdf

The Location and Trafficking of Offenders Using GPS Based Systems
http://www.correctionstech.org/2004Conference/Presentations/m-Oper-GPS2/
Location_&_Tracking.ppt

The Long Arm of the Law
http://www.corrections.com/ezine/
this%20week%20on%20corrections_com%20special%20report.htm

Tracking Prisoners with Biometrics
http://www.ojp.usdoj.gov/nij/journals/253/tracking.html

F) Crime Prevention

School Safety – U.S. Department of Education
http://www.connectlive.com/events/edschoolsafety/

G) Government Agencies and Departments

Bureau of Alcohol, Tobacco, Firearms, and Explosives
http://www.atf.gov

Bureau of Justice Statistics
http://www.ojp.usdoj.gov/bjs/

Campbell Collaboration
http://www.campbellcollaboration.org/

Central Intelligence Agency
http://www.cia.gov

Drug Enforcement Agency
http://www.dea.gov

Federal Bureau of Investigation
http://www.fbi.gov

Federal Bureau of Prisons
http://www.bop.gov/

National Crime Information Center (NCIC)
http://www.fas.org/irp/agency/doj/fbi/ncic.htm

National Institute of Justice
http://www.ojp.usdoj.gov/nij/

United States Secret Service
http://www.secretservice.gov

H) Websites on Violence

CDC's National Center for Injury Prevention and Control
http://www.cdc.gov/ncipc/dvp/dvp.htm

Free lectures for CJ Professors and Students
http://www.newtexts.com/newtexts/cluster.cfm?cluster_id=16

Indicators of School Crime and Safety, 2004 (Bureau of Justice Statistics)
http://www.ojp.usdoj.gov/bjs/abstract/iscs04.htm

National Center for the Analysis of Violent Crime (FBI)
http://www.fbi.gov/hq/isd/cirg/ncavc.htm

National Consortium on Violence Research
http://www.ncovr.org/

National Domestic Violence Hotline
http://www.ndvh.org/

Office of Juvenile Justice and Delinquency Prevention News at a Glance
http://ojjdp.ncjrs.org/publications/PubAbstract.asp?pubi=11965

Satanic Ritual Abuse
http://www.religioustolerance.org/sra.htm

Southern California Center of Excellence on Youth Violence Prevention
http://www.stopyouthviolence.ucr.edu/index.html

The National Institute for the Prevention of Workplace Violence
http://www.workplaceviolence911.com

United States Secret Service National Threat Assessment Center
http://www.secretservice.gov/ntac.shtml